Credit Risk

Credit Risk: Pricing, Measurement, and Management
IS A PART OF THE
PRINCETON SERIES IN FINANCE

SERIES EDITORS

Darrell Duffie   Stephen Schaefer
Stanford University   *London Business School*

Finance as a discipline has been growing rapidly. The number of researchers in academy and industry, of students, of methods and models have all proliferated in the past decade or so. This growth and diversity manifests itself in the emerging cross-disciplinary as well as cross-national mix of scholarship now driving the field of finance forward. The intellectual roots of modern finance, as well as the branches, will be represented in the Princeton Series in Finance.

Titles in the series will be scholarly and professional books, intended to be read by a mixed audience of economists, mathematicians, operations research scientists, financial engineers, and other investment professionals. The goal is to provide the finest cross-disciplinary work, in all areas of finance, by widely recognized researchers in the prime of their creative careers.

OTHER BOOKS IN THIS SERIES

Financial Econometrics: Problems, Models, and Methods by Christian Gourieroux and Joann Jasiak

Credit Risk

Pricing, Measurement, and Management

Darrell Duffie
and
Kenneth J. Singleton

Princeton University Press
Princeton and Oxford

Copyright © 2003 by Princeton University Press
Published by Princeton University Press, 41 William Street,
Princeton, New Jersey 08540
In the United Kingdom: Princeton University Press, 3 Market Place, Woodstock,
Oxfordshire OX20 1SY

Library of Congress Cataloging-in-Publication Data

Duffie, Darrell.
    Credit risk : pricing, measurement, and management / Darrell Duffie and
Kenneth J. Singleton.
        p.   cm. — (Princeton series in finance)
    Includes bibliographical references and index.
    ISBN 0-691-09046-7 (alk. paper)
    1. Credit—Management. 2. Risk management. I. Singleton, Kenneth J.
II. Title. III. Series.
HG3751 .D84   2003
332.7'42—dc21   2002030256

British Library Cataloging-in-Publication Data is available

This book has been composed in New Baskerville by Princeton Editorial Associates,
Inc., Scottsdale, Arizona

Printed on acid-free paper ∞

www.pupress.princeton.edu

Printed in the United States of America

10 9 8 7 6 5 4 3 2 1

Contents

Preface

THIS BOOK PROVIDES an integrated treatment of the conceptual, practical, and empirical foundations for modeling credit risk. Among our main goals are the measurement of portfolio risk and the pricing of defaultable bonds, credit derivatives, and other securities exposed to credit risk. The development of models of credit risk is an ongoing process within the financial community, with few established industry standards. In the light of this state of the art, we discuss a variety of alternative approaches to credit risk modeling and provide our own assessments of their relative strengths and weaknesses.

Though credit risk is one source of market risk, the adverse selection and moral hazard inherent in the markets for credit present challenges that are not present (at least to the same degree) with many other forms of market risk. One immediate consequence of this is that reliable systems for pricing credit risk should be a high priority of both trading desks and risk managers. Accordingly, a significant portion of this book is devoted to modeling default and associated recovery processes and to the pricing of credit-sensitive instruments.

With regard to the default process, we blend in-depth discussion of the conceptual foundations of modeling with an extensive discussion of the empirical properties of default probabilities, recoveries, and ratings transitions. We conclude by distinguishing between historical measures of default likelihood and the so-called risk-neutral default probabilities that are used in pricing credit risk.

We then address the pricing of defaultable instruments, beginning with corporate and sovereign bonds. Both the *structural* and *reduced-form* approaches to pricing defaultable securities are presented, and their comparative fits to historical data are assessed. This discussion is followed by a comprehensive treatment of the pricing of credit derivatives, including credit swaps, collateralized debt obligations, credit guarantees, and spread options. Finally, certain enhancements to current pricing and management practices that may better position financial institutions for future changes in the financial markets are discussed.

The final two chapters combine the many ingredients discussed throughout this book into an integrated treatment of the pricing of the credit risk in over-the-counter derivatives positions and the measurement of the overall (market and credit) risk of a financial institution.

In discussing both pricing and risk measurement, we have attempted to blend financial theory with both institutional considerations and historical evidence. We hope that risk managers at financial intermediaries, academic researchers, and students will all find something useful in our treatment of this very interesting area of finance.

Acknowledgments

WE ARE GRATEFUL for early discussions with Ken Froot and Jun Pan, and for conversations with Ed Altman, Angelo Arvanitis, Steve Benardete, Arthur Berd, Antje Berndt, Michael Boulware, Steve Brawer, Eduardo Canaberro, Ricard Cantor, Steve Carr, Lea Carty, James Cogill, Pierre Collin-Dufresne, Ian Cooper, Didier Cossin, Michel Crouhy, Qiang Dai, Josh Danziger, Sanjiv Das, Mark Davis, David Dougherty, Adam Duff, Greg Duffee, Paul Embrechts, Steve Figlewski, Chris Finger, Gifford Fong, Jerry Fons, Benoit Garivier, Bob Geske, Bob Goldstein, Martin Gonzalez, David Heath, Tarek Himmo, Taiichi Hoshino, John Hull, Bob Jarrow, Vince Kaminsky, Stephen Kealhofer, David Lando, Joe Langsam, Jean-Paul Laurent, David Li, Nicholas Linder, Robert Litterman, Robert Litzenberger, Violet Lo, Mack MacQuowan, Erwin Marten, Jim McGeer, Maureen Miskovic, Andy Morton, Laurie Moss, Dan Mudge, Michael Norman, Matt Page, Vikram Pandit, Elizabeth Pelot, William Perraudin, Jacques Pezier, Joe Pimbley, David Rowe, John Rutherford, Patrick de Saint-Aignan, Anurag Saksena, James Salem, Stephen Schaefer, Wolfgang Schmidt, Philip Schönbucher, Dexter Senft, Bruno Solnik, Roger Stein, Lucie Tepla, John Uglum, Len Umantsev, Oldrich Vasicek, Matthew Verghese, Ravi Viswanathan, Allan White, Mark Williams, Fan Yu, and Zhi-fang Zhang.

Excellent research assistance was provided by Andrew Ang, Arthur Berd, Michael Boulware, Joe Chen, Qiang Dai, Mark Fergusen, Mark Garmaise, Nicolae Gârleanu, Yigal Newman, Jun Pan, Lasse Heje Pedersen, Michael Rierson, Len Umantsev, Mary Vyas, Neng Wang, and Guojun Wu. We also thank Sandra Berg, Melissa Gonzalez, Zaki Hasan, Dimitri Karetnikov, Glenn Lamb, Wendy Liu, Laurie Maguire, Bryan McCann, Ravi Pillai, Betsy Reid, Paul Reist, Brian Wankel, and, especially, Linda Bethel, for technical support. We benefited from helpful and extensive comments on early drafts by Suresh Sundaresan and Larry Eisenberg.

We have had the advantage and pleasure of presenting versions of material from this book to a series of excellent participants in our M.B.A.,

Ph.D., and executive programs at the Graduate School of Business of Stanford University. Participants in our executive program offerings on Stanford's campus, in London, and in Zurich who have helped us improve this material over the past years include Peter Aerni, Syed Ahmad, Mohammed Alaoui, Morton Allen, Jeffery Amato, Emanuele Amerio, Charles Anderson, Nels Anderson, Naveen Andrews, Fernando Anton, Bernd Appasamy, Eckhard Arndt, Javed Ashraf, Mordecai Avriel, Bhupinder Bahra, Paul Barden, Rodrigo Barrera, Reza Behar, Marco Berizzi, Frederic Berney, Raimund Blache, Francine Blackburn, Christian Bluhm, Thomas Blummer, Dave Bolder, Luca Bosatta, Guillermo Bublik, Paola Busca-Pototschnig, Richard Buy, Ricardo Caballero, Lea Carty, Alberto Castelli, Giovanni Cesari, Dan Chen, Wai-yan Cheng, Francisco Chong Luna, Michael Christieson, Meifang Chu, Benjamin Cohen, Kevin Coldiron, Daniel Coleman, Radu Constantinescu, Davide Crippa, Peter Crosbie, Michel Crouhy, Jason Crowley, Rabi De, Luiz De Toledo, Andre de Vries, Mark Deans, Amitava Dhar, Arthur Djang, David Dougherty, Rohan Douglas, J. Durland, Steven Dymant, Sebastien Eisinger, Carlos Erchuck, Marcello Esposito, Kofi Essiam, Francine Fang, John Finnerty, Earnan Fitzpatrick, Claudio Franzetti, David Friedman, Ryuji Fukaya, Birgit Galemann, Juan Garcia, Francesco Garzarelli, Tonko Gast, Claire Gauthier, Ruediger Gebhard, Soma Ghosh, G. Gill, Claudio Giraldi, Giorgio Glinni, Benjamin Gord, Michael Gordy, Anthony Gouveia, Brian Graham, Robert Grant, Patrick Gross, Anil Gurnaney, Beat Haag, Robert Haar, Isam Habbab, Tariq Hamid, Jose Hernandez, Peter Hoerdahl, Kathryn Holliday, Jian Hu, Houben Huang, W. Hutchings, John Im, Jerker Johansson, Georg Junge, Theo Kaitis, Vincent Kaminski, Anupam Khanna, Pieter Klaassen, Andrea Kreuder-Bruhl, Alexandre Kurth, Asif Lakhany, Julian Leake, Jeremy Leake, Daniel Lehner, James Lewis, Ying Li, Kai-Ching Lin, Shiping Liu, Robert Lloyd, Bin Lu, Peter Lutz, Scott Lyden, Frank Lysy, Ian MacLennan, Michael Maerz, Haris Makkas, Robert Mark, Reiner Martin, Gilbert Mateu, Tomoaki Matsuda, Andrew McDonald, Henry McMillan, Christopher Mehan, Ruthann Melbourne, Yuji Morimoto, Anthony Morris, Philip Morrow, Gerardo Munoz, Jones Murphy, Theodore Murphy, Gary Nan, Hien Nguyen, Toshiro Nishizawa, Jaesun Noh, Gregory Nudelman, Mark Nyfeler, Nick Ogurtsov, Erico Oliveira, Randall O'Neal, Lorena Orive, Ludger Overbeck, Henri Pagès, Deepanshu Pandita Sr., Ben Parsons, Matthias Peil, Anne Petrides, Dietmar Petroll, Marco Piersimoni, Kenneth Pinkes, Laurence Pitteway, H. Pitts, Gopalkrishna Rajagopal, Karl Rappl, Mark Reesor, Sendhil Revuluri, Omar Ripon, Daniel Roig, Emanuela Romanello, Manuel Romo, Frank Roncey, Marcel Ruegg, John Rutherfurd, Bernd Schmid, David Schwartz, Barry Schweitzer, Robert Scott, James Selfe, Bryan Seyfried, Anurag Shah, Vasant Shanbhogue, Sutesh Sharma, Craig Shepherd, Walker Sigismund, Banu Simmons-Sueer, Herman Slooijer, Sanjay Soni, Arash Sotoodehnia, Gerhard Stahl, Sara Strang, Eric Takigawa,

Michael Tam, Tanya Tamarchenko, Stuart Tarling, Alexei Tchernitser, David Thompson, Fumihiko Tsunoda, James Turetsky, Andrew Ulmer, Edward van Gelderen, Paul Varotsis, Christoph Wagner, Graeme West, Stephen West, Andre Wilch, Paul Wilkinson, Todd Williams, Anders Wulff-Andersen, Dangen Xie, Masaki Yamaguchi, Toshio Yamamoto, Xiaolong Yang, Toyken Yee, Kimia Zabetian, Paolo Zaffaroni, Omar Zane, Yanan Zhang, Hanqing Zhou, and Ainhoa Zulaica.

We are grateful for administrative support for this executive program from Gale Bitter, Shelby Kashiwamura, Melissa Regan, and, especially, Alicia Steinaecker Isero, and for programmatic support from Jim Baron, Dave Brady, Maggie Neale, and Joel Podolny, and in general to Stanford University.

While there are many more Stanford M.B.A. and Ph.D. students to thank for comments related to this material than we can recall, among those not already mentioned, we would like to thank Muzafter Akat, Daniel Backal, Jennifer Bergeron, Rebecca Brunson, Sean Buckley, Albert Chun, David Cogman, Steven Drucker, Nourredine El Karoui, Cheryl Frank, Willie Fuchs, Enrique Garcia Lopez, Filippo Ginanni, Jeremy Graveline, Michel Grueneberg, Ali Guner, Christopher Felix Guth, John Hatfield, Cristobal Huneeus, Hideo Kazusa, Eric Knyt, Eric Lambrecht, Yingcong Lan, Peyron Law, Chris Lee, Brian Jacob Liechty, Dietmar Leisen, Haiyan Liu, Ruixue Liu, Rafael Lizardi, Gustavo Manso, Rob McMillan, Kumar Muthuraman, Jorge Picazo, Shikhar Ranjan, Gerardo Rodriguez, Rohit Sakhuja, Yuliy Victorovich Sannikov, Devin Shanthikumar, Ilhyock Shim, Bruno Strulovici, Alexei Tchistyi, Sergiy Terentyev, Kiran M. Thomas, Stijn Gi Van Nieuwerburgh, Leandro Veltri, Faye Wang, Ke Wang, Wei Wei, Pierre-Olivier Weill, Frank Witt, Wei Yang, Tao Yao, Assaf Zeevi, Qingfeng Zhang, and Alexandre Ziegler.

One of our foremost debts is to our faculty colleagues here at Stanford's Graduate School of Business, for listening to, and helping us with, our questions and ideas during the years taken to produce this book. Among those not already named are Anat Admati, Peter DeMarzo, Steve Grenadier, Harrison Hong, Ming Huang, Ilan Kremer, Jack McDonald, George Parker, Paul Pfleiderer, Manju Puri, Myron Scholes, Bill Sharpe, Jim Van Horne, and Jeff Zwiebel.

Our final thanks go to Peter Dougherty of Princeton University Press, for his enthusiastic support of our project.

We wish to acknowledge the following copyrighted materials: Figures 6.6 and 6.7 are from Duffie, D., and K. Singleton (1999), "Modeling Term Structures of Defaultable Bonds," *Review of Financial Studies* **12**, no. 4, 687–720, by permission of the Society for Financial Studies; Figure 5.6 is from Duffie, D., and D. Lando (2001), "Term Structures of Credit Spreads with Incomplete Accounting Information," *Econometrica* **69**, 633–664, copyright

Credit Risk

1

Introduction

OUR MAIN GOAL is modeling credit risk for measuring portfolio risk and for pricing defaultable bonds, credit derivatives, and other securities exposed to credit risk. We present critical assessments of alternative conceptual approaches to pricing and measuring the financial risks of credit-sensitive instruments, highlighting the strengths and weaknesses of current practice. We also review recent developments in the markets for risk, especially credit risk, and describe certain enhancements to current pricing and management practices that we believe may better position financial institutions for likely innovations in financial markets.

We have in mind three complementary audiences. First, we target those whose key business responsibilities are the measurement and control of financial risks. A particular emphasis is the risk associated with large portfolios of over-the-counter (OTC) derivatives; financial contracts such as bank loans, leases, or supply agreements; and investment portfolios or broker-dealer inventories of securities. Second, given a significant focus here on alternative conceptual and empirical approaches to pricing credit risk, we direct this study to those whose responsibilities are trading or marketing products involving significant credit risk. Finally, our coverage of both pricing and risk measurement will hopefully be useful to academic researchers and students interested in these topics.

The recent notable increased focus on credit risk can be traced in part to the concerns of regulatory agencies and investors regarding the risk exposures of financial institutions through their large positions in OTC derivatives and to the rapidly developing markets for price- and credit-sensitive instruments that allow institutions and investors to trade these risks. At a conceptual level, market risk—the risk of changes in the market value of a firm's portfolio of positions—includes the risk of default or fluctuation in the credit quality of one's counterparties. That is, credit risk is one source of market risk. An obvious example is the common practice among

1

broker-dealers in corporate bonds of marking each bond daily so as to reflect changes in credit spreads. The associated revaluation risk is normally captured in market risk-management systems.

At a more pragmatic level, both the pricing and management of credit risk introduces some new considerations that trading and risk-management systems of many financial institutions are not currently fully equipped to handle. For example, credit risks that are now routinely measured as components of market risks (e.g., changes in corporate bond yield spreads) may be recognized, while possibly offsetting credit risks embedded in certain less liquid credit-sensitive positions, such as loan guarantees and irrevocable lines of credit, may not be captured. In particular, the aggregate credit risk of a diverse portfolio of instruments is often not measured effectively.

Furthermore, there are reasons to track credit risk, by counterparty, that go beyond the contribution made by credit risk to overall market risk. In credit markets, two important market imperfections, *adverse selection* and *moral hazard*, imply that there are additional benefits from controlling counterparty credit risk and limiting concentrations of credit risk by industry, geographic region, and so on. Current practice often has the credit officers of a financial institution making *zero-one* decisions. For instance, a proposed increase in the exposure to a given counterparty is either declined or approved. If approved, however, the increased credit exposure associated with such transactions is sometimes not "priced" into the transaction. That is, trading desks often do not fully adjust the prices at which they are willing to increase or decrease exposures to a given counterparty in compensation for the associated changes in credit risk. Though current practice is moving in the direction of pricing credit risk into an increasing range of positions, counterparty by counterparty, the current state of the art with regard to pricing models has not evolved to the point that this is done systematically.

The informational asymmetries underlying bilateral financial contracts elevate *quality pricing* to the front line of defense against unfavorable accumulation of credit exposures. If the credit risks inherent in an instrument are not appropriately priced into a deal, then a trading desk will either be losing potentially desirable business or accumulating credit exposures without full compensation for them.

The information systems necessary to quantify most forms of credit risk differ significantly from those appropriate for more traditional forms of market risk, such as changes in the market prices or rates. A natural and prevalent attitude among broker-dealers is that the market values of open positions should be re-marked each day, and that the underlying price risk can be offset over relatively short time windows, measured in days or weeks. For credit risk, however, offsets are not often as easily or cheaply arranged. The credit risk on a given position frequently accumulates over long time horizons, such as the maturity of a swap. This is not to say that credit risk is a distinctly long-term phenomenon. For example, settlement risk can be significant, particularly for foreign-exchange products. (Conversely, the market risk of default-free positions is not always restricted to short time windows. Illiquid positions, or long-term speculative positions, present long-term price risk.)

On top of distinctions between credit risk and market price risk that can be made in terms of time horizons and liquidity, there are important methodological differences. The information necessary to estimate credit risk, such as the likelihood of default of a counterparty and the extent of loss given default, is typically quite different, and obtained from different sources, than the information underlying market risk, such as price volatility. (Our earlier example of the risk of changes in the spreads of corporate bonds is somewhat exceptional, in that the credit risk is more easily offset, at least for liquid bonds, and is also more directly captured through yield-spread volatility measures.)

Altogether, for reasons of both methodology and application, it is natural to expect the development of special pricing and risk-management systems for credit risk and separate systems for market price risk. Not surprisingly, these systems will often be developed and operated by distinct specialists. This does not suggest that the two systems should be entirely disjoint. Indeed, the economic factors underlying changes in credit risk are often correlated over time with those underlying more standard market risks. For instance, we point to substantial evidence that changes in Treasury yields are correlated with changes in the credit spreads between the yields on corporate and Treasury bonds. Consistent with theory, low-quality corporate bond spreads are correlated with equity returns and equity volatility. Accordingly, for both pricing and risk measurement, we seek frameworks that allow for interaction among market and credit risk factors. That is, we seek integrated pricing and risk-measurement systems. A firm's ultimate appetite for risk and the firmwide capital available to buffer financial risk are not specific to the source of the risk.

1.1. A Brief Zoology of Risks

We view the risks faced by financial institutions as falling largely into the following broad categories:

- *Market risk*—the risk of unexpected changes in prices or rates.
- *Credit risk*—the risk of changes in value associated with unexpected changes in credit quality.
- *Liquidity risk*—the risk that the costs of adjusting financial positions will increase substantially or that a firm will lose access to financing.
- *Operational risk*—the risk of fraud, systems failures, trading errors (e.g., deal mispricing), and many other internal organizational risks.

- *Systemic risk*—the risk of breakdowns in marketwide liquidity or chain-reaction default.

Market price risk includes the risk that the degree of volatility of market prices and of daily profit and loss will change over time. An increase in volatility, for example, increases the prices of option-embedded securities and the probability of a portfolio loss of a given amount, other factors being held constant. Within market risk, we also include the risk that relationships among different market prices will change. This, aside from its direct impact on the prices of cross-market option-embedded derivatives, involves a risk that diversification and the performance of hedges can deteriorate unexpectedly.

Credit risk is the risk of default or of reductions in market value caused by changes in the credit quality of issuers or counterparties. Figure 1.1 illustrates the credit risk associated with changes in spreads on corporate debt at various maturities. These changes, showing the direct effects of changes in credit quality on the prices of corporate bonds, also signal likely changes in the market values of OTC derivative positions held by corporate counterparties.

Liquidity risk involves the possibility that bid-ask spreads will widen dramatically in a short period of time or that the quantities that counterparties are willing to trade at given bid-ask spreads will decline substantially, thereby reducing the ability of a portfolio to be quickly restructured in times of financial stress. This includes the risk that severe cash flow stress forces dramatic balance-sheet reductions, selling at bid prices and/or buying at ask prices, with accompanying losses or financial distress. Examples of recent experiences of severe liquidity risk include

- In 1990, the Bank of New England faced insolvency, in part because of potential losses and severe illiquidity on its foreign exchange and interest-rate derivatives.
- Drexel Burnham Lambert—could they have survived with more time to reorganize?
- In 1991, Salomon Brothers faced, and largely averted, a liquidity crisis stemming from its Treasury bond "scandal." Access to both credit and customers was severely threatened. Careful public relations and efficient balance-sheet reductions were important to survival.
- In 1998, a decline in liquidity associated with the financial crises in Asia and Russia led (along with certain other causes) to the collapse in values of several prominent hedge funds, including Long-Term Capital Management, and sizable losses at many major financial institutions.

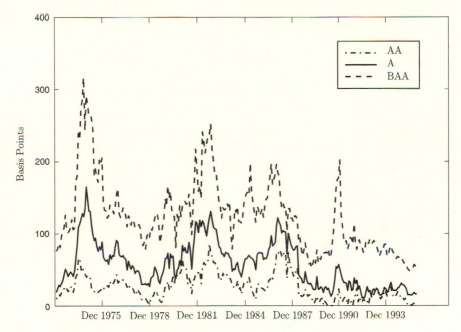

Figure 1.1.   *Corporate bond spreads. (Source: Lehman Brothers.)*

- In late 2001, Enron revealed accounting discrepancies that led many counterparties to reduce their exposures to Enron and to avoid entering into new positions. This ultimately led to Enron's default.

Changes in liquidity can also be viewed as a component of market risk. For example, Figure 1.2 shows that Japanese bank debt (JBD) sometimes traded through (was priced at lower yields than apparently more creditworthy) Japanese government bonds (JGBs), presumably indicating the relatively greater liquidity of JBDs compared to JGBs. (Swap-JGB spreads remained positive.)

Systemic risk involves the collapse or dysfunctionality of financial markets, through multiple defaults, "domino style," or through widespread disappearance of liquidity. In order to maintain a narrow focus, we will have relatively little to say about systemic risk, as it involves (in addition to market, credit, and liquidity risk) a significant number of broader conceptual issues related to the institutional features of financial systems. For treatments of these issues, see Eisenberg (1995), Rochet and Tirole (1996), and Eisenberg and Noe (1999). We stress, however, that co-movement in market prices—nonzero correlation—need not indicate systemic risk per se. Rather, co-movements in market prices owing to normal economic

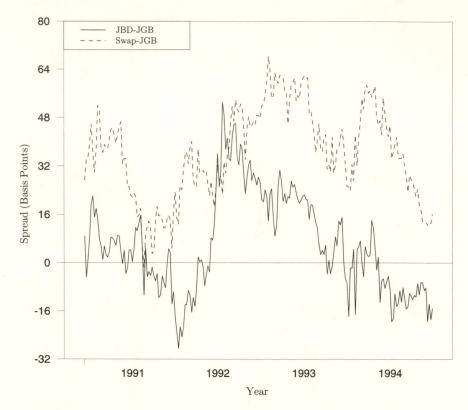

Figure 1.2. *Japanese bank debt trading through government bonds.*

fluctuations are to be expected and should be captured under standard pricing and risk systems.

Finally, *operational risk,* defined narrowly, is the risk of mistakes or break-downs in the trading or risk-management operations. For example: the fair market value of a derivative could be miscalculated; the hedging attributes of a position could be mistaken; market risk or credit risk could be mis-measured or misunderstood; a counterparty or customer could be offered inappropriate financial products or incorrect advice, causing legal exposure or loss of goodwill; a "rogue trader" could take unauthorized positions on behalf of the firm; or a systems failure could leave a bank or dealer without the effective ability to trade or to assess its current portfolio.

A broader definition of operational risk would include any risk not already captured under market risk (including credit risk) and liquidity risk. Additional examples would then be:

- *Regulatory and legal risk*—the risk that changes in regulations, account-ing standards, tax codes, or application of any of these, will result in unforeseen losses or lack of flexibility. This includes the risk that the legal basis for financial contracts will change unexpectedly, as occurred with certain U.K. local authorities' swap positions in the early 1990s. The risk of a precedent-setting failure to recognize netting on OTC derivatives could have severe consequences. The significance of netting is explained in Chapter 12.

- *Inappropriate counterparty relations*—including failure to disclose information to the counterparty, to ensure that the counterparty's trades are authorized and that the counterparty has the ability to make independent decisions about its transactions, and to deal with the counterparty without conflict of interest.
- *Management errors*—including inappropriate application of hedging strategies or failures to monitor personnel, trading positions, and systems and failure to design, approve, and enforce risk-control policies and procedures.

Some, if not a majority, of the major losses by financial institutions that have been highlighted in the financial press over the past decade are the result of operational problems viewed in this broad way and not directly a consequence of exposure to market or credit risks. Examples include major losses to Barings and to Allied Irish Bank through rogue trading, and the collapse of Enron after significant accounting discrepancies were revealed.

Our focus in this book is primarily on the market and, especially, credit risk underlying pricing and risk-measurement systems. Given the relatively longer holding periods often associated with credit-sensitive instruments and their relative illiquidity, liquidity risk is also addressed—albeit often less formally. Crouhy et al. (2001) offer a broad treatment of risk management for financial institutions with a balanced coverage of market, credit, and operational risk, including a larger focus on management issues than we offer here.

1.2. Organization of Topics

We organize subsequent chapters into several major topic areas:

- Economic principles of risk management (Chapter 2).
- Single-issuer default and transition risk (Chapters 3 and 4).
- Valuation of credit risk (Chapters 5–9).
- Default correlation and related portfolio valuation issues (Chapters 10 and 11).
- The credit risk in OTC derivatives positions and portfolio credit risk measurement (Chapters 12 and 13).

We begin our exploration of credit risk in Chapter 2, with a discussion of the economic principles guiding credit risk management for financial firms, along with an overview of some procedural risk-management issues. As a set of activities, risk management by a financial firm may involve: (1) measuring the extent and sources of exposure; (2) charging each position a cost of capital appropriate to its risk; (3) allocating scarce risk capital to traders and profit centers; (4) providing information on the firm's financial integrity to outside parties, such as investors, rating agencies, and regulators; (5) evaluating the performance of profit centers in light of the risks taken to achieve profits; and (6) mitigating risk by various means and policies. An important objective that applies specifically to credit risk is assigning and enforcing counterparty default exposure limits. Chapter 2 also provides an assessment of several measures of market and credit risk, based on such criteria as how closely they are related to the key economic costs of financial risk or how easily measures of risk at the level of individual units or desks can be meaningfully aggregated into an overall measure of risk for the firm. We also discuss here, at an introductory level, the challenges that arise in attempting to implement these measures and aggregate market and credit risks.

In developing frameworks for the measurement and pricing of credit risks, our initial focus is the modeling of *default risk* and *ratings-transitions risk*. Chapter 3 introduces a convenient and tractable class of models of the default process for a given counterparty that is based on the concept of *default intensity*. Intuitively, the default intensity of a counterparty measures the conditional likelihood that it will default over the next small interval of time, given that it has yet defaulted and given all other available information. Here, we also review the historical experience with corporate defaults in the United States, and relate these experiences to calibrations of models of default. Similar issues regarding ratings-transition risk—the risk that a counterparty will have its credit rating upgraded or downgraded—are taken up in Chapter 4. Both of these chapters explore alternatives for a computationally tractable algorithm for simulating future defaults and ratings transitions, an essential ingredient of credit risk measurement and pricing systems.

These two foundational modeling chapters are followed by a series of chapters that develop models for, and empirical evidence regarding, the pricing of defaultable instruments. Chapter 5 provides an overview of alternative conceptual approaches to the valuation of securities in the presence of default risk. Initially, we focus on the most basic instrument— a defaultable zero-coupon bond—in order to compare and contrast some of the key features of alternative models. We review two broad classes of models: (1) *reduced-form*, those that assume an *exogenously* specified process for the migration of default probabilities, calibrated to historical or current market data; and (2) *structural*, those based directly on the issuer's ability or willingness to pay its liabilities. This second class is usually framed around a stochastic model of variation in assets relative to liabilities. Most pricing models and frameworks for inferring default probabilities from market data adopt one of these two approaches. A review of their conceptual under-pinnings will prove useful in addressing many other issues.

Chapter 5 also includes a discussion of the differences between *risk-neutral* and *actual* default probabilities. Our discussion of default processes in Chapters 3 and 4 and the mappings of these models to historical experience focus on actual probabilities. Virtually all pricing models in use in the financial industry and studied by academics are based instead on risk-neutral probabilities. That is, building on the pathbreaking result of Black and Scholes (1973) and Merton (1974) showing that *plain-vanilla* (conventional) equity options can be priced, given the underlying price, as though investors are neutral to risk, one may compute the market values of future cash flows, possibly from defaultable counterparties, from the expectation of discounted cash flows, under risk-neutral probabilities.

Chapter 6 discusses the pricing of corporate bonds in more detail, paying particular attention to the practical and empirical aspects of model implementation. We begin here with a discussion of another key component of default risk: the recovery in the event of default. Though bond covenants are often clear about the payoff owed by the defaulting counterparty, we emphasize that renegotiation out of bankruptcy, as well as in bankruptcy courts, does not always result in strict adherence to the terms of bond covenants. Faced with the real-world complexity of default settlements, a variety of tractable approximations to the outcomes of settlement processes have been used to develop simple pricing models. We illustrate some of the practical implications of different recovery assumptions for the pricing of defaultable securities.

For certain defaultable instruments, an important indicator of credit quality is the credit rating of the counterparty. Credit ratings are provided by major independent rating agencies such as Moody's and Standard & Poor's. In addition, many financial institutions assign internal credit ratings. Ratings are often given as discrete indicators of quality, so a transition from one rating to another could, if not fully anticipated, introduce significant *gapping* risk into market prices, that is, the risk of significant discrete moves in market prices as a rating is changed. The formal introduction of this gapping risk into pricing systems presents new challenges, which are reviewed briefly at the end of Chapter 6.

Drawing upon our discussions of default, recovery, and dynamic models of the prices of reference securities (e.g., Treasuries or swaps), we turn in Chapter 7 to an overview of alternative empirical models of corporate and sovereign yield spreads. We also review in this chapter some standard term-structure models for the time-series behavior of the benchmark yield curves from which defaultable bonds are spread. Sovereign bonds present their own complications because of the more diverse set of possible credit events, including various types of restructuring, changes in political regimes, and so on, and the nature of the underlying risk factors that influence default and restructuring decisions. We discuss the nature of the credit risks inherent in sovereign bonds and review the evidence on default and recovery. Additionally, we present an in-depth analysis of a model for pricing sovereign debt with an empirical application to Russian bonds leading up to the default in August 1998.

Next, we direct our attention to the rapidly growing markets for credit derivatives. Among these new derivatives, credit swaps have been the most widely traded and are taken up in Chapter 8. An important feature of credit swaps is that the exchange of cash flows between the counterparties is explicitly contingent on a credit event, such as default by a particular issuer. Indeed, the most basic default swap is essentially insurance against loss of principal on a defaulting loan or bond. The chapter focuses on the structure of these contracts as well as on pricing models.

Chapter 9 treats the valuation of options for which the underlying security is priced at a yield spread. An obvious example is a spread option, conveying the right to put a given fixed-income security, such as a corporate or sovereign bond, at a given spread to a reference bond, such as a Treasury note. A traditional lending facility, for example, an irrevocable line of credit, can also be viewed in these terms. The chapter also treats callable and convertible corporate debt, examining the manner in which both interest-rate risk and credit risk jointly determine the value of the embedded options.

In order to address instruments with payoffs that are sensitive to the joint credit risks of multiple issuers, we consider alternative conceptual formulations of default correlation in Chapter 10.

One of the most important recent developments in the securitization of credit risk is the growing issuance of *collateralized debt obligations* (CDOs). The cash flows of loans or bonds of various issuers are pooled and then tranched by priority into a hierarchy of claims, much as with the earlier development of collateralized mortgage obligations. The pricing of CDOs is presented in Chapter 11, along with a critical discussion of how rating agencies are assessing the credit risks of these relatively complex instruments.

Chapter 12 examines the impact of credit risk on OTC derivatives. The key issues here are exposure measurement and the adjustment for credit risk of valuations based on midmarket pricing systems. For many such derivatives, such as forwards and interest-rate swaps, credit risk is two sided: either counterparty may default and, depending on market conditions, either counterparty may be at risk of loss from default by the other. For example, with a plain-vanilla at-market interest-rate swap,[1] the market

---

[1] A standard arrangement is for counterparty A to pay counterparty B a fixed coupon, say semiannually, in return for receiving a floating payment at the 6-month London Interbank Offer Rate (LIBOR) rate, also every 6 months. Payments are based on an underlying notional amount of principal. No money changes hands at the inception of an at-market swap.

value of the swap at the inception date is zero. Going forward, if interest rates generally rise, then the swap goes *in the money* to the receive-floating side, whereas if rates fall then the swap has positive value to the pay-floating side. Since, over the life of the swap, rates may rise and fall, the credit qualities of both counterparties are relevant for establishing the market value of a swap.

Chapter 13 addresses integrated market and credit risk measurement for large portfolios. We provide several examples of the risk measurement of portfolios of option and loan positions. In developing the market risk component, we address the implications for risk measurement of alternative parameterizations of the risk factors driving portfolio returns. In particular, we explore the implications of changes in volatility (*stochastic volatility*) and of the possibility of sudden jumps in prices for the measurement of market risk. Additionally, we review the *delta-gamma* approach to approximating the prices of OTC derivatives and discuss its reliability for revaluing derivative portfolios in risk measurement. Finally, through our examples, we discuss the use of computationally efficient methods for capturing the sensitivity of derivative prices to underlying prices and to changes in credit quality and default. We contrast the types of portfolios whose profit-and-loss *tail risks* are driven largely by changes in credit quality from types of portfolios whose tail losses are mainly a property of exposure to market prices and rates.

Appendix A presents an overview of *affine* models, a parametric class of Markov jump diffusions that is particularly tractable for valuation and risk modeling in many of the settings that are encountered in this book, including the dynamics of the term structure of interest rates, stochastic volatility and jump risk in asset returns, option valuation, and intensity-based models of default probabilities and default correlation risk. Appendix B reviews alternative approaches to estimating the parameters of the affine models overviewed in Appendix A. Appendix C outlines an approach to modeling term structures of credit spreads that is based on forward-rate models in the spirit of Heath, Jarrow, and Morton (1992).

2

Economic Principles
of Risk Management

WHY DO MANAGERS of financial institutions care about financial risks? Are the economic incentives for managing market and credit risks the same, or does credit risk present different challenges, calling for distinct measurement systems or tools? These are some of the questions that we begin to address in this chapter. The economics of risk management for financial firms is far from an exact science. While rigorous and empirically testable models can be brought to the task of measuring financial risks, some of the benefits and costs of bearing these risks are difficult to quantify.

In a hypothetical world of perfect capital markets—as we know from the work of Modigliani and Miller (1958), widely held to be the basis for the Nobel prizes awarded to Franco Modigliani and Merton Miller—any purely financial transaction by a publicly traded firm has no impact on that firm's total market value. Capital markets, however, are not perfect. Market imperfections underlie significant benefits for banks and other financial institutions for bearing and controlling financial risks. Indeed, we name and characterize many of these benefits. One should not, however, anticipate a model allowing a practical cost-benefit analysis of risk that leads to precise quantitative trade-offs. Some of the important channels through which risk operates to the detriment or benefit of a financial corporation are not readily priced in the market.

For instance, there are no obvious formulas to determine the market value that can be created by a financial firm willing to bear a given amount of risk through proprietary trading or intermediation. In perfect capital markets, after all, securities are priced at their fair market values, and trading could therefore neither add nor subtract market value. Any such formula relating financial risk bearing to the market value of the firm would, in the reality of imperfect capital markets, depend on such difficult-to-capture variables as the human abilities of traders and management, the information flows available to the firm, its reputation, its access to customers, and its organization of the risk-management function itself, not to mention a host of economic variables that characterize its economic environment.

One can imagine how difficult it might be to capture numerically the impact on the market value of the firm of adding a given amount of risk through such channels as

- The ongoing value of a corporation's reputation, in evidence, for example, from the franchise value of a corporate name such as J. P. Morgan or Deutsche Bank.
- The incentives of risk-averse managers acting as agents of shareholders.
- Financing-rate spreads, especially when the firm is better informed about its risks than are its creditors.

So, rather than a recipe providing in each case the appropriate amounts of each type of risk to be borne in light of the costs and benefits, one should aim for a critical understanding of the nature of these risks, the channels through which they affect performance, and the methods by which they can be measured and mitigated. An appropriate appetite for risk is ultimately a matter of judgment, which is informed by quantitative models for measuring and pricing risk and based on a conceptual understanding of the implications of risk.

2.1. What Types of Risk Count Most?

The primary focus of risk-management teams at financial institutions is not on traditional financial risk, but rather on the possibility of *extreme losses*. As discussed in the next section, the benefits of this particular focus of risk management usually come from the presence of some kind of nonlinearity in the relationship between the market value of the firm and its raw profits from operations. Such a nonlinearity is typically associated with events that create a need for quick access to additional capital or credit, *whether or not accompanied by severe reductions in market value*. It happens that a need for quick access to funds is often associated with a sudden reduction in market value, especially at financial firms, because of the relatively liquid nature of their balance sheets.

Before exploring some economic motives for managing the risk of extreme loss in more depth, it is instructive to expand briefly on what we mean by this risk. We let P_t denote the market value of a portfolio held by a firm (or a particular profit center) at date t. The probability distribution of the change $P_s - P_t$ in market value between the current date t and a future date s is shown in Figure 2.1 for various s. For a given time horizon, say 1 day, the bell-shaped curve represents the likelihood of various potential changes in market value, or profit and loss (P&L). (As we emphasize later, the simple bell shape that is illustrated is not often found in practice.) Financial risk, as typically discussed in the context of portfolio management, is captured by the shape of this P&L distribution. Risk reduction is often, though not always, concerned with reductions in the volatility of P&L and focuses in particular on the leftmost regions of the probability density curves shown in Figure 2.1, those regions where P&L is extremely negative.

Risk management is the process of adjusting both the risk of large losses and the firm's vulnerability to them. This vulnerability depends on the portfolio of positions *and* on the amount of capital that is backing the firm's investment activities. Vulnerability to risk depends as well on the quality of the institution's risk-management team, its risk-measurement systems, the liquidity of its positions, and many other attributes.

As suggested by Figure 2.1, the shapes of P&L distributions, and in particular the shapes of the leftmost tails, depend on the horizon (a day, a week, and so on) over which P&L is measured. As will be discussed, an appropriate risk-measurement horizon is, in practice, partly a property of the liquidity of the balance sheet of assets and liabilities and may also depend on the requirements of regulatory agencies. A balance sheet composed entirely of liquid marketable securities, for example, could be rapidly adjusted so as to maintain risk and capital at desired levels. At, or just before, the point

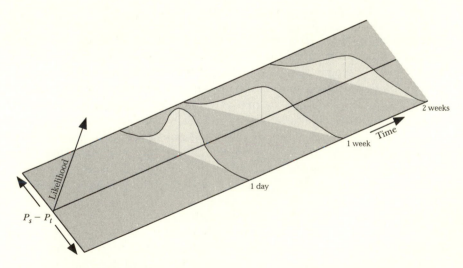

Figure 2.1.   *Probabilities of changes in market value by time.*

of insolvency, a firm with a liquid balance sheet could potentially be re-capitalized at low cost. For a financial firm that holds a significant amount of illiquid assets (e.g., a portfolio of real estate or exotic collateralized mort-gage obligations), however, there may be a sudden need for cash, whether or not accompanied by a large reduction in market value, which forces a costly balance-sheet reduction, perhaps including asset *firesales*. When, as Lowen-stein (2000) relates in the case of the demise of Long-Term Capital Manage-ment, the positions to be sold are large relative to the market, the associated illiquidity costs can be particularly large. Thus, a natural time horizon for measuring and managing risk increases with the degree of balance-sheet illiquidity.

Measures of risk also depend on the state of the economy. That is, risk managers focus on the *conditional distributions* of profit and loss, which take full account of current information about the investment environment (macroeconomic and political as well as financial) in forecasting future market values, volatilities, and correlations. This is to be contrasted with the *unconditional* distributions, which can be thought of as representing the average frequencies of different results over long periods in history. To make this distinction concrete, let a given bell curve in Figure 2.1 represent the distribution of $P_s - P_t$, conditional on all the information about market conditions (financial, macroeconomic, political, and so on) available at date t. As shown, the conditional variance of $P_s - P_t$ typically increases as one looks further into the future. (The bell curves become more dispersed for longer holding periods.) Not only are the prices of underlying market indices changing randomly over time, the portfolio itself is changing, as are the volatilities of prices, the credit qualities of counterparties, and so on. The farther into the future that we measure the conditional probability distribution of market value, the less confident we are about each of these determinants.

Moreover, for a fixed investment horizon $s - t$, as economic conditions change, so might the reliability of one's forecast of the future value of a given portfolio of securities. We capture this by letting the conditional means, variances, and other moments of the distribution of $P_s - P_t$ change with the measurement date t, holding the investment horizon $s - t$ fixed. That the riskiness of a position can change rapidly and adversely was illustrated, for example, in the fall of 1998 with the turmoil in Asian and Russian financial markets.

2.2. Economics of Market Risk

We elaborate on some of the nonlinearities that give rise to incentives for risk management, including risk allocation and capital budgeting. At the outset, we stress that risk management is *not* expressly for the purpose of

protecting shareholder equity value from the losses represented directly
by changes in market prices, but is rather for the purpose of reducing
the frictional costs that are sometimes associated with changes in market
value, such as financial distress costs. Shareholders can, on their own, adjust
their overall exposures to market risks, one of the key points of the theory
of Modigliani and Miller (1958) that, to some degree, holds true even in
imperfect capital markets.

2.2.1. Profit-Loss Asymmetries

An operating loss of a given amount x may reduce the market value of
the firm by an amount that is greater than the increase in market value
caused by an operating gain of the same size x. An obvious example of
this asymmetry arises from taxation. With a progressive tax schedule, as
illustrated in an exaggerated form in Figure 2.2., the expected after-tax
profit generated by equally likely before-tax earnings outcomes of $X_1 = \overline{X} + x$ and $X_2 = \overline{X} - x$ is less than the after-tax profit associated with the
average level $\overline{X}$ of before-tax earnings. Reducing risk therefore increases
the market value of the firm merely by reducing the expected present value
of its tax liability. On average, with a progressive tax scheme such as that
illustrated in Figure 2.2., a firm would prefer to have a before-tax profit of
$\overline{X}$ for sure than uncertain profits with a mean of $\overline{X}$.

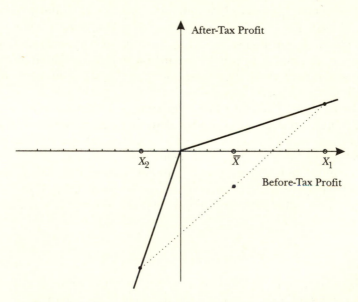

Figure 2.2.   *Concavity effect of a progressive tax schedule.*

The effect of risk shown in Figure 2.2. is an example of what is known as *Jensen's inequality*, which states that the expectation of a concave function of a random variable X is less than the concave function evaluated at the expectation $\overline{X}$ of X. (In this example, the concave function is defined by the schedule of after-tax P&L associated with each before-tax level of P&L.)

Another source of concavity, and thus benefit for risk management, is illustrated in Figure 2.3, which shows how the trading profits of a financial firm are translated into additions to, or subtractions from, the firm's total market value. This hypothetical schedule, which ignores tax effects, is illustrated as linear over a wide range, within which trading profits merely flow through the income statement to the balance sheet. With sufficiently large losses, however, financial distress costs become apparent. These costs may be associated with financing premia for replacing capital (especially on an emergency basis), the liquidity costs of asset firesales, losses associated with reductions in lines of business or market share, and, in severe cases, the threat of loss of reputation or of some portion of franchise value. If risk management reduces the likelihood of such large losses, then it increases the market value of the firm, in light of a reduced present market value of future distress costs. Jensen's inequality is again at play.[1] Froot et al. (1993) model how risk management can increase market value in the presence of concavities such as these.

Because of its overhead and operating expenses, the hypothetical firm pictured in Figure 2.3 must have significantly positive trading profits before "breaking even." While this plays no role in the Jensen effect that we have just described, it does signal that a firm whose core business is financial trading must take risks in order to generate additions to market value. It follows that risk reduction is not to be pursued at all costs. A financial firm's core business, whether through proprietary trading or intermediation, calls for bearing risk in an efficient manner.

2.2.2. Minimum Capital Requirements

Distinctions can arise between the interests of equity shareholders and those of other stakeholders, such as creditors, concerning the desired amount of risk to be borne by the firm. At sufficiently low levels of capital, equity shareholders, because they have limited liability and are the residual claimants of the firm, have an incentive to "gamble." That is, shareholders

---

[1] This is actually a corollary of Jensen's inequality stating that a reduction in the risk of X increases the expectation of a concave function of X. This corollary is sometimes known as the Blackwell-Girschick theorem. A *reduction in risk* means the elimination of a mean-preserving spread in the distribution of X. While risk management may not literally eliminate mean-preserving spreads, the intuition is clear and robust. For details, see, e.g., DeMarzo and Duffie (1991).

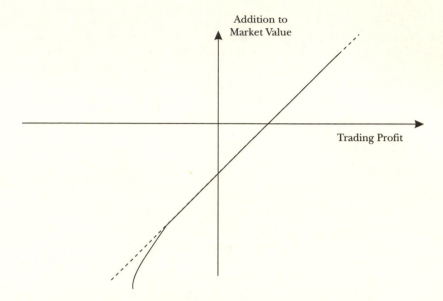

Figure 2.3.   *Financial distress and trading profit and loss.*

hold an effective option on the total market value of the firm. For purposes
of this simple illustration, we assume that debtholders exercise a protec-
tive covenant that causes liquidation of the firm if its total market value
falls below the total principal K of the outstanding debt, in which case
the liquidation value of the firm goes to creditors. Under this absolute-
priority rule, the schedule relating the liquidation value of the net assets
of the firm to the liquidation value of equity is convex, as illustrated in
Figure 2.4. Jensen's inequality therefore operates in a direction opposite
to that illustrated in Figures 2.2. and 2.3. Equity shareholders may actually
prefer to *increase* the risk of the firm, perhaps by substituting low-risk positions with high-risk positions or by increasing leverage. In the corporate-
finance literature, this is called *asset substitution.* Unless restricted by other
debt covenants or by regulation, equity shareholders can play a "heads-I-
win, tails-I-don't-lose" strategy of increasing risk in order to increase the
market value of their share of the total value of the firm. This effect is illustrated in Figure 2.5, which shows the market value of equity as an option
on net assets struck at the liability level K for two levels of asset volatility,
L (low) and H (high). The market value of debtholders who retain the
concave portion of the firm illustrated in Figure 2.4 is therefore reduced
by such an increase in risk. (The illustration is based on the Black-Scholes
formula.)

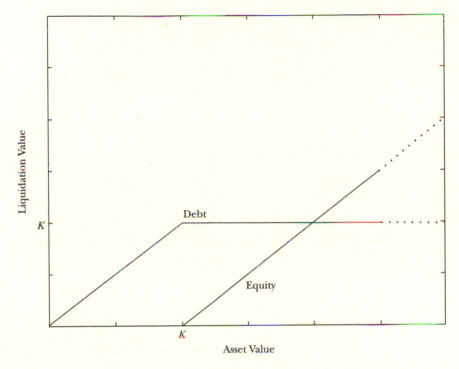

Figure 2.4.   *Liquidation values of debt and equity.*

While this potential conflict between shareholders and creditors is, in principle, present at all levels of capital, its impact is mitigated at high-capital levels, at which the benefits of increasing risk through the convex Jensen effect illustrated in Figure 2.5 may be dominated by the benefits of reducing risk from the concave Jensen effect illustrated in Figure 2.3.

As financial distress at a given firm has negative spillover effects for the remainder of the financial system, such as systemic risk, and implicit or explicit financial guarantees provided by taxpayers, regulators of financial institutions are typically empowered to enforce minimum levels of capital relative to risk. If well formulated, risk-based minimum-capital regulations can inhibit socially inefficient gambles. They may also leave equityholders with little or no incentive to add inefficient gambles. The distortions and frictional costs of capital regulations are of course to be considered as well. For additional discussion, one may refer to Dewatripont and Tirole (1993).

Section 2.5.2 contains a brief summary of recent and proposed minimum capital standards for the credit-sensitive instruments held by regulated banks.

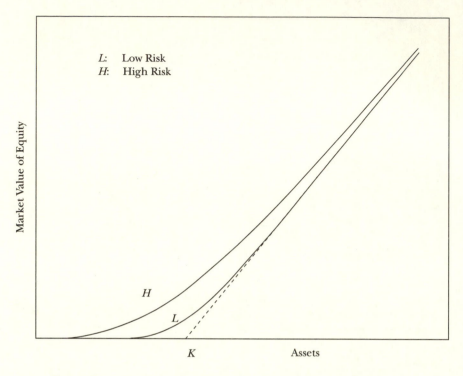

L: Low Risk
H: High Risk

Market Value of Equity

H

L

K   Assets

Figure 2.5.   *Exposure of market value of equity to low and high risks.*

2.2.3. Principal-Agent Effects

It may be difficult for equityholders to coordinate "optimal" risk management, given that the firm's managers may be risk-averse and wary of the
potential impact of their firm's losses on their job security, compensation,
and apparent performance. For this reason, traders and managers are often given implicit or explicit contractual incentives to take risks. Finding an
effective balance between incentives for taking and for limiting risk can be
delicate. In any case, the costs of retaining managers and of keeping their
incentives relatively well aligned with those of shareholders are generally
increasing in the firm's level of risk, other things being equal.

2.2.4. Capital—A Scarce Resource

If new capital could be obtained in perfect financial markets, we would
expect a financial firm to raise capital as necessary to avoid the costs of
financial distress illustrated in Figure 2.3, so long as the firm has positive

market value as an ongoing operation (see, e.g., Haugen and Senbet, 1978). In such a setting, purely financial risk would have a relatively small impact, and risk management would likewise be less important.

In fact, however, externally raised capital tends to be more costly than retained earnings as a source of funding. For example, external providers of capital tend to be less well informed about the firm's earnings prospects than is the firm itself and therefore charge the firm a *lemon's premium*, which reflects their informational disadvantage, a term that arose from a seminal article (the basis of a Nobel prize) by Akerlof (1970), who uses as an illustration the market for used cars, some of which are known by sellers, but not buyers, to be lemons. Leland and Pyle (1977) and Myers and Majluf (1984) provide examples of the application of Akerlof's model to the lemon's premium on corporate debt or equity. External providers of capital may also be concerned that the firm's managers have their own agendas and may not use capital efficiently from the viewpoint of shareholders' interests, which is the principal-agent problem mentioned above. For these and other reasons, for each dollar of capital raised externally, the firm may not be able to generate future cash flows with a present market value of $1. In order to obtain new capital, the firm's current owners may therefore be forced to give up some of their current share-market value, for instance, through dilution. Retained earnings are therefore normally a preferred source of funds, if available.

As raising capital externally is relatively costly, replacing capital after significant losses is one of the sources of financial distress costs illustrated in Figure 2.3. The present market value of these distress losses can be traded off against the benefits of bearing financial risk, as we have already discussed, through the activity of risk management.

2.2.5. Leverage and Risk for Financial Firms

Compared to other types of corporations, such as utilities, financial firms have relatively liquid balance sheets, made up largely of financial positions. This relative liquidity allows a typical financial firm to operate with a high degree of leverage. An incremental unit of capital, optimally levered, allows a significant increase in the scale of the firm and is relatively easily deployed. Financial firms therefore tend to operate at close to the full capacity allowed by their capital. For example, major broker-dealers regulated by the U.S. Securities and Exchange Commission (SEC) frequently have a level of accounting capital that is close to the regulatory minimum of 8% of accounting assets (after various adjustments), implying a debt-equity ratio on the order of 12 to 1, which is high relative to the norm for nonfinancial corporations. Minimum capital standards for regulated banks are also framed around a benchmark of 8%.

Ironically, in light of the relatively high degree of liquidity that fosters high leverage, a significant and sudden financial loss (or reduced access to credit) can cause dramatic illiquidity costs. For example, a moderate reduction in capital accompanied by high leverage may prompt a significant reduction in assets in order to recover a desirable capital ratio, as was the case in several of the illiquidity episodes described in Chapter 1. Quick and major reductions in balance sheets tend to be expensive, especially as they are often accompanied by significant reductions in marketwide liquidity or the bid prices of commonly held assets or both. A notable example is the demise of Long-Term Capital Management in 1998.

In summary, we expect many financial firms to operate "close to the edge," relative to nonfinancial firms, in terms of the amount of capital necessary to sustain their core businesses and that this sustaining level of capital is determined in large part by the volatility of earnings. Firms with more volatile earnings would seek a higher level of capital in order to avoid frequent or costly recapitalizations and emergency searches for refreshed lines of credit and reductions in balance sheets. We should therefore think of capital as a scarce resource, whose primary role is to act as a buffer against the total financial risk faced by the firm. Lowenstein (2000) reviews the role of high leverage in the losses incurred by Long-Term Capital Management and the difficulties that it faced in reducing its balance sheet.

2.2.6. Allocation of Capital or Risk?

Capital is a common resource for the entire firm. It would be counterproductive to ration capital itself among the various profit centers within the firm, for that would limit the availability of this common resource to all users as the need arises.[2] What is to be rationed instead is the *risk* that can be sustained by the given pool of capital.

One can envision a system of risk limits or internal pricing of risk usage that allocates, in some sense to be defined and measured, the risk of loss of firmwide capital from positions within each profit center. By any reasonable measure, however, risk is not additive across profit centers. For example, suppose we measure risk in terms of the standard deviation of earnings.[3] Suppose further that the firm has two profit centers: *A* with 4 units of risk,

---

[2] There are nevertheless circumstances in which capital is rationed, as between a parent bank and its subsidiary derivative product company (DPC). The emergence of DPCs is, however, the result of a rather subtle set of strategic marketing circumstances and might be counterproductive from the viewpoint of risk management of the parent firm.

[3] The standard deviation of earnings is the square root of the expected squared difference between earnings and expected earnings. For a random variable X, i.e., its standard deviation is $\sqrt{E\{[X - E(X)]^2\}}$. We ignore cases in which the standard deviation is not mathematically well defined.

and B with 3 units. The total risk of the firm could be as little as 1 (if the profits of A and B are perfectly negatively correlated) or as much as 7 units (if the profits of these centers have perfect positive correlation). Moreover, an increase in risk usage by B *could decrease the total risk of the firm,* if the earnings of A and B are sufficiently negatively correlated. If this correlation is sufficiently negative, profit center B should indeed be encouraged to *increase* its risk (ignoring other effects and assuming that additional risk bearing by B is, on its own, a profitable activity). Even if the earnings of A and B are uncorrelated, the total risk of the firm is not obtained by adding the individual risks for a total of 7, for there are diversification benefits. The total risk in the case of zero correlation, for instance, is $\sqrt{3^2 + 4^2} = 5$ units.

Allocation of risk to the various profit centers within the firm therefore calls for coordination. If each profit center determines the risk that it will bear based on its own business opportunities, the firm as a whole loses the potential to make effective use of diversification as a way to conserve costly capital. We also expect central management of the level of capital, in light of the costs of firmwide risk, such as financial distress, and the marginal costs and benefits of raising external capital or returning capital to shareholders.

One can envision a role not only for a coordinated allocation of risk to profit centers but also for additional market positions, perhaps chosen by a central risk manager, that are designed to manage the overall risk of the firm, given the positions of individual profit centers.

2.2.7. Risk-Adjusted Return on Capital?

The allocation of risk to profit centers may reflect the relative abilities of the profit centers to generate earnings. A profit center that, on average, generates relatively large additions to market value per unit of incremental risk is presumably one to be given larger risk limits (or a lower marginal charge for carrying risk), holding other effects equal.[4]

One such performance-based allocation scheme would have each profit center "bid" the amount of market value that it could add to its own position if it were allowed to change its portfolio of positions so as to increase the total risk of the firm by 1 unit. In order to make this computation, each profit center would need to know the sizes of the market values of all active positions within the firm as well as their volatilities and correlations. This calculation is hypothetical. Any profit center with the ability to add market value by *reducing* the firm's total risk would be automatically permitted to

---

[4] This is not a setting in which the usual reasoning of equilibrium capital-asset pricing theory can be applied. The intuition of the capital-asset pricing model, e.g., suggests that the expected return on an asset is increasing in its *systematic* risk. In perfect capital markets, however, no purely financial transaction can add market value. For more discussion, see Crouhy et al. (1998).

do so. This could arise, for example, through negative correlations. If, with this auction, the capital currently available to the firm were found capable of supporting one more unit of risk at a lower marginal financial distress cost than the highest bid, then the profit center offering the highest bid would be allowed to implement its own plan to increase the total risk of the firm by 1 unit. (The process would operate in reverse if the marginal financial distress cost exceeded the highest bid, in which case the lowest-bidding profit center would be asked to reduce the firm's total risk by 1 unit, unless more capital could be obtained at an even lower marginal cost.) Ideally, this auction would be operated continually.

As an example, suppose that we measure risk by standard deviation and that the contemplated increments to the firm's portfolio at each profit center are small relative to the entire firm's risk. Then the marginal impact on the firm's total risk of adding one additional unit of risk at profit center i is the correlation ρ_i between the incremental earnings of the proposed portfolio change at profit center i and the firm's total earnings.[5] Suppose, for simplicity, that all market value–adding increments with zero or negative correlations have already been exhausted, so that $\rho_i > 0$ for all i. If the position contemplated by profit center i adds a market value of v_i, then profit center i can bid $b_i = v_i/\rho_i$. The firm's central risk manager bids the incremental financial distress cost b_0 associated with a unit increase in the firm's risk. The highest bid is awarded the right to implement its planned change. (If b_0 is high, the low bidder must reduce the firm's risk by 1 unit.) At any time, the firm should raise capital whenever the net incremental market value of doing so is positive, considering the direct costs of raising capital and the benefits associated with reductions in financial distress costs.

As a practical matter, however, it seems difficult to implement the calculations necessary to estimate the incremental market value b_i that could be offered by profit center i per unit of firmwide risk. On top of this, casual discussion with high-level managers at financial-services firms suggest that individual managers are often not competing to add risk in any case, as they are risk-averse and carry personal reputational and other costs for losses.

We can sum up as follows. While the notion of a decentralized risk-management system that charges for risk based on relative earnings performance sounds clever in principle, it seems a difficult practical matter (with current technology) to find reasonably implementable formulas for

---

[5] Let D be the standard deviation of the firm's earnings and d the standard deviation of the proposed new position. Suppose we are to add t units of the proposed position. At correlation ρ, the total standard deviation is $v(t) = (D^2 + 2tdD\rho + t^2 d^2)^{1/2}$. Then $v'(0) = d\rho$. We can assume $d = 1$ by scaling. Obviously, this analysis only applies to "small" incremental positions (see Garman, 1996).

internal pricing of risk that: (1) appropriately compensate for the different
opportunities available to different profit centers, (2) exploit diversification opportunities across profit centers, and (3) account for the risk aversion of managers and traders. At some point in the risk-allocation process,
it seems appropriate that judgment and centralized decisions play significant roles.

2.2.8. Performance Incentives

Performance incentives that consider the risk taken to obtain a given profit
may generate better risk-return choices by traders, but should not be con-
fused with the allocation of risk limits based on expected returns. These are
related but not synonymous issues. For example, even if (for sake of discussion) a given trader is immune to incentives, and performance bonuses
that would encourage the trader to obtain higher expected profits by taking a given level of risk are therefore pointless, there may nevertheless be
an important role for risk limits that consider the expected profitability of
the trader's positions. For another example, two traders with identical skills
and effort that operate in different markets would be expected to perform
differently in terms of the expected earnings that they can produce for given
marginal additions to the firm's risk.

This is not to say that risk-based performance incentives are ineffectual,
but rather that one should not equate earnings performance per unit of
risk with ability or effort. The relative earnings of different profit centers
depend in part on their opportunities. The benefit of offering a given
profit incentive to a trader depends in part on that trader's alternative
opportunities.

Suppose, for example, that an investment bank has four divisional profit
centers, whose relative contributions to the firm's overall earnings are, on
average, as follows: equities, 35%; fixed income, 45%; foreign exchange,
15%; and commodities, 5%. In practice, would we expect the risks of the various profit centers to be in equal proportion to their relative contributions
to earnings? Probably not! How should we plan to charge different businesses for the risks they take? As we have seen, the answer to this question
depends on diversification effects, at least. We would also expect to see distinctions among lending, investment banking, market making, insurance,
and proprietary trading in terms of such variables as: (1) the importance
of the credit quality of customers, (2) the difficulty of measuring customer
credit quality, (3) the degree of flexibility in the choice of business configu-
ration, and (4) opportunities for developing profitable long-term customer
relationships that may benefit other profit centers. It therefore seems appropriate to view risk allocation within the firm as a process that is distinct
from, although related to, the evaluation of individual performance.

2.3. Economic Principles of Credit Risk

Credit risk acts through most of the same channels followed by other forms of market risk and also operates via other mechanisms.

2.3.1. Adverse Selection and Credit Exposure

Suppose, as is often the case in the business of lending, that a borrower knows more than its lender, say a bank, about the borrower's credit risk. Being at an informational disadvantage, the bank, in light of the distribution of default risks across the population of borrowers, may find it profitable to limit borrowers' access to the bank's credit, rather than allowing borrowers to select the sizes of their own loans without restriction.

An attempt to compensate for credit risk by increasing a borrower's interest rate or by a schedule of borrowing rates that increases with the size of the loan may have unintended consequences. A disproportionate fraction of borrowers willing to pay a high interest rate on a loan are privately aware that their own poor credit quality makes even the high interest rate attractive. An interest rate so high that it compensates for this adverse selection could mean that almost no borrower finds a loan attractive and that the bank would do little or no business.[6] Depending on the variation in credit risk over the population of borrowers, it may be (and, in practice, usually is) more effective to limit access to credit. Even though adverse selection can still occur to some degree, the bank can earn profits on average, depending on the distribution of default risk and private information in the population of borrowers.

In the case of an over-the-counter (OTC) derivative, such as a swap, an analogous asymmetry of credit information often exists. For example, counterparty A is typically better informed about its own credit quality than about the credit quality of counterparty B. (Likewise B usually knows more about its own default risk than about the default risk of A.) By the same adverse-selection reasoning described above for loans, A may wish to limit the extent of its exposure to default by B. Similarly, B does not wish its potential exposure to default by counterparty A to become large. Rather than limiting access to credit in terms of the notional size of the swap or its market value (which in any case is typically zero at the inception of a swap), it makes sense to measure credit risk in terms of the probability distribution of the exposure to default by the other counterparty. We return to this in Chapter 12.

---

[6] That is, the lemons premium that banks would extract from borrowers in order to make loans profitable could cause certain loan markets to break down, as proposed by Akerlof (1970) and by Stiglitz and Weiss (1981), in a model of credit rationing.

Based on adverse selection, quantitative exposure limits are analogous to a stock specialist's limit on size for market orders. Setting a smaller limit reduces volume and thereby limits profits. Setting a larger limit encourages the selection of positions with adverse credit quality. An "optimal" limit is one that trades off these two effects.

We expect that limits should be based on any information available on credit quality. For example, Aaa-rated counterparties should have higher limits than Baa-rated counterparties, for there is a relatively small likelihood that a large position initiated by an Aaa-rated counterparty is designed to exploit the broker-dealer's incomplete information of the counterparty's credit quality.

2.3.2. Credit Risk Concentrations

Banks and OTC derivatives broker-dealers measure and limit credit risk not only to individual counterparties, but also to industry groups, geographic regions, and sometimes other classifications. For example, the Derivatives Policy Group (1995)[7] recommended measurement (and disclosure) of credit exposure by industry, by geographic location, and by credit rating. Unless one supposes that such classifications define groups that might act in concert to take advantage of their private information, it may not be obvious from our discussion of loans to a privately informed borrower why one wishes to measure (or limit) credit concentration by groups. Here again, however, adverse selection can play a role.

For example, suppose that different banks are differentially informed about default risk in the real estate industry. Suppose that banks set rates naïvely, according to their own best estimates of the expected rate of losses owing to default. Simply from "noise," some banks will have lower default loss estimates than others and so set lower interest rates. Borrowers migrate to banks offering the most attractive rates, even if they have no private information about their own credit quality. Those banks with the lowest default-loss estimates will therefore end up offering an unusually large number of loans to real estate developers, even if the loans to individual borrowers are limited in size. These banks will therefore suffer an expected loss on their real estate loans, unless the interest rates that they charge are elevated sufficiently to offset this *winner's curse,* another form of adverse selection. At a mundane level, this could be as simple as a story in which the credit officer at "our bank" was sloppy or by chance neglected to consider, say, the risk of political instability in a region. Assuming that other banks were sufficiently "smart," or lucky, to have arrived at higher estimates of default risk, our

---

[7] The DPG was made up of representatives of CS First Boston, Goldman Sachs, Morgan Stanley, Merrill Lynch, Salomon Brothers, and Lehman Brothers.

bank will undertake a disproportionate share of loans with expected losses. The point of the adverse selection is that the law of averages does *not* offer protection. Rather, when we charge too much, we lose business; when we charge too little, we win business we should not want.

Banks can use both borrowing rates *and* credit risk concentration limits, by area of concentration to reduce the impact of the winner's curse. A full analysis would involve modeling equilibrium in loan markets with correlated default among borrowers and with asymmetrically informed lenders.[8] This is beyond our objectives here.

Another reason to measure concentrations of credit risk is to provide information for the coordination of the lending business. For example, suppose that, in aggregate, loans to a particular industry appear to be profitable. We may wish to monitor that level of profitability against the aggregate credit risk, so as to make judgments regarding the allocation of the firm's capital to loans made to firms in that industry. Measures of concentration risk can also be useful for crisis management. For example, a major news release, say a natural catastrophe or war, may prompt concern over default losses in a particular area of concentration. Timely information could be valuable in managing liquidity or laying off risk.

2.3.3. Moral Hazard

Within banking circles, there is a well-known saying: "If you owe your bank $100,000 that you don't have, you are in big trouble. If you owe your bank $100 million that you don't have, your bank is in big trouble." (The numbers and currency vary with the storyteller.) One of the reasons that large loans are more risky than small ones, other things being equal, is that they provide incentives for borrowers to undertake riskier behavior.

For example, it has often been noted that the U.S. savings-and-loan debacle of the 1980s was a consequence of giving savings-and-loan institutions access to extensive credit through federal deposit insurance, while at the same time not enforcing sufficient limits on the riskiness of savings-and-loan investments. This encouraged some savings-and-loan owners to take on highly levered and risky portfolios of long-term loans, mortgage-backed securities, and other risky assets. If these "big bets" turned out badly (as they ultimately did in many cases), and if a savings-and-loan institution failed as a result, its owners "walked away." If the big bets paid off, the owners of the savings-and-loan institution earned large gains.[9]

An obvious defense against the moral hazard induced by offering large loans to risky borrowers is to limit access to credit. The same story applies,

---

[8] We are not aware of any relevant literature. The model would be akin to that of a multiunit auction with asymmetric information.

[9] For a regulatory discussion and further references see Dewatripont and Tirole (1993).

in effect, with OTC derivatives. Indeed, it makes sense, when examining the probability distribution of credit exposure on an OTC derivative to use measures that place special emphasis on the largest potential exposures, providing some justification for high-percentile credit exposure measures, such as those considered in Chapter 12.

Large borrowers in default are often in a better bargaining position and can thereby extract more favorable terms for bankruptcy or restructuring than can small borrowers. This could, on average, reduce the profitability of larger loans, putting aside fixed costs for setting up loan arrangements. As with a bank, a derivatives broker-dealer may wish to limit the extent of credit exposure for particular counterparties. Large concentrations of credit risk, for example, with Latin American countries in the 1980s, might also induce coordinated responses by groups of defaulting borrowers, again reducing the bargaining power of the lender.

2.4. Risk Measurement

In addition to considering the broader strategic dimensions of risk management that we have discussed, senior managers of financial institutions, in collaboration with their research staffs, develop policies and systems. Key ingredients of their credit risk pricing and risk-measurement systems include: (1) the sources of risk (the risk factors) to be examined and their joint probability distribution, and (2) methodologies for measuring changes in credit quality and default over a large set of counterparties. We organize our outline of these ingredients around the basic schematic of the risk system presented in Figure 2.6.

The box labeled *Counterparty Data Bases* in Figure 2.6 represents a data

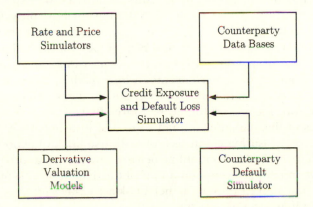

Figure 2.6. *Key elements of pricing and risk-measurement systems.*

base of portfolio positions, including the contractual definitions of each position (derivative, bond, and so on) and its collateralization and netting arrangements. For example, a single counterparty can create exposures under the names of thousands of different legal entities. The basic items in such a data base are important for pricing and risk management even in the absence of significant credit risk. For example, one needs the contractual definitions of each position in order to mark it to market. More challenging, however, is organizing information related to credit risk, including details regarding collateral and netting arrangements. Though the construction of such a data base is a formidable challenge and essential to the success of both pricing and risk-management systems, it is largely a firm-specific problem that is beyond our scope.

The box in Figure 2.6 labeled *Counterparty Default Simulator* is treated in Chapters 3 and 4, where we address default and credit-rating transition risk for a single counterparty, and then later in Chapter 10, where the correlation of default and transition risk among multiple counterparties is broached. Chapter 13 treats the box labeled *Rate and Price Simulators*, exploring the implications for market risk measurement of alternative parameterizations of the risk factors driving portfolio returns. Chapter 13 also addresses the revaluation of derivatives, illustrated in the box labeled *Derivative Valuation Models*, including the efficient estimation of the responses of the market values of derivatives positions to changes in underlying prices and rates and to changes in credit quality, including default.

The selection of a risk measure involves judgments about whether it is: (1) closely related to the key economic costs of financial risk; (2) estimable at a reasonable cost and within a reasonable tolerance; (3) easily communicated to, and understood by, those that use it; and (4) meaningfully aggregated from individual units or desks into an overall measure of risk for the firm. In computing both market and credit risks, we expect trade-offs among these criteria. For example, high-dimensional risk measures, such as the entire probability distribution of unexpected changes in market value, at all future dates, captures most of the risk-related information about the economic costs of market risk (given the firm's capital and holding other cost determinants constant). This much information, however, is difficult to estimate accurately, to communicate, and to digest. Market risk assessment therefore focuses on simple measures that summarize some of the key aspects of this high-dimensional source of information. Similarly, the challenges of measuring credit risk for a diverse book of exposures, many of which have embedded optionlike features, mean that approximate pricing models and implied representations of the default process may be used. Moreover, not all measures of financial risk are easily aggregated across individual trading desks or divisions.

The larger economic consequences of market risk are normally felt over relatively short time horizons. Over a matter of a few weeks, if not days, provided the firm's *franchise* has positive market value as an ongoing business, it would become apparent whether external capital can be refreshed at reasonable cost, or balance sheets can be reduced, or credit lines can be reestablished or extended. For example, in the aftermath of its Treasury auction "scandal" of 1991, which caused significant loss of business and liquidity problems, Salomon Brothers was able to quickly reduce its balance sheet by roughly $50 billion over a period of about 6 weeks,[10] using a previously established emergency plan based on increasing internal financing rates as an incentive for traders to reduce position sizes.

We therefore expect, because of both the difficulty of determining market risk over longer time horizons and the greater relevance of market risk over short horizons for many types of financial firms, to see a focus on risk measures that are based on the probability distribution of the change in market value of the firm over a relatively short time horizon.

Thus, in light of the preceding discussion, market risk measures should place more weight on those aspects of market risk that are more often accompanied by financial distress, such as: (1) severe negative cash flow events, (2) reductions in liquidity, and (3) relatively large losses in total market value, for example, exceeding some threshold at which distress costs typically become relevant, as illustrated in Figure 2.3. As we shall see, most conventional measures of market risk have emphasized the last of these.

2.4.1. Value at Risk

Regulators and their constituent financial institutions have generally focused on a widely applied measure of market risk called value at risk (VaR). Fixing a confidence level p such as 99% and a time horizon (e.g., 2 weeks), the VaR of a given portfolio is the loss in market value that is exceeded with probability $1 - p$, as illustrated in Figure 2.7. In other words, if $p = 0.99$, then, with 99% probability, the loss exceeds the VaR with 1% probability.[11]

Under normality of the distribution of market value, the VaR is approximately the mean change minus 2.33σ, where σ is the standard deviation of the daily change in market value. If, in addition, daily changes in market value are independently and identically distributed, then the VaR over n days is n times the daily mean change less $2.33\sigma\sqrt{n}$. With nonnormal or serially correlated returns, however, these well-known formulas for confidence levels are merely rough guidelines.

---

[10] See the *Wall Street Journal*, October 24, 1991.

[11] The VaR is not the difference between the expected value and the p-critical value of losses, but rather is the p-critical value itself. There is not much difference in practice for the error tolerance of current modeling techniques and for short time horizons.

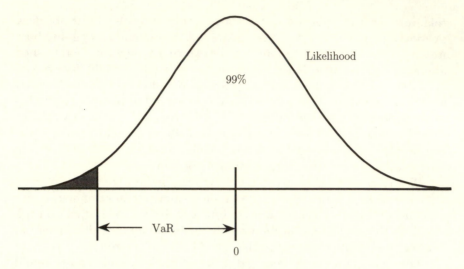

Figure 2.7.   *Value at risk.*

The concept of VaR is easy to grasp and communicate. The 99% confidence level, as opposed to some other confidence level, is rather arbitrary. If one is to use a risk measure based on a confidence level, and we shall have more to say on this point, then the choice of a confidence level should be linked somehow to the level of losses at which financial-distress costs become relevant, at least on average. With changes in market value that are independently distributed across time, a 99% 2-week VaR is actually exceeded by a 2-week loss roughly once every 4 years, a short life for a bank with a large franchise value! Clearly, then, given the goal of protecting the franchise value of the firm, one should not treat such a VaR measure, even if accurate, as the level of capital necessary to sustain the firm's risk.

It may be helpful, instead, to view VaR as merely a benchmark for *relative* judgments, such as the risk of one desk relative to another, the risk of one portfolio relative to another, the relative impact on risk of a given trade, the modeled risk relative to the historical experience of marks to market, the risk of one volatility environment relative to another, and so on. Even if accurate, comparisons such as these are specific to the time horizon and the confidence level associated with the VaR standard chosen.

With regard to how VaR is used in practice, the DPG proposed two uses of VaR: (1) reporting risk exposures to the SEC for their use in assessing overall systemic risk in the financial system; and (2) internal monitoring of risk exposures. For the purpose of preparing reports to the SEC on OTC derivatives activities, the DPG set a VaR time horizon of 2 weeks and a confidence level of 99%. Firms are permitted to use their own proprietary in-house models to determine their exposures. At a minimum, the models must include *core shocks* in the form of parallel yield-curve shifts, changes in yield-curve steepness, parallel yield-curve shifts in combination with changes in steepness, changes in yield volatilities, changes in the value and volatility of equity indices, changes in currency levels and volatilities, and changes in swap spreads. The responses of portfolios to the specified core shocks must be reported in addition to an overall VaR.[12] The models may use historical or market-implied volatilities and correlations. This approach explicitly recognizes that markets are correlated and that the degree of correlation affects the overall risk profile of a derivatives portfolio.

For the purposes of internal monitoring, risk management, and external disclosure of risks, any firm using VaR as a risk measure is free to choose its own confidence level and time horizon, as well as the nature of the risk factors underlying changes in value of their derivatives position. Many banks have chosen a 1-day time horizon for internal calculations of VaR, though 10 days is also common, and we are aware of one example of a 30-day horizon.[13] Firms also differ in their choices of confidence levels. For example, J. P. Morgan has disclosed its daily VaR at the 95% level. Before being acquired by Deutsche Bank, Bankers Trust disclosed statistics based on its daily VaR at the 99% level.

The Bank for International Settlements (BIS) accord allows a version of VaR to be used in the formula for the minimal capital that banks maintain as backing for their traded portfolios of financial instruments. The BIS has set a confidence level of 99% and a time horizon of 10 days for this purpose. The capital charge for users of a proprietary model is the higher of the previous day's VaR and three times the average daily VaR over the preceding 60 business days. This multiplier of three is intended to capture nonlinearities in price reactions to shocks that are not captured in VaR calculations, nonnormality of shocks, unexpected changes in such model parameters as volatility or correlation, and the residual risks not captured by the modeled risk factors. As with the DPG, the BIS provides explicit guidance on the nature of the risk factors that must be incorporated into proprietary models.[14] Banks have the discretion to account for correlations among price changes within broad risk categories (e.g., interest rates and

---

[12] These include, e.g., parallel yield-curve shifts of 100 basis points, up and down, steepening and flattening of the yield curves (2-year to 10-year) by 25 basis points, changes in swap spreads (up and down) of 20 basis points, among other scenarios.

[13] See Basle Committee on Banking Supervision and IOSCO (1997).

[14] See, e.g., Basle Committee on Banking Supervision and IOSCO (1996).

equity prices) and, with regulatory approval, can use proprietary measures of correlations across broad risk categories when aggregating risks.

Whether the VaR of a firm's portfolio of positions is a relevant measure of the risk of financial distress over a short time period depends in part on the liquidity of the portfolio and the risk of adverse extreme net cash outflows or of severe disruptions in market liquidity. In such adverse scenarios, the firm may suffer costs that include unanticipated short-term financing costs, opportunity costs of foregone profitable trades, and forced balance-sheet reductions involving market-impact costs. Whether the net effect actually threatens the ability of the firm to continue to operate profitably depends in part on the firm's net capital. VaR, coupled with some measure of *cash flow at risk*,[15] is relevant in this setting because it measures the extent of potential forced reductions of the firm's capital over short time periods, at some confidence level. Clearly, however, VaR captures only one aspect of market risk and is too narrowly defined to be used on its own as a sufficient measure of capital adequacy. Not surprisingly then, the BIS guidelines for risk capital based on VaR have been criticized by some members of the financial community.

2.4.2. Expected Tail Loss

A disadvantage of VaR is that it is not sensitive to the likelihoods of losses in excess of the VaR itself. Two different portfolios, for example, could have the same 99% VaR of, say, $50 million, but one may have significantly higher likelihood of losses in excess of $50 million than the other.

Instead of, or in addition to, VaR, one could measure the conditional expected loss, given that the loss is at least as large as some given level ℓ. If we let $L = -(P_s - P_t)$ denote the loss, this risk measure is defined by

$$T_\ell = E(L \mid L \geq \ell). \tag{2.1}$$

This measure is illustrated in Figure 2.8 for the case of $\ell = L_{0.99}$, the 99% confidence level on loss. In some cases the expected tail loss can be computed analytically and, otherwise, Monte Carlo simulation can be used by simply averaging the losses over all scenarios in which the loss exceeds the threshold level ℓ.

If the market value is normally distributed, then the expected tail loss and the VaR are in fixed proportion to the standard deviation σ of the change in market value, and these measures thus provide equivalent information. With normality, for example, $E(L \mid L \geq L_{0.99}) \simeq 2.67\sigma$. If, on the

---

[15] By cash flow at risk we mean a similarly high confidence level for the net cash outflow over the relevant time horizon.

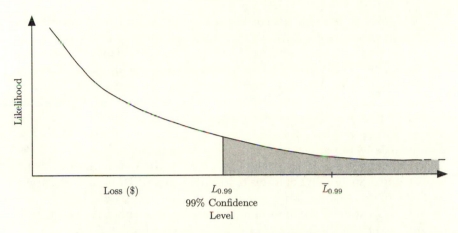

Figure 2.8. *Expected tail loss,* $\overline{L}_{0.99} = E(L \mid L \geq L_{0.99})$.

other hand, changes in market value are not normally distributed, then the standard deviation, the VaR, and the expected tail loss would be distinct sources of information on market risk.

2.4.3. The Price of Market Value Insurance

An alternative measure of the market risk of a firm's portfolio is the cost of an insurance policy guaranteeing that the market value does not fall by more than a given amount, say ℓ. In efficient markets, this insurance premium is the price of a put option on the portfolio, struck at ℓ out of the money. This measure of risk is the actual economic price of eliminating a given portion of the market risk.

For the short time horizons of a few days or weeks over which market risk measures are often applied, the price of an insurance policy that guarantees that market value will not drop by more than ℓ would be reasonably approximated by the expected claim against the policy. (The theoretical impact of discounting for time and for risk premia is typically small for short time horizons, unless there can be large jumps in prices.) This expected claim is $c_\ell = E[\max(L - \ell, 0)]$, where, as above, L is the loss in market value over the given time horizon. This expected insurance claim c_ℓ and the expected tail T_ℓ are closely related, in that

$$c_\ell = q(T_\ell - \ell), \tag{2.2}$$

where q is the probability that the loss exceeds ℓ. That is, for fixed q, the two measures c_ℓ and T_ℓ provide equivalent information.

A closely related measure of market risk, proposed for broader purposes by Merton and Perold (1993), is the cost of insuring against losses in the market value of *net assets*. By net assets, Merton and Perold mean gross assets net of default-free versions of customer liabilities, such as deposits, swaps, property or casualty insurance policies, guaranteed investment contracts, and so on. Merton and Perold use the term *risk capital* to describe this insurance premium. For example, suppose (to take one of the examples provided by Merton and Perold) a firm has $2.5 billion in risky assets and a single liability whose default-free market value is $1 billion. The net asset value is therefore $1.5 billion. Suppose it would cost $500 million to insure against any reduction in net assets below $1.5 billion. Then the risk capital is $500 million.

The risk capital is the minimum investment that would be necessary to obtain default-free financing for the firm. In effect, creditors, customers, equityholders, and any other stakeholders implicitly or explicitly provide the risk capital of a financial firm.

One can also view the risk capital as the premium of an at-the-money put option on net assets. For practical purposes, the risk capital could be computed in essentially the same manner as one would compute the expected tail loss or the price of insurance on the firm's total market value.

2.4.4. Volatility as a Measure of Market Risk

All of the risk measures that we have discussed are sensitive to the volatility (standard deviation) σ of market value. Indeed, one can make a strong case for volatility itself as a risk measure, at least over short time periods and for many types of financial firms. Relative to other conventional risk measures, volatility is easily estimated and communicated. For example, the language of volatility is well understood in the financial industry, and statistical measures of volatility are more reliable, and more readily validated from historical experience, than are VaR and some of the other risk measures that we have discussed. (Under normality, of course, these measures all provide the same information once one ignores mean effects, which are typically small.)

A disadvantage of volatility is that it does not focus specifically on large losses.

2.4.5. Coherency of Risk Measures

The risk measures that we have discussed, while meaningful, are not equally attractive from the perspective of the decentralization of risk management within a firm or from the viewpoint of aggregation of risk measures across positions or trading units. Artzner et al. (1999) analyze desirable properties for a portfolio risk measure. Such a measure $m(\cdot)$ assigns, to any portfolio whose market value at the test horizon is a random variable X, the risk measure $m(X)$.[16] These authors call such a risk measure $m(\cdot)$ *coherent* if it satisfies the four axioms,[17]

1. Subadditivity: For any portfolio payoffs X and Y,

$$m(X + Y) \leq m(X) + m(Y).$$

2. Homogeneity: For any number $\alpha > 0$, $m(\alpha X) = \alpha m(X)$.
3. Monotonicity: $m(X) \geq m(Y)$ if $X \leq Y$.
4. Risk-free condition: $m(X + k) = m(X) - k$, for any constant k.

VaR satisfies homogeneity, monotonicity, and the risk-free condition, but is not subadditive. This is a potentially serious limitation when aggregating risk measures across business units (e.g., trading desks or divisions), for a failure of subadditivity implies that there are cases in which the benefits of diversification are not recognized. For example, suppose X and Y are the independently and identically distributed payoffs on two loans, each of which pays the full principal of 100 with probability 0.994, and otherwise defaults and pays nothing. If our risk measure $m(\cdot)$ is VaR at the 99% confidence level, then $m(X) = m(Y) = 0$, for the likelihood of loss is "below the radar" of the VaR measure, which captures only losses that occur with at least probability 0.01. Consider, on the other hand, a portfolio that includes one-half of each of the loans. We have $m(X/2 + Y/2) = 50$, because the event that at least one bond defaults has a probability just over 1%, and the event of default by both is less than 1%. As a risk measure, VaR therefore discourages diversification.

Artzner et al. (1999) provide natural conditions under which the expected-tail-loss risk measure T_ℓ is coherent. Unfortunately, the simple risk measure that is given by the mean loss plus a multiple of the standard deviation of loss is not coherent. This risk measure is defined by

$$m(X) = E(-X) + \beta \sigma_X, \tag{2.3}$$

where σ_X denotes the standard deviation of X, and $\beta > 0$ is a fixed coefficient. Regardless of β, this measure fails the monotonicity axiom.

---

[16] There are technical limitations. Artzner et al. (1999) assume a finite number of states of the world in order to simplify the technical issues.

[17] We are implicitly using *cash* as a reference point for measuring losses, which is slightly less general than allowed by Artzner et al. (1999).

2.5. Measuring Credit Risk

Credit risk should be treated as part of market risk. The measurement of credit risk, however, provides its own set of challenges. Many credit-sensitive instruments are relatively illiquid, remain on a firm's books for lengthy periods of time, and cannot be reliably marked to market.

Here, we first discuss the integration of credit risks and other forms of market risk into conventional market risk systems. Then, we examine various specialized measures of credit risk for regulatory reporting, internal monitoring, and the setting of counterparty exposure limits.

2.5.1. Specialized Measures of Credit Risk

Adverse selection and moral hazard imply that there are additional benefits, beyond the contribution of credit risk to market risk, of controlling counterparty credit risk and limiting concentrations of credit risk by industry, geographic region, and so on. In order to better understand the nature of their exposures to credit risk, risk managers have explored several complementary measures of credit risk, including:

- *Market value of default loss.* Reliable estimates of the impact of credit risk on fair market values contribute to the accuracy of pricing and the profitability of making markets. Chapter 12 discusses relevant methodologies. This information is also useful for determining a financial institution's liquidity "buffer" for default losses, or the fraction of a financial firm's capital that underpins credit risk.
- *Exposure.* The exposure to a given counterparty (or collection of counterparties) is the loss in the event of default. For example, one could measure, by date, the expected exposure or the 99% confidence level of exposure. As explained in Chapter 12, it is common to condense this information into a single potential exposure measure, such as the lifetime maximum of the period-by-period 99% confidence limit on exposure. Exposure measures are often used when enforcing policy limits for granting additional credit, on the basis of the impact of a candidate new position on the exposure measure.

As noted by the Counterparty Risk Management Policy Group (1999), in broad terms, these specialized measures of risk are used somewhat differently by financial institutions, depending on the nature of their credit-sensitive businesses. Those institutions primarily emphasizing trading (including most global investment banks) set counterparty exposure limits based on estimates of future *potential credit exposures* of derivatives positions and generally focus on credit risk from a counterparty perspective. In contrast, traditional banks engaged primarily in direct lending have tended to view credit risk more from the viewpoint of current credit granted, including some summary measure of lines of loan guarantees and contractual lines of credit. As credit risk systems evolve and the activities of banks and investment banks become more common, these distinctions become increasingly blurred. Investment banks should be expected to continue to set counterparty exposure limits, to mitigate adverse-selection problems, using measures of exposure. At the same time, as they develop the informational and technological systems to measure the sensitivities of the prices of OTC derivatives to changes in credit factors, credit risk is being increasingly folded into market risk–measurement systems. That is, the treatment of credit risk in OTC derivatives is increasingly being approached from the same firmwide portfolio perspective that is used in assessing the risks of corporate bonds or loans.

Besides these and other internal measures of credit risk, financial institutions are required to measure and report credit risk to the appropriate regulatory authorities. Regulators have focused primarily on measures of exposure. We proceed with an overview of measures of credit risk for regulatory reporting and then return to measures of loss risk and the value of potential default losses. A more formal treatment of model-based versions of these specialized measures of credit risk is presented in Chapter 13.

2.5.2. *Capital Guidelines for Credit Exposures*

The "original" 1988 Basel Accord, organized under the auspices of the BIS, became the standard for capital requirements for internationally active banks, first in the Group-of-Ten (G10) countries and Switzerland and subsequently in more than 100 countries. The basic idea of the accord is that banks must hold capital of at least 8% of total *risk-weighted* assets. In order to calculate this total measure of assets, each asset is multiplied by a risk weighting factor that, in principle, represents the credit quality of the asset. As for market risks of other types, such as the risk of changes in interest rates and market prices, regulated banks have been required since the mid-1990s to hold capital against their trading books, as described in our earlier discussion of the use of VaR as a benchmark for capital requirements. A bank's trading book is the portion of the bank's portfolio, containing, for example, OTC derivatives, that is marked to market in its accounts because of the lack of an indicated intent of the bank to hold these investments to maturity.

As of June 2001, the risk weights for the nontrading portion of bank portfolios set by the 1988 BIS accord are:

0%   Cash and claims on central governments and central banks, denominated and funded in their national currency.

20%   Claims on banks incorporated in OECD countries and cash items in the process of collection.

50%   Loans fully secured by mortgages on residential property that is rented or occupied by the borrower.

100% Claims on the private sector, claims on banks outside the OECD with a residual maturity of more than 1 year, and real estate investments.

This schedule notably calls for corporate loans to receive a 100% risk weighting, regardless of the corporation's credit rating, whereas loans to banks domiciled in OECD countries, regardless of their credit quality, receive the lower 20% weighting. For example, the capital required to back a loan to an AAA-rated corporation is five times that required to back the same size loan to any regulated bank in, say, Turkey, which happens to be a speculatively rated OECD country. (Notably, loans to governments of OECD countries, regardless of credit quality, would carry no capital requirement.)

In order to address the obvious imbalances created by the 1988 accord, a new capital accord is approaching approval. The new accord, planned for implementation in 2005, reflects the relative credit qualities of obligors based on their credit ratings, according to one of two approaches—standardized and internal-ratings-based.

Table 2.1 shows the proposed risk weights for the standardized approach. Each jurisdiction will choose one of two options for the treatment of loans to banks. Under option 1, loans to banks are assigned the rating

Table 2.1.   Proposed BIS Accord Standardized Risk Weights

Security type	Risk weights (percent)					
	AAA to AA−	A+ to A−	BBB+ to BBB−	BB+ to B−	Below B−	Unrated
Asset-backed	20	50	100	150[1]	Deducted	Deducted
Banks, option 1[2]	20	50	100	100	150	100
Banks, option 2[3]	20	50[4]	50[4]	100[4]	150	50[4]
Corporates	20	100	100	100	150	100
Sovereigns	0	20	50	100	150	100

Source: BIS Reports.

Notes: [1] Securitization tranches rated BB+ to BB− would be risk weighted 150%. Tranches rated below B+ and unrated tranches would be deducted from capital.

[2] Risk weighting based on the risk weighting of sovereign in which the bank is incorporated.

[3] Risk weighting based on the rating of the individual bank.

[4] Claims on banks with an original maturity of less than 6 months would receive a weighting that is one category more favorable than the risk weight shown above (e.g., 20% instead of 50%), subject to a floor of 20%.

of their sovereign. Under option 2, loans to banks are assigned the obligor bank's own rating, with special lower risk weights for loans maturing in less than 6 months.

The standardized approach will better recognize the benefits of credit risk mitigation. Compared to the 1988 accord, the standardized approach allows for a wider range of acceptable collateral (subject to volatility-based haircuts) and for offsets for a wider range of acceptable guarantees and credit derivatives. For example, guarantees and credit derivatives supplied by an OECD government, by a bank with a rating higher than that of the obligor, or by any corporation rated A or higher will be recognized as offsets to assets, after haircuts. For the trading portfolio of the bank, similar offsets to market risk will be allowed, including recognition of an 80% offset for default swaps.

A disadvantage of the standardized approach is that exposure to un-rated obligors (which are numerous in some countries) will receive a 100% risk weight. As indicated in Table 2.1, because certain low-rated obligors carry an even higher risk weight of 150%, the standardized approach sets up a perverse incentive for obligors to become unrated or for banks to loan to poor-quality unrated borrowers over certain rated borrowers.

Under the internal-ratings-based approach, a bank could, subject to limits and approval, use its own internal credit ratings. The ratings must correspond to benchmarks for 1-year default probabilities. The internal ratings methodology must be recognized by the bank's regulator and have been in place for at least 3 years. Table 2.2, whose calculations are from Jackson and Emblow (2001), compares the capital required for senior un-secured corporate exposures under the 1988 accord, the proposed stan-dardized approach, and the proposed internal-ratings-based approach. (The 1-year default probabilities shown in this table for corporate borrow-ers rated AAA, AA, and A are the same because the Basel Committee on Banking Supervision set a minimum allowable estimate of 0.03% for 1-year default probabilities.) The committee provides a formula for the capital required for each interval of default probabilities, based on expected losses plus unexpected losses, allowing for recoveries based on seniority and type of security.

The currently proposed form of the internal-ratings-based approach also allows for a *granularity adjustment* that recognizes, albeit in a relatively imprecise manner, the benefits of diversification.[18] It appears, however, that regulatory acceptance of a full model-based estimate of credit risk for pur-poses of regulatory capital requirements is still some years away. A full

---

[18] Gordy (2001) provides some theoretical foundation for granularity-based diversifica-tion adjustments in a setting with at most one common credit risk factor that determines cor-relation among defaults.

Table 2.2.   Comparison of Capital Requirements for Senior Unsecured Corporate Debt

Credit rating	1-Year percent default probability	Capital requirements (percent of assets)		
		Current accord	Standardized approach	Internal-ratings-based approach
AAA	0.03	8.0	1.6	1.13
AA	0.03	8.0	1.6	1.13
A	0.03	8.0	4.0	1.13
BBB	0.20	8.0	8.0	3.61
BB	1.40	8.0	8.0	12.35
B	6.60	8.0	12.0	30.96
CCC	15.00	8.0	12.0	47.04

Source: Jackson and Emblow (2001).

model-based approach would directly recognize the benefits of diversification, for example, by Monte Carlo simulation of defaults with correlation.

The new accord will also introduce a capital charge for operational risk. The total capital charge will then be the sum of charges for market risk (for a bank's trading book), operational risk, and credit risk. The total capital required will remain at 8% of risk-weighted assets, but the calculation of risk-weighted assets will, as described above, be more sophisticated.

3

Default Arrival: Historical Patterns and Statistical Models

THE RISK OF default occupies a central role in the pricing and hedging of credit risk. Different approaches to modeling default probabilities, and their migration, have been pursued. We begin with a broad interpretation of causes for fluctuations in the default rates reported by the major U.S. ratings agencies. This is followed by a discussion of models of default probabilities and timing, beginning with structural models, in which the issuer's inability (or lack of incentive to pay) is explicitly modeled as the default-triggering event. We then turn to reduced-form models, in which default is treated as an unexpected event whose likelihood is governed by a default-intensity process. Under both approaches, the likelihood of default may be dependent on observable variables such as balance-sheet ratios or business cycle variables. This chapter also provides two basic methods for default-time simulation, one directly from the probability distribution of the default time, when it is easily calculated, and a compensator method based on simulation of the underlying intensity process. Finally, various statistical models of default likelihoods are reviewed, along with some of the empirical evidence on the economic factors most closely associated with default. Historical patterns in transitions to nondefault ratings are discussed in Chapter 4. Default probabilities can be adjusted for risk premia so as to be used for pricing, as explained in Chapter 5.

3.1. Introduction

Our main objective in this chapter is to model default probabilities conditional on reasonably available information, obligor by obligor, and also to model how these probabilities may fluctuate over time with the arrival of new information.

A naïve measure of default probability for a firm or sovereign that is

43

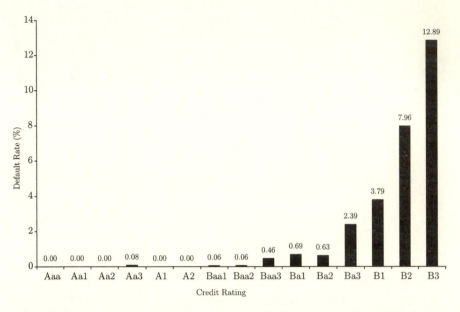

Figure 3.1. *Average 1-year default rates for 1983–2000 by Moody's modified credit rating. (Source: Moody's.)*

rated by an agency such as Moody's or Standard & Poor's is the average frequency with which obligors of the same rating have defaulted. For example, Figure 3.1 shows average 1-year corporate default rates, by rating, for the years 1983–2000, as published by Moody's[1] for senior unsecured debt.[2] The height of each bar is the fraction of those firms of the indicated rating at the beginning of a year that defaulted within the year, on average through the sample period.

We describe the use of these or similar average default rates as "naïve" estimates of default probabilities for several reasons, key among which are:

- Credit ratings are not intended by rating agencies to be a measure of a firm's default probability over some time horizon such as 1 year. Rating agencies also consider, to varying degrees, the extent of losses at default and other aspects of anticipated performance for investors

---

[1] Moody's defines a default to be: (1) a missed or delayed payment (including delays within a grace period), (2) a filing for bankruptcy (in the United States, Chapter 11 or Chapter 7) or a legal receivership, or (3) a distressed exchange, including restructuring amounting to a diminished obligation or an exchange for debt with the purpose of helping the borrower avoid default.

[2] Senior unsecured debt is unsecured debt with the highest contractual payment priority in the event of default.

over the life of a debt instrument. The degree to which other dimensions of default risk are considered varies over time and among rating agencies.[3]

- Credit ratings are, to some extent, measures of *relative* credit quality among firms. For instance, there is evidence (e.g., from Ederington and Yawitz, 1987) that ratings are more stable through business cycles than would be indicated by absolute default risk. We revisit this issue in this chapter and in Chapter 4.

- Average default frequencies are merely that, *averages*, and do not reflect newly available information as it arrives in the market nor distinctions among firms of the same rating that can be made from firm-specific data.

At the macroeconomic level, the average incidence of default in broadly constructed cohorts depends strongly on the current state of the economy. For example, Figure 3.2 shows, year by year, the rate of default of speculative-grade debt (i.e., debt rated below Baa by Moody's). The illustrated fluctuations in default rates support a widely held view that default rates are negatively correlated with real economic activity over the business cycle. (The spike shown in 1970 is an outlier caused by the collapse of Penn Central Railroad, which instigated numerous defaults on closely related issues.)

Probing more deeply, using quarterly, speculative-grade default rates compiled from Moody's data, we found that the correlation between the four-quarter moving averages of default rates and GDP growth rates for the sample period 1983–1997 was −0.78.[4] The close relationship between GDP growth rates and default rates during this period is illustrated in Figure 3.3. The illustrated data are standardized by subtracting from each time series its sample mean and dividing by its sample standard deviation. The post-1983 negative correlation is evident, especially in the 1990–1991 recession. During the earlier period of 1971–1982, however, this correlation was 0.07. Other than the fact that Moody's adjusted its ratings methodology in 1983, we have no convincing story for the lack of an apparent cyclical relationship between GDP growth rates and speculative default rates during the period before 1983.

Additional empirical support for the connection between the business cycle and default rates is provided by Fons (1991) and Jonsson and Fridson (1996). Fons (1991) finds a significant negative correlation between GNP growth rates and the deviations of actual speculative-grade default rates

---

[3] See Ederington and Yawitz (1987) and Moody's Investors Service (1993).

[4] We chose 1982 as the break point, because Moody's introduced a finer alpha-numeric ratings system in April 1982 and reclassified a large number of firms into different letter ratings.

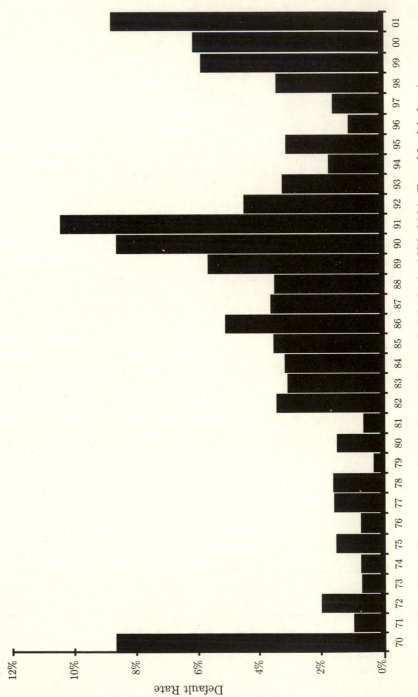

Figure 3.2. One-year annual rates of speculative-grade defaults for 1970–2001. (From Moody's data.)

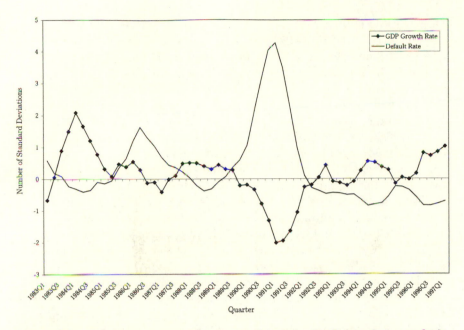

Figure 3.3. *Four-quarter moving averages of (standardized) speculative-grade default rates (solid line) and real GDP growth rates (diamonds) over the period 1983–1997. The vertical axis measures the number of standard deviations from sample mean.*

from expected default rates.[5] Jonsson and Fridson (1996) extended Fon's model to include various additional macroeconomic predictors of default. Their model explains approximately 50% of the variation in default rates within the sample for the period 1970–1994. More specifically, Blume and Keim (1991) found that default patterns of low-grade bonds issued in 1977 and 1978 were correlated with general business conditions.

3.1.1. The Changing Composition of Speculative Debt

Before the recession of 2001, by far the largest default rates shown in Figure 3.2 were experienced in 1990–1991. One obvious explanation is that 1990–1991 was a period during which the U.S. economy was in a recession.

---

[5] Expected default rates were computed by multiplying the number of firms in a given rating for a given year by the long-run average default rate for that rating. These products were then added across ratings to get a total expected default rate.

Upon further investigation, however, this explanation seems overly simplistic. The recession of 1981–1982 was much more severe in the United States, and yet default rates were much lower than in the early 1990s. Likewise, although the recession of 2001 was mild by conventional measures such as GDP growth, it was accompanied by unusually high rates of speculative-grade defaults of over 11% at their peak. As Lucas and Lonski (1992) and Jonsson and Fridson (1996), among others, have noted, default rates in the early 1990s were likely to have been influenced by the changing composition of the low-grade debt issues during the late 1980s, a period during which Michael Millken of Drexel Burnham Lambert was a particularly active catalyst for the issuance of large quantities of junk bonds.

According to calculations by Moody's reported in Lucas and Lonski (1992), from the beginning of 1988 to the end of the third quarter of 1990: (1) Ba-rated bonds fell from 38 to 27.6% of the face value of speculative-grade debt, and (2) the total face value of bonds rated B3 and Caa increased from 19 to 30.6% of the speculative-grade population.

The evolution of the composition of speculative-grade debt was precipitated in part by the unusually large levels of issuance of low-grade debt during the takeover and restructuring activities of the late 1980s. Figure 3.4 shows the par amounts of new issues of debt rated B− or below and debt rated B through BB+ by Standard & Poor's from 1980 through 1996. The quantity of very-low-grade debt issued between 1986 and 1989 was notably large. Figure 3.5 shows that the composition of speculative-grade debt continued to become more skewed toward lower ratings through the end of the twentieth century.

Some information about the effects of low-grade debt supply on default patterns is provided by Table 3.1. The numbers in square brackets next to each cohort year indicate the number of firms in the Standard & Poor's CCC-rated universe of bonds. For the early cohorts (those prior to 1986), the years 1986 and 1990 again stand out for their relatively high default rates. The number of CCC-rated firms more than tripled between 1986 and 1987. The default rates for subsequent cohorts are less concentrated in the years 1986 and 1990. The pattern of high 1-year default rates during the first year of the cohort, for all cohorts between 1988 and 1992, is particularly striking. The patterns suggest that these high first-year rates are not entirely caused by an aging effect for issues from previous years that may have experienced increased default rates. Rather, for a given cohort, the second-year default rate of the previous year's cohort is typically smaller than the 1-year rate for the given cohort.

In summary, these results present clear evidence of business cycle effects on default rates. At the same time, they suggest that knowledge of, say, GNP growth rates is not sufficient to capture the complexity of cycli-

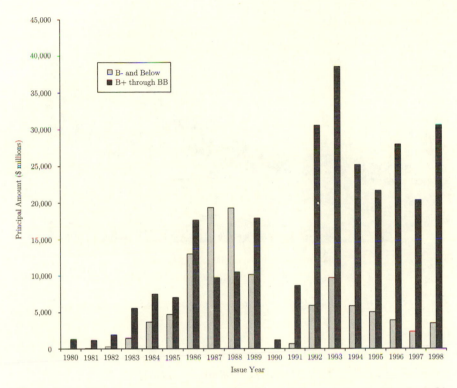

Figure 3.4. *Par issue amounts of straight debt rated B– or below by Standard &*
Poor's. (Tabulated using data from Securities Data Corporation.)

cal effects on default rates and spreads. Figure 3.3 suggests that industry-
specific developments such as the dramatic decline in oil prices in 1986
are missed by such aggregate measures of economic activity. Furthermore,
cyclical changes in supply are in part related to factors that influence waves
of takeovers and restructuring of the sort that occurred in the late 1980s.
The importance of an aging effect is less clear from these statistics and is
revisited in Section 3.7.

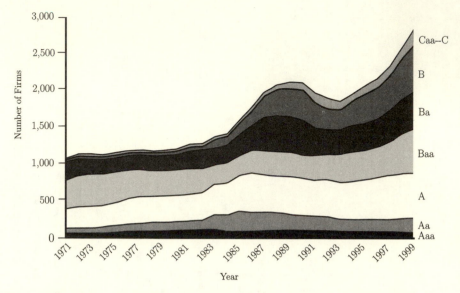

Figure 3.5.   *Changing composition of debt by rating. (Source: Moody's.)*

3.1.2. Forward Default Probabilities

For any model of default timing, we let $p(t)$ denote the probability of surviving t years. That is, as assessed at date 0, $p(t)$ is the likelihood that the firm will not default for at least t years. The probability of default between any times t and $s \geq t$ is thus $p(t) - p(s)$.

The probability of surviving to time s, given survival to time t, but given no other information about the issuer or economy, is, by Bayes's rule,[6]

$$p(s \mid t) = \frac{p(s)}{p(t)}. \tag{3.1}$$

We call $1 - p(s \mid t)$ the *forward default probability,* meaning the probability of default between times t and s, given survival to time t. Such conditional probabilities are important building blocks for modeling both default risk and credit-related prices. Figure 3.6 illustrates with a Venn diagram the

---

[6] Bayes's rule states that for any events A and B we have $P(A \text{ and } B) = P(A \mid B)P(B)$. Here, A is the event of survival for s years and B is the event of survival for t years. The event that both A and B occur is the event of survival for s years, so Bayes's rule leads to (3.1).

Table 3.1. *One-Year Cohort Default Rates (percent) for Standard & Poor's CCC-Rated Bonds*

Cohort		Calendar year													
		1981	1982	1983	1984	1985	1986	1987	1988	1989	1990	1991	1992	1993	1994
1981	[13]	0	7.69	0	0	0	7.69	0	0	0	7.69	0	0	0	0
1982	[16]		18.75	0	6.25	0	6.25	0	0	0	6.25	0	0	0	0
1983	[18]			0	11.11	0	5.56	5.56	0	0	5.56	5.56	0	0	0
1984	[21]				14.29	9.52	4.76	0	0	4.76	4.76	0	0	0	0
1985	[21]					9.52	4.76	0	0	4.76	4.76	0	0	0	0
1986	[20]						20.00	0	0	5.00	0	0	0	0	0
1987	[65]							7.69	12.31	6.15	3.08	12.31	1.54	3.08	0
1988	[58]								22.41	6.90	1.72	12.07	3.45	0	0
1989	[55]									25.45	3.64	10.91	5.45	5.45	0
1990	[51]										29.41	11.76	13.73	5.88	0
1991	[68]											30.88	10.29	2.94	2.94
1992	[55]												29.09	3.64	3.64
1993	[50]													12.00	4.00
1994	[24]														16.77

Note: The numbers in square brackets in the cohort column are the numbers of bonds in the Standard & Poor's CCC-rated universe of bonds for the cohort year.

calculation of the conditional probability of default between years 5 and 6 given survival to year 5.

Now, supposing that the survival probability $p(t)$ is strictly positive and is differentiable in t, we let

$$f(t) = \frac{-p'(t)}{p(t)}.$$ (3.2)

From a bit of calculus, it follows that

$$p(t) = e^{-\int_0^t f(u)\,du}.$$ (3.3)

Moreover, with an application of (3.1),

$$p(s \mid t) = e^{-\int_t^s f(u)\,du}$$ (3.4)

is the probability of survival to s given survival to t. Thus the forward default rate $f(t)$ is a useful basis for modeling the *term structure* of default risk. Indeed, $f(t)$ is analogous to a forward interest rate in a close mathematical analogy between zero-coupon bond prices and survival probabilities.

One can also think of $f(t)$ as the rate of default arrival at time t conditional only on survival up to time t. Indeed, if f is continuous then $f(t)\Delta$ is approximately equal to the probability of default between t and $t + \Delta$, conditional on survival to t. Sometimes the forward default rate is called the *hazard rate,* a term that is often found in the reliability literature.

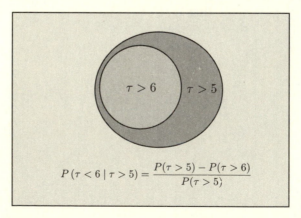

Figure 3.6. *Forward default probability by Bayes's rule.*

3.2. Structural Models of Default Probability

Firms default when they cannot, or choose not to, meet their financial obligations. In this section, we consider models that are based explicitly on the timing of such a default-triggering event. Most of these models are based on a balance-sheet notion of solvency, in that default occurs when assets are too small relative to liabilities.

We begin with the classic model of Black and Scholes (1973) and Merton (1974), under which default occurs at the maturity date of debt in the event that the issuer's assets are less than the face value of the debt. KMV Corporation has developed a successful empirical estimator of default probabilities, called the *estimated default frequency* (EDF), based on this model, which we review shortly. Moody's has also recently marketed an estimator of default probabilities that is based on balance-sheet information.

Then, we review a second structural approach based on the assumption that default occurs as soon as the asset value of a firm falls below a certain boundary, often taken to be the face value of its liabilities. We compare this *first-passage model* to the Merton model for their implications regarding default probabilities. In Chapter 5, we reconsider these structural models for their implications regarding bond pricing.

3.2.1. The Black-Scholes-Merton Default Model

For the case of a single bond of face value D maturing at T, the pathbreaking approach of Black and Scholes (1973) and Merton (1974) assumes default at time T in the event that $A_T \leq D$. As explained in Chapter 2, this model treats the process A, the market value of the firm's assets, as a log-normal diffusion, which allows the firm's equity to be priced with the Black-Scholes formula as though it is a call option on the total asset value A of the firm, struck at the face value of debt. The value of the debt is then simply obtained by subtracting this equity *option price* from the initial asset value, as we see later in Chapter 5.

The associated model of the default probability is illustrated in Figure 3.7, where the total value of assets A is approximated as the sum of the market value of equity and the book value of liabilities. Looking forward from "now," the default probability is obtained from the probability distribution of asset values at the maturity date T.

This model is based on a log-normal asset process, under which

$$\frac{dA_t}{A_t} = (\mu - \gamma) \, dt + \sigma \, dB_t, \tag{3.5}$$

where μ is the mean rate of return on assets, γ is the proportional cash payout rate, σ is the asset volatility, and B is a standard Brownian motion.

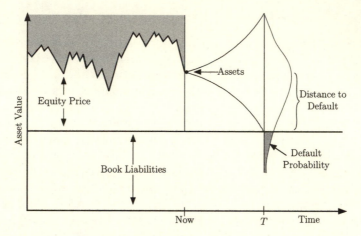

Figure 3.7.   The Black-Scholes-Merton structural model of default.

A key concept in this setting is the distance to default, which is the number of standard deviations by which assets exceed liabilities. Measured on a current basis, the distance to default is

$$X_t = \frac{\log A_t - \log D}{\sigma}. \tag{3.6}$$

We note that X is a Brownian motion with a unit variance parameter and a constant drift of $m = (\mu - \gamma - \sigma^2/2)/\sigma$, the rate of change of the mean distance to default. (This calculation follows from Itô's formula.) Under the Black-Scholes-Merton model, default occurs at the maturity date T with current conditional probability

$$P(X_T \leq 0 \mid X_t) = N\left[u(t, T)\right], \tag{3.7}$$

where $N(x)$ is the probability that a standard normal variable is less than x, and

$$u(t, T) = \frac{X_t + m(T - t)}{\sqrt{T - t}} \tag{3.8}$$

is the number of standard deviations by which the mean distance to default exceeds zero at the debt-maturity horizon T, using the fact that the standard deviation of X_T given X_t is $\sqrt{T - t}$.

That this style of model has predictive power for rating migrations and defaults is shown, for example, by Delianedis and Geske (1998).

3.2.2. First-Passage Models

Black and Cox (1976) introduced the idea that default would occur at the first time that assets drop to a sufficiently low default boundary, whether or not at the maturity date of the debt. They assumed a simple time-dependent default boundary, exploiting the fact that there is an explicitly known probability distribution (and Laplace transform) for the first time that a Brownian motion (with constant drift and volatility parameters) reaches a given level. Many subsequent structural models, including those of Fischer et al. (1989), Leland (1994), Anderson and Sundaresan (1996), and Mella-Barral (1999), have considered incentive-based models for the default boundary and the default recovery. Variants and extensions are due to Longstaff and Schwartz (1995) and Leland and Toft (1996), among many others.

Focusing for the moment on this simple first-passage model, suppose default occurs at the first time at which the log-normally distributed asset level, A_t defined by (3.5), reaches a constant default threshold D, which need not be the face value of debt, but rather may be chosen by the firm so as to maximize the market value of equity. For each time horizon T, the survival probability is then the probability $p(t, T)$ that the distance to default does not reach zero between t and T, or

$$p(t, T) = P(X_s \geq 0, t \leq s \leq T \mid X_t) = H(X_t, T - t), \qquad (3.9)$$

where

$$H(x, s) = N\left(\frac{x + ms}{\sqrt{s}}\right) - e^{-2mx} N\left(\frac{-x + ms}{\sqrt{s}}\right). \qquad (3.10)$$

The tractability of this model declines rapidly as one enriches the models used for the asset process A and allows for a time-varying default threshold D, although some extensions, including an allowance for jumps, have been introduced for purposes of bond pricing, and these are reviewed in Chapter 5.

The term structure of forward default rates for the classical first-passage model is illustrated in Figure 3.8. The illustrated firm has a net mean asset growth rate of $\mu - \gamma = 0.23\%$ and asset volatility of $\sigma = 5\%$. Its current leverage is roughly 8 to 1, as assets exceed the face value $D = 71.8$ of debt by approximately $A_t - D = 9.1$. This is a relatively risky firm, showing a forward default rate at the 2-year horizon of approximately 8% per year. That is, conditional on surviving for 2 years, the annualized default probability is about 8%. At the current date t, however, this firm has essentially no default risk for at least several months, after which, conditional on survival for the first few months, default risk climbs dramatically. This unrealistic term

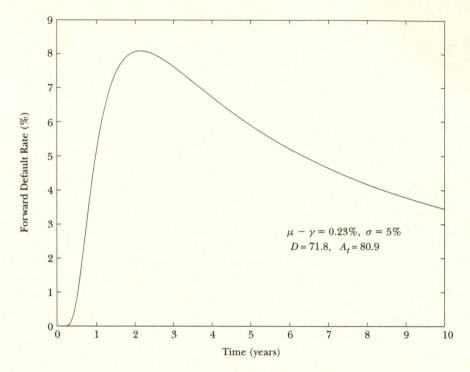

Figure 3.8. *Forward default rate for the classical first-passage model.*

structure of default probabilities is characteristic of first-passage models based on a diffusion process, such as a log-normal model, for assets. Even though a firm may be of rather low credit quality in terms of traditional measures of leverage and volatility, the likelihood of default within a short time horizon is extremely small because the asset process has continuous sample paths that "take time" to cross the default boundary at D.

The classical first-passage model assumes perfect knowledge of the firm's assets and default boundary. Allowing for imperfect information generates more realistic term structures of default probabilities, as shown in Figure 3.9, based on results in Duffie and Lando (2001). This figure, drawn for a firm of the same measured assets as that of Figure 3.8, assumes that assets are currently measured with a standard deviation of 25%, and that the previous year's asset measurement, $\hat{A}_{t-1}$, was accurate and was the same as the current measure, $\hat{A}_t = 80.9$. The term structure of forward default rates illustrated in Figure 3.9 correctly reflects the information that the firm has yet to default, but the investor recognizes the possibility that the actual distance to default, given a precise measure of assets, may be much closer to zero than the measured distance to default. A motivating example is the

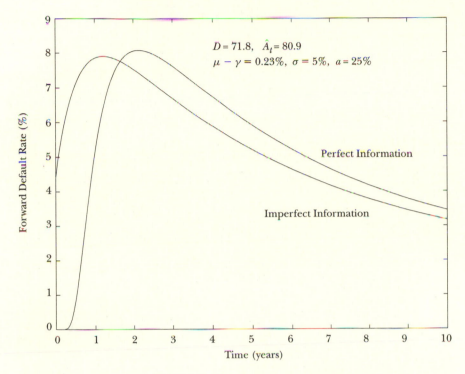

Figure 3.9. *Forward default rate for a first-passage model with imperfect asset information (noise a = 25%).*

default of Enron in 2001. Investors were surprised, apparently having been guided by a poor accounting measure of assets and liabilities. The dependence of the conditional default probabilities on the precision of the asset measure for various time horizons is illustrated in Figure 3.10.

The calculations of default probabilities with correct conditioning for imperfect measures of assets can be cumbersome for day-to-day business calculations. An alternative model for realistic short-term default probabilities can be based on introducing jumps in assets, as discussed in Chapter 5.

3.3. From Theory to Practice: Using Distance to Default to Predict Default

The Black-Scholes-Merton class of models is the theoretical underpinning of the popular commercial EDF measure of default probability supplied by KMV Corporation, reviewed by Kealhofer (1995), as well as the default probabilities computed by Moody's.

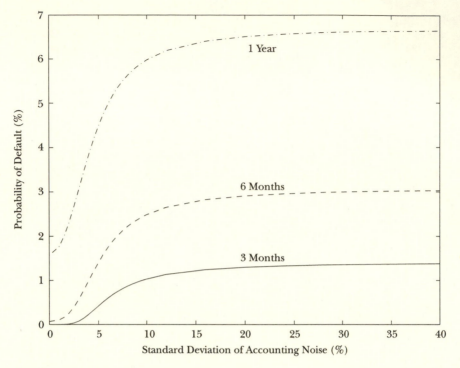

Figure 3.10. *Probability of default by a given time. (Source: Duffie and Lando, 2001.)*

KMV, rather than using the Black-Scholes-Merton model for the default probability, estimates the frequency with which firms of a given 1-year expected distance to default, as measured by a proprietary procedure, have actually defaulted in previous years. That is, a given firm's EDF is, roughly speaking, the fraction of those firms in previous years with the same distance to default that actually did default within 1 year, as illustrated in Figure 3.11. This figure is only illustrative; the actual EDF mapping used by KMV is proprietary.

In computing the distance to default, KMV uses a summary measure of the current book value of debt, the face value of near-term debt plus a fraction of long-term debt, rather than the actual amount of debt coming due within 1 year. The KMV asset volatility estimate is obtained from historical equity prices, recognizing the dependence of equity volatility on asset volatility through the firm's current leverage. The estimated level of assets is based on treating current assets as the sum of the debt measure and the current market value of equity.

Moody's approach to estimating default probabilities is also based on

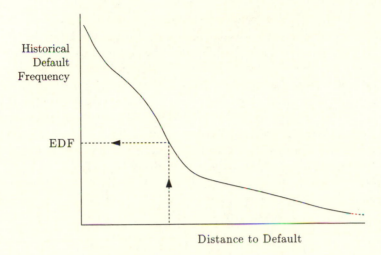

Distance to Default

Figure 3.11. *Mapping from distance to default to EDF (illustrative only).*

several key balance-sheet variables, but uses a logit-like statistical model fit to historical data with firm-specific information included as covariates.

3.4. Default Intensity

Many models of default probabilities and timing are based on the notion of the arrival intensity of default. The simplest version of such a model defines default as the first arrival time τ of a Poisson process with some constant mean arrival rate, called *intensity,* often denoted λ. With this:

- The probability of survival for t years is $p(t) = e^{-\lambda t}$, meaning that the time to default is exponentially distributed.
- The expected time to default is $1/\lambda$.
- The probability of default over a time period of length Δ, given survival to the beginning of this period, is approximately $\Delta\lambda$, for small Δ.

For example, at a constant default intensity of 0.04, the probability of default within 1 year is approximately 3.9%, and the expected time to default is exactly 25 years. Once the default event actually occurs, the intensity of course drops to zero. Whenever we speak of an intensity λ, however, unless otherwise qualified, we mean the intensity prior to default. For example, when we say that default occurs at an intensity λ, what we actually mean is that, as long as default has yet to occur, the intensity is λ.

The classic Poisson-arrival model is based on the notion of independence of arrival risk over time. For example, at constant default intensity λ and short time periods Δ, we can approximate the default time as the first time that a coin toss results in "heads," given independent tosses of coins, one each period, with each toss having a probability $\lambda \Delta$ of heads and $1 - \lambda \Delta$ of tails. This coin-toss analogy highlights the unpredictable nature of default in this model. Although one may be an instant of time away from learning that an issuer has defaulted, when default does occur, it is a "surprise." In the language of stochastic processes, one says in this case that the default time is *inaccessible*.

It is normally implausible to assume that the default intensity λ is constant over time. One simple extension of the basic Poisson model is to allow for deterministically time-varying intensities. Suppose, for instance, that the intensity of default is constant at rate $\lambda(1)$ during the first year and is a known constant $\lambda(2)$ during the second year, conditional on surviving the first year. Then, by Bayes's rule, the probability of survival for 2 years is

$$p(2) = p(1)p(2 \,|\, 1) = e^{-\lambda(1)} e^{-\lambda(2)} = e^{-[\lambda(1)+\lambda(2)]}.$$

If we carry out the same calculation over t years, recursively, the probability of survival for t years is

$$p(t) = e^{-[\lambda(1)+\cdots+\lambda(t)]}, \tag{3.11}$$

where $\lambda(i)$ is the default intensity during year i. Under technical conditions, we can pass to the case of deterministic continual variation in intensity to get

$$p(t) = e^{-\int_0^t \lambda(t)\, dt}, \tag{3.12}$$

where $\lambda(t)$ is the intensity at time t.

Comparing (3.3) and (3.12), we see that if the intensity process λ varies deterministically, then it coincides with the forward default rate function f. In effect, deterministic variation in intensity would thus imply that the only information relevant to default risk that arrives over time is the mere fact of survival to date.

More generally, as time passes, one would have new information, beyond simply survival, that would bear on the credit quality of an issuer. The default intensity would generally vary at random as this additional information arrives. Various models for this updating process are introduced as we proceed. For example, one could suppose that the intensity varies with an underlying state variable, or *driver*, such as the credit rating, distance to default, or equity price of an issuer, or with the business cycle.

In general, a natural model is to treat the arrival intensity, given all current information, as a random process. For example, suppose that in-

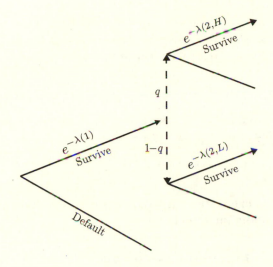

$$P(\text{Survival to Year 2}) = e^{-\lambda(1)}\left[qe^{-\lambda(2,H)} + (1-q)e^{-\lambda(2,L)}\right]$$

$$= e^{-\lambda(1)}E\left(e^{-\lambda(2)}\right) = E\left(e^{-[\lambda(1)+\lambda(2)]}\right)$$

Figure 3.12.   *Survival probability with randomly changing intensity.*

tensities are updated with new information at the beginning of each year and are constant during the year. The probability of survival to time t given survival to $t - 1$, and given all other information available at time $t - 1$, is then $p(t-1, t) = e^{-\lambda(t)}$. We emphasize that $p(t-1, t)$ is not typically known until time $t - 1$, because the default intensity $\lambda(t)$ for year t is based on information that is revealed at time $t - 1$.

In order to visualize the calculation of survival probabilities, we consider the simple case illustrated in Figure 3.12 of the calculation of a 2-year survival probability for a case in which the default intensity $\lambda(2)$ in the second year, assuming the firm survives the first, is uncertain and takes two possible levels, $\lambda(2, H)$ and $\lambda(2, L)$, with conditional probabilities q and $1 - q$, respectively. Given survival of the first year, the probability of surviving the second is the probability-weighted average, $qe^{-\lambda(2,H)} + (1 - q)e^{\lambda(2,L)}$, which is $E(e^{-\lambda(2)})$. By Bayes's rule, the probability of survival to year 2 is then

$$p(2) = p(1)\,p(2\,|\,1) = e^{-\lambda(1)}E\left[e^{-\lambda(2)}\right] = E\left[e^{-[\lambda(1)+\lambda(2)]}\right].$$

More generally, in this setting with a default intensity $\lambda(t)$ for year t that is uncertain but constant within each year, the probability for survival for t years is, again by applying Bayes's rule year by year back to year 0,

$$p(t) = E_0 \left[e^{-[\lambda(1)+\lambda(2)+\cdots+\lambda(t)]} \right]. \tag{3.13}$$

For a quarterly update model, taking an annualized intensity of λ_t at time t, the probability of survival for t years is

$$E \left[e^{-\frac{1}{4}[\lambda(0.25)+\lambda(0.5)+\lambda(0.75)+\cdots+\lambda(t)]} \right]. \tag{3.14}$$

In the next section, we extend the calculation of survival probabilities to the case of continual random variation in intensity.

3.4.1. Doubly Stochastic Default

As we let the update frequency become larger and larger, we are led from (3.14) to the doubly stochastic model of default. According to this model, conditional on the information given by the path of the intensity $\{\lambda(t) : t \geq 0\}$, default arrives according to a Poisson arrival with this time-varying intensity. In this setting, the survival probability is therefore

$$p(t) = E\left[P\left(\tau > t \mid \{\lambda(s) : 0 \leq s \leq t\}\right) \right] \tag{3.15}$$

$$= E \left[e^{-\int_0^t \lambda(s)\,ds} \right]. \tag{3.16}$$

The term *doubly stochastic* arises from the two layers of uncertainty: (1) random variation in the default-intensity process λ, and (2) conditional on the path of the default-intensity process λ, arrival of default as though by a Poisson process with time-varying intensity. Without the doubly stochastic assumption, the convenient formula (3.15) may not hold,[7] but we shall

---

[7] Aside from rather uninteresting technical problems, what may cause (3.15) to fail is a surprise piece of information regarding future credit quality that may arrive precisely at a time at which, with positive probability, default may occur. For example, suppose one monitors two issuers in the same industry, say banking. Banks A and B could, because of a potential for a common credit event, default simultaneously. If Bank A fails at time t, moreover, and Bank B survives past t, one might suppose that the perceived probability $p_B(t, s)$ of survival of Bank B to a future time s may jump suddenly at t, in response to the failure of Bank A. That is, in light of the failure of Bank A at t, perhaps the credit quality of Bank B is worse (or better) than believed just before time t. Thus, it is possible that default can occur for Bank B simultaneously with an event (failure of Bank A) that would cause a sudden revision of the probability that B will survive to time s, given all information available up to (but not including) time t. A precise mathematical example is provided by Kusuoka (1999). In this sort of situation, (3.15)

maintain the doubly stochastic assumption throughout, unless stating specifically otherwise.

The conditional probability at time t, given all available information at that time, of survival to a future time s, is then

$$p(t, s) = E_t \left[e^{-\int_t^s \lambda(u)\, du} \right]. \qquad (3.17)$$

Whenever we show such a calculation, it is implicit that we are treating a firm that has survived to the current time t, for otherwise the conditional probability of survival to a time $s > t$ is obviously zero.

Those familiar with term-structure modeling may see the analogy through (3.17) between an intensity process λ and a short interest-rate process r. According to (3.17), the relationship between survival probability and intensity is the same, from a mathematical viewpoint, as the relationship between a discount (i.e., a zero-coupon bond price) and the risk-neutral behavior of the short-rate process, as explained in Chapter 5. In this analogy, the forward default rate is in parallel with the forward interest rate.

One sometimes sees the terms *hazard rate* and *intensity* used interchangeably. We will attempt to use the terms *intensity* and, as a distinct concept, *forward default rate*, avoiding the term *hazard rate* in order to prevent confusion. In summary, the intensity $\lambda(t)$ is the arrival rate of default at t, conditioning on *all* information available at t. The forward default rate $f(t)$, however, is the mean arrival rate of default at t, conditioning *only* on survival to t. Of course, if the only information available is survival, then the forward default rate and the intensity coincide.[8]

We note that, given any nonnegative process λ, subject only to esoteric technical conditions, one can always define a default time τ so that λ is indeed its intensity process and (3.17) correctly characterizes the conditional survival probability. This is done as follows. Let Z be an exponentially distributed random variable, with mean 1, independent of the process λ. Then let the default time τ be the first time t that the accumulated intensity, $\int_0^t \lambda_s\, ds$, reaches[9] Z. This construction of τ actually defines an algorithm for simulation of default times, which we turn to shortly.

---

may not actually hold. Faced with this situation, it may be advantageous to directly model the arrival of the common credit event that could cause simultaneous failure of the two banks. Some illustrative examples are given in Chapter 13.

[8] This assumes that both the intensity and the forward default rate exist. There are cases, such as the first-passage structural model of default under perfect information, for which the forward default rate exists but the intensity process does not. The default intensity for this first-passage model does exist if the information concerning the assets is imperfect, as shown by Duffie and Lando (2001).

[9] For certain λ, the event that $\int_0^\infty \lambda(u)\, du < Z$ may have positive probability. In that event, we simply say that $\tau = +\infty$, meaning survival forever.

3.5. Examples of Intensity Models

This section describes several analytically tractable models of doubly stochastic default with an intensity process λ. In this section, we concentrate on an intensity process λ that is itself a Markov process. Drawing on the analogy between survival probabilities and discounts, several of these examples are based on term-structure models of short rates. More generally, based on results later in this chapter, one can formulate the intensity as a function of observable firm-specific and macroeconomic variables.

3.5.1. Mean-Reverting Intensities with Jumps

First we formulate an intensity process as a mean-reverting process with jumps. Specifically, the intensity process λ has independently distributed jumps at Poisson-arrival times, with independent jump sizes drawn from a specified probability distribution. Between jumps, λ reverts deterministically at rate κ to a constant γ. A simulated sample path for such an intensity, suffering four modest jumps over a 10-year period, is illustrated in Figure 3.13. For this illustration and our examples to follow, the mean-

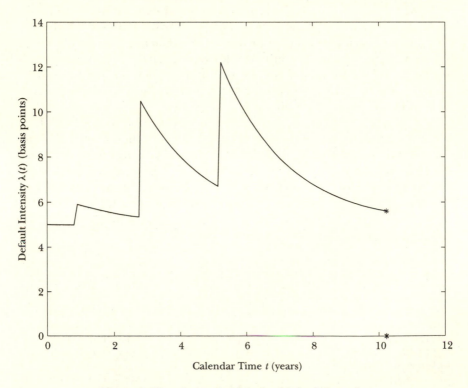

Figure 3.13. *A simulated path of default intensity.*

reversion rate is $\kappa = 0.5$, meaning a continual rate of 50% of expected movement of the process toward its long-run mean on an annualized basis. One can easily generalize.

With this simple model, the default intensity $\lambda(t)$, in between jump events, satisfies the ordinary differential equation

$$\frac{d\lambda(t)}{dt} = \kappa \left[\gamma - \lambda(t) \right]. \tag{3.18}$$

Thus, at any time t between jump times, we have a simple solution

$$\lambda_t = \gamma + e^{-\kappa(t-T)}(\lambda_T - \gamma), \tag{3.19}$$

where T is the time of the last jump and λ_T is the postjump intensity at time T.

For example, suppose that jumps occur at Poisson-arrival times with an intensity c and that the jump sizes are exponentially distributed with mean J. The initial condition $\lambda(0)$ and these parameters determine the probability distribution of the default time. In fact, this model for λ is a special case of a *basic affine process*, in the sense of Appendix A, where the calculation of the conditional probability at any $t < \tau$ of survival from t to s is shown to be

$$p(t, s) = e^{\alpha(s-t) + \beta(s-t)\lambda(t)}, \tag{3.20}$$

where

$$\beta(t) = -\frac{1 - e^{-\kappa t}}{\kappa}$$

$$\alpha(t) = -\gamma \left(t - \frac{1 - e^{-\kappa t}}{\kappa} \right) - \frac{c}{J + \kappa} \left[Jt - \ln\left(1 + \frac{1 - e^{-\kappa t}}{\kappa} J \right) \right].$$

For example, suppose $c = 0.001$, $\kappa = 0.5$, $\gamma = 0.001$, $J = 5$, and $\lambda(0) = 0.001$, meaning an initial mean arrival rate of default of once per thousand years (10 basis points). For comparison, the average rate of default arrival for both A-rated and Aa-rated corporate issuers from 1920 to 1997 was 9 basis points, according to Moody's (Moody's Global Credit Research, 1998). At these parameters, a jump in default risk is likely to be devastating, as a mean jump in intensity of 5 implies a mean expected remaining life of less than 3 months. This model is slightly less risky than one in which an issuer defaults at a constant intensity of 20 basis points.[10] (For reference, the

---

[10] This comparison follows from the fact that for the jump-intensity model, at these parameters, the first time of either default *or* a potentially survivable jump in intensity has a total mean arrival rate of 20 basis points.

average default arrival rate for all Baa-rated corporate issuers for 1920–1997, as measured by Moody's, is 32 basis points.)

In summary, this jump-intensity model is appealing on grounds of simplicity and tractability. As we shall see, it is also tractable and appealing as a foundation for modeling correlation in default times among various entities. In order to capture the effects of daily volatility in yield spreads (and quality), one can easily extend to multiple jump types at different respective arrival rates or dependence of λ on affine state variables, as reviewed in Appendix A.

3.5.2. CIR Intensity Models

A simple parametric intensity model often used for modeling interest rates is the so-called "CIR" process, named after an influential model of short rate processes of Cox, Ingersoll, and Ross (1985), for which

$$d\lambda_t = \kappa(\theta - \lambda_t)\,dt + \sigma\sqrt{\lambda_t}\,dB_t, \tag{3.21}$$

where B is a standard Brownian motion. The coefficients κ, θ, and σ (all positive) have natural interpretations:

- θ is the long-run mean of λ. That is, if the current date t is fixed, $E_t(\lambda_s)$ converges to θ as s goes to ∞.
- κ is the mean rate of reversion to the long-run mean. That is, at any time t, we have

$$E_t(\lambda_s) = \theta + e^{-\kappa(s-t)}(\lambda_t - \theta). \tag{3.22}$$

- σ is a volatility coefficient. The "vol" (in the Black-Scholes sense of "instantaneous" standard deviation as a fraction of level) is therefore $\sigma/\sqrt{\lambda_t}$.

Any CIR process is nonnegative.

This stochastic differential equation for λ can be interpreted in terms of its discrete-time approximation

$$\lambda_{t+\Delta t} - \lambda_t \simeq \kappa(\theta - \lambda_t)\,\Delta t + \sigma\sqrt{\lambda_t}\,\epsilon_t, \tag{3.23}$$

where Δ is the length of a "short" time period, and ϵ_t is a mean-zero independent normally distributed random variable with variance Δt. Because $\lambda(t)$ must be nonnegative in order to consider $\sqrt{\lambda_t}$ for this discrete-time approximation, any negative outcomes for $\lambda_{t+\Delta t}$ could be truncated at zero. Because of the appearance of the square root in (3.21), this process is sometimes called a *square-root diffusion,* and was introduced by Feller (1951) for applications in genetics.

The conditional survival probability $p(t, s)$ implied by (3.21) is known explicitly to be

$$p(t, s) = e^{\alpha(s-t)+\beta(s-t)\lambda(t)}, \qquad (3.24)$$

where α and β are time-dependent coefficients given in Appendix A. Indeed, the CIR process is, like the mean-reverting-jump process, a basic affine process, in the sense explained in Appendix A.

Figure 3.14 shows the effect of varying the volatility parameter σ on forward default rates, starting from the base case of a long-run mean of $\theta = 200$ basis points, $\lambda(0) = \theta$, a mean-reversion rate of $\kappa = 0.25$, and a choice for σ implying an initial volatility of $\sigma/\sqrt{\lambda(0)} = 100\%$. Increasing volatility tends to cause a decline in the probability of default given survival to a given future date, other things being equal. This is a consequence of Jensen's inequality, in that e^x is convex with respect to x, and noting the

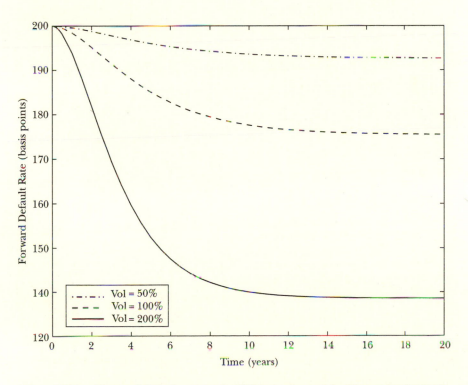

Figure 3.14. *Forward default rate in the CIR intensity model with varying intensity volatility.*

form (3.17) of the calculation of the survival probability. In our case, the random exponent to consider is $\int_0^t -\lambda(s)\,ds$. Increasing the volatility of the intensity process λ leaves the mean of $\int_0^t -\lambda(s)\,ds$ unchanged, but increases its dispersion around this mean. This in turn increases the survival probability, meaning lower forward default rates, as illustrated in Figure 3.14.

Figure 3.15 illustrates the effect on forward default rates of varying the mean-reversion parameter κ in the CIR intensity model from the same base case. From the preceding discussion of volatility, we see that as $\kappa \to 0$, the variance of λ_t increases. So, we would expect lower forward default curves for smaller κ. On the other hand, because $\lambda(0) = \theta$, a high rate of mean reversion keeps the forward default rate close to its initial level, as shown in Figure 3.15. These observations highlight a trade-off between the effects of the volatility parameter σ and the mean-reversion parameter κ. Mean reversion has the effect of reducing the impact of volatility on the shape of the curve of forward default rates. The distinct roles played by σ and κ could in principle be identified from time-series data, for example, a history

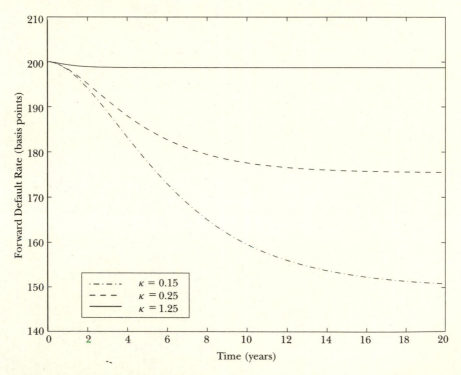

Figure 3.15. *Forward default rate in the CIR intensity model with varying mean-reversion rate.*

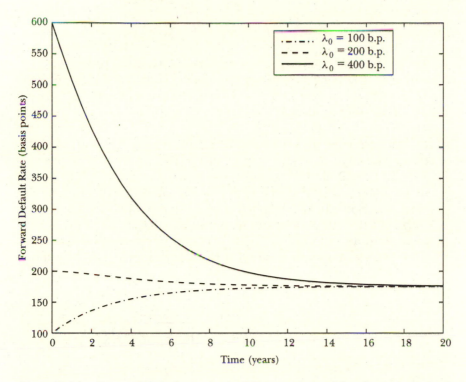

Figure 3.16. *Forward default rate in the CIR intensity model with varying initial intensity.*

of monthly EDFs from KMV or internal (to a financial institution) estimates of default probabilities.

Figure 3.16 shows the impact of the mean-reversion rate κ of the CIR model on the shape of the curve of forward default rates, as one varies the initial intensity $\lambda(0)$ above and below the long-run mean θ. A high initial λ means that the firm is a poor credit relative to its long-run mean level and that it will be expected to improve in quality, conditional on survival. The opposite is true of a firm with a below-mean initial intensity. These patterns are suggestive of the patterns in credit yield-spread curves that have been suggested for low-, medium-, and high-quality firms, an issue raised again in Chapter 5.

3.5.3. Comparison of Jump and CIR Intensities

In parallel to the CIR model, we can express the mean-reverting model with jumps of Section 3.5.1, with parameters (κ, c, J, γ), as the solution of a stochastic differential equation, in that

$$d\lambda_t = \kappa(\theta - \lambda_t)\,dt + dZ_t, \tag{3.25}$$

where Z_t is the total of all jumps by time t, net of the mean of this total, cJt. The increments of Z over equal nonoverlapping equally sized time periods are independent and identically distributed, just as are those of a Brownian motion. The long-run mean of $\lambda(t)$ for this model is $\theta = \gamma + cJ/\kappa$.

As we saw in Section 3.5.1, the associated survival probability $p(t, s)$ is of the same exponential-affine form (3.24) as for the CIR model, and the coefficients α and β are again known explicitly. The interpretations of κ and θ are as for the CIR model.

After choosing the jump parameters c and J of the jump-intensity model to match the moments of λ implied by the CIR model underlying Figure 3.16, we find that there is relatively little difference between the shapes of the forward default rates for the two models. For example, Figure 3.17 is created analogously with Figure 3.16 and shows similar effects of mean

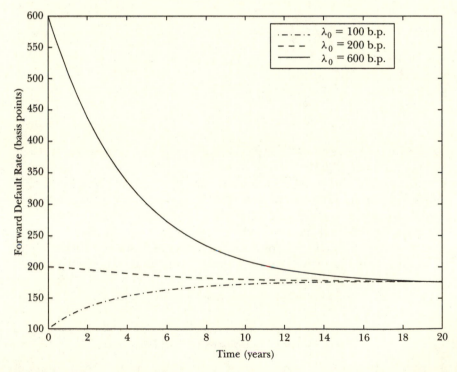

Figure 3.17.   *Forward default rate in the mean-reverting jump model with varying λ_0.*

reversion at similar parameters. This figure is drawn for a mean jump arrival rate of $c = 0.02$, and a mean jump size J chosen so that the variance of the steady-state (stationary) distribution of λ is the same as for the CIR model illustrated earlier.

Similarly, increasing the variance of changes in intensity for these two distinct types of intensity models has similar effects. Further similarities are revealed in Chapter 5, where we consider the implications of these and other model types for term structures of credit spreads.

3.5.4. Affine Intensity Models

A large class of intensity models with explicit formulas for default probabilities is based on the idea of an underlying Markov "factor" process X, possibly multidimensional. The two previous examples, the CIR and mean-reverting jump processes, are special cases in which the state process X is the intensity process λ itself, with one factor.

A multivariate example can be based on the n-dimensional CIR process, for which $\lambda_t = a + b \cdot X_t$ for some nonnegative constants a and $b = (b_1, \ldots, b_n)$, where $X = (X^{(1)}, \ldots, X^{(n)})$ is a vector of n independent CIR processes, possibly with time-dependent parameters. For this case, survival probabilities, similar to the univariate CIR form (3.24), are given by

$$p(t, s) = e^{\alpha(t,s) + \beta(t,s) \cdot X(t)}, \tag{3.26}$$

where the coefficient $\alpha(t, s)$ and the vector $\beta(t, s)$ depend on t and s. These coefficients can also be calculated as the solutions to ordinary differential equations, as explained in Appendix A.

One can allow correlation among the various elements of the state process X, as well as jumps, stochastic volatility, and many other features, while still maintaining the general solution form (3.26), under certain parametric restrictions on the state process X. Such models for (X, λ), those with survival probabilities of the form (3.26), are called *affine*. The theory is summarized in Appendix A. Some (or all) elements of the driving state vector X_t may be directly observable attributes of the firm or of the macro-economic environment.

3.5.5. HJM Forward Default Rate Models

It may be convenient in certain applications to suppose that default intensities are determined by a forward default rate model, in the spirit of the term-structure modeling approach of Heath, Jarrow, and Morton (HJM) (Heath et al., 1992). For this, we assume that

$$p(t, s) = \exp\left(-\int_t^s f(t, u)\, du\right), \qquad (3.27)$$

where, for each fixed s, we are to think of $f(t, s)$ as the forward default rate, conditional on all information available at time t. In parallel with an HJM model,[11] we suppose that

$$df(t, s) = \mu(t, s)\, ds + \sigma(t, s)\, dB_t,$$

where B is a standard d-dimensional Brownian motion, and μ and σ satisfy technical conditions.

By virtue of the same arguments used by HJM,[12] we can calculate the drift μ in terms of the volatility process σ, as

$$\mu(t, s) = \sigma(t, s) \cdot \int_t^s \sigma(t, u)\, du. \qquad (3.28)$$

The implied intensity process λ is then given, under technical conditions, by $\lambda(t) = f(t, t)$. One can likewise model forward default bond credit spreads with an HJM model, as reviewed in Appendix C.

3.6. Default-Time Simulation

We turn next to the simulation of default times, given a parametric model for the intensity λ. There are two well-known algorithms for simulation of the default time τ:

(A) *Inverse-CDF simulation:* Build a model in which the survival probability $p(0, t)$ is easily calculated. Simulate a uniformly distributed random variable U and let τ be chosen so that $p(0, \tau) = U$, as illustrated in Figure 3.18.[13]

The inverse-CDF method exploits a well-known method of constructing a random variable with a given probability distribution.[14] This approach is useful when one can calculate $p(0, t)$ easily.

---

[11] One can add jumps and extend the calculations easily.

[12] One uses the fact that, for fixed s, the process defined by $1_{\{\tau > t\}} p(t, s)$ must, by the law of iterated expectations, be a martingale, as well as the fact that $1_{\{\tau > t\}} + \int_0^t \lambda_s 1_{\{\tau > s\}}\, ds$ is a martingale and applies Ito's formula, as in Protter (1990).

[13] This assumes that $p(0, t) \to 0$ as $t \to \infty$. If not, then let $\tau = \inf\{t : p(0, t) \le U\}$, which may have $+\infty$ as an outcome.

[14] Suppose F is a given distribution function and Y is distributed uniformly on $[0, 1]$. Then the random variable $X = F^{-1}(Y)$ has distribution function F.

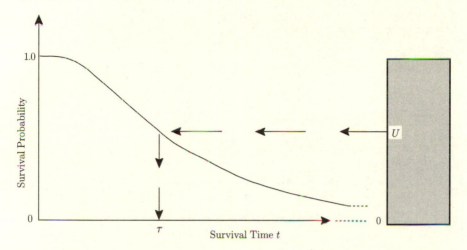

Figure 3.18. *Simulating a default time by the inverse-CDF method.*

(B) *Compensator simulation:* Build a model in which the cumulated intensity, $\Lambda(t) = \int_0^t \lambda(u)\, du$, often called the *compensator,* is feasibly simulated. Simulate, independently of the intensity process λ, a standard (unit-mean) exponentially distributed variable Z. Let τ be chosen so that $\Lambda(\tau) = Z$, as illustrated in Figure 3.19.[15]

For many models of intensity, in order to simulate by the compensator method, the sample paths must be approximated.[16] Figure 3.20 illustrates the simulation of the compensator with linear interpolation, assuming that the levels of intensity are constant over each unit of time.

The compensator method is based on the fact that, for unit-mean exponentially distributed Z, we have $P(Z > z) = e^{-z}$. Thus, conditional on the path of the intensity up to date t, $\{\lambda_t : 0 \le t < \infty\}$, the probability that the default time τ is larger than t is

$$P\left[Z > \int_0^t \lambda(s)\, ds \right] = e^{-\int_0^t \lambda(s)\, ds}.$$

---

[15] This assumes that $\Lambda(t) \to \infty$ as $t \to \infty$. If not, then let $\tau = \inf\{t : \Lambda(t) \ge Z\}$, which may have $+\infty$ as an outcome.

[16] One could use Euler or higher-order schemes for discrete-time approximate simulation of the stochastic differential equations underlying the intensities, but, bearing in mind the number of discrete time periods and the number of scenarios, this could be relatively expensive.

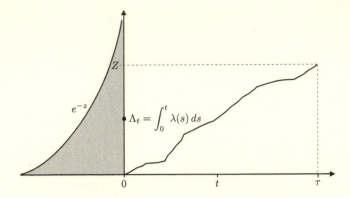

Figure 3.19. *Simulating a default time by the compensator method.*

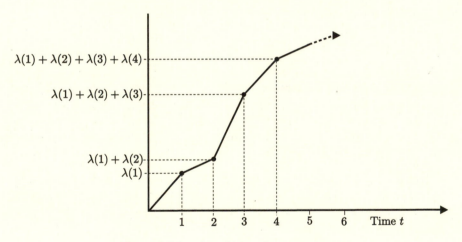

Figure 3.20. *Simulating the compensator.*

So, *conditioning down* to the information available at date 0, the probability of survival to t is indeed

$$p(0, t) = E_0 \left[e^{-\int_0^t \lambda(s)\, ds} \right],$$

as required.

3.7. Statistical Prediction of Bankruptcy

We have already reviewed several time-series models for describing aggregate frequencies of default, say among speculative-grade issuers. In this section we turn our attention to estimating the probability that a firm i will be bankrupt ($D^i_t = 1$) or not bankrupt ($D^i_t = 0$) in period t. The probabilities are conditional on information about the past performance of the firm and current market conditions, say X_{it}. Some studies focus on the *zero-one* indicator of whether or not a firm is legally bankrupt in the sense of having filed for protection under Chapter 7 or Chapter 11 of the U.S. bankruptcy laws. Other models include bankruptcy as one of several possible states that a firm might be in, captured for example by the "D" rating of Fitch.

Broadly speaking, we can classify models according to how the conditional probability of defaulting in the next period is modeled. We focus on three types of parameterizations: duration models, qualitative-response models, and discriminant analysis.

A duration model typically parameterizes the forward default rate $f(t)$, normally called the hazard rate in the duration literature. One classical parameterization is the Weibull model, for which

$$f(t) = \gamma p (\gamma t)^{p-1}, \tag{3.29}$$

for positive parameters p and γ to be estimated from survival-time data. In this case, the time to default, τ, has the Weibull distribution. Another parameterization is the log-logistic model, for which

$$f(t) = \frac{\gamma p (\gamma t)^{p-1}}{1 + (\gamma t)^p}, \tag{3.30}$$

so named because $\log \tau$, the logarithm of the survival time τ, has a logistic distribution, with mean $-\log \gamma$ and variance $\pi^2/(3p^2)$ (see, e.g., Kalbfleisch and Prentice, 1980). In these simple duration models, the hazard rate $f(t)$ depends only on t.

More advanced duration models allow dependence of the hazard rate $f(t)$ on a covariate vector X_i for each name i. With the proportional-hazards model, for example, the forward default rate $f_i(t)$ of firm i is assumed to be of the form

$$f_i(t) = f_0(t) g(X_i, \theta), \tag{3.31}$$

where $f_0(t)$ is a *baseline hazard rate* common to all i, while $g(X_i, \theta)$ depends on the covariate vector X_i of firm i in a manner depending on the parameter vector θ, common to all i, that is to be estimated. Linear dependence of $g(X_i, \theta)$ on X_i has been a popular model in some scientific applications (see Andersen et al., 1993). In some cases, the baseline function $f_0(t)$ is left nonparametric, especially if the main objective is the relative hazard rate, $g(X_i, \theta)/g(X_j, \theta)$ of two names.

For the proportional-hazards model (3.31), the covariate vector X_i does not depend on t. For default modeling applications, X_i could therefore include the industry of a firm, its domicile, its initial size, indicators for whether it is publicly traded, and so on.

In more advanced duration models, the covariates X_{it} may be stochastic processes, so that we are actually statistically modeling the default-intensity process λ_i, for example, extending from the proportional-hazards model (3.31) to

$$\lambda_i(t) = f_0(t)g(X_{it}, \theta). \tag{3.32}$$

Chapter 7 of Andersen et al. (1993) includes many sample applications of this type and many alternative formulations of duration models.

Qualitative-response models focus on the probability of default within one period (a month, say, or a year) for a firm i that has survived to the beginning of the period, conditional on current market conditions captured by the covariate vector X_{it}. A qualitative-response model typically takes the form

$$F(\theta \cdot X_{it}) = P\left[D_{t+1}^i = 1 \mid D_t^i = 0, X_{it}\right], \tag{3.33}$$

where $F(\cdot)$ is a given cumulative distribution function, usually parametrically specified, and θ is a vector of coefficients to be estimated. Two widely studied special cases are the probit and logit models. For the probit model,

$$F(z) = N(z), \tag{3.34}$$

where $N(\cdot)$ is the cumulative standard-normal distribution function. For the logit model, $F(\cdot)$ is the logistic distribution function, defined by

$$F(z) = \frac{e^z}{1 + e^z}. \tag{3.35}$$

The normal and logistic distributions have similar shapes, although the logistic distribution has somewhat heavier tails.

Discriminant analysis is based on a parametric specification of the conditional probability distribution of the covariate vector X_{it}, given the default indicator D_t^i. A typical formulation takes one conditional density $\varphi_0(\cdot)$ for X_{it} given $D_t^i = 0$ and a different conditional density $\varphi_1(\cdot)$ for X_{it} given $D_t^i = 1$. Firms are dropped from the data after they default. For firms that have survived to time $t - 1$, Bayes's rule implies that

$$P(D_t^i = 1 \mid X_{it}, D_{t-1}^i = 0) = \frac{\varphi_1(X_{it})q_{i1}}{\varphi_1(X_{it})q_{i1} + \varphi_0(X_{it})q_{i0}}, \tag{3.36}$$

where q_{i1} and q_{i0} are the marginal probabilities $P(D_1^i = 1)$ and $P(D_t^i = 0)$, respectively.

Altman (1968) introduced an early application of discriminant analysis to default probabilities, and he refined his approach in several subsequent studies. In many applications of discriminant analysis, φ_1 and φ_0 are taken to be densities of multivariate normal distributions with different mean vectors, but with the same covariance matrix. In this case, the conditional probability of default is of the form

$$P(D_t^i = 1 \mid X_{it}, D_{t-1}^i = 0) = \frac{e^{\theta_0 + \theta_X \cdot X_{it}}}{1 + e^{\theta_0 + \theta_X \cdot X_{it}}}, \qquad (3.37)$$

which is of the same form as the logit model. Although the logit and discriminant models have the same functional forms in this setting, some significant differences remain (see, e.g., Amemiya and Powell, 1983, and Lo, 1986). While the discriminant model specifies the distribution of the conditioning covariates parametrically, if this distributional assumption is wrong, then the maximum-likelihood estimator of parameters in the discriminant model is biased even in large samples. In addition, most discriminant studies use matched samples of firms from the same industry and year, which may introduce substantial sample selection bias. So, as implemented here, discriminant analysis has all of the limitations of qualitative-response models (e.g., it does not account for survival effects) and has greater scope for misspecification biases.

The data used for estimation of these three types of models are time series of the form

$$\{(D_1^i, X_{i1}), \ldots, (D_{T(i)}^i, X_{i,T(i)})\}, \; i = 1, \ldots, N, \qquad (3.38)$$

where $T(i) = \min(\tau_i, T)$, and T and N denote the number of time periods and firms, respectively. Truncation of the sample at date $T(i)$ presumes that data are not available for firms in default. We can easily accommodate the possibility that firms also enter into the sample at different times, rather than all at date 0, but we abstract from this possibility for notational simplicity. For more on biases introduced by endogenous sampling and censoring effects, see Amemiya (2001).

At the core of the differences among the three types of models are their implied default-time densities conditional on the sample $(X_{i1}, \ldots, X_{i,T(i)})$. As opposed to the duration model, which considers the distribution of the survival time through the specification of the hazard rate (or intensity), the qualitative-response and discriminant-analysis models address only the likelihood of survival for one period, based only on current conditions. A duration model also allows for the calculation of the one-period conditional surivival probability. For example, with the proportional-hazard model (3.31), the one-period conditional survival probability for a firm that has survived to time t is, from (3.4),

$$p(t+1 \mid t) = \exp\left[-\int_t^{t+1} f_0(u)g(X_i, \theta)\, du\right], \qquad (3.39)$$

for a parameter vector θ to be estimated. More generally, if the covariates X_{it} form a stochastic process, then a Markov assumption for the covariates leads to estimates of conditional one-period survival probabilities. Example parameterizations were mentioned in Section 3.5.4.

3.7.1. Comparing Prediction Methods

In spite of the potential limitations of discriminant analysis outlined above, in practice, early studies found that it was approximately as useful as probit models in predicting bankruptcy. For instance, Lo (1986) conducts formal specification tests on a sample of bankrupt firms and finds that he cannot reject the restrictions imposed by the form of discriminant-analysis model that he considered.

More recently, Lennox (1999) applied these methods to predict bankruptcies in a sample of 949 firms listed in the United Kingdom over the period 1987–1994. The covariate vector X_{it} for each firm includes business cycle indicators, industry dummies, and various balance-sheet variables. Lennox found that the most important determinants of bankruptcy were leverage and cash flow variables, the firm's size and industry, and the economic cycle.

Lennox also computed the rates of type-I errors (a company fails but is predicted to survive) and type-II errors (a company survives but is predicted to fail), for various threshold points, of probit and discriminant-analysis models. Specification of threshold points is necessary because the probit model, for instance, merely provides a predicted probability that a firm will go bankrupt. The predicted number of bankruptcies comes from selecting a survival probability below which firms are predicted to fail. The type-I and type-II error rates for his U.K. firms using a holdout sample (i.e., predicting outside the sample used to estimate the model's parameters) are given in Table 3.2. Of 3,288 observations in Lennox's holdout sample, there were thirty-three failures. The first column of the table shows the number of predicted failures. For instance, the first row gives the results for a threshold survival probability chosen so that, within this holdout sample, twenty firms were predicted to fail. The names of these firms are then compared to those that actually failed, and the type-I and type-II errors, expressed in percent,

Table 3.2. *Type-I and Type-II Errors (percent) for a Standard Probit Model (Probit), a Probit Model That Allows for Nonlinear Effects and Heteroskedasticity (Probit Nonlinear), and a Discriminant Analysis Model*

Number of predicted failures	Probit		Probit nonlinear		Discriminant analysis	
	Type-I	Type-II	Type-I	Type-II	Type-I	Type-II
20	87.88	0.049	75.76	0.039	100.0	0.061
40	72.73	0.095	69.70	0.092	90.91	1.14
60	63.64	1.47	63.64	1.47	72.73	1.57
80	57.58	2.03	63.64	2.09	66.67	2.12

are determined.[17] For small numbers of predicted failures, both variants of the probit model that Lennox studied outperformed the discriminant-analysis model. Interestingly, within the sample, Lennox found that the probit and discriminant-analysis models have comparable forecast errors. Thus, his results illustrate the importance of evaluating models for predicting bankruptcy on an out-of-sample basis.

Shumway (2001) criticized the static nature of probit and logit models, that is, their failure to account for the duration of survival. He proceeded to compare the out-of-sample forecasting accuracy of a duration model to Altman's (1968) prediction model, using the same conditioning variables (covariates) as in Altman's model. Firms are sorted in each calendar year into deciles based on their fitted default probabilities. Table 3.3 shows the percentage of bankrupt firms that are classified into each of the first five deciles (highest is decile 1) in the year in which they declared bankruptcy. The table shows that Shumway's model clearly outperforms Altman's model using the same conditioning information. Adding market variables (market capitalization, excess equity return, and equity-return volatility) to the information set further improves the forecasting performance (see column Shumway-M). The last column of Table 3.3, labeled CJ-Shumway, gives the results obtained by Chava and Jarrow (2001) using Shumway's model fit to a much larger data set on bankruptcies, confirming the superior performance of Shumway's duration model.

3.7.2. Default and Aging Effects

All of these formulations could be specified so that the probability of default depends on how long an issuer has been in existence or how long an issue has been outstanding. This is automatically the case for duration models. For example, with the proportional-hazards model (3.31), age enters the

---

[17] Given the small number of actual failures, the fraction of type-I errors is typically large.

Table 3.3.   Out-of-Sample Forecasting Accuracy, Expressed as Percent Classified

Decile	Percentage of bankrupt firms			
	Altman	Shumway	Shumway-M	CJ-Shumway
1	42.3	67.6	75.0	74.4
2	12.6	15.3	12.5	12.0
3	12.6	3.6	6.3	5.6
4	9.0	3.6	1.8	3.2
5	8.1	3.6	0.9	2.4

Note: Shumway refers to the model estimated with Altman's variables. Shumway-M is the model that includes market variables as well. CJ-Shumway shows the results obtained by Chava and Jarrow using the Shumway model with a larger data set.

conditional one-period survival probability in (3.39) through the baseline-hazard function $f_0(\cdot)$. For the qualitative-response and discriminant-analysis models, aging effects could be captured by introducing survival time as one of the conditioning variables in X_{it}.

Before discussing the evidence for aging effects within models of default probabilities, it is informative to review briefly the descriptive historical evidence for their presence. Aging effects cannot be studied directly with standard Moody's or Standard & Poor's default rates, because these rates are computed as the ratio of the number of debt issues that defaulted in a given year to the total number of speculative issues outstanding. There is no accounting for age in any form in these calculations. In an attempt to isolate any aging effects, Altman (1989) introduced the concept of a *mortality rate,* computed as the ratio of the total value of defaulting debt in a given year to the total value of the population of bonds at the start of this year. An important feature of his definition is that he held credit rating fixed as of the original issue date. More precisely, for the case, say, of debt rated A at the time of issue, he computed the mortality ratio for the first year of existence for all bonds issued between 1971 and 1987. These mortality rates were then averaged to obtain an average first-year mortality rate for all bonds with an original rating of A. This was repeated for years 2, 3, and so on, from issuance for A-rated bonds. The entire process was repeated for each of the other credit ratings. Mortality rates were found to increase as the time since issuance increased for low-rated bonds but not for investment-grade bonds. Similar aging effects were reported by Paul et al. (1989) and Altman (1991).

Recent evidence of this aging effect is shown in Figure 3.21, based on mortality rates for bonds rated BB, B, and CCC by Standard & Poor's and reported in Altman and Kishore (1995). For all three ratings, there is a pattern of increasing mortality rates over the first 3 years after a bond is issued. Moreover, the increase in mortality rates is particularly large for

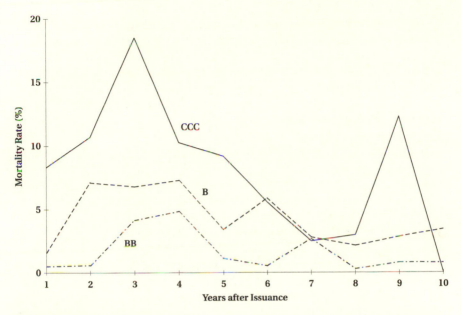

Figure 3.21. *Realized default rates by original rating. (Source: Altman and Kishore, 1995.)*

CCC-rated bonds. After 3 years of seasoning, mortality rates tend to decline, though there is a spike in year 9 for CCC-rated bonds. As was emphasized by Altman (1991) and Jonsson and Fridson (1996), this aging effect may have a significant impact on realized default rates if the quantity of new issuance and composition of issuance changes within the speculative ratings.

A reason sometimes given for an aging effect on default rates is that many corporate bonds are callable. As time passes from the issue date, it becomes increasingly likely that the call option owned by the issuer will go into the money. If higher-quality firms are more likely than low-quality firms to exercise their call options (because they are in a better position to refinance the debt issue), then there will be a deterioration over time in the average quality of the pool of bonds. This may lead to a rising default rate as the time since issuance increases, merely from the selection bias caused by calling. This explanation would seem to be weakened, however, by the standard call-protection clauses in many corporate bond covenants.

Whatever their sources, the aging effects displayed in Figure 3.21 are static measures. They represent an average aging effect over the sample period, without taking account of either the business cycles or issuance cycles (which may be correlated). Blume et al. (1991) argue that the aging effect is a manifestation of business cycle effects on default. In a sample of bonds from the issue cohort of 1977–1978, Blume and Keim (1991) show that the aging effect found in the original studies by Altman (1989) and Paul et al. (1989) may be largely attributable to changing economic conditions. Blume and Keim array default rates by year of default and age of bond. They find that there are notably more defaults in some years than others, regardless of age. Furthermore, when they adjust the aging results for the mean default rate of all bonds in a given calendar year, they find that a small aging effect remains but that it is not statistically significant.

Moody's and Standard & Poor's report aging effects in a different way. Cohorts of bonds are formed on the basis of the credit rating and year of purchase pair. The default experiences of these cohorts are tracked over time. The cohort consisting of B-rated bonds purchased in 1980, for example, represents the default experience in the years following 1980 of all B-rated bonds that could be purchased in 1980. This would include not only bonds that were newly issued in 1980 but also seasoned issues that may or may not have had an original rating at issue of B. Thus, the emphasis is not on time since issuance, as in the Altman studies, but rather on differences between cohorts indexed by calendar year and credit rating. Cyclical patterns in default, if important, would be more clearly revealed in these cohort default rates.

Moody's cohort data on the 1-year default rates for bonds purchased with an initial B rating are shown in Figure 3.22 for cohorts starting in 1980. The left "horizontal" axis indicates the calendar year during which the defaults were measured. The right "horizontal" axis indicates the cohort year during which the B-rated bonds were acquired. The vertical axis is the default rate for each cohort-calendar year combination. The most striking aspect of Figure 3.22 is the presence of distinct ridges along the cohort axis. Figure 3.23 shows in tabular form that these ridges are associated with the years 1986 and 1990–1991. In particular, default rates in 1986 and in 1990–1991 were much higher than those experienced by the 1980–1982 cohorts during the 1982 recession.

McDonald and Van de Gucht (1996) studied aging effects in the context of a duration model. Focusing on a sample of 579 high-yield, nonconvertible bonds issued between 1977 and 1989, they addressed the question of whether aging effects persist after controlling for business cycle effects on the default intensities, $\lambda_i(t)$ for firm i at time t. Survival was measured from the time of issuance of the bond. Cyclical variation in $\lambda_i(t)$ was captured by including changes in GNP in the vector X_{it} of covariates determining $\lambda_i(t)$. For their sample of high-yield bonds, estimated default intensities tended to increase as the bonds seasoned. McDonald and Van de Gucht attempt to control for supply effects by including covariates that indicate whether the bond was issued in the period 1980–1984 or after 1984. This approach, however, may not fully capture the substantial changes in composition of

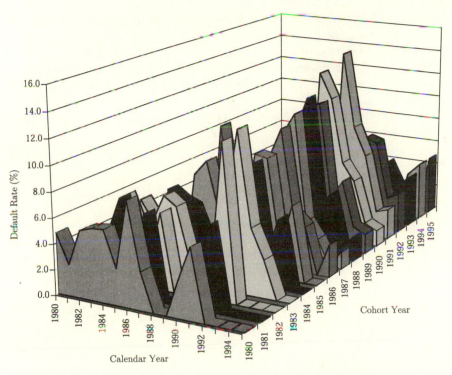

Figure 3.22. *One-year default rates for Moody's cohorts of B-rated bonds.*

Calendar Year

	1980	1981	1982	1983	1984	1985	1986	1987	1988	1989	1990	1991	1992	1993	1994	1995
1980	4.8	2.5	5.3	5.6	5.7	2.9	8.2	3.0	0.0	0.0	2.9	5.6	0.0	0.0	0.0	0.0
1981		4.7	4.5	4.9	7.5	2.3	6.6	0.0	0.0	0.0	2.2	6.5	0.0	0.0	0.0	0.0
1982			4.6	7.0	4.6	2.2	6.1	0.0	0.0	0.0	2.3	12.2	0.0	0.0	0.0	0.0
1983				6.1	4.6	6.7	6.0	2.1	2.4	2.7	6.4	12.6	5.3	3.0	0.0	0.0
1984					6.5	5.8	5.4	2.8	4.0	3.7	8.9	9.5	2.4	5.5	0.0	0.0
1985						7.3	8.5	4.5	4.2	3.2	9.6	9.4	2.5	6.0	0.0	0.0
1986							10.8	4.0	4.5	3.1	8.8	11.2	4.6	3.7	0.0	2.6
1987								5.2	7.0	6.1	10.2	11.9	3.4	2.1	0.0	1.4
1988									6.0	6.4	10.0	12.7	4.2	5.2	0.9	2.0
1989										8.7	11.4	11.8	4.2	5.7	2.1	1.6
1990											13.8	11.8	6.6	5.2	1.8	1.3
1991												15.1	9.1	6.8	2.2	2.5
1992													7.7	7.4	2.8	3.3
1993														5.2	3.3	4.2
1994															3.8	4.8
1995																4.8

Cohort Year (row labels)

Figure 3.23. *One-year cohort default rates for Moody's B-rated bonds.*

low-grade debt that occurred in the late 1980s and the associated increases in default rates. After controlling for "current liabilities of business failures" and for "corporate profits as a percentage of GNP," Jonsson and Fridson (1996) found a significant correlation between the quantity of unseasoned bottom-tier issues and default. This finding raises the possibility that the aging effects found by McDonald and Van de Gucht are spuriously affected by their omission of key cyclical factors. Further exploration of these issues seems warranted.

4

Ratings Transitions:
Historical Patterns and
Statistical Models

THE POSSIBILITY THAT major ratings agencies will change the credit rating of a bond issue is an important source of credit risk, above and beyond its implications for the direct risk of default. Changes in credit ratings may have an immediate effect on the values of defaultable bond portfolios, may mean that certain bonds are no longer admissible for investors who are subject to restrictions on the ratings of bonds in their portfolios, and may even lead to mandatory termination of some financial contracts. Certain *step-up* corporate bonds have coupon rates linked explicitly to credit rating. Proposed changes to the BIS accord, reviewed in Section 2.5.2, will determine the capital requirements of regulated banks based in part on the credit ratings of the debt instruments that they hold. These ratings-based regulatory capital charges will presumably be reflected in the market yield spreads charged for a given rating. Credit derivatives, and other contracts, sometimes have provisions for contingent payments based on changes in credit ratings. For these and related reasons, a model of the risk of ratings changes is a key ingredient for credit-risk management and for the valuation of many credit-sensitive instruments. This chapter reviews some of the historical patterns in ratings transitions as well as alternative approaches to modeling ratings transition risk.

4.1. Average Transition Frequencies

Major ratings agencies report the historical average incidence of transitions among credit ratings and into default in the form of a matrix of average transition frequencies. An example from Moody's is given in Table 4.1. Each row corresponds to the rating at the beginning of a year; the column heading gives the end-of-year rating. For example, of firms rated Baa at the beginning of a year, on average over this sample, 81% retained this rating,

85

Table 4.1.   Moody's All-Corporate Average Transition Frequencies for 1980–2000

	Rating at year end (percent)								
Initial rating	Aaa	Aa	A	Baa	Ba	B	Caa-C	Default	WR
Aaa	86.17	9.45	1.02	0.00	0.03	0.00	0.00	0.00	3.33
Aa	1.10	86.05	8.93	0.31	0.11	0.01	0.00	0.03	3.46
A	0.06	2.85	86.75	5.58	0.66	0.17	0.01	0.01	3.91
Baa	0.06	0.34	6.64	81.00	5.52	0.97	0.08	0.16	5.23
Ba	0.03	0.06	0.54	5.46	75.50	8.18	0.53	1.32	8.38
B	0.01	0.04	0.20	0.56	5.92	75.94	3.03	6.41	7.90
Caa-C	0.00	0.00	0.00	0.87	2.61	5.62	57.02	25.31	8.58

Source: Moody's Investor Services.

while approximately 5.5% made a transition to Ba. The fractions of transitions shown to WR correspond to withdrawn ratings. Although there may be some implications for credit quality for the event of becoming unrated, this effect is often ignored by normalizing each transition frequency by the total fraction of bonds that do not have a withdrawn rating.[1] The resulting normalized transition matrix is shown in Table 4.2.

It is not uncommon in industry practice to treat an annual average transition frequency matrix of the sort shown in Table 4.2 as though it is a matrix π of transition probabilities, with π_{ij} denoting the probability that a firm rated i at the beginning of the year is rated j at the end of the year. This implicitly assumes that transition probabilities are constant over time and that the sole determinant of an issuer's credit risk (including transition risk) is the issuer's current rating. This strong assumption would allow one to treat the rating of a firm as a Markov chain. As the number of years of data gets larger and larger, the historical transition frequency matrix would, under these assumptions, converge to the actual probability transition matrix π.

Such a Markov-chain assumption for ratings transitions is the basis for the popular CreditMetrics model (J. P. Morgan, 1997), although Credit-Metrics does not require that the user's transition probability matrix π is equal to a historical average 1-year transition frequency matrix. The Markov-chain assumption greatly simplifies multiyear ratings transition and default probability calculations. For example, the n-year probability transition matrix is π^n, the n-fold product of the 1-year transition matrix. That is, for a firm initially rated i, the probability of being rated j after n years is the (i, j) element of the matrix π^n. Because 1-year periods are too "coarse-grained" for many applications, later in this chapter we extend this annual-period

[1] Roundoff errors imply that the rows of Table 4.2 do not add precisely to 100.

Table 4.2.   Moody's Average Ratings Transition Frequency Matrix for 1980–2000, Normalized from Table 4.1 for Withdrawn Ratings

Initial rating	Rating at year end (percent)							
	Aaa	Aa	A	Baa	Ba	B	Caa-C	Default
Aaa	89.14	9.78	1.06	0.00	0.03	0.00	0.00	0.00
Aa	1.14	89.13	9.25	0.32	0.11	0.01	0.00	0.03
A	0.06	2.97	90.28	5.81	0.69	0.18	0.01	0.01
Baa	0.06	0.36	7.01	85.47	5.82	1.02	0.08	0.17
Ba	0.03	0.07	0.59	5.96	82.41	8.93	0.58	1.44
B	0.01	0.04	0.22	0.61	6.43	82.44	3.29	6.96
Caa-C	0.00	0.00	0.00	0.95	2.85	6.15	62.36	27.68

Markov chain into a continuous-time setting, in which ratings changes can happen at any time during the year.

One should beware of the potential traps associated with this elegant and simple treatment of the rating of an issuer as a Markov chain. The reported transition frequencies are only averages and do not condition on all available information. In particular:

- The reported transition matrix represents the average of 1-year transitions over a long history, during which economic conditions change.
- Even ignoring cyclical considerations, 1-year transition rates may not be fixed over the age of the bond, the age of the firm, the previous rating, or time in current rating category. As with default risk, there is dependence of transition probabilities on duration in a rating category or age, often called an *aging effect,* documented by Carty and Fons (1994), Lando and Skødeberg (2000), and Kavvathas (2001). Moreover, Behar and Nagpal (1999), Lando and Skødeberg (2000), and Kavvathas (2001) all find that, for firms of certain ratings, the prior rating is an important determinant of the likelihood of a downgrade, versus that of an upgrade, over a given time horizon. There is indeed apparent *momentum* in ratings transitions data.
- Generally, different firms of the same rating have different credit qualities, and a given firm of a fixed rating has a credit quality that changes over time.

4.2. Ratings Risk and the Business Cycle

In order to assess the relationships between rating transitions and the business cycle, we computed four-quarter moving averages of the ratio of the total number of Moody's ratings upgrades to the the total number of downgrades (the *U/D* ratio). The *U/D* ratio was computed separately for the investment and speculative-grade (below Baa) ratings categories. These ratios were then correlated with the four-quarter moving average of U.S. gross domestic product (GDP) growth over various sample periods. The sample was split in 1983, because Moody's introduced a new alpha-numeric rating system in April 1982. Inspection of ratings transition activity during 1982 shows clearly that, with this new system, a large number of firms were reclassified to new coarse (letter) ratings. For instance, during the quarter in which Moody's introduced their alpha-numeric system, nearly 50% of Baa-rated U.S. industrial firms transitioned to new letter ratings. Such a large transition rate is well out of line with typical transition rates. The analysis of Kliger and Sarig (1997) suggests that the information release implicit in the new classification system was economically significant, in that there was a significant reaction of corporate bond yield spreads to the ratings refinements.

We report the sample correlations in Table 4.3, and show the underlying (standardized) time series of U/D ratios and GDP growth in Figure 4.1 for the postrevision sample period 1983–1997. The correlation is low during the first sample period but positive during the later sample period. The trends in upgrades relative to downgrades for speculative-grade issues, in particular, are strikingly well correlated with GDP growth during the second half of the sample. In Chapter 3, for example, we reported a consistent large negative correlation between default rates and GDP growth.

In order to analyze the impact of business cycles on ratings transitions probabilities, Nickell et al. (2000), extending work by Wilson (1997a, b), estimated an ordered probit model, a class of statistical models explained in Section 4.4, for the likelihood of a given transition, using: (1) domicile (Japan, U.S., U.K., and non-U.K. European domiciles); (2) ten industry categories; and (3) the business cycle (peak, normal, and trough) as explanatory variables.

Nickell et al. (2000) allocated the years of their sample period, 1970–1997, into "peak," "normal," and "trough" categories, depending on whether GDP growth was in the upper, middle, or lower third of realized growth rates over the sample period. For U.S. industrial and banking Aa-rated firms (treated separately), they found only a few statistically significant differences between the transition probabilities for peak and trough

Table 4.3.   Sample Correlations of GDP Growth and U/D Ratios for Investment and Speculative-Grade Issues, as rated by Moody's

Sample period	Investment grade	Speculative grade
1971–1982	0.076	−0.012
1983–1997	0.198	0.652
1971–1997	0.068	0.230

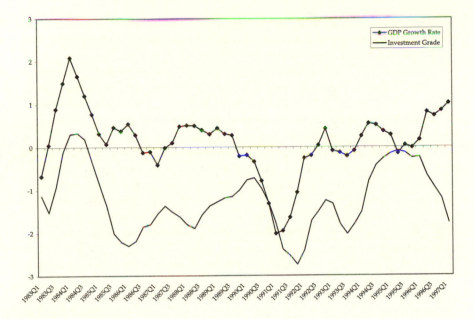

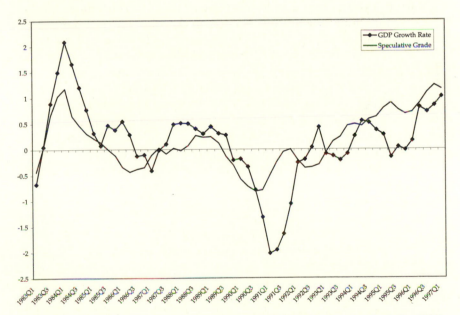

Figure 4.1. *Upgrade/downgrade ratios for 1983–1997 (standardized for 1971–1997).*

periods. There were significant differences, however, between peaks and troughs for lower-rated firms, between U.S. banks and industrial firms, and between U.S.- and foreign-domiciled firms.

Such a model and estimation procedure implicitly assume independence across issuers within a year, given the business cycle. Correlation is induced only by business cycle changes (which affect all issuers the same way). A selection of the results of Nickell et al. (2000) is given in the estimated peak-conditional and trough-conditional transition probabilities shown in Table 4.4, where "A↑" represents the subset of firms rated A or higher. The entries shown in bold type are the percentage transition probabilities estimated for troughs of the business cycle. Those shown in standard type are associated with the peaks. One notes the obvious adverse influence on ratings of troughs relative to peaks.

In order to extend our Markov-chain setting for transitions so as to allow for the influence of the business cycle (or some other state variable), we can let $\Pi_{ij}(x)$ denote the probability of a transition from rating i to rating j over 1 year if the underlying driving state variable (such as the business cycle) is at x. For example, with three business cycle states, as in Nickell et al. (2000), x is one of {peak, normal, trough}.

Then, in order to deal with multiyear transition probabilities, we can make the additional simplifying assumption that the time series of underlying covariate vectors, $X_1, X_2, \ldots, X_t, \ldots$, forms a Markov process. Moreover, conditional on the path taken by this Markov state process X, the probability that a given issuer makes a transition from rating i at year t to j at year $s > t$ is the (i, j) element of the product $\Pi(X_t)\Pi(X_{t+1}) \cdots \Pi(X_{s-1})$ of 1-year conditional transition matrices. The unconditional multiyear transition probabilities can be calculated, for example, by simulating the paths of X and averaging the conditional transition probabilities over independently generated paths for X. This is called a doubly stochastic transition model. More computationally tractable doubly stochastic ratings-transition models, in continuous time settings, are introduced in Section 4.5.2.

Table 4.4.   Comparison of Peak and Trough
(bold) Estimated Transition Probabilities (percent)

	A↑	Baa	Ba	B	Caa↓	D
A↑	(**93.9**, 95.7)	(**5.6**, 3.9)	(**0.4**, 0.3)	(**0.0**, 0.1)	(**0.0**, 0.0)	(**0.0**, 0.0)
Baa	(**6.9**, 4.6)	(**86.8**, 92.2)	(**5.6**, 2.8)	(**0.4**, 0.3)	(**0.2**, 0.1)	(**0.1**, 0.1)
Ba	(**0.6**, 0.6)	(**5.9**, 4.8)	(**83.1**, 88.5)	(**8.4**, 5.0)	(**0.3**, 0.3)	(**1.7**, 0.7)
B	(**0.3**, 0.1)	(**0.8**, 0.3)	(**6.6**, 7.2)	(**79.6**, 85.8)	(**3.2**, 2.1)	(**9.4**, 4.5)
Caa	(**0.0**, 0.0)	(**0.0**, 0.9)	(**1.9**, 2.7)	(**9.3**, 5.4)	(**64.9**, 77.5)	(**23.1**, 12.6)

Source: Based on results from Nickell et al. (2000).

More generally, we can treat the pair (X_t, C_t) as a Markov chain. Suppose, for instance, that X_t has three outcomes, as in the example above with peak, normal, and trough. With, say, seven ratings, we can now treat the entire system as a Markov chain with $3 \times 7 = 21$ states. If we follow the doubly stochastic assumption, we can let $p_{x,y}$ denote the conditional probability that $X_{t+1} = y$, given that $X_t = x$. In this case, the one-period transition probability from (x, i) to (y, j) is given by $p_{x,y} \times \Pi_{i,j}(x)$. Multiperiod ratings transition probabilities are now easy, following the matrix-product rule.

4.3. Ratings Transitions and Aging

There is evidence that the transition rates to new ratings depend on the length of time that an issue has held its current rating and also on an *aging effect*. These effects are explored by Carty and Fons (1994), who assumed that the probability distribution for the time spent continually in a given credit rating was described by the Weibull duration model introduced in Chapter 3 in the context of default time. The Weibull duration model has a hazard rate for transition out of the current rating of

$$h(t) = \gamma p (\gamma t)^{p-1}, \tag{4.1}$$

where p and γ are constants, and the time t should be interpreted as time since entering a given rating category. If $p > 1$, then $h(t)$ is increasing in t, so the hazard function $h(\cdot)$ is said to exhibit *positive duration dependence*. If $p = 1$, then $h(t)$ does not depend on t, whereas $p < 1$ implies that there is negative duration dependence. Positive duration dependence implies that the longer a bond has a given credit rating, the more likely it is that there will be a change in rating in the near term. The Weibull distribution implies only monotonically increasing or decreasing hazard rates for nonzero p. A "humped" pattern, for instance, cannot be captured by the Weibull model.

Carty and Fons estimated positive duration dependence for Aaa-rated bonds, approximately no duration dependence for Baa-rated bonds, and negative duration dependence for B-rated and Caa-rated bonds (see Figure 4.2). For the lowest credit rating, the negative duration dependence suggests that the intensity of default declines with the duration of survival time from issuance. However, these forward survival probabilities are not conditioned on information about the state of the economy or other credit covariates.

The study by Carty and Fons (1994) also examined the presence of ratings *drift* and *momentum*. They found that, since the mid-1970s, the differences between the percentage of firms upgraded and the percentage of firms downgraded generally declines with later calendar years. This was

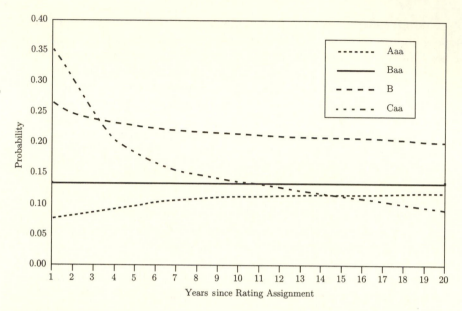

Figure 4.2.   *Hazard functions for selected long-term ratings. (Source: Carty and Fons, 1994.)*

interpreted as a downward drift in the Moody's ratings. Additionally, they examined whether prior ratings changes have predictive power for future ratings changes, that is, whether there is *ratings momentum*. Using data from January 1938 through June 1993, Carty and Fons (1994) found that, for all ratings between Aa and B, there was a significantly higher probability of a downgrade within a year given that the previous rating change had been a downgrade. They found essentially no evidence of a comparable upgrade momentum. Extending from this work, Behar and Nagpal (1999), Lando and Skødeberg (2000), and Kavvathas (2001) all find that for firms of a given rating, the prior rating is an important determinant of the likelihood of a downgrade, versus that of an upgrade, over a given time horizon.

4.4. Ordered Probits of Ratings

Most of the statistical analyses linking credit ratings to observable credit-related covariates are special cases of qualitative-response models, such as ordered probit. As opposed to ratings-transition probabilities, these studies focus on an explanation of how ratings are assigned at a given time as a function of currently observable variables related to credit quality.

An ordered qualitative-response model is obtained by assuming that ratings are linked to a credit-quality index Z_t that depends on observable covariates measured in a vector X_t, in that

$$Z_t = \alpha + \beta \cdot X_t + \epsilon_t, \tag{4.2}$$

for an intercept coefficient α and a vector β of slope coefficients to be estimated, where ϵ_t is a *noise* variable that is generally assumed to be independent and identically distributed across observations. We let $C(t)$ denote the credit rating of a bond at date t and suppose that there are K credit ratings, as well as default $(K+1)$. The ratings of bonds are then assumed to be determined by

$$C(t) = j, \qquad \text{if} \quad z_{j-1} \le Z_t < z_j, \tag{4.3}$$

for boundary coefficients $z_1, z_2, \ldots, z_K$, which are also to be estimated from the data on the covariates X_t and ratings $C(t)$ of issuers. [In (4.3), we take $z_0 = -\infty$ and $z_{K+1} = +\infty$.] In other words, the probability that the rating of this bond is j is the probability that the credit index Z_t is in the interval $[z_{j-1}, z_j)$.

Ordered probit models were estimated by Kaplan and Urwitz (1979), Ederington and Yawitz (1987), Cheung (1996),[2] and Blume et al. (1998).

Blume et al. (1998) examined a data set of over 14,000 observations covering the period 1973–1992. The covariate vector X_t included balance-sheet information about the firm as well as information about the firm's stock-return beta. Blume et al. also allowed the intercept coefficient α in (4.2) to depend on the year. They found that these estimated time-varying intercepts became increasingly negative over time, especially after 1980, and interpreted this finding to mean that the standards used in assigning ratings became more stringent over time. This conclusion comes from the implication that a firm with a given credit rating in one year is more likely to have a lower credit rating in subsequent years, holding the conditioning variables (X_t) fixed. These results may reflect the same ratings-drift phenomenon documented by Carty and Fons (1994). They, however, interpreted ratings drift as being due to "a prolonged deterioration in overall credit quality that started in 1980," and not to changes in the stringency of the criteria used by Moody's to rate firms. Blume et al. (1998) also omit business cycle effects on both the likelihood that a given firm will default and possible cyclical changes in the ranges of characteristics that define the credit ratings (the boundary coefficients z_j).

---

[2] Cheung (1996) focused on provincial debt ratings in Canada and thus considered a quite different set of explanatory variables.

4.5. Ratings as Markov Chains

We now extend the notion of rating as a Markov chain by using the intensity approach of Chapter 3, in this case to allow for ratings transition that may occur at any time within a year, as follows.

We allow for K nondefault ratings as well as the default rating, numbered $K + 1$. For any current rating i, there is a transition intensity for a jump to any other rating j given at time t of $\Lambda_{ij}(t)$. For example, any firm currently rated i has a default intensity of $\Lambda_{i,K+1}(t)$. We suppose that there is no transition out of default, so that $\Lambda_{K+1,i}(t) = 0$ for all $i < K + 1$. This is a technical convenience and is not to be taken as a statement of whether a firm can be reorganized after default. For now, we can suppose that these transition intensities are deterministic and constant. Later, we consider deterministic time variation, and then stochastic variation, in intensities.

For example, we could take the $K = 6$ nondefault ratings, Aaa, Aa, A, Baa, Ba, B, and let default be rating number 7, labeled D. The total intensity of a change in rating (including default) by a B-rated issuer is then

$$\Lambda_{B,Aaa} + \Lambda_{B,Aa} + \Lambda_{B,A} + \Lambda_{B,Baa} + \Lambda_{B,Ba} + \Lambda_{B,D}.$$

Similarly, for each rating i, the total intensity of a change in rating is $-\Lambda_{ii}$, where

$$\Lambda_{ii} = -(\Lambda_{i,1} + \Lambda_{i,2} + \cdots + \Lambda_{i,i-1} + \Lambda_{i,i+1} + \cdots + \Lambda_{i,7}). \qquad (4.4)$$

This implies that, starting in rating i at time t, the probability of remaining within rating i continually until some time $s > t$ is $e^{(s-t)\Lambda_{ii}}$, analogous to the modeling in Chapter 3 of survival probabilities based on a constant default intensity.

The *generator* for the Markov chain is the 7×7 matrix Λ, with the ith diagonal element Λ_{ii}, given by

$$\Lambda = \begin{pmatrix} \Lambda_{11} & \Lambda_{12} & \Lambda_{13} & \cdots & \Lambda_{1,6} & \Lambda_{1,D} \\ \Lambda_{21} & \Lambda_{22} & \Lambda_{23} & \cdots & \Lambda_{2,6} & \Lambda_{2,D} \\ \vdots & \vdots & \vdots & \ddots & \vdots & \vdots \\ \Lambda_{61} & \Lambda_{62} & \Lambda_{63} & \cdots & \Lambda_{6,6} & \Lambda_{6,D} \\ 0 & 0 & 0 & \cdots & 0 & 0 \end{pmatrix}. \qquad (4.5)$$

The zero bottom row of the generator Λ in (4.5) reflects our standing assumption that default is a *trapping state*.

For example, extrapolating from estimates in work by Jarrow et al.

(1997), a constant generator that is "close" in some sense to that implied by the average transition frequencies of Figure 4.1 is given by

	A ↑	BBB	BB	B	CCC	D
A ↑	−0.086	0.069	0.011	0.005	0.000	0.001
BBB	0.077	−0.171	0.070	0.017	0.002	0.005
BB	0.012	0.081	−0.252	0.118	0.014	0.027
B	0.005	0.007	0.057	−0.192	0.048	0.075
CCC	0.014	0.014	0.025	0.093	−0.432	0.286
D	0	0	0	0	0	0

after collapsing AAA, AA, and A into a single rating denoted A↑.

Israel et al. (2001) provide alternative techniques for the "calibration" of a generator to a 1-year transition probability matrix (or a transition matrix of any discrete period length). It is well known, however, that for certain 1-year transition matrices, there need not be any generator.[3] This would mean that the 1-year transition matrix could not be that of a continuous-time Markov chain. Moreover, as pointed out by Israel et al. (2001), there can be distinctly different generators consistent with a given 1-year transition matrix, and these different generators imply different transition probabilities for time horizons other than 1 year.

In any case, assuming that we have a generator Λ in hand, we are ready to calculate the probability $\Pi_{ij}(t, s)$, beginning at time t in rating i, of being in rating j at time $s > t$. In particular, $\Pi_{i,K+1}(t, s)$ gives the probability, for an i-rated firm at time t, of having defaulted by time s. (This uses the assumption that default is a trapping state, for once having defaulted at any time before s, the firm is assured of being in default at time s.) This transition matrix is

$$\Pi(t, s) = e^{\Lambda(s-t)}, \tag{4.6}$$

where the exponential of any matrix A is defined by

$$e^A = I + A + \frac{A^2}{2!} + \frac{A^3}{3!} + \cdots.$$

4.5.1. Time-Varying Transition Intensities

If the ratings-transition generator $\Lambda(t)$ varies over time, then special methods are required to compute ratings-transition probabilities. It is *not*

---

[3] Israel et al. (2001) provide sufficient conditions on a transition matrix for the existence of a generator and conditions for the failure of the existence of a generator.

generally true that one can extend (4.6) to get $\Pi(t, s) = e^{\int_t^s \Lambda(u)\,du}$. Instead, for a time-varying but deterministic generator $\{\Lambda(t) : t \geq 0\}$, $\Pi(t, s)$ solves the linear ordinary differential equation (ODE)

$$\frac{\partial}{\partial s}\Pi(t, s) = -\Lambda(s)\Pi(t, s). \tag{4.7}$$

Without special structural assumptions on the generator Λ, (4.7) is solved numerically.

In one of the most comprehensive empirical studies of a time-varying generator, Kavvathas (2001) assumed that the ijth entry of $\Lambda(t)$ is given by

$$\Lambda_{ij}(t) = \exp\left[\eta_{ij} + \gamma'_{ij}X(t)\right]. \tag{4.8}$$

The parameters were estimated using historical ratings-transition information from Standard & Poor's and with various choices of $X(t)$, including bond, equity, and credit market variables. He found that his econometric model with state-dependent intensities out-performed, in out-of-sample forecasting, various reference models (including the constant-intensity model).

Computation of $\Pi(t, s)$ from a model such as Kavvathas's can be burdensome, however, so it is instructive to examine cases where the linear ODE can be solved more explicitly. One such case is when

$$\Lambda(s)\Lambda(t) = \Lambda(t)\Lambda(s), \tag{4.9}$$

for all s and t. This commutativity property obviously holds if the transition intensities are constant. More generally, commutativity applies if, for all t, $\Lambda(t)$ can be diagonalized in the form

$$\Lambda(t) = B\mu(t)B^{-1}, \tag{4.10}$$

where B is the matrix whose columns are the eigenvectors of $\Lambda(t)$, and $\mu(t)$ is the diagonal matrix whose ith diagonal element is the eigenvalue of $\Lambda(t)$ associated with the ith eigenvector. By assuming that B does not depend on t, while $\mu(t)$ may, we have commutativity (4.9). Under this commutativity condition, it follows from the theory of linear ODEs that

$$\Pi(t, s) = B\exp\left[\int_t^s \mu(u)\,du\right]B^{-1}. \tag{4.11}$$

For example, from (4.11), the probability, beginning in rating i at time t, of being in some other given rating k at time $s > t$, is

$$\Pi_{ik}(t,\,s) = \sum_{j=1}^{K+1} B_{ij} \exp\left[\int_t^s \mu_j(u)\,du\right] B_{jk}^{-1}$$

$$= \sum_{j=1}^{K+1} \beta_{ijk} \exp\left[\int_t^s \mu_j(u)\,du\right], \qquad (4.12)$$

where $\beta_{ijk} = B_{ij}B_{jk}^{-1}$.

4.5.2. Lando's Stochastic Transition-Intensity Model

In order to allow for stochastic transition intensities, which are natural given random fluctuations over time in the economic environment that deter-mines default risk, but still maintain tractability, Lando (1998) provides the following insightful model. He maintains the special diagonalizability assumption (4.10) on the generator $\Lambda(t)$, now assumed to be a stochastic process, and moreover assumes that we have the affine dependence,

$$\mu_j(t) = \gamma_{j0} + \gamma_{j1} \cdot X_t, \qquad (4.13)$$

of the eigenvalues of $\Lambda(t)$ on some n-dimensional affine state process X that reflects changing economic conditions determining ratings-transition intensities.

Lando's model is doubly stochastic in the sense that, conditional on the entire future path of the state process X, the transition probabilities from rating to rating are given by (4.12). It follows from (4.12) that, for an issuer currently rated i, the conditional probability at time t, given X_t, of being in rating k at a future time s is

$$\pi_{ik}(t,\,s,\,X_t) = E_t\left(\sum_{j=1}^{K+1} \beta_{ijk} \exp\left[\int_t^s \mu_j(u)\,du\right]\right)$$

$$= \sum_{j=1}^{K+1} \beta_{ijk} E_t\left(\exp\left[\int_t^s (\gamma_{j0} + \gamma_{j1} \cdot X_u)\,du\right]\right)$$

$$= \sum_{j=1}^{K+1} \beta_{ijk}\, e^{a_j(t,s)+b_j(t,s)\cdot X(t)}, \qquad (4.14)$$

for coefficients $a_j(t,\,s)$ and $b_j(t,\,s)$, which can be easily calculated, as in any affine model setting, in the manner explained in Appendix A. For example, if the coordinates of X are CIR (square-root) diffusions, or mean reverting with jumps, or variants discussed in Appendix A, then we can use the explicit formulas for affine processes that were applied in Chapter 3 to calculate default probabilities.

In order to consider the special structure associated with Lando's generator-decomposition assumptions (4.10) and (4.13) for the correlations among the various transitions and default intensities, we momentarily specialize to the case of $K = 2$ nondefault ratings. We label rating 1 as I, for investment grade, and rating 2 as S, for speculative grade. The ratings-transition intensities $\Lambda_{IS}(t)$ and $\Lambda_{SI}(t)$ governing the transitions from rating I to S, and conversely, can be calculated from (4.10) as

$$\Lambda_{IS}(t) = \eta_1[\mu_1(t) - \mu_2(t)]$$

$$\Lambda_{SI}(t) = \eta_2[\mu_1(t) - \mu_2(t)],$$

where

$$\eta_1 = -\frac{B_{11}B_{12}}{B_{11}B_{22} - B_{12}B_{21}}$$

$$\eta_2 = \frac{B_{21}B_{22}}{B_{11}B_{22} - B_{12}B_{21}}.$$

It follows that the ratings-transition intensities are proportional to each other in this model and, hence, perfectly correlated. In particular, with $K = 2$, this model cannot capture asymmetric upgrade/downgrade patterns, such as the tendency for there to be more upgrades than downgrades in economic expansions and the opposite during contractions. We note that this conclusion is independent of assumptions such as (4.13) regarding the behavior of the eigenvalues $\mu_1(t)$ and $\mu_2(t)$.

Turning to the intensities for default, after computing $B\mu(t)B^{-1}$ and selecting the relevant elements of this matrix, we obtain[4] the default intensity from ratings I and S of

$$\Lambda_{ID}(t) = -[\Lambda_{IS}(t) + \omega\mu_1(t) + (1 - \omega)\mu_2(t)]$$

$$\Lambda_{SD}(t) = -[\Lambda_{SI}(t) + (1 - \omega)\mu_1(t) + \omega\mu_2(t)],$$

respectively, where $\omega = B_{11}B_{22}/(B_{11}B_{22} - B_{12}B_{21})$. As $\Lambda_{IS}(t)$ and $\Lambda_{SI}(t)$ are

---

[4] Here, we use the facts that

$$B_{13}^{-1} = \frac{B_{12} - B_{22}}{B_{11}B_{22} - B_{12}B_{21}}, \qquad B_{23}^{-1} = \frac{B_{21} - B_{11}}{B_{11}B_{22} - B_{12}B_{21}}.$$

perfectly correlated, these default intensities are also perfectly correlated if $\omega = 0.5$.

More generally, by counting the equations restricting the transitions intensities with K nondefault ratings, Lando (1998) finds that the K^2 transition intensities vary in a $(K - 1)$-dimensional subspace. As we have already found for $K = 2$, this implies that these intensities must be perfectly correlated.

In Chapter 6, we reinterpret these results in order to consider the effect of stochastic variation in transition intensities on the term structures of credit spreads for each rating.

5

Conceptual Approaches to Valuation of Default Risk

A VARIETY OF alternative approaches to the valuation of default risk have been explored in the literature and implemented by practitioners. This chapter introduces some of the most popular of these through the lens of a central building block in most valuation problems—zero-coupon defaultable bonds. In order to highlight key differences among models of default timing, we generally maintain in this chapter the assumption of no recovery by bond investors in the event of default. In Chapters 6 and 7, we extend the pricing frameworks introduced here to treat corporate and sovereign coupon bonds with nonzero recovery. Subsequent chapters examine more complex instruments such as callable and convertible debt and structured products that securitize credit risk in various ways.

Following the increasingly common nomenclature in the financial literatures on default, we classify pricing models into those that are *reduced form*, meaning that they are based on an assumed form of default intensity, and those that are *structural*, based for example on *first-passage* of assets to a default boundary. Both reduced-form and structural models have their proponents in industry and academia. One of the primary objectives of this chapter is to highlight some of the key implications of standard formulations of these models, with particular emphasis on their differences and similarities.

5.1. Introduction

To be concrete, consider a loan promising to pay $1 at date T. If the issuer is default-free, then valuation can proceed using a conventional default-free term-structure model. Such models are usually based on some short-rate process r, whose stochastic behavior is modeled under *risk-neutral* probabil-

100

ity assessments.[1] By *risk-neutral probabilities,* we mean probability assessments under which the market value of a security is the expectation of the discounted present value of its cash flows, using the compounded short rate for discounting. For example, if the short-rate process changes only at discrete time intervals of length 1, then the value of a default-free zero-coupon bond maturing at date T, with promised payoff of 1 at maturity, has a price at time T of

$$
\begin{aligned}
\delta(t, T) &= E_t^* \left[e^{-r(t)} e^{-r(t+1)} \cdots e^{-r(T-1)} \right] \\
&= E_t^* \left[e^{-[r(t)+r(t+1)+\cdots+r(T-1)]} \right],
\end{aligned}
\tag{5.1}
$$

where E_t^* denotes risk-neutral expectation conditional on information available at date t. There are computational advantages, particularly when working with default, to modeling in a continuous-time setting, for which the analogue to (5.1) is

$$
\delta(t, T) = E_t^* \left[e^{-\int_t^T r(u)\, du} \right].
\tag{5.2}
$$

Risk-neutral probabilities exist under extremely weak no-arbitrage conditions, as shown by Harrison and Kreps (1979) and Delbaen and Schachermayer (1999). When pricing default-free securities, these probabilities are often specified so as to make computation of the expectation in (5.2) tractable. When markets are not financially complete, there are in fact many alternative choices for risk-neutral probabilities that are consistent with the pricing of traded securities. Whether in complete or incomplete markets, however, knowledge of risk-neutral probabilities is generally not enough information to assess the fit of a model to historical data, because the behavior over time of observed prices reflects the *actual,* that is, "real-world," likelihoods that generate history. Thus, when the objectives are both to price securities and to assess the implications of one's pricing model for, among other purposes, the financial risks of positions, it is typically necessary to specify both the actual and risk-neutral probabilities. For now, we take as given the probabilities underlying the risk-neutral expectation E_t^* and defer until the end of this chapter a discussion of some parametric specifications of actual and risk-neutral probabilities.

---

[1] All random variables are defined on a fixed probability space $(\Omega, \mathcal{F}, P)$. A filtration $\{\mathcal{F}_t : t \geq 0\}$ of σ-algebras, satisfying the usual conditions, is fixed and defines the information available at each time. It is not necessary to restrict attention to models that are based on a short-rate process. For example, certain discrete-tenor forward rate models, such as the *market model* of Miltersen et al. (1997), can be used to treat the term structure of default probabilities (see, e.g., Bielecki and Rutkowski, 2000b).

If the issuer might default prior to the maturity date T, then, in addition to the risk of changes in r, both the magnitude and timing of the payoff to investors may be uncertain. In this case, it is often convenient to view a zero-coupon bond as a portfolio of two securities: a security that pays \$1 at date T if and only if the issuer survives to the maturity date T and a security that pays the random amount W of recovery received at default if default occurs before maturity. We shall see various models of the default time τ. We let $1_{\{\tau > t\}}$ be the indicator of the event that $\tau > t$, which has outcome 1 if the issuer has not defaulted prior to time t and zero otherwise.[2] The price $d(t, T)$ of this defaultable zero-coupon bond is then

$$d(t, T) = E_t^* \left[e^{-\int_t^T r_s \, ds} 1_{\{\tau > T\}} \right] + E_t^* \left[e^{-\int_t^\tau r_s \, ds} W 1_{\{\tau \le T\}} \right]. \qquad (5.3)$$

In this chapter we make the simplifying assumption of zero recovery ($W = 0$), in which case the last term in (5.3) is zero and we are left with the price of the *survival-contingent* security,

$$d_0(t, T) = E_t^* \left[e^{-\int_t^T r_s \, ds} 1_{\{\tau > T\}} \right]. \qquad (5.4)$$

Our goal is to characterize this defaultable no-recovery price $d_0(t, T)$ under various parameterizations of reduced-form and structural models. This will involve characterizations of the joint distribution of the default-free term structure and the default time, based on risk-neutral probabilities. Before going into this basic pricing problem in more depth, we discuss the meaning of risk-neutral probabilities for a setting in which there is the possibility of default.

5.2. Risk-Neutral versus Actual Probabilities

Just as with interest-rate risk, differences between actual and risk-neutral default probabilities reflect risk premia required by market participants to take on the risks associated with default. In general, default-risk premia reflect aversion to both the risk of timing of default and to the risk of severity of loss in the event of default. For reasons that we hope to make clear by the conclusion of this chapter, modeling default-risk premia is conceptually more challenging than modeling interest-rate risk. Furthermore, particularly in credit markets, the price of a new security could differ according to which (among the set of nonunique) risk-neutral probabilities are

---

[2] More precisely, if τ is viewed as a random variable mapping the sample space Ω to $[0, \infty]$, then $1_{\{\tau > t\}}$ is a random variable with outcome 1 in the event $\{\omega : \tau(\omega) > t\}$ and zero otherwise.

used. With these observations in mind, we start with a brief nontechnical overview of actual and risk-neutral default probabilities in the context of a simple example and comment briefly on the likely magnitudes of default-risk premia. The construction of risk-neutral from actual probabilities, or vice versa, will be taken up subsequently when we describe alternative pricing models.

The historical default probabilities discussed in Chapter 3 are *actual* default probabilities and, as such, are not the relevant probabilities for use in pricing. To illustrate the difference between risk-neutral and actual default probabilities, suppose as in Figure 5.1 that we are pricing a 1-year par bond (i.e., whose price is its face value) that promises its face value and an 8% coupon at maturity. The 1-year riskless rate is 6%. If the issuer survives, then the investor receives $108 at maturity, and this happens with actual probability 0.99. On the other hand, if the issuer defaults before maturity (which happens with actual probability 0.01), then the investor is assumed to recover 50% of the par value, or $50. Because the default recovery is known with certainty in this example, there is no recovery risk premium.

It is natural, especially because default risk is correlated with downturns in the business cycle, to presume that investors demand a premium, above and beyond expected default losses, for bearing default risk. If so, then our pricing must somehow account for this risk premium. In particular, simply discounting, at the risk-free rate of 6%, the expected payoff computed with actual probabilities, $108 \times 0.99 + 50 \times 0.01$, presumes no default-risk premia and thus overstates (by 1.31) the actual market price of 100 for this security.

For our illustration of a 1-year defaultable par bond, we let p^* denote the risk-neutral probability that the issuer will survive through the maturity date of the bond. Then, according to the risk-neutral valuation paradigm, the fact that the security is priced at par (100) implies that its price is the present value of the risk-neutral expected payoff, so that

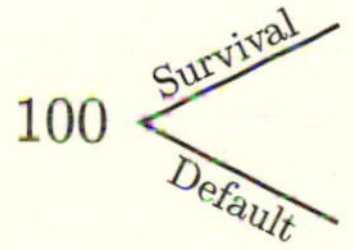

8% Par 1-Year Bond Pays	Actual Probability	Risk-Neutral Probability
108	0.99	p^*
50	0.01	$1 - p^*$

100 < Survival / Default

Figure 5.1. *Backing out the implied risk-neutral default probability.*

$$100 = \frac{1}{1.06}\left[p^* \times 108 + (1 - p^*) \times 50\right].$$ (5.5)

Solving (5.5) yields the market-implied risk-neutral survival probability of $p^* = 0.965$. In a setting of constant risk-neutral default intensity, in the sense of Chapter 3, it follows that the risk-neutral default intensity underlying this model is $\lambda^* = -\log 0.965 = 0.0356$. (The superscript asterisk will henceforth be used to indicate risk-neutral variables or properties.)

We note that $p^* = 0.965$ is less than the actual survival probability ($p = 0.99$). Equivalently, this bond is priced as though it were a breakeven trade for a hypothetical "stand-in" investor who is not averse to risk and who assumes a default probability of 0.0356, which is larger than the actual default probability of 0.01. This makes sense if investors are averse to default-timing risk. The difference between $\lambda = 0.01$ and $\lambda^* = 0.0356$ reflects the premium for default-timing risk.

We also note that because there is no recovery uncertainty nor random fluctuation over time in default rates, the risk-neutral survival probability p^* is uniquely determined in this simple example.

More generally, the risk-neutral default-intensity process $\{\lambda^*(t) : t \geq 0\}$ may fluctuate randomly over time as new information comes into the market. Moreover, the level and random behavior over time of λ^* need bear no simple relationship to the actual default-intensity process λ.[3] Not only can λ and λ^* differ in their current levels, but they can also have different degrees of persistence, time-varying volatility, and jump behavior. Indeed, one may experience jumps and the other might not. At a practical level, this raises the challenging question of how to parameterize λ^* for pricing if the available historical observations are based on the actual intensity λ. One way of proceeding, as we have just done in a crude example, is to infer information about λ^* from the market prices of defaultable bonds. However, this direction is unlikely to be productive when an issuer has little or no actively traded debt or other securities and there are no reasonable proxy security prices. A second approach is to parameterize the transformation between λ and λ^* explicitly. Examples of both approaches are discussed later in this chapter and in Chapters 6 and 7.

Before turning to pricing methods in more depth, it is instructive to informally consider the likely magnitude of risk-neutral default intensities relative to their actual counterparts. That is, how important are default-risk premia? If spreads are due to default and recovery risk, and there is zero recovery upon default, we will see subsequently that the credit spread on an issuer's short-term debt should be approximately the same as the

---

[3] See Artzner and Delbaen (1995) for the existence of a risk-neutral intensity λ^*, given knowledge of the risk-neutral probabilities and an actual intensity λ.

risk-neutral default intensity λ_t^*. If we take the short-spread process s to be stationary, it can be shown (by Jensen's inequality) that, on average over time, bond yield spreads are *smaller than* $\bar{\lambda}^*$, the long-run average of λ^*. In a manner that we analyze in the next chapter, positive recovery upon default narrows spreads. Thus, on average, credit spreads, such as those shown by generic issuers with B or Ba ratings in Figure 5.2, are lower than risk-neutral default intensities, assuming zero recovery, and of course spreads are yet smaller with some default recovery.

Actuarial credit spreads are those implied by assuming that investors are neutral to risk and use historical frequencies of default and average recoveries to estimate default probabilities and expected recoveries, respectively. Figure 5.3, taken from Fons (1994), suggests that corporate yield spreads are larger than the spreads suggested by actuarial default losses alone. For example, the actuarially implied credit spreads on A-rated 5-year U.S. corporate debt were estimated by Fons to be 6 basis points. The corresponding

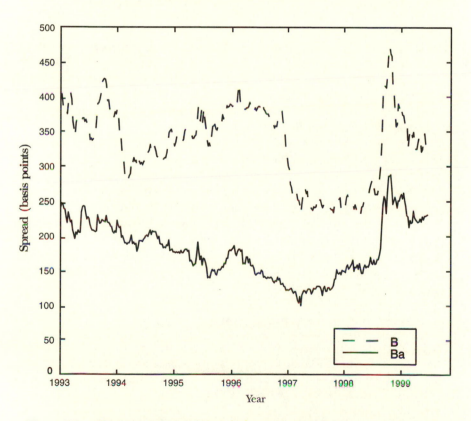

Figure 5.2. *Five-year industrial speculative-grade spreads. (Source: Bloomberg.)*

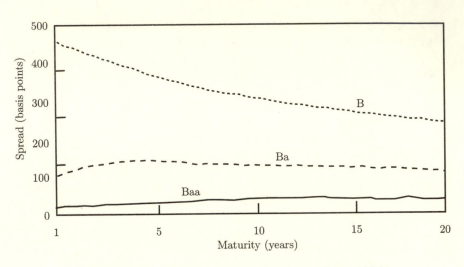

Figure 5.3. *Actuarial credit spreads. (Source: Fons, 1994.)*

market spreads, relative to those of U.S. Treasury securities of similar maturities, have been on the order of 100 basis points, as indicated in Table 5.1, computed from Lehman Brothers data. (See Chapter 7 for details on these data.) The actuarial credit spread of 5-year Ba-rated bonds is about 100 basis points. The corresponding market yield spreads have been on the order of 200 basis points, as indicated in Figure 5.2.

Differences between *actuarial credit spreads* and *actual yield spreads* are due to many effects, including risk premia for bearing default risk, tax shields on treasuries (Elton et al., 2001), special repo rates for on-the-run Treasuries (Duffie, 1996), and liquidity effects. Even after measuring spreads relative to AAA yields (thereby stripping out Treasury effects), actuarial credit spreads are smaller than actual market spreads, especially for high-quality bonds. An assumption that history is a guide leaves a significant fraction of this difference to be allocated to risk premia and to illiquidity. We will bear this in mind as we discuss alternative formulations of defaultable bond pricing models.

5.3. Reduced-Form Pricing

This section briefly reviews reduced-form debt pricing for a default time τ that has an assumed risk-neutral default-intensity process λ^*. An implication of this modeling framework, as shown by Lando (1998), is that the zero-recovery defaultable bond price of (5.4) is

$$d_0(t, T) = E_t^* \left[e^{-\int_t^T (r(u) + \lambda^*(u))\, du} \right], \tag{5.6}$$

provided that default has not already occurred by time t. An intuitive interpretation of this pricing relation is as follows. First, conditional on the path of r and λ^*, the risk-neutral survival probability is $e^{-\int_t^T \lambda^*(u)\,du}$ and the discount factor for interest rates is $e^{-\int_t^T r(u)\,du}$. Thus, the discounted expected cash flow, given the paths of r and λ^*, is $e^{-\int_t^T [r(u)+\lambda^*(u)]\,du}$. Now we can calculate the expectation over the possible paths of r and λ^*, as in (5.6), to get the bond price. All of these calculations are with respect to risk-neutral probabilities and are based on the assumption of a doubly stochastic default model.[4]

The pricing relation (5.6) accommodates correlation between the riskless interest-rate process r and the risk-neutral default-intensity process λ^*. In particular, the conditional (risk-neutral) likelihood of default can fluctuate with the stage of the business cycle, consistent with evidence summarized in Chapter 3, just as interest rates depend on economic conditions. For example, suppose that n risk factors, $X = (X^{(1)}, \ldots, X^{(n)})$, are relevant for pricing this bond and that X is a multivariate square-root process. That is, $X^{(i)}$ is, for each i, a CIR (also known as a square-root or a Feller) diffusion, as introduced in Chapter 3, and these risk factors are risk-neutrally independent. We will suppose for this illustration that

$$r(t) = a_r(t) + b_r(t) \cdot X(t)$$

$$\lambda^*(t) = a_{\lambda^*}(t) + b_{\lambda^*}(t) \cdot X(t),$$

for deterministic (possibly time-dependent) coefficients a_r, b_r, a_{λ^*}, and b_{λ^*}. This allows for correlation between $r(t)$ and $\lambda^*(t)$ through their joint dependence on $X(t)$. For this specification, from (5.6), we get simple, tractable representations of both defaultable and default-free bond prices in the form

$$d_0(t, T) = e^{\alpha_d(t,T)+\beta_d(t,T)\cdot X(t)} \qquad \text{and} \qquad \delta(t, T) = e^{\alpha_\delta(t,T)+\beta_\delta(t,T)\cdot X(t)}, \quad (5.7)$$

respectively, for coefficients $\alpha_d(t, T)$, $\beta_d(t, T)$, $\alpha_\delta(t, T)$, and $\beta_\delta(t, T)$, which are well known from the work of Cox et al. (1985). (The CIR model is a special case of the basic affine model, whose coefficients are shown explicitly in Appendix A.) Variants of this approach in the affine class have similar analytical advantages, as outlined in Appendix A, and generate the same form (5.7) of solutions.

---

[4] It does not necessarily follow, given a doubly stochastic default model under actual probabilities, that default is also doubly stochastic under risk-neutral probabilities. In this setting, the doubly stochastic assumption is that, conditional on all of the information necessary to determine the paths of the risk-neutral default-intensity process λ^* *and* the short-term default-free interest-rate process, default occurs at the first arrival of a risk-neutral Poisson process whose (conditionally deterministic) intensity process is λ^*.

A Gaussian model for X_t, say of the *Vasicek* (1977) type, is in the affine family, but is not literally consistent as a source of random fluctuation in λ^* in an affine setting because an intensity process must be nonnegative. In certain cases, however, the computational advantages may be worth the approximation error associated with such a Gaussian formulation.

Owing to potential correlation between r_t and λ^*_t, variation in credit spreads, even with zero recovery, is not determined purely by changes in credit quality. The zero-coupon bond credit spread for maturity $(T - t)$ is

$$s(t, T) = -\frac{\log d_0(t, T) - \log \delta(t, T)}{T - t}, \tag{5.8}$$

which, in the case of the affine model (5.7), simplifies to

$$s(t, T) = -\frac{\alpha_s(t, T) + \beta_s(t, T) \cdot X(t)}{T - t}, \tag{5.9}$$

for α_s and β_s obtained by subtraction of the respective α's and β's in (5.7). In general, $s(t, T)$ and $r(t)$ are correlated through their joint dependence on $X(t)$.

For the special case in which the default time τ and the default-free short-rate process r are risk-neutrally independent, the bond price formula (5.4) can be decomposed into

$$d_0(t, T) = E_t^* \left[e^{-\int_t^T r(u)\, du} \right] E_t^* \left[1_{\{\tau > T\}} \right] = \delta(t, T) p^*(t, T). \tag{5.10}$$

Provided that default has not already occurred by time t,

$$E_t^* \left[1_{\{\tau > T\}} \right] = p^*(t, T) = E_t^* \left[e^{-\int_t^T \lambda^*(u)\, du} \right] \tag{5.11}$$

is the risk-neutral conditional survival probability, which gives a *markdown* to the price of a default-free zero that can be used to get the price of a defaultable zero-coupon bond.

It follows from (5.10) and (5.11) that

$$d_0(t, T) = \exp \left[-\int_t^T [F(t, u) + f^*(t, u)]\, du \right], \tag{5.12}$$

where $F(t, u)$ is the default-free forward rate at t for maturity u, and $f^*(t, u)$ is the risk-neutral forward default rate (the latter was explained in Chapter 3). Thus, under risk-neutral independence of r and λ^*, defaultable bonds are priced at a default-risk-corrected forward rate, an idea developed in a discrete-time setting by Pye (1974) and Litterman and Iben (1991).

As a further illustration, consider the simple mean-reverting-with-jumps model of Section 3.5.1 for the risk-neutral default-intensity process λ^* and suppose once again that there is risk-neutral independence between r and λ^*. The parameters governing the behavior of λ^* are its mean-reversion rate κ^*, the rate γ^* to which the intensity reverts between jumps, the Poisson mean-arrival rate c^* of jumps, and the mean jump size J^* for exponentially distributed jumps. Each of these parameters, κ^*, γ^*, c^*, and J^*, is risk-neutral, that is, adjusted to account for risk premia. We take a constant default-free short rate r for simplicity. This model for spreads is also affine, and, based on Chapter 3, the parameters in (5.9) are

$$\beta_s(t, t+u) = -\frac{1 - e^{-\kappa^* u}}{\kappa^*}$$

$$\alpha_s(t, t+u) = -\gamma^* \left(u - \frac{1 - e^{-\kappa^* u}}{\kappa^*} \right)$$

$$- \frac{c^*}{J^* + \kappa^*} \left[J^* u - \ln \left(1 + \frac{1 - e^{-\kappa^* u}}{\kappa^*} J^* \right) \right].$$

The associated credit spreads for a low-risk and a high-risk issuer are plotted in Figure 5.4. The two issuers have the same parameters ($\gamma^* = 10$, $\kappa^* = 0.5$, $J^* = 5$, and $c^* = 10$ basis points). They differ in their initial risk-neutral default intensities λ_0^* in that the low-risk issuer has an initial risk-neutral default intensity λ_0^* of 5 basis points, whereas the high-risk issuer has an initial intensity of 400 basis points. (For reference, the average annual default frequency of B-rated corporate issuers over the period 1920–1997, as measured by Moody's, was 442 basis points.)

Empirically, as for this simple model, the term structure of yield spreads is downward sloping for low-quality issuers and upward sloping for relatively high-grade issuers, as indicated in Table 5.1, which displays average yield spreads for various industrial sectors, investment-grade ratings categories, and maturities. More systematic analyses in Jones et al. (1984), Sarig and Warga (1989), and He et al. (2000) find that, historically, the term structures of credit spreads for high-grade issuers tend to be upward sloping, whereas those for lower-rated investment grade issuers (e.g., Baa) are close to flat, or perhaps hump shaped.

The shape of the term structure of credit spreads for low-grade bonds has been more controversial. The actuarial yield spreads of Fons illustrated in Figure 5.3 show a downward-sloping term structure of spreads for low-

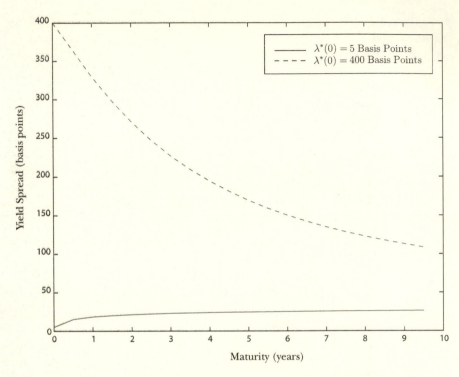

Figure 5.4.   *Term structure of coupon-strip (zero-recovery) yield spreads.*

grade bonds. Helwege and Turner (1999) argue that the findings in many
previous studies of spreads reflect a selection bias associated with a tendency for better-quality speculative-grade issuers to issue longer-term bonds.
As these authors show, because the spreads of all speculative-grade issuers
are averaged, this bias might induce a spurious downward slope to spread
curves. By matching bonds by issuer and ratings, Helwege and Turner conclude that spread curves for B-rated U.S. industrial issues are upward sloping. Subsequently, He et al. (2000) refined this matching method and ex-
panded the set of ratings examined. They found that spread curves for firms
rated CCC and CC are downward sloping, whereas those for firms rated BB
and B are slightly upward sloping out to about 15 years and then show somewhat humped shapes for longer maturities.

From Table 5.1, we also see that the volatilities of spreads are inversely
related to maturity for investment-grade issues. This pattern is implied by
many reduced-form models as a consequence of the typical assumption
of mean reversion of the intensity λ^*. By analogy, the term structure of
volatilities of yields on zero-coupon bonds is typically downward sloping
provided the short rate r exhibits mean reversion.

Table 5.1. Averages and Standard Deviations of Spreads by Sector

Average spreads

Rating	All			Financial			Industrial			Utility		
	Short	Medium	Long	Short	Medium	Long	Short	Medium	Long	Short	Medium	Long
AA	0.69	0.73	0.90	0.75	0.83	1.06	0.56	0.71	0.87	0.55	0.58	0.55
A	0.95	1.03	1.17	0.58	1.19	1.28	0.73	0.96	1.16	0.76	0.80	1.01
BBB	1.42	1.49	1.82	1.51	1.58	1.45	1.53	1.49	1.86	1.12	1.30	1.57

Standard deviations of spreads (percent)

Rating	All			Financial			Industrial			Utility		
	Short	Medium	Long	Short	Medium	Long	Short	Medium	Long	Short	Medium	Long
AA	19.49	17.52	17.93	20.87	22.50	17.37	13.51	15.78	19.47	7.97	9.57	10.23
A	26.25	24.47	22.88	64.00	35.50	30.02	43.53	19.25	21.29	19.20	16.13	24.65
BBB	51.13	40.42	36.13	77.84	69.92	14.03	50.49	36.72	32.19	28.26	28.70	23.11

5.4. Structural Models

Structural credit pricing models are based on modeling the stochastic evolution of the balance sheet of the issuer, with default when the issuer is unable or unwilling to meet its obligations.

5.4.1. The Black-Scholes-Merton Debt Pricing Model

As explained in Chapter 3, Black and Scholes (1973) and Merton (1974) suppose that default occurs at the maturity date of debt provided the issuer's assets are less than the face value of maturing debt at that time. (Default before maturity is not considered.) That is, for the case of a single bond of face value D maturing at T, they assume default at time T in the event that $A_T \leq D$. The bond price is thus the initial market value of assets less the initial market value of equity, which is priced using the Black-Scholes formula as though equity is a call option on assets struck at the face value of debt.

Specifically, suppose for now that the default-free short rate r is constant and that the process A of the market value of assets is risk-neutrally lognormal, in that

$$\frac{dA_t}{A_t} = (r - \gamma)\, dt + \sigma\, dB_t^*, \tag{5.13}$$

for a given volatility parameter σ and cash payout rate γ, where B^* is a risk-neutral standard Brownian motion. (This satisfies the required property that the risk-neutral mean rate of return on any asset, including equity, is the default-free short rate r.) We consider the price $d(t, T)$ at time t of a zero-coupon bond of face value D maturing at date T, assuming that no other liabilities mature between t and T, and assuming recovery of all assets in the event of default (absolute priority). We have

$$d(t, T) = A_t - C(A_t, D, r, \gamma, T - t, \sigma), \tag{5.14}$$

where $C(\cdot)$ is the Black-Scholes call-option pricing formula, given by

$$C(z, D, r, \gamma, s, \sigma) = z e^{-\gamma s} N(d_1) - D e^{-rs} N(d_2), \tag{5.15}$$

where

$$d_1 = \frac{\log z - \log D + (r - \gamma + \sigma^2/2)s}{\sigma \sqrt{s}}$$

$$d_2 = d_1 - \sigma \sqrt{s}.$$

Geske (1977) extended this debt pricing model to the case of bonds maturing at different dates.

5.4.2. First-Passage Debt Pricing

From Chapter 3 we also recall the first-passage structural model, especially popular in the academic literature, in which default occurs at the first time that assets fall to a sufficiently low boundary (which may or may not be the face value of debt). Focusing for the moment on this simple first-passage model, suppose default occurs at the first time at which assets A_t reach a constant threshold D, which need not be the face value of debt. Leland (1994) showed how this default-triggering boundary D may be chosen by the firm so as to maximize the market value of equity.

We suppose for now that the riskless rate is constant at r and that assets are risk-neutrally log-normal, satisfying (5.13).

For each maturity time horizon T, the risk-neutral survival probability is the probability that the distance to default, $X_t = (\log A_t - \log D)/\sigma$, does not reach 0 between t and T. Based on the analogous result (3.10) of Chapter 3 for actual survival probabilities, this risk-neutral survival probability is

$$H^*(x, s) = N\left(\frac{x + m^* s}{\sqrt{s}}\right) - e^{-2m^* x} N\left(\frac{-x + m^* s}{\sqrt{s}}\right), \qquad (5.16)$$

where $m^* = (r - \gamma - \sigma^2/2)/\sigma$ is the risk-neutral drift of the distance to default process X, and $N(x)$ is the probability that a standard normal variable is less than or equal to x. With zero recovery, under these assumptions, the price of a defaultable zero-coupon bond maturing at date T is

$$d_0(t, T) = e^{-r(T-t)} p^*(t, T). \qquad (5.17)$$

Longstaff and Schwartz (1995) extended this model to the case of stochastic interest rates using the Gaussian one-factor model of Vasicek (1977) for the short-rate process r and allowing A and r to be correlated. Section 7.4 reviews further extensions and some of the empirical evidence for this model. Collin-Dufresne and Goldstein (1999) subsequently provided an efficient method for computing the defaultable discount $d_0(t, T)$ for this setting. Although this approach extends to much richer stochastic environments, its tractability declines rapidly as one enrichs the models used for A and r and allows for a time-varying default threshold D.

Pricing for the first-passage model remains tractable, however, if one extends the basic model by allowing for a jump in the asset-value process A. Following Zhou (2000), for instance, suppose that

$$\frac{dA_t}{A_t} = (r - \gamma - c)\, dt + \sigma\, dB_t^* + dZ_t, \qquad (5.18)$$

where, under risk-neutral probabilities, Z is a compound Poisson jump process (i.e., Z has independently and identically distributed jumps at Poisson
event times), and c is the mean jump size multiplied by the arrival intensity of jumps. Zhou (2000) assumes that jump sizes have the distribution of
$J - 1$, where J is log-normal. With (5.18), A may reach the default threshold either through continuous fluctuations of the Brownian motion B^* or
by jumps. Zhou (2000) provides a closed-form expression for the associated risk-neutral survival probability. Boyarchenko (2000) and Hilberink
and Rogers (2001) extend this approach to more general jump-diffusion
models.

5.5. Comparisons of Model-Implied Spreads

The solid and dashed lines in Figure 5.5 show, from Collin-Dufresne and
Goldstein (1999), typical term structures of credit spreads from a reduced-
form model that is based on an exogenously specified square-root (CIR)
risk-neutral default-intensity process and from the first-passage model of the
previous section, with a log-normal asset process and constant interest rates.
There is a striking difference in the shapes of the spread curves at both short
and long maturities. We address each of these in turn.

As explained in Chapter 3, a first-passage model without jumps has the
property that, even for extremely highly levered firms, the likelihood of

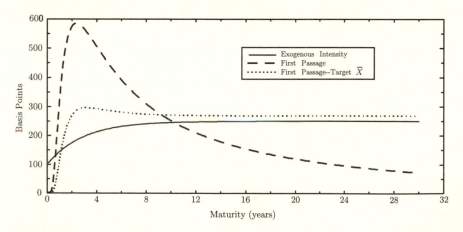

Figure 5.5.   *Credit spreads implied by reduced-form and structural models. (Source:
Collin-Dufresne and Goldstein, unpublished paper, 1999).*

default is essentially zero for short horizons. The associated credit spreads are therefore essentially zero for short maturities. This explains the location of the dashed line in Figure 5.5, near zero for the first several months and then rapidly increasing over the first several years of maturity. In contrast, the solid line for the reduced-form model starts at a nonzero spread and increases gradually, much as we see in the empirical data.

The credit spreads of the log-normal first-passage model can be made to look more like those of a reduced-form model over short maturities by introducing a jump in the model of the asset process, as in (5.18). This allows default at jump times, which occur with a positive intensity and therefore cause nontrivial short spreads.[5] As the jump-arrival intensity of assets, or the variance of the jump amplitude, ranges from zero (no jump) to positive numbers, short-term credit spreads range from near zero to potentially large magnitudes. Consequently, the term structure of credit spreads takes a shape similar to that of the reduced-form case illustrated in Figure 5.5.

The differences between the spread curves implied by reduced-form and structural models at longer maturities reflect different implicit assumptions about the likelihood of survival over long horizons. In the reduced-form model,

$$p^*(t, T) = E_t^* \left[\exp \left(- \int_t^T \lambda^*(u) \, du \right) \right] = \exp \left(- \int_t^T f^*(t, u) \, du \right), \quad (5.19)$$

where $f^*(t, u)$ is the risk-neutral forward default rate for date u. Suppose, for illustrative purposes, that λ^* is a square-root process with parameters (σ^*, θ^*, κ^*). Then it can be shown that

$$\lim_{T \to \infty} f^*(t, T) = \frac{2\kappa^* \theta^*}{\sqrt{\kappa^{*2} + 2\sigma^{*2}} + \kappa^*}, \quad (5.20)$$

a nonzero constant. In other words, the forward probability of default remains bounded away from zero even over long horizons and, consequently,

$$\lim_{T \to \infty} p^*(t, T) = 0. \quad (5.21)$$

Negligible survival probabilities over long horizons imply that credit spreads level off at a positive constant for long maturities, as depicted in Figure 5.5.

---

[5] The default intensity associated with jumps is, roughly speaking, the intensity of a jump arrival multiplied by the probability that, at the current level A_t of assets, the downward jump size is at least as large as $A_t - D$. Strictly speaking, as explained by Duffie and Lando (2001), there is no default intensity because default can also occur through diffusion across the boundary.

These features are shared by many of the commonly used default-intensity models.[6]

In the structural model, however, based on (5.16), provided the risk-neutral drift m^* of the distance to default is positive, the risk-neutral probability that the issuer never defaults is positive, in that

$$\lim_{s \to \infty} H^*(x, s) = 1 - e^{-m^* x} > 0. \tag{5.22}$$

It follows that for a first-passage model based on a distance-to-default process X whose risk-neutral drift $m^* = (r - \gamma - \sigma^2/2)/\sigma$ is strictly positive, we have

$$\lim_{T \to \infty} f^*(t, T) = 0. \tag{5.23}$$

The decline in $f^*(t, T)$ with increasing T leads to the declining long-term credit spreads in Figure 5.5. If the drift m^* of the distance to default is negative (owing to high volatility or a high cash-payout rate γ), then of course the opposite conclusion applies.

Collin-Dufresne and Goldstein (2001) recognize that firms are often viewed as having a target leverage ratio, which in our setting may be viewed as a target $\overline{X}$ for the distance-to-default process X. That is, over time, so long as they are able to survive, firms tend to adjust the components of their balance sheets so as to move on average toward their target leverage. Introducing this feature into the first-passage model leads to the spread curve shown with dots in Figure 5.5, which, at longer maturities, is similar to that of the illustrated reduced-form model. (Having a target leverage ratio does not significantly affect the probability of default over short horizons, so short-term spreads remain near zero, still counter to market-observed spreads.)

In assessing the relative merits of structural versus reduced-form models, we should recognize that it is unrealistic to assume, especially at low levels of capital, that balance-sheet data provide a precise view of default risk, particularly over short time horizons. Accounting data tend to be noisy. One often finds, for example, that the assets of a defaulting firm that are reported just before default are not representative of the actual assets of the firm. (An obvious example is the demise of Enron in 2001.) If one assumes uncertainty about the true asset level, then one obtains a default intensity under natural conditions, and the term structure of default risk and spreads

---

[6] As noted in Chapter 3, forward default probabilities are conceptually analogous to forward interest rates in term-structure models. Dybvig et al. (1996) showed that, under mild regularity, forward interest rates must converge to a nonzero constant as the horizon of the forward loan increases. Analogous properties of the forward probabilities follow immediately.

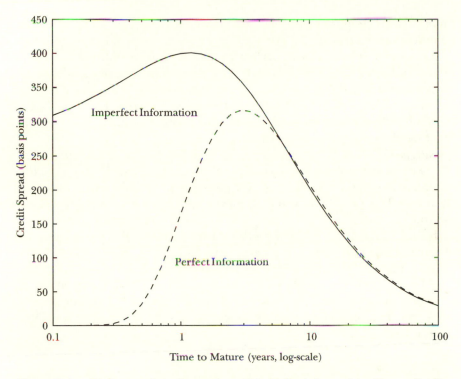

Figure 5.6. *Credit spreads under perfect and imperfect information. (Source: Duffie and Lando, 2001.)*

at short maturities are, as a consequence, like those of a typical reduced-form model.

For instance, suppose, as in Duffie and Lando (2001), that default occurs when assets, modeled as the log-normal process (5.13), hit a default-triggering boundary level D. Suppose, however, that assets are imperfectly observed in the market through an accounting report with a standard deviation of 10% of true assets. Figure 5.6 shows illustrative model-implied spreads under both perfect and imperfect information about firm assets.[7]

---

[7] We assume that the asset value 1 year ago, $A_0 = 88.5$, was observed perfectly and that we have just received a noisy accounting report showing assets at the same level. In computing the conditional distribution of the current value of assets, and from that credit spreads and hazard rates for default, we condition not only on the noisy asset report but also on the fact that the firm has not yet defaulted. The firm defaults when assets reach as low as 80. (This is the optimal default boundary, in the sense of Leland, 1994, as explained in Duffie and Lando, 2001.) Recovery at default is 43.7% of face value. The other key parameters are an asset volatility of $\sigma = 25\%$; a risk-neutral mean growth rate of assets of $m = 1\%$; and a riskless interest rate of $r = 6\%$.

A particularly important aspect of imperfect accounting information is that credit spreads are strictly positive at short maturities, and nontrivially so as compared with the case of perfect accounting information, which would imply (as shown) zero credit spreads at zero maturity. Moreover, with imperfect information, default occurs at some intensity (that is calculated for this example by Duffie and Lando, 2001), so one may view this structural model with imperfect information as formally equivalent to a reduced-form model that has the endogenously determined default intensity associated with first passage.

For the example illustrated in Figure 5.6, the risk-neutral drift m^* of the distance to default is positive, so zero-coupon spreads also go to zero with maturity. This would not be the case if the cash-payout rate were increased so that $m^* < 0$.

Pursuing a reduced-form model does not mean that accounting or balance-sheet information is irrelevant for predicting default. Such information may well have imperfect but substantial predictive power. As we saw in Chapter 3 for the estimation of actual default probabilities, and will see in Chapter 7 when pricing corporate bonds, it can be useful to include observable information about a firm's balance sheet as a determinant of default intensities.

5.6. From Actual to Risk-Neutral Intensities

Though pricing depends on risk-neutral default probabilities, in many circumstances it would be useful to know the mapping between actual and risk-neutral probabilities. For example, risk-neutral probabilities are not easily inferred from market prices when one is pricing a newly issued security. In such circumstances, it may be desirable to use historical information about actual default probabilities for the firm or for comparable issuers to infer information about the risk-neutral probabilities that would be used for pricing the new issue. Conversely, one may wish to use the risk-neutral probabilities implicit in credit spreads as a source of information when estimating actual default probabilities for trading, risk-management, or credit allocation purposes. This section describes some of the mappings used by practitioners that connect actual and risk-neutral probabilities.

5.6.1. Reduced-Form Models

In the context of reduced-form models, actual and risk-neutral default probabilities are determined by the intensity processes λ and λ^*. In general, the dependence of these intensities on both the state and the likelihood of a given path are different under the actual and risk-neutral measures.[8] One could examine the implications of a simple mapping between λ and λ^*, such as $\lambda_t^* = \psi \lambda_t$, for some scalar $\psi \geq 1$. Equipped with data on both actual survival probabilities and spreads on defaultable bonds, we could then treat ψ as an issuer-specific parameter that is chosen to best match the historical data on default probabilities and spreads. Except in the trivial case of deterministic intensities, credit spreads respond nonlinearly to the risk-premium coefficient ψ because of the convex response to λ^* in (5.6) and Jensen's inequality. It remains an empirical issue, yet to be explored, whether simply scaling λ to obtain λ^* is sufficient to match the historical data on both default incidence and yield spreads.

We could paramerterize a much richer but still tractable relationship between λ and λ^* as follows. Suppose that X is an underlying state process, assumed to be affine under both actual and risk-neutral probabilities, although perhaps with different actual than risk-neutral parameters. If, for example, $\lambda_t^* = \psi_0 \lambda_t + \psi_1 \cdot X_t$ or, more generally, if λ and λ^* are affine in X, then

$$\log p(t, T) = \alpha_\lambda(t, T) + \beta_\lambda(t, T) \cdot X(t), \tag{5.24}$$

for coefficients α_λ and β_λ that are known (essentially) in closed form, as explained in Appendix A. A similar linear relationship holds for $\log p^*(t, T)$ and λ_t^*.

One would want time-series data on both credit spreads and default probabilities (say EDFs), as well as any market-observable components of the state vector X, in order to estimate the coefficients ψ_0 and ψ_1.

5.6.2. Structural Models

In order to translate from actual to risk-neutral probabilities for structural models, practitioners have focused on the Black-Scholes-Merton model, in which firms may default only at the maturity date T of a bond. Here, the

---

[8] Jarrow et al. (2000) argue that, under certain diversification conditions, one may find that $\lambda = \lambda^*$. This would not, however, imply that actual and risk-neutral survival probabilities are the same. We have

$$p^*(t, T) = E_t^* \left(e^{-\int_t^T \lambda^*(u)\,du} \right)$$

$$p(t, T) = E_t \left(e^{-\int_t^T \lambda(u)\,du} \right),$$

so, even if $\lambda^* = \lambda$, a difference between $p(t, T)$ and $p^*(t, T)$ can arise from the fact that E_t and E_t^* may assign different likelihoods to the paths of λ. A default-risk premium could in this case be due, for example, to an expected growth rate in future default intensities that is risk-neutrally higher than it is in actuality.

firm's total value is modeled as the log-normal diffusion (3.5), whose risk-neutral form is (5.13), for a constant default-free interest rate r.

As in (3.7), the actual default probability is

$$q(t, T) = P(X_T \leq 0 \mid X_t) = N \left(\frac{X_t + m(T - t)}{\sqrt{T - t}} \right), \qquad (5.25)$$

where X_t is the current distance to default, $N(x)$ is the probability that a standard normal variable is less than x, and $m = (\mu - \gamma - \sigma^2/2)/\sigma$ is the drift of the distance-to-default process X. Likewise, the risk-neutral default probability is

$$q^*(t, T) = P^*(X_T \leq 0 \mid X_t) = N \left(\frac{X_t + m^*(T - t)}{\sqrt{T - t}} \right), \qquad (5.26)$$

where $m^* = (r - \gamma - \sigma^2/2)/\sigma$ is the risk-neutral drift of the distance to default.

In order to calibrate this model to market data for the purposes of their internal risk management and credit-derivative pricing systems, J. P. Morgan focuses on the *Sharpe ratio*

$$\eta = \frac{\mu - r}{\sigma}, \qquad (5.27)$$

a measure of the risk premium associated with uncertainty about the firm's asset growth. A calibration based on the idea of the capital-asset pricing model (CAPM) of Sharpe (1964) sets $\eta = \rho\theta/\sigma$, where ρ is the correlation between the firm's return on assets and the "market" return, and θ is the Sharpe ratio of the CAPM market portfolio (a proxy for which is often taken to be a major stock index; see Demchak, 2000). A similar formulation is applied to the valuation of corporate bonds in Bohn (1999) and related studies by KMV Corporation.

From (5.25) and (5.26), the mapping between risk-neutral and physical default probabilities is then

$$q^*(t, T) = N \left(N^{-1} \left[q(t, T) \right] - \eta\sqrt{T - t} \right), \qquad (5.28)$$

where $N^{-1}(\cdot)$ is inverse of the standard normal cumulative distribution function. So long as $\theta > 0$ (i.e., investors demand a positive return premium for bearing market risk) and $\rho > 0$ (i.e., the underlying firm has a positive CAPM β), we know that $q^*(t, T) > q(t, T)$ or, equivalently, that the risk-neutral default probability is larger than the actual default probability.

At a practical level, a user of this framework has the option of fixing the components of $\eta = \rho\theta/\sigma$ at values computed from historical data or letting either ρ or θ be free parameters. For instance, given historical estimates of $p(t, T)$ and η, the risk-neutral survival probability $p^*(t, T)$ can be estimated directly from (5.28) and then plugged into a present-value model in order to estimate the price of a corporate bond. This approach does not use market bond price information, but rather infers the model-implied price from historical default information. Alternatively, using data on $p(t, T)$ and, say, an estimate of ρ, the parameter θ can be chosen to best match the term structure of corporate bond yields of an issuer. In this manner, one of the parameters is calibrated to the corporate yield curve, which might be useful for valuing firm-related credit derivatives. As part of model validation, after this calibration, one can check whether the market Sharpe ratio implied by the corporate yields and that implied by the model are consistent with what has been observed historically. Using a somewhat different model, Huang and Huang (2000) have shown that there is some degree of inconsistency between the risk premium on corporate debt and that on equity, which might be interpreted as a source of information regarding the liquidity component of spreads on bonds.

The reader should bear in mind that this formulation based on distance to default, though analytically convenient, is formally justified only under the special assumptions of the Black-Scholes-Merton pricing framework. In more general settings, the distributional assumptions underlying the calculation (5.28) might not be consistent with one's model for the random evolution of assets or for the determinants of default. Nevertheless, this approach provides one tractable and economically motivated approximate mapping between actual and risk-neutral survival probabilities.

6

Pricing Corporate and Sovereign Bonds

THIS CHAPTER EXPLORES in more depth the pricing of defaultable bonds. Focusing initially on corporate debt, we begin by extending the basic reduced-form models introduced in Chapter 5 to allow for nonzero recovery and for potentially different liquidities between the corporate and reference bonds over which corporate yields are spread. We then turn to conventional structural models of corporate bond prices. This is followed by a discussion of some extensions of our pricing framework that accommodate ratings-transition risk. Finally, we address several new issues that arise in pricing sovereign debt, including the need to allow for multiple types of credit events.

Chapter 7 provides some of the empirical evidence on the fit of pricing models to U.S. corporate and sovereign data.

6.1. Uncertain Recovery

A variety of recovery assumptions appears in the bond pricing literature, with sometimes material differences in tractability and pricing behavior. Reduced-form models used for term-structure modeling, including credit-derivative pricing among other applications, are distinguished mainly by their treatments of recovery. In their simplest forms, all assume that, conditional on the arrival of default in the next instant, the bond in question has a given expected fractional recovery. But this recovery is a fraction of what? One class of models, introduced by Jarrow and Turnbull (1995), has taken recovery at default to be a given fraction of a default-free but otherwise equivalent bond. Another, owing to Duffie and Singleton (1999), has taken recovery to be a fraction of the market value of the bond just prior to default (or, equivalently, the same fraction of an otherwise equivalent bond that has yet to default). Finally, there is a class of models that takes recovery to be a specified expected fraction of face value, based on a legal interpretation of the prioritization of bankruptcy rights.

Measuring recovery on defaulted debt is difficult. In principle, one would like to discount the eventual actual payouts to bondholders, net of procedural costs, back to the date of default. However, this information is rarely available. Carey (1998) presents recovery results on this basis for private debt. For traded debt, as a proxy for recovery, Moody's uses the trading price of the defaulted debt, expressed as a percentage of par and measured approximately 1 month after default. This proxy is likely to be imperfect, but, as it is based on market prices, it is in principle the value that bondholders would receive by selling their positions following default. Figure 6.1 shows summary statistics from the frequency distributions of recovery, by seniority, as measured by Moody's, for the period 1974–1999. Median recovery rates for bank loans and equipment trusts were higher than those for all rated, publicly issued corporate debt in the United States. Median recovery rates for bonds naturally decline with seniority. For junior subordinated bonds, the median recovery rate was only about 10 cents on the dollar.

The rectangles in Figure 6.1 capture the range between the 25th and

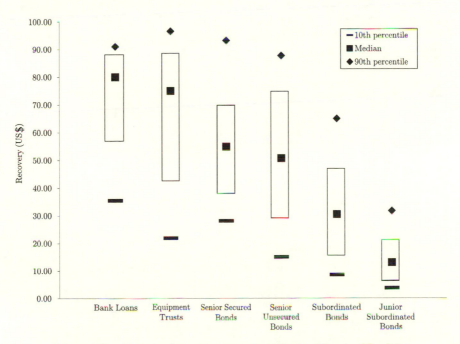

Figure 6.1. *Distributions of recovery by seniority. (Source: Moody's.)*

75th percentiles of the recovery distributions. For each seniority, there was substantial variation in recovery. Senior secured and senior unsecured bonds had similar median recovery rates, but the distribution of recoveries for senior unsecured bonds is more spread out and has a longer lower tail. The 10th percentile of the distribution for unsecured bonds is substantially below that for secured bonds.

Overall, these distributions suggest a significant idiosyncratic component to the recovery experience for bonds with the same seniority. The dispersion within each seniority classification may be due in part to variation in rating among bonds at the time of default or to different recovery patterns for different industrial classifications. There may also be substantial heterogeneity within a seniority category in terms of collateral, the existence of sinking funds, maturity, and so on. For these reasons, simply setting the recovery of a bond of a given seniority to the median value in Figure 6.1 for that seniority is likely to lead to inferior pricing compared to recovery assumptions that condition on the characteristics of a bond, including its rating and industrial classification. One's internal credit analysis may shed some extra light on prospective default recovery. In the end, however, even after conditioning on all public information available prior to default, it is natural to presume uncertainty regarding default recovery.

Figure 6.2 provides a temporal perspective on default recovery rates. For the illustrated sample period, recoveries were lowest, especially for subordinated debt, during 1990–1991, when default rates among speculative-grade bonds were highest (see Figure 3.2). On the other hand, average

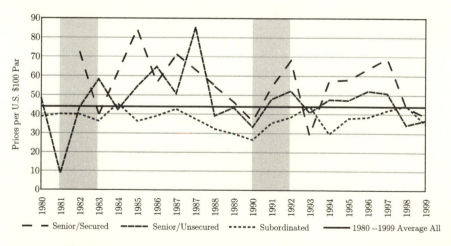

Figure 6.2.   *Bond recovery by seniority and year. (Source: Moody's.)*

recovery rates remained high in 1986 even though this was a period in which default rates increased.

Gupton and Stein (2002) present a statistical model of the distribution of recoveries, controlling for macroeconomic conditions as well as the seniority, rating, and industry of the issuer. The study is based on 1,800 default recovery observations, over 900 firms, for loans, bonds, and preferred stock. The macro factors studied were 1-year median RiskCalc default probabilities, Moody's bankrupt bond index, the trailing 12-month speculative-grade average default rate, and the change in the index of leading economic indicators. Recoveries were measured based on market-quoted bid prices from Goldman Sachs, Citibank, BDS Securities, Loan Pricing Corporation, Merrill Lynch, and Lehman Brothers. Gupton and Stein (2002) found that debt type and seniority accounted for the greatest influence on recoveries, followed in order by macroeconomic environment, industry, and the degree of relative seniority (as opposed to absolute seniority). (For example, the most senior obligation of an issuer might be a subordinated note.) The model was fit based on a beta distribution of recoveries, after controlling for the above covariates.

In testing the ability of their model to forecast recovery rates out of sample, Gupton and Stein (2002) compared the model's mean-squared recovery rate prediction error to that based on traditional historical average default-recovery rates, by seniority type. They found that the mean-squared prediction errors produced by their statistical model were roughly a third less than those of the traditional historical averages.

6.2. Reduced-Form Pricing with Recovery

For our analysis of reduced-form pricing models, we focus on two recovery assumptions: fractional recovery of face value and fractional recovery of market value. We extend the pricing frameworks introduced in Chapter 5 in order to add in the market value of recovery cash flows received at default.

6.2.1. Fractional Recovery of Face Value

The assumption of fractional recovery of face value is based on a legalistic interpretation of bond covenants that would have defaulting firms liquidating their assets and returning to bondholders some fraction of the face values of their bonds according to the priority of their holdings. While this formulation is conceptually straightforward and well motivated, there is in fact substantial evidence that bankruptcy courts, and negotiations outside of courts, do not fully honor priority in setting recoveries. (For example, holders of senior bonds do not always, in practice, take absolute precedence over holders of more junior issues.) For cases in which default occurs through a restructuring that does not lead into bankruptcy, legal priority need not play a direct role in recoveries. For sovereign debt valuation, moreover, legal priority in the event of default is sometimes a secondary consideration, given the ability of the sovereign to influence eventual payments to different classes of debtholders based on many (e.g., macroeconomic and political) considerations. Accordingly, recovery of face value is an approximation and one that we will compare to alternative assumptions.

In order to see the basic idea of valuation with fractional recovery of face value, suppose that recovery payments are made at the time of default and that default occurs only at discrete time intervals of length Δ. For example, with $\Delta = \frac{1}{365}$, recovery is measured as of the end of the day of default. We assume purely for notational simplicity that the number of periods before maturity, $n = (T-t)/\Delta$, is an integer. We let $Z(t, i)$ denote the market value at time t of any default recoveries to be received between times $t + (i-1)\Delta$ and $t+i\Delta$. As usual, we let $d(t, T)$ denote the price at time t of a defaultable zero-coupon bond maturing at time T. We have

$$d(t, T) = d_0(t, T) + \sum_{i=1}^{n} Z(t, i), \tag{6.1}$$

where $d_0(t, T)$ is the market value of the survival-contingent payment at maturity, as calculated in Chapter 5, for example, in (5.6). The second term in (6.1) is the market value at time t of any cash flows received (through default and subsequent recovery) before maturity.

We start by assuming independence (risk-neutrally) between interest rates and default risk, and with a known constant fraction w for the fraction of face value recovered at default. Later, we consider the more complex case of correlation between interest rates and the default time. Because the risk-neutral time t conditional probability of default during any time interval $(u, T]$ is $p^*(t, u) - p^*(t, T)$ (the difference in the survival probabilities to the beginning and end of the period), we have

$$Z(t, i) = \delta(t, t + i\Delta)w \left(p^*[t, t + (i-1)\Delta] - p^*(t, t + i\Delta)\right), \tag{6.2}$$

recalling that $\delta(t, s)$ is the price at time t of a default-free zero-coupon bond maturing at time s.

The case of continuous-time recovery is obtained from (6.1) and (6.2) by letting the length Δ of a recovery period go to zero, leaving[1]

$$d(t, T) = d_0(t, T) + w \int_t^T \delta(t, u)\pi^*(t, u) \, du, \tag{6.3}$$

[1] See Duffie et al. (1996), Duffie (1998b), or Lando (1998) for further discussion and technical regularity conditions under which (6.3) holds.

where, conditioning on information available at time t, $\pi^*(t, \cdot)$ is the risk-neutral density of the default time. That is,

$$\pi^*(t, u) = -\frac{d}{du} p^*(t, u). \tag{6.4}$$

For example, consider the typical reduced-form pricing model for defaultable debt of Chapter 5, based on a risk-neutral doubly stochastic default time with risk-neutral intensity process λ^*. In order to compute $\pi^*(t, u)$ from (6.4), we differentiate $p^*(t, u)$ with respect to u in (5.11), passing the derivative through the expectation (when justified by technical conditions), to obtain

$$\pi^*(t, u) = E_t^* \left[e^{-\int_t^u \lambda^*(s)\,ds} \lambda^*(u) \right]. \tag{6.5}$$

The following intuition may be helpful in unraveling this calculation. For deterministic λ^*, the risk-neutral probability at time t of survival to u is $e^{-\int_t^u \lambda^*(s)\,ds}$, and $\lambda_u^*\,du$ is the probability of default during the "small" time interval $[u, u+du]$, conditional on survival to u. Applying Bayes's rule then gives the risk-neutral default-time density, $e^{-\int_t^u \lambda^*(s)\,ds} \lambda_u^*\,du$. For a random intensity process λ^*, we first condition on the path of λ^*, then make this intuitive calculation based on conditionally deterministic intensity, and, finally, by taking the expectation of the result, we average over possible intensity paths with weights given by their risk-neutral likelihoods, arriving at (6.5).

With an affine intensity model for λ^*, the density $\pi^*(t, u)$ is often available in closed form, as shown in Chapter 3. For example, if $\lambda_t^* = a + b \cdot X_t$ for a (risk-neutrally) affine process X, then $p^*(t, u) = e^{\alpha(t, u) + \beta(t, u) \cdot X(t)}$, for coefficients $\alpha(t, u)$ and $\beta(t, u)$ whose derivatives with respect to u, denoted $\alpha_u(t, u)$ and $\beta_u(t, u)$, are easily calculated. From (6.4), we have

$$\pi^*(t, u) = -e^{\alpha(t, u) + \beta(t, u) \cdot X(t)} [\alpha_u(t, u) + \beta_u(t, u) \cdot X_t]. \tag{6.6}$$

With correlation between the default-free short-rate process r and the default time τ, the natural extension of (6.3) is

$$d(t, T) = d_0(t, T) + \int_t^T k(t, u)\,du, \tag{6.7}$$

where

$$k(t, u) = w E_t^* \left[e^{-\int_t^u [r(s) + \lambda^*(s)]\,ds} \lambda^*(u) \right] \tag{6.8}$$

may be viewed as the market value, calculated as of time t, of a claim to any recovery paid during the "small" time interval $[u, u + du]$. This valuation "density" incorporates the default-free term structure, the likelihood of default, the recovery fraction w, as well as any correlation and volatility effects. For special cases in which r_t and λ_t^* are affine functions of an affine state vector X_t (e.g., a square-root or Gaussian process, under risk-neutral probabilities), one has a closed-form solution for (6.8) of the form

$$k(t, u) = we^{\alpha_d(t,u)+\beta_d(t,u)\cdot X(t)}[\hat{\alpha}_d(t, u) + \hat{\beta}_d(t, u) \cdot X(t)], \qquad (6.9)$$

where $\alpha_d(t, u)$ and $\beta_d(t, u)$ are the same coefficients appearing in the discount formula (5.7) and $\hat{\alpha}_d(t, s)$ and $\hat{\beta}_d(t, s)$ are given by other, also explicit, formulas (see Duffie et al., 2000).

In some models, it has been supposed that the fractional recovery of face value is actually paid at the original maturity date T of the debt and is independent of the default time and interest rates. While this is a strong assumption, its main virtue is its simplicity. Regardless of the default-time model, structural or reduced-form, this recovery-at-maturity assumption implies that at its original maturity date T the bond pays the contingent amount

$$1_{\{\tau>T\}} + \overline{w}1_{\{\tau\leq T\}} = 1_{\{\tau>T\}} + \overline{w}(1 - 1_{\{\tau>T\}})$$

$$= (1 - \overline{w})1_{\{\tau>T\}} + \overline{w}, \qquad (6.10)$$

where $\overline{w}$ is the risk-neutral mean amount recovered, as a fraction of face value, when measured as of maturity date. From (6.10), the price at time t under this recovery assumption, for any model of the default time, is

$$d(t, T) = (1 - \overline{w})d_0(t, T) + \overline{w}\delta(t, T), \qquad (6.11)$$

which is easily computed for most models, whether reduced-form or structural, for we saw in Chapter 5 how to compute the zero-recovery zero-coupon price $d_0(t, T)$ for many different default models.

As for coupon bonds, bankruptcy claims are normally proportional to the face values of bonds held, irrespective of coupon rate, and it is therefore common when using a model based on fractional recovery of face value to assume that coupons have zero recovery. As we have noted, even putting aside the issue of violations of absolute priority in bankruptcy, default need not arise only through legal bankruptcy proceedings, so this zero-recovery assumption for coupons is an approximation of reality. Based on this assumption, however, we can treat each coupon as though it is a zero-coupon bond with zero recovery, in which case the price at time t of a bond promising to pay a coupon of c at each of m payment dates $t(1), t(2), \ldots, t(m)$ is

$$V(t, T) = d(t, T) + c \sum_{j=1}^{m} d_0(t, t(j)), \qquad (6.12)$$

where, as usual, $d(t, T)$ is the market value of the zero-coupon claim to the face value at maturity.

In practice, one typically has as data the prices of coupon bonds and wishes to "calibrate" a risk-neutral intensity process λ^* to the term structure of coupon bond prices or yield spreads. Unfortunately, given only the current term structure of yield spreads, there is relatively little that can be said about the degree of *jumpiness* or volatility of λ^*. For example, a given term structure of credit spreads can often be matched equally well for practical purposes by using a default-intensity process λ^* that is either a CIR diffusion model or a mean-reverting-with-jumps (MRJ) model of the type considered in Chapter 5. This observation is simply a translation into the world of spread curves of the observation made in Chapter 3 that, once the moments of the diffusion and MRJ intensity processes are matched, the implied forward default probabilities are nearly identical (see Figures 3.16 and 3.17). Of course, the diffusion and MRJ models would be distinguished by the time-series behaviors of their implied term structures of credit spreads. In Chapter 7, we turn to the issue of econometric estimation of such models from historical data on spreads for many past dates.

Figure 6.3 shows the impact of increasing the volatility of the intensity process: Higher volatility implies tighter credit spreads.[2] The basic intuition for this comes from the related discussion in Chapter 3 of the effects of volatility on forward default rate curves and the pricing formula for the survival-contingent zero-coupon bond given by (5.6). Increasing the volatility of $r + \lambda^*$ increases zero-coupon bond prices, and the effect is greater at longer maturities, all as a consequence of Jensen's inequality. An analogous narrowing of credit spreads comes from lowering the mean-reversion rate of the (risk-neutral) intensity process, as suggested by the analysis in Chapter 3 of the term structure of forward default rates.

---

[2] The underlying model is a four-factor CIR model, in which the risk-neutral intensity has an initial volatility of 100% and an initial level of 200 basis points, with 25% mean reversion (except for mean-reversion effects caused by correlation with short rates, which are themselves matched to the behavior of U.S. LIBOR swap rates). The model is calibrated to the fit by Duffie and Singleton (1997) of U.S. LIBOR swap data. We present this model in more depth subsequently. Low, medium, and high volatilities are 50, 100, and 200%, respectively.

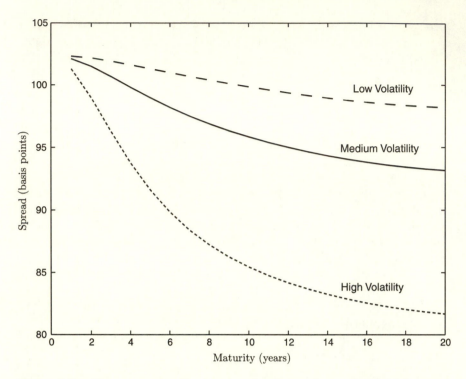

Figure 6.3.   *Term structure of par-coupon bond spreads, varying initial proportional intensity volatility, with 50% fractional recovery of face value at default.*

6.2.2. Conditional Expected Recovery

We now introduce the treatment of uncertainty regarding the fractional recovery rate W. We allow for the possibility that W may be revealed only at the default time τ, for example, through observing the defaulted debt price. For the purpose of pricing bonds prior to default, one can replace W with $E^*(W \mid \mathcal{F}_{\tau-})$, where $\mathcal{F}_{\tau-}$ denotes the information in the market up to, *but not including*, the default time τ. In fact, it can be shown that there is a process, say w, that at any time t, if default has yet to occur, is in effect the conditional risk-neutral expectation of recovery in the event of default at time t, based on information available up to but not including time t. Under technical conditions (Duffie, 1998a; Schönbucher, 1998) it then simplifies the bond pricing calculation to replace W with w_τ. The distinction is that w_τ is known based on information available before τ, whereas W is not.

We can simply replace w with w_u in our previous pricing formulas, leaving

$$d(t, T) = d_0(t, T) + \int_t^T k(t, u)\, du, \tag{6.13}$$

where the recovery valuation density $k(t, u)$ is now given by

$$k(t, u) = E_t^* \left[e^{-\int_t^u [r(s) + \lambda^*(s)]\, ds} \lambda^*(u) w(u) \right]. \tag{6.14}$$

Though seemingly more complicated, $k(t, u)$ can also be computed in closed form for certain affine specifications of the risk-neutral expected recovery rate $w(u)$ as a function of the underlying risk factors.

6.2.3. Fractional Recovery of Market Value

An alternative and more tractable recovery assumption is that, at each time t, conditional on all information available up to but not including time t, a specified risk-neutral mean fraction L_t of market value is lost if default occurs at time t. One can also view the recovery fraction $1 - L_t$ as relative to the market value of another bond, yet to default, that is otherwise of the same quality. Whether or not this recovery assumption leads to reliable pricing of other instruments, such as corporate bonds, is an empirical question that we take up subsequently. Because strict priority is not always observed, specifying recovery assumptions in terms of the fraction of market value lost at default is not obviously less plausible than specifying the expected recovery of face value.

With a risk-neutral default-intensity process λ^*, the risk-neutral conditional expected rate of loss of market value at time t owing to default is $s_t = \lambda_t^* L_t$. It is therefore natural to presume that the associated price of a zero-coupon bond at any time t before default is

$$d(t, T) = E_t^* \left[e^{-\int_t^T [r(u) + s(u)]\, du} \right]. \tag{6.15}$$

This relatively simple pricing result is in fact justified under technical conditions given in Duffie and Singleton (1999). Notably, this formula accounts for nonzero recovery and for correlation between default risk and interest-rate risk, all through a single *default-adjusted* short rate $R = r + \lambda^* L$. As we shall see, additional adjustments to the short rate can be made for illiquidity costs.

An attractive feature of this recovery convention, and the associated pricing relation (6.15), is that one may use a model for the default-adjusted short-rate process $R = r + s$ of a type that admits an explicit discount $d(t, T)$ from (6.15). With this, one can build tractable models for defaultable bond pricing on the same computational platforms used for default-free bond pricing. Indeed, as we illustrate subsequently, many of the same formulations of the default-free short-rate process r can be applied directly (albeit with different parameters) to modeling the components of R, r, and s, or to modeling R directly.

In order to promote intuition for this pricing result, we illustrate with a simple example. We will price a 2-year defaultable zero-coupon bond in a simple event-tree setting, supposing that the default-free annual interest rate r, now and in each state 1 year from now, is as shown in Figure 6.4. Upward and downward changes in r are assumed to have equal risk-neutral probabilities. Moreover, we assume for simplicity that the bond may default in any year with a 6% (risk-neutral) probability, conditional on survival to the beginning of that year. We also assume that the bond loses 60% of its market value if and when it defaults.

If the default-free interest rate moves up to 12%, the value of the bond at year 1, assuming that it has not defaulted, will be the risk-neutral probability of surviving another year without default, multiplied by the payoff given survival, plus the risk-neutral default probability multiplied by the payoff given default. At the 12% node, assuming no default before then, the bond price is therefore

$$0.94 \times \frac{100}{1.12} + 0.06 \times \frac{(1-0.6) \times 100}{1.12} = 83.93 + 2.14 = 86.07.$$

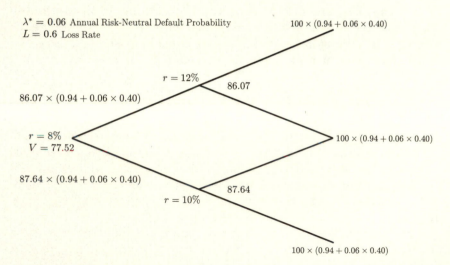

$\lambda^* = 0.06$ Annual Risk-Neutral Default Probability
$L = 0.6$ Loss Rate

$100 \times (0.94 + 0.06 \times 0.40)$

$r = 12\%$

86.07

$86.07 \times (0.94 + 0.06 \times 0.40)$

$r = 8\%$
$V = 77.52$

$100 \times (0.94 + 0.06 \times 0.40)$

$87.64 \times (0.94 + 0.06 \times 0.40)$

87.64

$r = 10\%$

$100 \times (0.94 + 0.06 \times 0.40)$

Figure 6.4. *Valuation of a 2-year zero-coupon bond with default risk.*

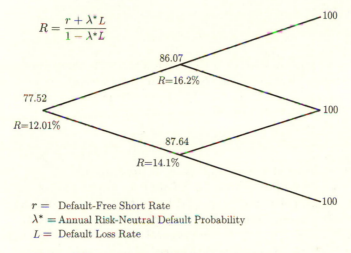

$$R = \frac{r + \lambda^* L}{1 - \lambda^* L}$$

$r =$ Default-Free Short Rate
$\lambda^* =$ Annual Risk-Neutral Default Probability
$L =$ Default Loss Rate

Figure 6.5. *Valuation at default-adjusted short rates.*

This means that the impact of default can be captured by an effective default-adjusted interest rate at that node of the tree of

$$\frac{100.0 - 86.07}{86.07} = 16.2\%.$$

In general, the effective discount rate at any node in the tree is R, where

$$\frac{1}{1 + R} = \frac{1}{1 + r}[\lambda^*(1 - L) + (1 - \lambda^*)], \tag{6.16}$$

with λ^* the risk-neutral probability of default at that node and L the risk-neutral expected loss in market value, as a fraction of the market value at that node, conditional on default in the next period.[3]

When we use (6.16) as a specification for a default-risk-adjusted short-rate process R, there is no loss of generality, when pricing a defaultable claim, in treating the claim as though it is default-free, once the short-term default-free discounting rate r is replaced by the default-adjusted short rate R. In other words, the simplified valuation tree in Figure 6.5 is sufficient for pricing defaultable zero-coupon bonds. We can solve for the default-adjusted short rate R from (6.16):

---

[3] We are abusing notation by writing λ^* for the default probability, using the symbol we usually reserve for an intensity, but we will be taking limits under which the default probability per unit of time converges to λ^* as the time period Δ converges to zero.

$$R = \frac{r + \lambda^* L}{1 - \lambda^* L}. \tag{6.17}$$

This tree-based discrete model is actually simpler in its continuous-time counterpart, at least notationally and intuitively. For time periods of length Δ, we can repeat (6.17), replacing r, R, and λ^* in annualized form, as

$$R\Delta = \frac{r\Delta + L\lambda^*\Delta}{1 - L\lambda^*\Delta}. \tag{6.18}$$

Dividing through by Δ and allowing Δ to converge to zero leaves the continuous-time default-risk-adjusted short-rate process $R = r + s$, where $s = \lambda^* L$ is the risk-neutral expected loss rate. Under technical conditions found in Duffie and Singleton (1999), this leaves the pricing model (6.15).

For example, suppose the risk-neutral default intensity λ^* is constant at 1%, and that the bonds have a risk-neutral expected loss in market value at default of 50%. Then the credit yield spread on any bond issued by that counterparty is 50 basis points, neglecting illiquidity. At a constant risk-neutral mean loss rate $s = \lambda^* L$, the associated credit spread at any maturity is s. In this simple (constant credit risk) setting, a continuously compounding yield spread of s would therefore imply a risk-neutral default intensity of $\lambda^* = s/L$ per year. For example, a spread of 100 basis points would imply a risk-neutral default intensity of 2% per year if one assumes that half of the market value of the issuer's bonds is lost, in risk-neutral expectation, at default. The same spread would imply a risk-neutral default intensity of 4% per year if one assumes a risk-neutral expected fractional loss at default of only 25%.

It follows that (within this pricing framework) knowledge of defaultable bond prices (before default) alone is not sufficient to separately identify λ^* and L. At most, we can extract information about the risk-neutral mean loss rate $\lambda^*_t L_t$. In order to learn more about the default intensities and recovery rates implicit in market prices, it is necessary to examine either: (1) a collection of bonds that share some, but not all, of the same default characteristics, or (2) derivative securities with payoffs that depend in different ways on λ^* and L (see Chapter 9).

As an illustration of the former strategy, suppose that one has the prices V_t^J of junior debt and V_t^S of senior debt of the same issuer, along with the prices of one or more default-free bonds. In this case, it seems reasonable to assume that junior and senior debt share the same risk-neutral default intensity λ^* but have different conditional expected fractional losses at default, say L_t^J and L_t^S, respectively, consistent with the evidence in Figure 6.1. Using the econometric approaches discussed later may make it possible (for given parameters determining the dynamics of r and $\lambda^* L$) to extract observations of $\lambda_t^* L_t^J$ and $\lambda_t^* L_t^S$ from junior and senior bond prices as well as default-free bond prices. Then, although the junior and senior bond spreads are determined by "two equations and three unknowns" (λ_t^*, L_t^J, and L_t^S), we can infer the relative expected recovery rate, L_t^J/L_t^S. However, it is still not possible to extract the risk-neutral intensity λ_t^* or the individual expected recovery rates.[4] Of course, if the risk-neutral default intensity and either of the recovery rates were observable, as known functions of observable variables, then the identification problem would be solved. The prices of both junior and senior debt would in this case provide enough market information for the estimation of λ^*.

With a valuation model based on assumed fractional recovery of face value, it is seen from (6.8) that the default intensity λ^* and fractional recovery w enter the basic pricing relation asymmetrically and thus can, in principle, be separately identified from two different bond yields of the same priority. As we shall see, however, for practical purposes the degree of identification in this sense is weak. For example, the impact on bond prices of halving the assumed risk-neutral default intensities is nearly the same as that of halving the assumed fractional loss $1 - w$ of face value, at reasonable parameters.

The framework based on recovery of market value is easily modified to account for different degrees of liquidity. For example, suppose that there is a risk-neutral expected fractional loss ℓ_t in market value associated with frictional trading costs, along the lines of Amihud and Mendelson (1991). One can view ℓ_t as the risk-neutral intensity of the arrival of a trade multiplied by the risk-neutral expected rate of frictional cost associated with trade as a fraction of market value. One must take care, as emphasized by Gârleanu and Pedersen (2001), to exclude the portion of bid-ask spreads associated with adverse selection that do not affect the present value of trading costs. The resulting short discount rate, adjusted for both default risk and liquidity costs, is $R_t = r_t + \lambda_t^* L_t + \ell_t$. This clearly complicates the task of backing out information about the market's assessment of the issuer's credit risk, at least in the absence of an observable measure of ℓ_t.

6.2.4. Comparing Recovery Assumptions

One may well be concerned about the implications of choosing one recovery formulation over another. A legalistic interpretation of recovery at default, assuming liquidation and absolute priority, would impose equal

---

[4] Using an approach that has elements of both reduced-form and structural models, Madan and Unal (1998) used data on junior and senior certificates of deposit of thrift institutions to estimate default intensities, assuming strict priority and recovery by both junior and senior debt from a given pool of assets.

recovery for bonds of equal seniority of the same issuer, favoring the recovery-of-face-value (RFV) formulation. On the other hand, the recovery-of-market-value (RMV) parameterization offers additional tractability. The fact that discounts, including the effects of recovery, can be computed in an RMV model by the same formulas used for default-free bonds, with new default-adjusted parameters, is attractive when one is calibrating or estimating a model or conducting a sensitivity analysis of parameters.

In the end, is there a significant difference between the pricing implications of the two models? In order to gain insight on this issue, we consider a simple, noncallable defaultable coupon bond (a corporate or sovereign straight bond) with semiannual coupon payments of c, face value 1, and a market price of

$$c \sum_{j=1}^{2T} d_C(t, t + 0.5j) + d_P(t, T), \qquad (6.19)$$

where $d_C(t, s)$ is the defaultable discount applied to coupons, and $d_P(t, s)$ is the defaultable discount applied to principal. For a reduced-form RMV model, we illustrate with an example in which $d_C(t, s)$ and $d_P(t, s)$ are computed with the same risk-neutral mean loss rate $\lambda_t^* L_t$. For the RFV reduced-form model, we assume zero recovery for coupons. Our example is based on a multifactor CIR model of risk-neutral intensity and short rate, with 25% mean reversion in intensity and an initial proportional intensity volatility of 100%.

For the estimation of par-bond spreads or risk-neutral default intensities implied by par spreads, we find rather little difference between the RFV and RMV formulations, even with identical default-intensity processes and the same parameter for the fractional recovery of par as for fractional recovery of market value. For example, Figure 6.6 shows the initial (set equal to long-run mean) risk-neutral intensity $\bar{\lambda}^*$ implied by the fractional recovery of market and face value models at various levels of 10-year par-coupon credit spreads. That is, given the 10-year par-coupon spread and a fractional recovery w of face value and the same fraction $1 - L = w$ recovery of market value, we infer the model-implied intensity $\bar{\lambda}^*$ consistent with each given spread. For a wide range of recovery rates and levels of par spreads, the model-implied default intensities are rather close.

The assumption that initial and long-run mean intensities are equal makes for a rather gentle test of the distinction between the RMV and RFV formulations, as it implies that the term structure of risk-neutral default rates is rather flat and therefore that the risk-neutral expected market value, given survival to a given time, is close to face value. The present value of recoveries for the RMV and RFV models would therefore be rather similar. In order to show the impact of upward- or downward-sloping term structures

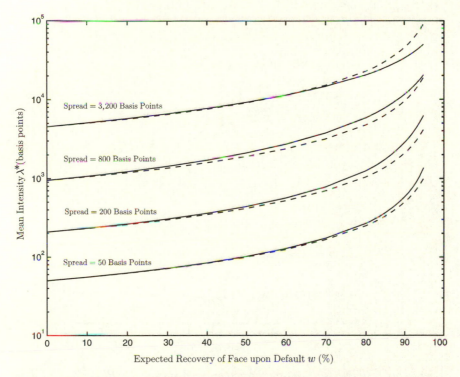

Figure 6.6. *For fixed 10-year par-coupon spreads, the dependence of mean risk-neutral default intensity $\overline{\lambda}^*$ implied by assumed expected fractional default recovery w. The solid lines correspond to the model with fractional recovery of face value, while the dashed lines are for the model with fractional recovery of market value. (Source: Duffie and Singleton, 1999.)*

of forward default rates, we provide in Figure 6.7 the term structures of par-coupon yield spreads (semiannual, bond equivalent) for cases in which the initial risk-neutral default intensity $\lambda^*(0)$ is much higher or lower than its long-run mean, $\theta = 200$ basis points. (The model is otherwise identical to that used for Figure 6.6.) The assumed recovery fractions are 50% for both the RMV and RFV formulations. We now see larger differences between the pricing models, particularly for low-quality firms—those with an initial risk-neutral default intensity that is well above its long-run mean. Even larger differences are possible, of course, for bonds trading at a discount or premium to par.

6.3. Ratings-Based Models of Credit Spreads

This section presents several econometrically tractable, reduced-form models of term structures of credit spreads that are based on using the issuer's

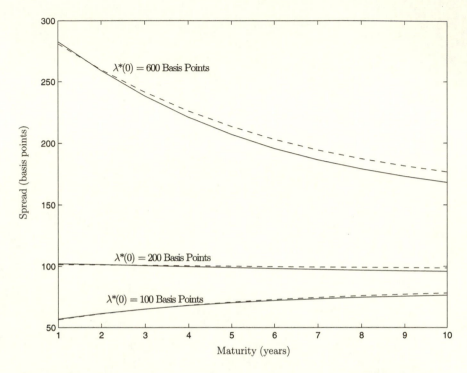

Figure 6.7. *Term structures of par-coupon yield spreads for RMV (dashed lines) and RFV (solid lines), with 50% recovery upon default, a long-run mean intensity $\theta_\lambda^* = 200$ basis points, a mean reversion rate of $\kappa = 0.25$, and an initial intensity volatility of 100%. (Source: Duffie and Singleton, 1999.)*

credit rating as a key state variable determining the risk-neutral default intensity. Some of these models allow for stochastic variation of credit quality within each rating class as well as random transitions in rating, as modeled in Section 4.5. Associated with each rating is a risk-neutral default intensity. One's goal, as usual, is a pricing model that is sufficiently computationally tractable to make empirical estimation feasible, yet sufficiently rich to capture important features of historical fluctuations in yield spreads.

The defaultable bond pricing models discussed up to this point are normally estimated issuer by issuer, using issuer-specific data. A ratings-based model, however, is typically applied to generic issuers, rating by rating, although one could estimate different ratings-based models by country or industry classification.

One of the advantages of a ratings-based term-structure model, in addition to the opportunity to apply it generically to all rated issuers, is the fact that it captures the *gapping* risk that can be associated with a downgrade or upgrade. While, in principle, gap risk can be captured in issuer-specific models by allowing jumps in risk-neutral default intensities, some institutional sources of shocks to supply or demand are linked directly to credit rating. For example, internal risk-management systems are often linked to the rating of the issuer, and certain institutional investors are precluded by charter or by regulation from investing in speculatively rated debt. Moreover, the likely implementation of ratings-based capital requirements under the proposed interim BIS accord explained in Chapter 2 implies an effective cost to regulated banks of holding investments in debt instruments that are based on the credit rating of the instrument. These new capital regulations will further influence the dependence of yield spreads on rating.

Allowing for ratings-transition risk is also motivated by such applications as:

- Valuing securities with credit triggers tied explicitly to ratings, such as downgrade protection in swap contracts and step-up bonds whose coupon rates depend contractually on the issuer's rating.
- Exploiting ratings as a factor structure for pooling sparse and noisy yield data at the corporate or sovereign issuer level, both for valuation and risk analysis of multicredit portfolios.
- The use of an estimated ratings-based term-structure model to estimate option-adjusted yields at the issuer level for cases in which valuation of the call feature commonly bundled with corporate bonds would otherwise be difficult.
- Parsimonious analysis of the empirical relationship between credit spreads and selected business cycle variables and default-free yields, issues addressed in previous work by Stock and Watson (1989), Bernanke (1990), Friedman and Kuttner (1993), Duffee (1998), and Collin-Dufresne et al. (2001), among others.

6.3.1. General Pricing Framework

We describe a ratings-based defaultable bond pricing model that is structured along the lines of the model of stochastic ratings-transition intensities of Section 4.5.2, reinterpreted as a risk-neutral ratings-transition model. This framework for pricing is due to Lando (1998).

Suppose that, risk-neutrally, an issuer's credit rating, $C(t)$ at time t, makes transitions among K nondefault ratings, as well the default rating, labeled $K + 1$, according to risk-neutral stochastic transition intensities $\{\Lambda^*_{ij}(t)\}$. As usual, we assume no transition out of default, in that $\Lambda^*_{K+1,j} = 0$ for all j. The issuer's risk-neutral default intensity at time t is $\lambda^*_t = \Lambda^*_{C(t),K+1}(t)$. The risk-neutral conditional probability at time t of survival (no default) to time T is

$$p^*(t, T) = E_t^* \left(e^{-\int_t^T \lambda^*(u)\, du} \right). \tag{6.20}$$

If we were to make the same assumptions on the structure of risk-neutral ratings-transition intensities that were made (for actual transitions intensities) in Section 4.5.2, we would immediately obtain a model for risk-neutral default and ratings-transition probabilities. By a slight extension, we would get zero-coupon defaultable bond prices under zero recovery. In order to allow for nonzero recovery, however, we proceed as follows.

We suppose for simplicity that, for a bond currently rated i, the event of immediate default carries a risk-neutral expected fractional loss of market value of $L_i(t)$. The default-free short-rate process r is given.

As with any model based on recovery of market value, we have, from (6.15), the defaultable bond price

$$d(t, T) = E_t^* \left(e^{-\int_t^T R(u)\, du} \right), \tag{6.21}$$

where $R(t) = r(t) + L_{C(t)}(t)\Lambda^*_{C(t), K+1}$ is the default-adjusted short rate.

In order to reduce the calculation of $d(t, T)$ to that of a survival probability in the setting of ratings transitions of Section 4.5.2, we introduce, purely as a helpful computational device, a fictitious ratings-transition model with risk-neutral transition intensity from any rating i to any non-default rating j of $H_{ij}(t) = \Lambda^*_{ij}(t)$, identical to that of our actual model but with the special substitution

$$H_{i, K+1}(t) = r(t) + \Lambda^*_{i, K+1}(t) L_i(t) \tag{6.22}$$

for the risk-neutral intensity of transition from rating i into default. Now, under our usual doubly stochastic assumption, the probability of survival (no transition into default for this model) for this fictitious transition model is equivalent to the bond price (6.21). The result is intuitive and can be confirmed by comparing it with equation (8) of Huge and Lando (1999).[5]

The natural next step is to suppose that the generator matrix $H(t)$ for this fictitious ratings-transition model is diagonalizable, following (4.10) as a guide, in that

$$H(t) = b\mu^*(t) b^{-1}, \tag{6.23}$$

where b is a constant matrix whose columns are the eigenvectors of $H(t)$,

---

[5] Another derivation is obtained by comparing equation (10) of Li (2000) with the corresponding equation for survival probability with the fictitious default intensities indicated.

and $\mu^*(t)$ is the diagonal matrix whose ith diagonal element is the eigenvalue of $H(t)$ associated with the ith eigenvector. By assuming that b does not depend on t, while $\mu^*(t)$ may, we have the same commutativity property exploited in Section 4.5.2.[6] From this, following (4.14) by analogy, we have

$$d(t, T) = \sum_{j=1}^{K+1} \beta^*_{C(t),j} E^*_t \left[\exp \left(\int_t^T \mu_j^*(u) \, du \right) \right], \qquad (6.24)$$

where $\beta^*_{ij} = b_{ij} b^{-1}_{j,K+1}$.

Finally, following the approach of Lando (1998), we suppose that there is a risk-neutrally affine state vector process X with the property that the eigenvalues of $H(t)$ have affine dependence on $X(t)$, in that

$$\mu_j^*(t) = \theta_{j0} + \theta_{j1} \cdot X(t), \qquad (6.25)$$

for constant coefficients $\{\theta_{jk}\}$. With this assumption, (6.24) and the affine property of the state process X imply that

$$d(t, T) = \sum_{j=1}^{K+1} \beta^*_{C(t),j} \, e^{a_j^*(t,s) + b_j^*(t,s) \cdot X(t)}, \qquad (6.26)$$

for coefficients $a_j^*(t, s)$ and $b_j^*(t, s)$, which can be easily calculated, as in any affine setting. For example, if the coordinates of X are CIR (square-root) diffusions, or affine jump diffusions, or multivariate variants discussed in Appendix A, then we can use the explicit formulas for $a_j^*(t, s)$ and $b_j^*(t, s)$ that were used to calculate default probabilities in Chapter 3. A straightforward extension of these affine calculations, as explained in Appendix A, allows time dependency in the coefficients, for example, in order to calibrate yield spreads and their volatilities and correlations, across issues and maturities, to current market or time-series data. It will be noted that the short rate r_t plays a trivial role in the diagonalization of $H(t)$, for the ith eigenvalue of $H(t) - r(t)I$ is $\mu_i^*(t) - r(t)$. Thus, an affine short-rate model estimated for other purposes can be easily adapted for this application.[7]

Changing the assumed fractional-recovery coefficients $L_i(t)$ has potentially complicated effects on bond prices because this typically influences the eigenvectors and eigenvalues of $H(t)$. The eigenvectors may become

---

[6] We have no reason to suspect that diagonalizability of H follows from diagonalizability of Λ^*.

[7] A more complicated pricing model based on a given fractional recovery of face value can be derived by combining the results in Chapter 5 with the preceding discussion.

time varying, thereby ruling out this simple approach, or such eigenvectors may even no longer exist.

Jarrow et al. (1997) assume both zero recovery and that the risk-neutral transition intensities $\{\Lambda_{ij}^*(t)\}$ are constants. It then follows that credit spreads on zero-coupon bonds of a given rating are constant over time. Though tractable, this formulation is clearly counterfactual. Some state dependence in recovery, as in the ratings-based model of Das and Tufano (1996), or in the risk-neutral ratings-transition and default intensities, would be necessary to explain historical fluctuation in credit spreads.

As a special example of his general results, Li (2000) assumes that ratings-transition intensities among nondefault ratings are constants and that risk-neutral default intensities as well as the default-free short-rate process are affine with respect to a risk-neutrally affine state vector process X.

The ratings-based pricing model of Arvanitis et al. (1999), which assumes zero default recovery, can be viewed as a special case of this model. In their basic formulation, these authors assume that the state process X is, risk-neutrally, a one-dimensional affine process and that the eigenvalues of the risk-neutral transition generator matrix $\Lambda^*(t)$ are linear in $X(t)$. These assumptions imply that all pairs of risk-neutral ratings-transition intensities, as well as zero-coupon spreads, are perfectly correlated across different credit ratings. This extreme correlation assumption can be relaxed by assuming instead that the eigenvalues are affine with respect to a multivariate affine process. Arvanitis et al. (1999) also assumed for simplicity that X is a Gaussian process, which is not strictly consistent with the requirement of nonnegative default intensities, default probabilities, and spreads. Nakazato (1997) also adopts a Gaussian ratings-based model of spreads.

Bielecki and Rutkowski (2000b) take the HJM approach to modeling spreads by rating, extending the HJM model of spreads in Appendix C.

6.3.2. Calibrating a Model to Historical Data

In order to examine the sensitivity of ratings-based term-structure models to alternative dynamic specifications of the intensities, we calibrate a simple version of Lando's model to the term structures of credit spreads on September 14, 1998, reported by CreditMetrics for generic new issues rated AAA, AA, A, BBB, BB, and B-CCC. (We combined the ratings B and CCC and averaged the yield spreads for these two ratings because of the small number of CCC-rated firms.) Our goal is not a formal estimate of a ratings-based model, but rather an examination of the properties of a model with benchmark parameter values chosen to approximately match market spreads.

For the purposes of this exercise, we assume zero recovery, so that the eigenvectors of $\Lambda^*(t)$ and $H(t)$ (assuming they exist) are the same. We fit a matrix b of eigenvectors as follows. Matrices of 1-year ratings-transition frequencies were computed from Moody's historical 1-year ratings-transition data over the period 1983–1997. These 1-year frequency matrices were approximated, by least-squares fit, to eigenvector-eigenvalue decompositions with the same constant eigenvector matrix b for all years, allowing year-dependent eigenvalues. Only the fitted eigenvector matrix b was kept for the purpose of our illustration. This rough fitting exercise, designed only for the purposes of this illustrative example, has several shortcomings, including the fact that actual transition frequencies are used as the basis to fit the risk-neutral ratings-transition intensities, which implicitly assumes that default-timing risk premia are captured by adjustments to the eigenvalues of the transition generator.

As a model of the riskless term structure, we adopt the two-factor affine square-root (CIR) model estimated by Duffie and Singleton (1997). Using these estimated parameter values, we chose the values of the two term-structure state variables to minimize the squared deviations between the model-implied and the actual 1-, 2-, 3-, 5-, 7-, and 10-year risk-free, par-coupon yields obtained from CreditMetrics on September 14, 1998.

In order to introduce state-dependent risk-neutral ratings-transition intensities, the eigenvalues μ_{it}^* of the risk-neutral generator $\Lambda^*(t)$ were assumed to be of the form $\mu_i^*(t) = -X_{it}$, where the

$$dX_{it} = \kappa(\theta\gamma_i - X_t^i)\,dt + \sigma\sqrt{X_t^i}\,dB_{it}^* \tag{6.27}$$

are independent risk-neutral CIR processes with common mean-reversion κ and volatility σ parameters. The risk-neutral transition and default intensities are therefore linear combinations of these (X_{it}) state variables.[8]

The actual and fitted term structures of par-coupon spreads are shown in Figure 6.8 for the speculative-grade issues. The fit is uniformly good for short and intermediate maturity bonds of all ratings. For 10-year bonds, there is a tendency for this model to overstate the quality (understate spreads) on BB-rated bonds. (This model also understates the credit quality

---

[8] As a benchmark, we choose the free parameters and the initial value $X(0)$ as follows. Letting Θ be the set of free model parameters [including $X(0)$], we calibrated the model by minimizing

$$\Delta(\beta) = \sum_{i,j}\left(1 - \frac{\hat{S}_{i,j}}{S_{i,j}(\beta)}\right)^2,$$

over $\beta \in \Theta$, where $\hat{S}_{i,j}$ is the market observed T_i-year par-coupon spread for rating α_j, where $T_i = 1, 2, 3, 5, 7, 10$ and $\alpha_i =$ AAA, AA, A, BBB, BB, and B-CCC, with $i = 1, \ldots, 6$, and $S_{i,j}(\beta)$ is the model-implied T_i-year par-coupon spread for rating α_j with model parameters fixed at value β. The estimates are: $\gamma_2 = 4.00$, $\gamma_3 = 4.85$, $\gamma_4 = 2.41$, $\gamma_5 = 2.67$, $\gamma_6 = 5.47$, $\kappa = 0.0265$, $\theta = 0.1212$, $\sigma = 0.0231$, and $X(0) = 0.0135$. The initial values of the state variables are taken to be $\gamma_i X(0)$, while γ_1 is normalized to unity.

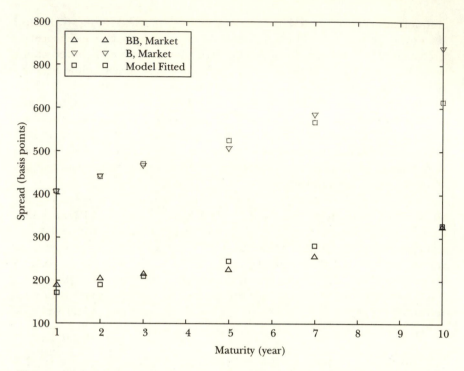

Figure 6.8. *Market-observed and model-fitted (squares) term structures of par-coupon bond spreads for speculative grades; $n = 1$ and $L = 1$.*

[overstates spreads] on BBB-rated bonds.) The zero-recovery assumption, taken for illustration of the technique, could be at fault.

Next, we examine the relative contributions of ratings-transition risk and default risk to the spread curves computed for the benchmark model. This is accomplished by computing spreads using the corporate bond pricing model of Duffie and Singleton (1999), with a risk-neutral default intensity equal to that calibrated to the ratings-based model for a fixed rating. More precisely, for rating i, the risk-neutral default intensity in the benchmark model is

$$\Lambda_{i,K+1}^{*}(t) = \sum_{j=1}^{K} -b_{ij} b_{j,K+1}^{-1} X_j(t). \tag{6.28}$$

Assuming a fractional loss of market value upon default of 100% ($L = 1$), we valued par-coupon corporate bonds that are assumed to have the risk-neutral default-intensity process $\{\Lambda_{i,K+1}^{*}(t) : t \geq 0\}$, that is, with no transition from rating i prior to default. The resulting spread curves for these refreshed BBB and B-CCC qualities are shown in Figures 6.9 and 6.10, respectively. These figures show that, within this model, most of the credit spread for any given bond is induced by the risk-neutral probability of default directly from the fixed rating, and not indirectly through predefault ratings transitions. In the case of BBB-rated bonds, however, as well as bonds of higher credit ratings (not shown), this artificial pricing model based on assuming refreshed BBB credit quality by remaining in this rating understates the credit spreads for the respective ratings. Evidently, the potential for a ratings downgrade to noninvestment grade has a significant effect on the term structure of credit spreads for this rating, and this effect is increasing in maturity.

In the case of debt rated B and below, ignoring transition risk leads to an overstatement of credit spreads. The latter may be interpreted as a statement that there is a high risk-neutral default probability for bonds rated

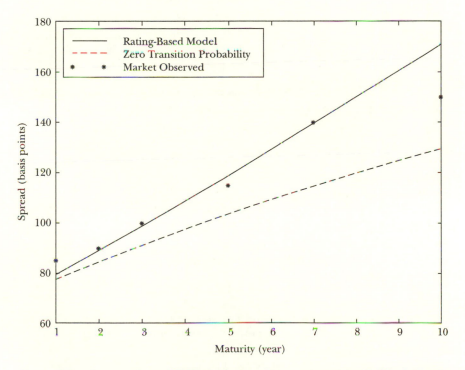

Figure 6.9. *A comparison of BBB-grade spread term structure implied by the benchmark Markov-chain model with ratings transitions and the model assuming zero probabilities of ratings transitions. Zero fractional recovery is assumed.*

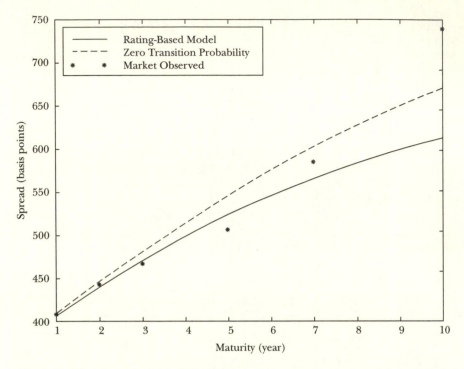

Figure 6.10. *A comparison of B-and-below-grade spread term structure implied by the benchmark Markov-chain model with ratings transitions and the model assuming zero probabilities of ratings transitions. Zero fractional recovery is assumed.*

B and below, but that the prospect of upgrades has a significant impact on spreads. This "upside" potential implies that the ratings-based spread curve lies below the spread curve implied by the model with zero transition probabilities. Again, the effect is increasing in maturity.

6.4. Pricing Sovereign Bonds

The determinants of default for a sovereign are typically quite different from those of a corporation. A sovereign default is largely a political decision, influenced by such macroeconomic factors as the balance of payments, central bank reserves, and so on. Governments trade off the cost of making debt payments against reputation costs (Eaton and Gersovitz, 1981), the costs of having assets abroad seized, and the costs of having international trade impeded (Bulow and Rogoff, 1989b; Gibson and Sundaresan, 1999). A sovereign rarely makes an outright default. Rather, it may force a restructuring or renegotiation of its debt. Indeed, the same bond may be repeatedly renegotiated (Bulow and Rogoff, 1989a). A holder of sovereign debt, moreover, may not have recourse to a bankruptcy code. A sovereign also trades off the costs of default (or forced restructuring) of internal versus external debt. As we shall see, this trade-off can have interesting implications for the pricing of different classes of sovereign debt.

In this section, we take up these new issues, which arise when analyzing the credit risks of sovereign bonds. We begin by reviewing the nature of sovereign credit risk (ratings and recovery). Then we extend our basic pricing models for corporate bonds to accommodate the new types of credit events that may be prominent in the case of sovereign debt. Recent empirical work on the pricing of sovereign bonds is reviewed in Chapter 7.

6.4.1. Credit Risk in Sovereign Bonds

Credit risk is rarely one-dimensional, and this is particularly true of sovereign risk. Among the types of credit events that holders of sovereign debt might experience are:

- *Default or repudiation:* The sovereign announces that it will stop making payments on its debt.
- *Restructuring or renegotiation:* The sovereign and the lenders "agree" to reduce (or postpone) the remaining payments.
- *A regime switch,* such as a change of government or the default of another sovereign bond that changes the perceived risk of future defaults.

Depending on the type of credit event, the recoveries of bondholders may also differ. Before discussing pricing models that can potentially accommodate these considerations, we briefly review the nature of the credit risks of sovereign bonds.

The incidence of default on publicly traded, foreign-currency-denominated sovereign bonds has been low over the past two decades. There were six defaults by South and Central American issuers in the 1980s and early 1990s, and a default by Russia in 1999. All of these defaults were on bonds issued *outside* of the Eurocurrency markets. Indeed, until the late 1990s, there had never been a restructuring or default on a sovereign Eurocurrency bond. A watershed event occurred in November 1999, when Pakistan launched an offer to exchange or restructure some its Eurobonds. Aside from some piecemeal restructurings and exchanges by Ukraine during 1998, at the maturity of some Eurobonds, this was the first time that private investors faced a loss on Eurobonds. Equally important, the widely held view that private investors faced an implicit guarantee from the International Monetary Fund (IMF) was undermined by these experiences, as private investors were "bailed in," to share in the losses (see, e.g., McBrady and

Seasholes, 2000, and Roubini, 2000). In both cases, Pakistan and Ukraine, the Eurobonds in question were restructured prior to an actual default event, given that investors viewed the threat of default as credible in the absence of a restructuring (International Monetary Fund, 2001). Subsequently, Ecuador defaulted on some of its Eurocurrency bonds, and these bonds were in default for about a year. This was the first default on bonds that were, at the time, widely traded on secondary markets and included in J. P. Morgan's Emerging Market Bond Index.

In order to put these developments into perspective, we note that there are many types of foreign-currency-denominated sovereign debts, three of which are: (1) debts governed by the domestic law of the issuer (e.g., Russian Ministry of Finance bonds denominated in U.S. dollars), (2) Eurocurrency bonds, and (3) debt, such as Brady bonds, that arise from prior restructurings of bank loans or bonds. The available avenues of response by debtholders to a default or proposed restructuring may be very different in each of these cases. For instance, domestic law may not include cross-default clauses that would force, upon the default of one bond, the simultaneous default of other bonds of the same type but of a different maturity. For various strategic reasons related to internal or external political or economic considerations, sovereign issuers may choose to default on, or to renegotiate, the terms of one bond (or one set of bonds), but not on others. Further, as in the Russian case, which we discuss in more detail shortly, portions of the outstanding debt may have been issued under different political regimes. In this situation, the current regime may feel, or be perceived to feel, a stronger obligation to make contractual payments on the debt issued during its own regime.

Most Eurocurrency bonds are governed by the laws of either the United Kingdom (approximately 25% of issues) or the United States (approximately 75% of issues). The differences between these systems can be crucial for the experiences of debtholders in a credit event. Specifically, under U.K. law, in order to modify the payment terms of a bond, consent by a quorum of 75% of bond investors is needed, with a reduction to 25% in the event that a quorum of 75% cannot be reached. In contrast, under U.S. law, a quorum of 100% is needed to initiate a restructuring of bond issues in a credit event. Thus, U.K. law is more likely to encourage collective action on the part of bondholders and perhaps lead to less time between a credit event and the consumation of a restructuring. The restructured Pakistani bonds were governed by U.K. law, as are the restructured Russian Eurodollar bonds. On the other hand, the restructured bonds from Ukraine were governed by Luxumberg law (which included a collective-action clause) and German law (which did not include a collective-action clause). Finally, the Eurobonds on which Ecuador defaulted did not have a collective-action clause.

On the creditor side, there are (at least) three key players: (1) the London Club, representing more than 600 Western commercial lenders that own debts that have been restructured by sovereign issuers; (2) the Paris Club, consisting of Western governments that have lent money to developing nations and have agreed not to accept restructuring terms less favorable than those offered to the London Club; and (3) private lenders, which may form a relatively heterogeneous group. The actions of these players can have a significant effect on whether and how sovereign bonds are restructured. In particular, it was the insistence of the Paris Club that other bondholders receive comparable treatment of their claims that precipitated the restructuring of Pakistan's Eurobonds. Moreover, though collective-action clauses were in place under U.K. law, they were not exercised for strategic reasons by those creditors seeking a restructuring.

Although defaults and restructurings on Eurobonds are relatively recent phenomena, restructurings have been common on other foreign-currency-denominated debts. For instance, the Paris Club restructured its Soviet-era debts with Russia five times between April 1993 and August 1999. Moreover, restructurings can involve changes in not only the face values, coupons, or maturities of bonds, but also in their legal structure. In particular, a change in obligor status is possible.

Information about the credit qualities of sovereign issuers is provided by various agencies. Moody's and Standard & Poor's rate sovereign Eurobond and other issues based on their respective published criteria. Institutional Investor reports ratings, between 0 and 100, based on evaluations from the staffs of the largest 100 or so international banks. Similarly, Euromoney uses a panel of experts to rate sovereign issuers. The Lehman Brothers Eurasia Group Stability Index (LEGSI) publishes monthly a composite index based on twenty indicators of a country's capacity to withstand crises. These experts consider political, economic, and market indicators. Finally, the Economist Intelligence Unit rates sovereigns based on medium-term lending risk, political and economic policy risk, and balance-of-payments variables.

In assessing the creditworthiness of a sovereign, some have focused on its debt-service capacity. That is, the probability of default is linked to the sustainability of external debt and to problems associated with short-term illiquidity or long-run solvency. Among the macroeconomic variables that are likely to affect a sovereign's ability to service its debt (and the expected direction of the effect) are: current account to GDP (+), terms of trade (+), reserves to imports (+), external debt (−), income variability (−), export variability (−), and inflation (−).

Others have been concerned with possible debtor repudiations and have therefore focused on economic motives for issuing external debt (consumption smoothing, import demand, and disciplining of investment activities) as well as the consequent costs of repudiating debt. This focus leads to consideration of such variables as external debt $(-)$, income variability $(+)$, and imports/GNP $(+)$. In order to assess the importance of various types of information on actual sovereign ratings, Cantor and Packer (1996) estimate predictive regressions of Moody's and Standard & Poor's ratings of sovereign issues in the Eurobond markets. For a single cross section in 1995, over 90% of the variation in ratings is explained by their regressors. They found that ratings-change announcements lead to large changes in sovereign yield spreads. For example, in the case of Turkey, a downgrade from BBB to BB was associated with an increase in the spread from 371 basis points to 408 basis points. For Venezuela, a rating upgrade, from Ba3 to Ba1, was associated with a tightening of spreads from 274 to 237 basis points.

More recently, Reisen and Maltzan (1999), working with an extended sample covering the Mexican-peso and Asian-financial crises, found a much weaker relationship between ratings changes and sovereign bond yield spreads than was found by Cantor and Packer. They did find, however, a stronger effect for emerging-market bonds than for the sovereign issues of more "developed" economies. In other words, although yield spreads were found to move in anticipation of both upgrades and downgrades, there was nevertheless a mild market reaction for emerging-market bonds on the implementation date of a ratings change.

Measurement of recovery is particularly challenging for sovereign bonds because so many of the bonds are restructured, often many times, and even in the absence of a formal declaration of default. For the Latin American defaults during the 1980s, the losses at default range from 10 to 50%, with an average of approximately 25% (Deutsche Bank Research, 1999), implying relatively high recovery rates.

A different source of recovery information is the performance of commercial and industrial (C&I) loans by banks in Latin America. Citibank tabulated their average experience over a 27-year period (see Hurt and Felsovalyi, 1998) and found that recovery was larger on very small loans (26.1% loss on loans of less than $0.25 million) than on very large loans (38.0% loss on loans of more than $10 million). The reason appears to be that large loans were made to "economic groups" with relatively loose managerial structures and many banking relationships. Additionally, lenders had more leverage over small borrowers. The standard deviation of the loss rate was 21.8%.

This study also distinguished between "sovereign" and "nonsovereign" events, where the former were associated with changes in convertibility, strong devaluation, failure to make payments on external debt, and so on. The mean loss rates in the cases of sovereign and nonsovereign events were roughly the same, 30.9 and 31.5%, respectively, during the period 1987–

1996. Finally, the average loss in Latin America of 31.8% was comparable to the average of 34.8% on Citibank's U.S. commerical and industrial loans.

Within the sphere of Eurobonds, we would expect that the place of legal registration of the bonds might affect recovery. As noted previously, collective action by creditors to change the payment structure of debts is much easier under U.K. law than under U.S. law. Recovery may, on average, be correspondingly quicker and perhaps greater under U.K. law. Interestingly, some countries have Eurobonds outstanding that are denominated in the same currency but governed by different legal systems. Turkey and the Philippines are relevant examples. A natural question, then, is whether market prices reflect the different probabilities of default and restructuring associated with the relative ease of collective action. The analysis of Deutsche Bank Research (1999) suggests that prices do not reflect these differences. On the other hand, in a larger and more systematic study, Eichengreen and Mody (2000) find that such clauses lower borrowing costs for high-quality sovereign issues because of the benefits of easier restructuring and associated higher expected recoveries. On the other hand, for low-quality sovereign issuers, the costs of moral hazard and default risk associated with the relative ease of creditor-initiated restructurings seem to be associated with wider spreads.

6.4.2. Parametric Models of Sovereign Spreads

Following Duffie et al. (2003b), we proceed by discounting cash flows promised by a sovereign bond using a short-term discount rate adjusted for the risk-neutral mean loss rate of the various types of credit events discussed earlier. Additionally, we accommodate the possibility that bonds of exactly the same type but possibly of different maturities issued by the same sovereign may be priced in the market using different discount factors. That is, there may not be a common default-adjusted short-rate process that governs the prices of the entire term structure of sovereign bond yields. In this manner, we allow for the possibility of selective default by issuers, for different legal governance of bonds by the same issuer, and for different treatment of bonds issued under different political regimes. Finally, for these reasons and because of possible clientele-trading patterns, high transaction costs, or asymmetrically informed traders (including government insiders), we also allow for differential yields across bonds owing to illiquidity.

Several considerations influence our choice of a reduced-form over a structural model. Structural models can be problematic when empirically modeling sovereign debt. Countries have considerable latitude in reporting their balance sheets and balances of payments. Beyond this measurement issue, the incentives of a sovereign to default are relatively complex. When a sovereign defaults, it may lose assets held abroad, but assets held within the country need not be seized as collateral. Rather, the country loses

Table 6.1.   Contractual Characteristics of Russian
Dollar-Denominated MinFins and Eurobonds

Issue	Issue date	Maturity	Coupon	Amount issued (billions of U.S.$)
MinFin 3	5/14/1993	5/14/1999	3.00	1.32
MinFin 4	5/14/1993	5/14/2003	3.00	3.38
MinFin 5	5/14/1993	5/14/2008	3.00	2.84
MinFin 6	5/14/1996	5/14/2006	3.00	1.75
MinFin 7	5/14/1996	5/14/2011	3.00	1.75
Eurobond-01	11/27/1996	11/27/2001	9.25	2.40
Eurobond-07	6/26/1997	6/26/2007	10.00	1.00

reputation for its failure to make payments, which worsens its access to international capital markets and may impede international trade. Politicians trade off these costs against the cost of making debt payments, along with other political considerations (including their own personal incentives). The incentives of a corporation are usually simpler: It defaults (in theory) when it cannot make its payments or when equityholders find that assets have become worth less than liabilities. Gibson and Sundaresan (1999) present a formal model in which there are significantly different optimal default strategies for sovereign and corporate borrowers, in part because sovereign debt is not directly covered by a bankruptcy code.

The case of Russian bonds, and in particular the Russian MinFins that Duffie et al. (2003b) focus on in their empirical analysis, highlights the potential limitations of applying models that were developed for corporate bond pricing to sovereign debt. Table 6.1 lists five dollar-denominated MinFin[9] bonds issued in 1993 as payment to Russian exporters for accounts in the Vnesheconombank that were frozen in 1991. In 1996, two additional MinFins were issued, and Russia issued its first Eurobond. This was followed by several additional Eurobond issues in 1997 and 1998. The MinFins are domestic debt under the jurisdiction of Russian law, whereas the Eurobonds are subject to the stricter international covenants of the Eurobond markets.

The Russian Ministry of Finance has drawn a clear distinction between its commitment to fulfill the principal obligations of Soviet-era and post-Soviet-era debt. Although the MinFins issued in 1993 are technically from the post-Soviet era, they were issued to address Soviet-era problems. There has been no explicit commitment to repay principal at maturity. In fact, Russia defaulted on the principal obligation of the MinFin 3 bonds in 1999. In contrast, in 1999, the Russian Ministry of Finance publicly committed to fulfilling all of its payment obligations on the MinFin 6 and MinFin 7 bonds.

---

[9] The name MinFin is derived from Ministry of Finance. The MinFins are also known as Taiga bonds.

Moreover, though the MinFins are denominated in U.S. dollars, they are technically domestic debt under the jurisdiction of Russian law. This gives the Ministry of Finance some discretion in deciding which creditors are to be directly affected by a credit event (e.g., which set of bonds will default) as well as discretion over the nature of a credit event, including the effective recovery rate.

With these considerations in mind, we proceed with a model for pricing sovereign debt that is based on an exogenously specified risk-neutral intensity process. We also proceed under the assumption that credit events lead to a fractional loss in market value, while recognizing that this is a rough approximation to a complex process. That the Russian experience was roughly consistent with this assumption can be seen from Figure 6.11, which shows the prices of five MinFin bonds from July 31, 1998 (just prior to default in August 1998) to November 12, 1999, relative to the corresponding prices on July 31, 1998. We see that MinFin prices fell by approximately 80% during the week of the Russian default, suggesting that market participants were

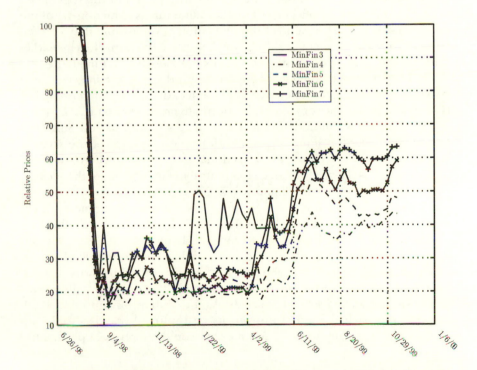

Figure 6.11. *Prices of the Russian MinFin 3–7 bonds over the time period from July 31, 1998 (just prior to default) to November 12, 1999, normalized so that they all have a market value of 100 at July 31, 1998.*

indeed surprised by this credit event right up to the time of the event itself. This is roughly consistent with default arrival at an inaccessible stopping time, as in our intensity-based modeling approach.

Initially, in the presence of multiple types of credit events, we characterize the price P_t of a nondefaulted sovereign security that promises to pay a single, possibly random, amount Z at some time $T > t$. This yields a pricing formula similar to that derived (in a less general setting) by Schönbucher (1998), who also considers multiple defaults. To accommodate multiple types of credit events, we let $N(t)$ be the number of credit events of any type that have occurred by time t, where N is a counting process with risk-neutral intensity process λ^*. We assume that, at the nth credit event, the promised payment of the security is lowered to a (risk-neutrally) expected fraction, $E_t^*(Y_n)$, of its pre-credit-event value. For example, a sovereign issuer may simply unilaterally announce at the first credit event that the principal that it recognizes as an obligation is reduced by 50%, in which case the outcome of Y_1 is 0.5. This leaves open the possibility of a further repudiation at a later date. Also, at the nth credit event, investors may receive, or prospectively value, cash flows paid by the issuer in lieu of the repudiated portion of the debt, with a current market value that is a fraction W_n of the pre-credit-event market value of the obligation.[10] We assume that λ^*, $\{Y_n\}$, and $\{W_n\}$ are given exogenously. The total effective fractional loss in market value caused by the nth credit event is thus $1 - Y_n - W_n$. At time t, the risk-neutral expected fractional loss associated with the next credit event, were it to occur immediately, is denoted L_t^*.[11] Hence, the process describing the risk-neutral mean fractional loss rate (owing to credit events) is $\lambda^* L^*$.

We also allow liquidity to affect pricing. As in Duffie and Singleton (1999), we make the simplistic assumption that illiquidity of the security translates into a risk-neutral mean fractional cost rate of ℓ, where ℓ is a predictable process. Hence, the total risk-neutral mean loss rate of the security owing to credit events and illiquidity is $\lambda^* L^* + \ell$.

If the repudiated fraction Y_n is observable at the event time τ_n, then, at time t, the security is worth the fraction $Y_1 Y_2 \cdots Y_{N(t)}$ of an otherwise identical security that has not yet experienced credit events. Even without formal econometric analysis, the behavior of the prices of MinFin 3 shown in Figure 6.11 suggests that allowing for the risk of write-downs that are instigated by a credit event (in this case the default on domestic GKOs) may be critical for pricing sovereign bonds. As the MinFin 3 matured in 1999, its price approached about a third of its face value. A standard reduced-form model based on only one credit event would, however, imply that the

---

[10] Here, Y_n and W_n are random variables with outcomes in $[0, 1]$.

[11] Specifically, L^* is a predictable process such that for each integer $n > 0$, $L_\tau^* = E^*(1 - Y_n - W_n | \mathcal{F}_{\tau-})$.

modeled price of any nondefaulted bond would continually approach its face value at maturity, which was not the case for the MinFin 3. Not only does the observed pattern call for a write-down effect, but it also challenges the strong assumption that the fraction Y_n of the notional that is recovered owing to the nth credit event is observable at the associated credit event time τ_n. An empirically more plausible view is that, as a consequence of the default on GKOs in August 1998, bond prices reflected investors' expected payment at maturity and investors' expectations were subsequently revised upward over time toward one-third of face value as market and economic conditions changed.

Duffie et al. (2003b) formalize the idea of "expected payments at maturity" by allowing bond investors to learn more about the extent of the write-down after the credit event itself, including the possibility that the final resolution of the impact of a restructuring is learned only at maturity. Although such knowledge substantially increases the difficulty of pricing sovereign bonds, they extend their pricing relation under the strong assumption of *independent recovery*: Risk-neutrally, $\{Y_1, Y_2, \ldots\}$ are independent, and they are also independent of $\{Z, r, l, N, W_1, W_2, \ldots\}$. With this assumption, the price at date t of the random payoff Z at date T is

$$P_t = E_t^* \left(e^{-\int_t^T R_u \, du} Z \right) \prod_{n \leq N(t)} E_t^*(Y_n). \qquad (6.29)$$

Coupon bond prices are built up, as usual, from zero-coupon prices, as explained earlier in this chapter. The independent recovery assumption is strong because, for instance, as economic conditions in a sovereign domain improve, we would expect both that $E_t^*(Y_n)$ is revised upward and that the credit-event risk-neutral intensity λ_t^* declines. The independence assumption does, however, allow for the expected write-down factor $E_t^*(Y_n)$ to be state dependent, which substantially increases the flexibility of this model in capturing market price movements. In particular, subsequent to the first credit event, when at least one such term, $E_t^*(Y_n)$, is present in (6.29), bond prices may jump up or down as investors revise their expectations about the consequences of past credit events for eventual receipts at maturity. Such jumps can occur at any time, including just prior to the maturity of the bond. A notable example of this type of jumpiness is the rather saw-toothed time pattern of the price of MinFin 3 in 1999 prior to its default at maturity, illustrated in Figure 6.11. We note that jumps in $E_t^*(Y_n)$ are conceptually distinct from jumps in prices that might occur as a consequence of jumps in the short spread $s = \lambda^* L^* + \ell$, owing to, say, a jump in the risk-neutral intensity of credit events.

Empirical Models of
Defaultable Bond Spreads

This chapter emphasizes empirical aspects of corporate and sovereign bond yields. We begin with an examination of the historical properties of corporate yield spreads in the U.S. markets, including an exploration of their correlations with business cycles. After setting up a framework for the modeling of reference yield curves, we turn to the empirical evidence on the fit of pricing models, both reduced-form and structural, to U.S. corporate bond data. Finally, we overview recent empirical studies of pricing models for sovereign bonds.

7.1. Credit Spreads and Economic Activity

Before discussing the empirical implementation of corporate bond pricing models, we briefly review some historical properties of U.S. corporate bond credit spreads. Though the concept of credit spread is easily described, numerous data problems compromise the informativeness of spreads about default risk. The difficulties include: (1) many corporate and sovereign bonds are relatively illiquid, so reliable transactions data for individual bonds are not readily available, (2) "credit" spreads therefore reflect such noncredit factors as liquidity risk, and (3) many corporate bonds have embedded options, so changes in spreads are not associated purely with changes in default risk. (We review callable and convertible bond pricing models in Chapter 9.) Fortunately, some of these problems can be reduced by careful use of the data. Our strategy for dealing with these data limitations is to present results for several different data bases. With the limitations of each data set in mind, we attempt to identify patterns that are unlikely to have been spuriously induced by measurement problems.

One of the data sets on which we focus is constructed from historical spreads on corporate bonds compiled from the Lehman Brothers data base, as was shown earlier in Figure 1.1. An attractive feature of this data set is its relatively long history. Matching the peaks in yields to business cycle activity, we see that credit spreads tended to be larger during recessions, a pattern that is consistent with the intuition that default probabilities (or default risk premia, or both) increase during weak economic times. The magnitudes of the fluctuation in Figure 1.1, at least as a reflection of credit risk, must be interpreted with some caution, however, because many of the bonds entering the Lehman index have embedded call options.

From the raw Lehman data, we used an "option-cleansed" data set that was constructed by selecting U.S. corporate bonds with no embedded call or sinking fund options.[1] Owing to the illiquidity of many corporate bonds, it is common practice for investment banks to form a "matrix" of prices of relatively liquid bonds for various maturity-rating pairs within a given industrial grouping. The prices of less liquid bonds are set as a spread to the relevant entries in this matrix. In order to reduce distortions owing to "matrix pricing," we select only trader quotes. For each bond, at each month's end, we computed the difference between the yield on the bond and a constant-maturity-Treasury (CMT) yield for a nearby maturity. These yield spreads were then averaged across all industries within the maturity ranges 2–7 years ("short"), 7–15 years ("medium"), and 15–30 years ("long"). The data are monthly, from January 1985 through December 1994.[2]

Looking ahead to parameterizations of intensities that might be suitable for the empirical implementation of pricing models, we use this data set to explore some relationships between spreads and other economic variables. Recent empirical evidence generally supports negative correlations between credit spreads and yields on Treasury bonds of comparable maturities (see, e.g., Duffee, 1998). We found similar negative correlations using both the Lehman Brothers data and the Bloomberg "fair market value" yield spreads.[3] Three possible interpretations of the negative sign of these correlations are: (1) the effects of macroeconomic business cycles on spreads, (2) the illiquidity of corporate bonds relative to Treasury bonds, and (3) supply responses of issuers to changing market conditions.

If the likelihood of default increases during recessions, as suggested earlier in Section 3.1, and if Treasury rates tend to fall during cyclical down-

---

[1] Data bases constructed in this fashion underlie most of the empirical studies discussed subsequently. We are grateful to Greg Duffee for making his version of option-cleansed corporate yields available to us.

[2] Data for the long-term bonds start in April 1987, because of the lack of data on non-callable long-term bonds for some of the credit classes over some subperiods between January 1985 and early 1987.

[3] These data represent Bloomberg's estimates of new-issue par-coupon bond yields for a given rating. Par-coupon yield spreads are computed using market quotes on industrial bonds, after an adjustment for the values of embedded options.

turns, then we might expect a negative correlation between Treasury rates and spreads. This result is also consistent with the implications of a model in which default occurs the first time that the total value of the firm falls below a default-triggering boundary, such as the face value of its liabilities (see Chapter 5). An increase in the default-free rate implies a higher risk-neutral mean growth rate of assets, and, fixing the initial value of the firm and the default boundary for assets, risk-neutral survival probabilities go up, lowering spreads. One can easily take issue with the idea of holding the market value of the firm fixed for purposes of this calculation. In theory, the market value of the firm is the risk-neutral expectation of the discounted present value of its future cash flows, using market interest rates for discounting. If we instead take the firm's cash flow process as given and raise interest rates, then the entire path of the market value of the firm is *lowered*, thus advancing its default time and widening spreads. Of course, the effect of market rates on the cash flow process itself must also be considered.

An alternative explanation for negative correlations is that corporate bond markets are less liquid than Treasury markets. In the Lehman data, we have controlled somewhat for illiquidity by focusing on trader quotes. In the Bloomberg data, this problem is mitigated somewhat by the use of actively traded bonds to construct the par curves. Nevertheless, there may be some stale prices, in which case an increase in the Treasury rate may be associated with a decline in spreads, at least until the corporate market reacts to changing conditions.

Third, we hear anecdotally that issuers tend to reduce their supply of new corporate debt when Treasury rates rise. If the demand for corporate debt remains largely unchanged or increases when Treasury rates rise, then corporate yield spreads would tend to narrow. More generally, there are pronounced bond "issuance cycles," as illustrated in Figure 7.1, suggesting a business cycle component to supply-and-demand effects on yield spreads.

The performance of equity prices also reflects business cycle developments, through both changes in discount rates and expectations about future corporate earnings. Furthermore, the likelihood of default for a firm depends on the value of the firm's assets relative to its liabilities. Both of these observations suggest that equity returns should be negatively correlated with corporate spreads, and, in fact, this is what we found with our data sets. These correlations also change with the stage of the business cycle and the credit quality of the issuers, with high-yield firms showing more correlation with equity returns than low-leverage firms (Shane, 1994).

Credit spreads also show evidence of substantial persistence over time. Therefore, in developing a model of risk-neutral default intensities based on historical bond yield spreads, it is not sufficient to know the contemporaneous correlations among spreads, interest rate levels, and other variables

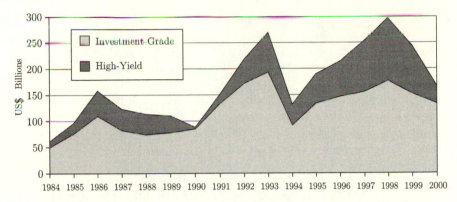

Figure 7.1. *Corporate bond issuance by credit quality. (Source: Moody's.)*

that might influence default intensities. It is also helpful to have information about the temporal interactions among these variables. In order to explore the dynamic correlations among spreads and other macroeconomic
variables, we estimate a linear equation that expresses contemporaneous
yield spreads as linear functions of the past histories of four variables: yield
spreads (its own history, say, *SPREAD*), an index of consumer confidence
(*ConConf*), the CMT 30-year Treasury yield (*CMT*30), and the Standard &
Poor's 500 stock index return (*S&P*500). Specifically,

$$SPREAD_t = \alpha_0 + \sum_{j=1}^{J} \beta_{1j} SPREAD_{t-j} + \beta_{2j} ConConf_{t-j}$$

$$+ \beta_{3j} CMT30_{t-j} + \beta_{4j} S\&P500_{t-j} + \epsilon_t, \qquad (7.1)$$

where ϵ_t is the regression error. We then calculate the response over time in
SPREAD to a "shock" in each of these four variables, holding the other three
variables fixed. The size of each shock is equal to one standard deviation of
the regression errors. For instance, in the case of the response of *SPREAD*
to its own shock, we compute an estimate of the standard deviation of ϵ_t in
(7.1) and then trace out the effects on *SPREAD* of a shock to ϵ_t while setting
the shocks to the other three variables equal to zero.

In (7.1), we allow lagged values of all of the variables to affect *SPREAD*,
and we suppose that the corresponding representations of *ConConf*,
*CMT*30, and *S&P*500 have the same feature. Thus, if we change one of
the variables today, it may affect all four variables over time through these
dynamic interactions. It is the timing and magnitude of these interactions
that we are attempting to capture with our linear regression model.

Responses of long-term BAA spreads are displayed in Figure 7.2. The horizontal axis measures elapsed time, in months, from the initial shock. The size of the response on the vertical axis is measured in basis points. Each solid line represents the expected response pattern. The dashed lines trace out two-standard-deviation confidence bands around these responses. An increase in the index of consumer confidence leads to a prolonged decline in long-term BAA spreads that persists for a period of about 8 months. An increase in equity prices also leads to a narrowing of short-term spreads, but the effect is smaller than for *ConConf*. The corresponding plot of the responses of short-term BAA spreads shows an even more pronounced response, with a shock to *ConConf* being associated with a decline of about 15 basis points in the short-term BAA spread after 3 months. The signs of these responses are as we would expect, although their magnitudes relative to the effects of other shocks may be surprising. Indeed, *ConConf* has a larger effect on short-term BAA spreads than either of the other two macro variables.

From our regression analysis, we also obtain information about the fraction of the variation over time in credit spreads attributable to each of the explanatory variables over various forecast horizons. For instance, when forecasting long-term (short-term) BAA spreads 1 month ahead, 76% (74%) of the variation in the forecast error is due to unexpected spread shocks, 1% (9.8%) is due to unexpected shocks to *ConConf*, and 23% (9.9%) is due to the 30-year Treasury rate. For long horizons, the variance of the forecast error approaches the variance of the spread itself. In particular, variation in *ConConf* is associated with 8.7% (32.9%) of the variation in the long-term (short-term) BAA spread over long horizons.

Interestingly, for long-term BAA spreads, nearly 23% of the forecast-error variance in the long spread over the first month is attributable to variation in *CMT*30, consistent with the impression gained from Figure 7.2. The near-term effects of *CMT*30 shocks on the short-term spread are smaller. In both cases, moreover, the effects of Treasury shocks on spreads dissipate relatively quickly, becoming statistically insignificant after a period of less than 2 months following the shock. This finding is consistent with a conjecture that the negative correlation between *CMT*30 and long BAA spreads is due to the relative illiquidity of the corporate bond market. It is also consistent with the view that the supply of new issues temporarily diminishes after increases in Treasury yields. More extensive studies of the dynamic correlations among corporate bond yields and macroeconomic variables are presented in Neal et al. (2000) and Collin-Dufresne et al. (2001). The latter study finds that a large proportion of the variation in yield spreads is unexplained by the macro information included in their statistical analyses. Their principal-component analysis also suggests that a single, corporate market–specific factor also explains most of the variation in spreads that is not accounted for by the macro variables.

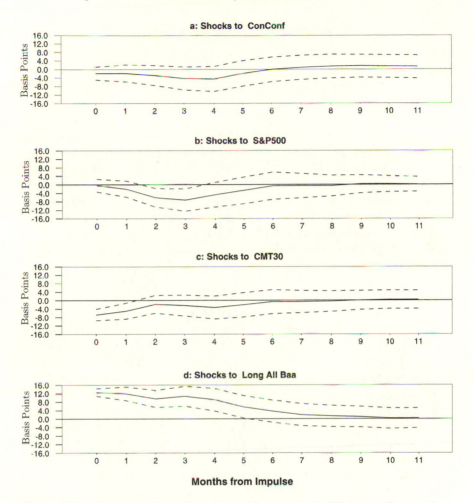

Figure 7.2. *Responses, in basis points, of long-maturity BAA spreads to various shocks.*

We also find that, for both short-term and long-term BAA spreads, substantial fractions of their variation over time are explained by their own prior "spread" shocks. This suggests that there are important economic factors underlying spread variability that are not well proxied by any of the three predictor variables used in our time-series analysis. In other words, when modeling the market and credit risks of corporate bond portfolios, it seems essential to allow for variation that is idiosyncratic to the corporate bond market relative to the Treasury and equity markets.

7.2. Reference Curves for Spreads

Although in the preceding descriptive analysis we used U.S. Treasury yields as a benchmark for the purpose of calculating corporate yield spreads, this is only one among several sensible choices. Other natural candidates for reference curves are the term structures of swap, agency, and high-grade corporate bond yields. The choice among these is typically influenced by: (1) pricing conventions in markets, (2) data availability, (3) desires by financial institutions to standardize pricing models across markets and countries, and (4) institutional considerations that affect the relative pricing of the reference and corporate markets. For example, in many countries, swap markets are relatively unencumbered by institutional, tax, and regulatory factors that influence Treasury yields. This may suggest the use of the swap curve as a reference curve, even in countries where the pricing convention is to quote defaultable bonds at spreads to Treasuries. Owing to the large federal budget surpluses in 2000 and 2001 and the associated decline in both issuance and outstanding principal of U.S. Treasury bonds, many financial institutions were reevaluating their use of the U.S. Treasury yield curve as a reference curve. For example, in some settings, J. P. Morgan started using government agency yield curves as reference curves (Demchak, 2000). Other financial institutions have focused on the swap curves. In fact, in late 2001, the U.S. Treasury announced that it will discontinue issuing 30-year bonds.

Of course, the interpretation of the "credit spread" that results from the selection of a particular reference curve must depend on the choice of the latter curve. Choosing a non-Treasury reference curve has the potential advantage of removing some of the liquidity premium associated with Treasuries over most corporates. At the same time, swap and high-grade corporate yields themselves reflect credit risk, so when spreading to these curves one ends up with a relative credit spread. Any estimates of (risk-neutral) default probabilities implied by these spreads should be interpreted in this relative sense. For low-grade issuers, in particular, little ambiguity about the credit quality of the issuer is likely to be created by using these non-Treasury reference curves. With these caveats in mind, we proceed by allowing reference curves themselves to be based on defaultable bonds.

In this section, we present some illustrative models for the reference curve to be used in pricing corporate bonds. The motivation for this first step is the development of a benchmark reference curve for a wide variety of different defaultable debt issues (in the same currency). With such a reference curve in place, the pricing of the defaultable bonds of a given issuer is obtained by specifying the risk-neutral joint distribution of the reference curve and the issuer's default-adjusted short-term credit-spread process. This second step is taken up in the next section. For illustrative purposes, we focus on the swap curve as a reference curve, but the same pricing models could be applied equally to Treasury or agency curves. Chapter 12 addresses the influence of default risk on swap rates.

Much (though not all) of the academic literature on the term structure of interest rates fits the parameters of term-structure models to data using methods very different from those commonly used by practitioners. Academic studies often address the time-series properties of yield curves, holding the parameters of the model fixed. In contrast, for the purpose of pricing interest-rate derivatives, practitioners normally calibrate a reference yield-curve model using a contemporaneous cross section of yields and interest-rate option prices. The models we discuss can be used either way. In order to convey a sense of the dynamic properties of corporate bond pricing models, however, we proceed by treating the model parameters as fixed over time and examine the fit of these models to historical time series of yields.

The most frequently studied reduced-form models are those based on "affine" parameterizations for the reference curve, summarized in Appendix A.[4] In this section, we focus on an affine family of two-factor models for the instantaneous interest rate underlying the pricing of the reference curve. We will write r_t for this instantaneous short rate, in light of its benchmark status, even though the reference curve may not itself be default-free. We suppose that

$$r_t = \gamma_0 + \gamma_1 X_{1t} + \gamma_2 X_{2t}, \tag{7.2}$$

for a risk-neutral affine state vector $X_t = (X_{1t}, X_{2t})'$ satisfying

$$dX_t = \mathcal{K}(\Theta - X_t)\, dt + \Sigma \sqrt{S_t}\; dB_t^*, \tag{7.3}$$

where B^* is a risk-neutral standard two-dimensional Brownian motion. The 2×1 vector Θ is the long-run risk-neutral mean of state X_t. The 2×2 matrix $\mathcal{K}$ governs the rate at which the conditional means of the state variables revert to Θ. Since $\mathcal{K}$ may be nondiagonal, X_{1t} may be used to forecast future changes in X_{2t}, and conversely. The 2×2 matrix Σ contains instantaneous correlations, whereas the diagonal matrix S_t contains instantaneous variances.

This model can be visualized from the standard Euler discretization of (7.3),

$$X_{t+\Delta} - X_t \simeq \mathcal{K}\Delta\,(\Theta - X_t) + \Sigma\sqrt{S_t}\sqrt{\Delta}\,\epsilon_{t+\Delta}, \tag{7.4}$$

---

[4] Another tractable family is the "quadratic-Gaussian" family in which $r(t)$ is a quadratic function of a Gaussian state vector. See, e.g., Beaglehole and Tenney (1991), Constantinides (1992), Leippold and Wu (2001), and Ahn et al. (2002).

where Δ is the length of the discretization interval and $\epsilon_{t+\Delta}$ is a standard normal "shock" (of zero mean, with identity covariance matrix, independent over time). For example, if X_{1t} is below Θ_1, then the conditional expectation of the change $X_{1,t+\Delta} - X_{1t}$ over the next interval of time is influenced by the degree to which X_{2t} is above or below its long-run mean Θ_2. The parameter determining this "cross-state" mean reversion is $\mathcal{K}_{12}$, the upper-right element of $\mathcal{K}$.

The structure of volatility in these models is governed by the matrices Σ and S_t. The correlation matrix Σ is constant, whereas

$$[S_t]_{ii} = \alpha_i + \beta_{i1} X_{1t} + \beta_{i2} X_{2t}, \tag{7.5}$$

allowing for dependence of the instantaneous variances on the risk factors. (The conditional *volatility* of the ith risk factor is therefore $\sqrt{[S_t]_{ii}}$.) Among the interesting special cases of this model are:

(A) $[S_t]_{ii} = \alpha_i$: The risk factors are Gaussian (possibly correlated) processes with constant variances. Such models were introduced by Vasicek (1977) and Langetieg (1980).

(B) $[S_t]_{ii} = X_{it}$, and $\mathcal{K}$ and Σ are diagonal matrices[5]: The risk factors are independent square-root (or CIR) processes. The instantaneous volatility of X_{it} is $\sqrt{X_{it}}$.

(C) $[S_t]_{11} = X_{1t}$, $[S_t]_{22} = \alpha_2 + \beta_{21} X_{1t}$: This is a hybrid model, with X_{1t} determining the conditional volatility of *both* risk factors and correlation in X_{1t} and X_{2t} through both cross-state mean reversion (nondiagonal $\mathcal{K}$) and the instantaneous correlation matrix Σ.

For all three cases, as with any affine model, the zero-coupon bond price at maturity date T is

$$\delta(t, T) = E_t^* \left[e^{-\int_t^T r(u)\, du} \right] = e^{\alpha_\delta(t,T) + \beta_\delta(t,T) \cdot X(t)}, \tag{7.6}$$

where $\alpha_\delta(t, T)$ and $\beta_\delta(t, T)$ are known functions of the parameters governing X_t and the parameters γ_0, γ_1, and γ_2 relating r to X, as explained in Chapter 5 and Appendix A.

By calculating the derivative of this equation for the bond price $\delta(t, T)$ with respect to $X_i(t)$, we see that the proportional sensitivity of the bond price to changes in $X_i(t)$ is the ith element of the vector $\beta_\delta(t, T)$, which is

---

[5] We can relax the assumption that $\mathcal{K}$ is diagonal, while preserving the tractability of this model, in which case X_{1t} and X_{2t} are correlated (see Dai and Singleton, 2000, for further discussion).

therefore often called the *factor-loading* vector. With this, one can express the "instantaneous" expected excess return on a zero-coupon bond maturing at date T in the form

$$e(t, T) = \beta_\delta(t, T) \cdot Q(t), \tag{7.7}$$

where the ith element of $Q(t)$ is the excess expected rate of return on any security whose returns are instantaneously perfectly correlated with $X_i(t)$.[6]

A convenient specification of $Q(t)$ that allows us to match the historical predictability of excess returns on bonds, while preserving analytic tractability, has (see Dai and Singleton, 2002, Duffee, 2002, and Appendix B)

$$Q(t) = \psi^0 + \psi^X X(t), \tag{7.8}$$

where ψ^0 is a two-dimensional vector and ψ^X is a 2×2 matrix. This parameterization of risk premia implies that the state process X is affine under both actual and risk-neutral probabilities, although with different parameters. It turns out (Duffee, 2002) that there are no-arbitrage restrictions on the risk-premia coefficients ψ^0 and ψ^X that depend on the preceding specifications of $S(t)$. In case (A), the Gaussian model, ψ^0 and ψ^X are unconstrained, so excess expected returns are time varying, even though the instantaneous variances of the risk factors X_t are constant. For the CIR model, case (B), one must have $\psi^0 = 0$ and ψ^X diagonal. Finally, in the hybrid case (C), we must have

$$Q(t) = \begin{pmatrix} 0 \\ \psi_2^0 \end{pmatrix} + \begin{pmatrix} \psi_{11}^X & 0 \\ \psi_{21}^X & \psi_{22}^X \end{pmatrix} \begin{pmatrix} X_{1t} \\ X_{2t} \end{pmatrix}. \tag{7.9}$$

In order to illustrate these ideas, we show an estimate from Duffie et al. (2003b) of the two-factor hybrid model (C), based on weekly data on generic U.S. swap rates for the period April 1987 through October 2000 (678 observations).[7] Estimation is accomplished using the method of maximum likelihood within a parameterization in which Σ is normalized to the identity matrix (see Duffie et al., 2003b, for details). The estimates are:

$$r_t = 0.0503 + 0.000656\, X_{1t} + 0.000042\, X_{2t} \tag{7.10}$$

---

[6] Those familiar with the use of Ito calculus in asset pricing theory can also view these risk premia in terms of the "market price of risk." We have $Q(t) = \Sigma\sqrt{S(t)}\Lambda(t)$, where $\Lambda(t)$ is the market price of risk.

[7] The 6-month LIBOR and 10-year swap rates are assumed to be observed without error. One-year LIBOR and swap rates of 2, 3, 4, 5, and 7 years are assumed to be measured with first-order autoregressive errors that may be correlated across maturities.

$$dX_t = \begin{pmatrix} 0.0402 & 0 \\ -23.8 & 0.276 \end{pmatrix} \left[\begin{pmatrix} 12.4 \\ 0 \end{pmatrix} - X_t \right] dt + \sqrt{S_t}\, dB_t^* \qquad (7.11)$$

$$Q(t) = \begin{pmatrix} 0 \\ 0.0005 \end{pmatrix} + \begin{pmatrix} -0.026 & 0 \\ -16.7 & 0.227 \end{pmatrix} X_t \qquad (7.12)$$

$$[S(t)]_{11} = X_{1t}, \quad [S(t)]_{22} = 1 + 3516\,X_{1t}. \qquad (7.13)$$

As is not atypical in estimates of affine models, one of the state variables (X_1) has a much slower rate of mean reversion than the other (X_2). This means that variation in yields at the longer end of the yield curve is due primarily to variation in X_1. Further, $\mathcal{K}_{21} < 0$, which implies that the two risk factors are positively correlated in this model.

For this estimated model, expected excess rates of returns of bonds are state dependent. Moreover, X_{2t} affects the time variation in expected excess returns even though it has no effect on the volatilities of the risk factors (the latter depend only on X_1). Finally, X_1 affects the risk premium associated with exposure to movements in X_2, in that $\psi_{21}^X = -16.7$.

7.3. Parametric Reduced-Form Models

Reduced-form models with fractional recovery of market value have been implemented empirically for corporate bonds under various assumptions about the determinants of intensities and the reference curves.

7.3.1. Square-Root Diffusion Models of Spreads

As a reference curve, Duffee (1999) used the U.S. Treasury yield curve, modeled by a two-factor risk-neutral CIR state process X, with

$$r_t = -1 + \gamma_1 X_{1t} + \gamma_2 X_{2t}, \qquad \gamma_1 > 0,\ \gamma_2 > 0. \qquad (7.14)$$

This is case (B), explained in Section 7.2.1, of two-factor affine models.

For the pricing of default risk, Duffee took a model based on fractional recovery of market value, as in Section 6.2.3, whose default-adjusted short rate R_t exceeds the reference short rate r_t by a short spread s_t, where

$$s_t = \varphi_0 + \varphi_1 X_{1t} + \varphi_2 X_{2t} + \varphi_3 Y_t, \qquad (7.15)$$

where Y is also a CIR (square-root) process, risk-neutrally independent of (X_{1t}, X_{2t}). We recall from Chapter 6 that, absent liquidity spreads, we may interpret s_t as the risk-neutral mean fractional rate of loss of market value owing to default and illiquidity. Correlation between the credit spread and riskless term structure is induced in this model by the joint dependence of s_t and r_t on (X_{1t}, X_{2t}).

Using the Lehman Brothers data on trader quotes for noncallable corporate bonds, Duffee obtained negative estimates of (φ_1, φ_2) for most of the U.S. issuers that he studied. This is consistent with the descriptive findings in Section 7.1 that corporate yield spreads are negatively correlated with U.S. Treasury rates. Capturing this feature of historical data, however, comes at the cost of allowing the short spread s_t to become negative, given Duffee's negative estimates of φ_1 and φ_2 in (7.15). Absent negative relative liquidity effects, this would not be consistent with nonnegative risk-neutral mean fractional loss at default. Nevertheless, the latter may occur with a small probability at the estimated parameters. Duffee found that the average error in fitting noncallable corporate bond yields was less than 10 basis points.

This model can be extended in a number of ways while preserving its tractability. First, the riskless short rate could be allowed to depend on all three state variables (X_1, X_2, Y). This does not present any problems for the analysis of a given issuer, but would require that the reference and issuer curves be studied simultaneously for estimation. With a large number of issuers, this would quickly become intractable. Additionally, much more flexibility with regard to the factor correlations can be achieved by adopting richer affine parameterizations of the state vector, while having strictly positive λ^*.

7.3.2. Jump-Diffusion Spreads

Collin-Dufresne and Solnik (2001) also implement a version of a defaultable bond term-structure model based on fractional recovery of market value, but one in which the default-free short-rate process r is based on a two-factor Gaussian state process X, case (A) in Section 7.2.1. They modeled the short-spread process s based on an affine jump-diffusion state model of the form

$$ds_t = \kappa_s(\theta_{st} - s_t)\, dt + \sigma\, dW_t^* + v\, dN_t \tag{7.16}$$

$$d\theta_{st} = v\, dN_t, \tag{7.17}$$

where W^* is a risk-neutral standard Brownian motion and N is, risk-neutrally, a Poisson process with constant jump intensity. The introduction of jumps allows for sudden big changes in credit quality other than default. The Brownian motion W^* driving spreads may be correlated with the two-dimensional standard Brownian motion B^* of (7.3) that affects changes in the reference curve. This model for the state (X_t, θ_t, s_t) is, once again, affine.

Treating the U.S. Treasury curve as the reference curve and taking LIBOR-quality bonds as the defaultable securities, they estimate negative correlation between changes in r_t and s_t, again consistent with the U.S. experience for corporate issuers. The average fitting errors for maturities ranging up to 10 years were less than 1 basis point for the sample period of October 1988 through January 1997.

7.3.3. Accommodating Observable Credit Factors

Up to this point, the econometric models that we have examined treat the state variables determining the short spread s_t as unobservable. Alternatively, one or more of the state variables could be an observable economic time series that is thought to be related to the degree of credit risk. Using a model based on recovery of market value, Bakshi et al. (2001) assumed that the short spread s_t depends on the reference short rate r_t and an observed credit-related state variable, say Y_t, in that

$$s_t = \alpha_0 + \alpha_r r_t + \alpha_Y Y_t, \tag{7.18}$$

for coefficients α_0, α_r, and α_Y to be estimated. In their various formulations, Y_t is one of: (1) the ratio of the book value of debt to the total of the book value of debt and the market value of equity, (2) the ratio of the book value of equity to the market value of equity, (3) the ratio of operating income to net sales, (4) a lagged credit spread, and (5) the logarithm of the firm's stock price.

Bakshi et al. (2001) took the reference short rate r_t to be determined by a two-factor Gaussian state vector $(X_{1t}, X_{2t})'$, as in case (A) of Section 7.2.1. The observable credit factor Y was assumed to be a mean-reverting Gaussian diffusion, so that the state vector $(X_{1t}, X_{2t}, Y_t)'$ upon which r_t and the short spread s_t depends is a three-factor affine process. The various versions of the model, differing only in terms of the choice of the observable credit variable Y_t, were estimated using the Lehman Brothers data on individual U.S. corporate issuers.

For cases in which Y_t is a leverage measure, Bakshi et al. (2001) found that, after controlling for interest-rate risk, higher leverage indeed implies a higher short spread s_t. They estimated a sensitivity α_Y of the short spread to leverage that is highest among AA-rated firms and lowest among utilities. They also found that leverage-related credit risk is more pronounced for long-maturity than for short-maturity corporate bonds. Similar results were found if Y_t is taken to be the book-to-market ratio.

For the time-series analysis of U.S. credit spreads discussed in Section 7.1, we found that a substantial fraction of the variation in spreads is unrelated to such macro variables as aggregate equity returns and consumer confidence. Spread variation must be captured within (7.18) by firm-specific variables. An interesting question, then, is whether there is an incremental role for a latent spread factor, over and above those in (7.18).

7.4. Estimating Structural Models

Whereas reduced-form models hinge on the specification of the risk-neutral default intensity λ^* and the fractional loss model, structural models normally call for parameters determining the behavior of the assets of the issuer, such as the asset volatility σ. One must also make assumptions concerning the capital structures of issuers, which are in practice quite complex and include multiple types of debt and other forms of liabilities. As with reduced-form models, one must specify a term-structure model for the reference yield curve in terms of the short-rate process r. In addition, one may allow for correlation between assets and r, when relevant. Finally, one must specify a model of recovery.

Empirical implementations of structural models have varied widely in their resolutions of these issues. Focusing first on the "naïve" first-passage structural models introduced in Section 5.4, as in the original models of Black and Scholes (1973) and Merton (1974), the asset-value process A is typically assumed to be risk-neutrally log-normal in that

$$\frac{dA_t}{A_t} = (r - \gamma)\, dt + \sigma\, dB_t^*, \tag{7.19}$$

where γ is the constant cash payout rate and r is the constant short rate. When applying estimates of this model to corporate debt pricing, the empirical literature typically assumes that: (1) the firm is capitalized with common stock and one bond, (2) default occurs when $A_T < D$, where D is a default-triggering boundary, usually estimated in terms of book liabilities, (3) the default-free short rate r is allowed to vary deterministically so as to capture the spot yield curve on the day valuation is undertaken, and (4) coupon bonds are priced as though they are a portfolio of zero-coupon bonds corresponding to coupons and principal.

Jones et al. (1984) implemented this Merton model for a sample of callable coupon bonds for the sample period 1977–1981. They found average absolute pricing errors of 8.5%. Model prices were too high, so spreads were too narrow. Ogden (1987) showed that, for primary market prices for bonds over the period 1973–1985, the model underpredicted spreads by an average of 104 basis points. More recently, Lyden and Sariniti (2000) used data from Bridge (which provides actual transactions prices) and found mean absolute errors in yield spreads of roughly 80 basis points. The model-implied spreads were particularly low (bonds were overpriced) for small firms and long maturities.

Extending the one-factor log-normal model (7.19), the two-factor structural model of Longstaff and Schwartz (1995) assumes that

$$\frac{dA_t}{A_t} = (r_t - \gamma) \, dt + \sigma \, dB_t^* \tag{7.20}$$

$$dr_t = \kappa(\mu - r_t) \, dt + \sigma_r \, dW_t^*, \tag{7.21}$$

where W^* is a risk-neutral Brownian motion, with $\mathrm{corr}(W_t^*, B_t^*) = \rho$. The risk-neutral short-rate model is thus of the type introduced by Vasicek (1977). Kim et al. (1993) and Cathcart and El-Jahel (1998) considered a variant of this model in which the short-rate process r is a one-factor CIR process.[8]

Empirical implementations of the two-factor Longstaff-Schwartz model have typically assumed that: (1) default occurs at the first time that A_t falls below a prespecified boundary, typically the face value of outstanding bonds; and (2) in the event of default, bondholders recover a constant fraction w of the face value. Collin-Dufresne and Goldstein (2001) provide a numerical procedure for computing zero-coupon bond prices in this setting. Again, risky coupon bonds are priced as a portfolio of risky zero-coupon bonds.

Lyden and Sariniti (2000) found that the Longstaff-Schwartz model performs roughly as well as the naïve one-factor model (7.19). Moreover, their findings for the Longstaff-Schwartz model were remarkably insensitive to correlation between A and r. Indeed, the Merton model dominated the Longstaff-Schwartz model (they are not strictly nested) when a common, aggregate recovery fraction w was used for all firms. Use of industry-specific recovery values for individual issuers only worsened the fit.

Eom et al. (2002) have undertaken the most comprehensive empirical analysis of structural models to date. Using time-series data from Lehman Brothers on the prices of noncallable bonds, they estimate the Black-Scholes-Merton and Longstaff-Schwartz models, as well as the model of Collin-Dufresne and Goldstein (2001), which allows firms to have a target debt-equity ratio. Interestingly, Eom et al. find that all of these models have difficulty in accurately predicting credit spreads and that the difficulties are not limited to underprediction. Their version of the Black-Scholes-Merton model does underpredict spreads. The Longstaff-Schwartz model, however, predicts spreads that are too large on average. More precisely, the model predicts excessive spreads for the riskiest bonds, and underpredicts spreads on the safest bonds. The extension by Collin-Dufresne and Goldstein helps with the underprediction problem, but on average, also over-

---

[8] Related first-passage structural models include Nielsen et al. (1993) and Briys and de Varenne (1997).

predicts spreads. Eom et al. conclude that "the challenge for theoretical bond pricing models is to raise the average predicted spread relative to the Merton model, without overstating the risks associated with volatility, leverage or coupon."

7.5. Parametric Models of Sovereign Spreads

The empirical literature on the pricing of sovereign bonds has also focused primarily on affine models.[9] Merrick (1999) calibrates a discrete-time model to Russian and Argentinian bonds that can be reinterpreted as a model with a constant risk-neutral default intensity.

More generally, Pagès (2001) adopted a special case of the modeling framework in Duffie and Singleton (1999) in which

$$r_t = \delta_0 + \delta_X X_{1t}, \tag{7.22}$$

$$\lambda_t^* = \varphi_0 + \varphi_1 X_{1t} + \varphi_2 X_{2t}, \tag{7.23}$$

where X_{1t} and X_{2t} (under both actual and risk-neutral probabilities) are independent CIR processes. Using data on Brazilian Brady bonds, he found that $\hat{\varphi}_1$ was negative, implying negative correlation between the default-free curve and the risk-neutral default intensity. Other things being equal, a 1% increase in r_t implies an expected reduction of λ_t^* of 60 basis points. Potential explanations for this negative correlation that are discussed by Pagès include: (1) the sensitivity of the supply of sovereign debt to rising U.S. interest rates, and (2) a "flight-to-quality" phenomenon. In another study of Brady bond prices, Keswani (2002) implemented Duffee's (1999) formulation of a three-factor model based on fractional recovery of market value using data from Argentina, Mexico, and Venezuela. Like Pagès, Keswani finds a negative correlation between the level of the default-free curve and instantaneous credit spreads and interprets this finding as a flight-to-quality phenomenon.

Interestingly, Keswani also implements a version of the Longstaff-Schwartz structural model to price the same Latin American bonds. The distance to default was computed using the ratio of the value of the government assets of a country to its default floor. He finds that the structural model produces smaller fitting errors prior to the devaluation in Mexico in December 1994 but that the reduced-form model performs better subsequent to this "structural break."

Implicit in all of these formulations are the assumptions that holders of sovereign debt face a single credit event—default with liquidation upon

---

[9] An exception is Keswani (2002), who applies the model of Longstaff and Schwartz (1995) to Brady bonds.

default—and that the bonds issued by a given sovereign are homogeneous
with regard to their credit characteristics.

Duffie et al. (2003b) estimate a three-factor model using Russian bond
yields that relaxes these assumptions and calibrate their model "through"
the Russian default of August 1998. The reference curve was the two-factor
hybrid model (C) defined in Section 7.2.1. In order to accommodate idiosyncratic components in the (relative) credit risk-adjusted discount rate
$R = r + s$, they selected the MinFin 4 as the benchmark bond, and modeled
the joint behavior of the riskless term structure and the benchmark short
spread as

$$
d \begin{bmatrix} v_t \\ r_t \\ s_t \end{bmatrix} = \begin{bmatrix} K^{vv} & 0 & 0 \\ K^{rv} & K^{rr} & 0 \\ K^{sv} & K^{sr} & K^{ss} \end{bmatrix} \left(\begin{bmatrix} \theta^v \\ \theta^r \\ \theta^s \end{bmatrix} - \begin{bmatrix} v_t \\ r_t \\ s_t \end{bmatrix} \right) dt
$$
$$
+ \begin{bmatrix} 1 & 0 & 0 \\ \Sigma^{rv} & \Sigma^{rr} & 0 \\ \Sigma^{sv} & \Sigma^{sr} & \Sigma^{ss} \end{bmatrix} \begin{bmatrix} \sqrt{v_t} & & \\ & \sqrt{v_t} & \\ & & 1 \end{bmatrix} dW_t,
$$

(7.24)

where $W = (W^v, W^r, W^s)'$ is a standard three-dimensional Brownian motion. For any nonbenchmark bond, numbered $i \in \{1, \ldots, I\}$, of the same
issuer, they modeled its short-spread process in the form $s_t^i = s_t + \gamma_t^i$, where

$$
d\gamma_t^i = \kappa^i \left(\theta^i - \gamma_t^i \right) dt + \sigma^i d\xi_t^i,
$$

(7.25)

and ξ^i is a standard Brownian motion independent of $\{W, \xi^j, j \neq i\}$.

Their analysis suggests that market participants applied substantial
"write-downs" to their MinFin holdings subsequent to the Russian default
on domestic treasury debt. Additionally, while the curve associated with the
default-adjusted short rate $R = r + s$ for MinFin 4 provided reasonable
pricing for the Eurobonds prior to the default, afterward market participants were clearly treating the Eurobonds as higher-quality credits. Finally,
prior to the default on the MinFin 3 in May 1999, there were several periods
during which market participants seemed to price MinFin 3 with a different
discount curve than MinFin 4. That is, the idiosyncratic factor $\gamma_t^{\text{MinFin3}}$ was
nontrivial in magnitude.

8

Credit Swaps

THIS CHAPTER EXPLAINS some basic aspects of credit swaps, with a focus on valuation. A credit swap is a form of derivative security that can be viewed as default insurance on loans or bonds. Credit swaps pay the buyer of protection a given contingent amount at the time of a given credit event, usually default of a stipulated bond or loan. If the insured event is a default, then the credit swap is known as a *default swap,* or sometimes as a *credit default swap* (CDS). The contingent amount is most often specified to be the difference between the face value of a bond and its market value, paid at the time of the credit event. In return, the buyer of protection pays a premium, in the form of an annuity, until the time of the credit event or until the maturity date of the credit swap, whichever is first.

Credit swaps are the most actively traded form of credit derivative and have become a benchmark for credit pricing. We briefly discuss some other forms of credit derivatives before turning to a focused discussion of credit swaps and their pricing.

8.1. Other Credit Derivatives

The two most active classes of credit derivatives are credit swaps, the focus of this chapter, and collateralized debt obligations (CDOs), which are typically tranches of a debt structure collateralized by a pool of individual loans or bonds whose cash flows are allocated, according to a specified prioritization schedule, to the individual tranches of the structure. We review CDOs in Chapter 11. In some cases, CDOs are constructed synthetically with the use of default swaps on the underlying debt instruments.

8.1.1. Total-Return Swaps

Another standard form of credit derivative is a *total-return swap,* sometimes called a TROR (for total rate of return), which pays the net return of one asset class over another. Often, the two asset classes are of obviously ordered credit qualities, and one counterparty is buying protection against a reduction in the credit quality of the lower-quality asset relative to the higher. For example, if one underlying asset is a corporate bond and the other is a government bond of the same or a similar maturity, then the net swap return is a partial hedge against the credit quality of the corporate bond. The hedge is not perfect, for the returns of the two underlying instruments usually reflect somewhat different exposures to interest-rate risk, illiquidity, taxes, and special terms in repurchase agreements (which we discuss later in this chapter). Even if the two bonds are of identical maturities, the corporate bond would typically have larger coupons and therefore a shorter duration and less exposure to interest-rate risk (in the sense of duration) than the government bond. Indeed, the potential for default before maturity further reduces the effective duration of the corporate bond and exacerbates the exposure of the total-return swap to interest-rate changes.

The contractual exchange of returns on the two instruments is normally based on mark-to-market price changes and coupons. In a pure version of a TROR, at each coupon date counterparty A pays counterparty B the fixed notional amount N of the contract multiplied by the difference between the mark-to-market return of the two underlying assets. The same notional exposure is maintained for the life of the contract, including through any default or restructuring events, although care must be taken to set the terms of the contract with regard to the treatments at default or restructurings. In a perfect-market setting, the pricing of a TROR of this simple type is trivial. The initial market value is zero, and the value immediately after each exchange of returns is zero, for one can synthetically recreate the position by forming a portfolio consisting of a quantity of one asset class with a market value equal to the notional N and a short position in the other asset class of the same market value N, for a total initial market value of zero, with rebalancing after each coupon date to form this balanced position. In practice, such a trading strategy is often not easy or costless, and there may be additional spread payments or fees by one counterparty to the other.

A variant of the TROR stipulates an exchange of only the cash flows on the two asset classes rather than their respective mark-to-market returns, resulting in a credit exposure of one TROR counterparty to the other as the prices of the two assets diverge over time.

One or more of the underlying asset classes of a total-return swap may be a portfolio, or an index representing a hypothetical portfolio or trading strategy. For example, a counterparty interested in obtaining a quick effective diversified position in speculative-grade bonds could request a total-return swap, receiving the total rate of return on a quoted bond index against, for example, LIBOR floating-rate payments. In some cases, one may wish to obtain the effect of a position in, or a hedge against, a portfolio representing the asset side of a specific balance sheet. Such a total-return swap has sometimes been called a *balance-sheet swap*.

Notably, a total-return swap offers exposure to, or protection from, changes in credit quality whether or not accompanied by a specific credit event such as a downgrade or default. For reasons that are not entirely obvious, however, total-return swaps have become dominated in popularity by credit swaps.

8.1.2. Spread Options

Spread options, discussed in Chapter 9, convey the right to trade bonds at a given yield spread over a reference yield, such as a Treasury yield or LIBOR swap rate. For example, one could purchase the right to sell a corporate bond at a given spread of, say, 400 basis points, to a Treasury bond of the same or a similar maturity. At expiration, if the corporate bond is trading at a spread of 600 basis points, then one may sell it at the price at which it would have a yield of 400 basis points above the specified Treasury yield. Like total-return swaps, spread options provide protection or exposure to changes in credit quality that need not be caused by specific credit events.

When a bank offers an irrevocable line of credit to a corporate borrower at a given spread over LIBOR, the corporation has, in effect, purchased a spread option on its own debt at this spread over LIBOR. Thus, spread options were effectively offered long before the advent of the market for *credit derivatives*.

8.2. The Basic Credit Swap

The basic credit-swap contract is as follows. Parties A and B enter into a contract, usually under terms standardized by The International Swaps and Derivatives Association (ISDA), terminating at the time of a given credit event or at a stated maturity, whichever is first. A commonly stipulated credit event is the default of a named issuer, say entity C, which could be a corporation, a private borrower, or a sovereign issuer. There are interesting applications, however, in which credit events may be defined instead in terms of downgrades, events such as currency nonconvertibility that may instigate the default of one or more counterparties, or other credit-related occurrences. The ISDA documentation of credit swaps allows for the specification of the covered credit event, such as bankruptcy, credit event upon merger, cross acceleration, cross default, downgrade, failure to pay, repudiation, or restructuring.

The credit event is to be documented with a notice, supported with evidence of public announcement of the event, for example, in the international press. The amount to be paid at the time of the credit event may

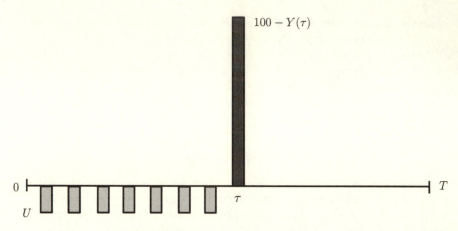

Figure 8.1.   *Credit swap cash flows.*

be based on physical or cash settlement, as indicated in the confirmation form of the OTC credit-swap transaction.

In compensation for what it may receive in the event of termination by the stated credit event, party B pays party A an annuity, at a rate variously called the credit-swap spread, CDS rate, or the credit-swap premium. This annuity stream is paid until the maturity of the credit swap or the designated credit event.

The cash flows of a credit swap are illustrated in Figure 8.1. The payment at the time τ of the credit event, if before the maturity date T of the credit swap, is the difference $100 - Y(\tau)$ between the face value, say 100, and the market value $Y(\tau)$ of a specified underlying note at time τ. With physical delivery, substitution of other debt of the same issuer is normally allowed, within contractually specified limits. The credit-swap annuity coupon rate is shown in the figure as U.

In some cases, the compensating annuity may be paid as a spread over the usual plain-vanilla interest-rate swap rate.[1] For example, if the 5-year fixed-for-floating interest-rate swap rate is 6% versus LIBOR, and if B is the buyer of protection and the fixed-rate payer in the default swap, then B would pay a fixed rate higher than the usual 6%. If, for example, B pays 7.5% fixed versus LIBOR and the defaultable note underlying the default swap is of the same notional amount as the interest-rate swap, then we would say that the default-swap spread is 150 basis points. If B is the floating-rate

---

[1] Discussions with a global bank in 1999 indicated that of more than 200 default swaps on its books, approximately 10% were combined with an interest-rate swap.

payer on the interest-rate swap, then B would pay floating plus a spread in return for the usual market fixed rate on swaps, or in effect would receive fixed less a spread. It is not necessarily the case that the theoretical default-swap spread is the same in the case of B paying fixed as in B paying floating. In general, combining the credit swap with an interest-rate swap affects the quoted credit-swap spread, because an interest-rate swap whose fixed rate is the at-market swap rate for maturity T, but with random early termination, does not have a market value of zero.

It is not unusual to see default swaps in which the payment to the buyer of protection at default is reduced by the accrued portion of the credit-swap premium. We consider this variation briefly later.

In short, the classic credit swap can be thought of as an insurance contract, under which the insured agent pays an insurance premium in return for coverage against a loss that occurs at a credit event. Indeed, default swaps of this type may be viewed as alternatives to traditional direct bond insurance, with the advantage of the standard treatment (e.g., netting with a master-swap agreement) of ISDA contracts.

For credit swaps, there are, in effect, two pricing problems:

1. At origination, the standard default swap involves no exchange of cash flows and therefore (ignoring broker margins and transactions costs) has a market value of zero. One must, however, determine the at-market annuity rate U illustrated in Figure 8.1, that for which the market value of the default swap is indeed zero.
2. After origination, changes in market interest rates and in the credit quality of the reference entity C, as well as the passage of time, typically change the market value of the default swap. For a given credit swap with a stated annuity rate U, one must determine the mark-to-market value, which is not generally zero.

When making markets, the former pricing problem is the more critical. When hedging or conducting a mark to market, the latter pricing problem is relevant. Solution methods for the two problems may call for similar capabilities. The latter problem is more challenging, generally, as there is less liquidity for off-market default swaps.

Physical settlement implies a cheapest-to-deliver option because there is normally a list of possible obligations of the named entity that may be delivered in exchange for the face value of the underlying. The alternative, cash settlement, is based on a poll of dealer quotes. Occasionally, settlement is *digital*, that is, for a fixed contractual payment.

ISDA 1999 contracts allow for default in several forms: bankruptcy, failure to pay, restructuring, repudiation/moratorium, obligation default, and obligation acceleration. The definition of bankruptcy, however, is broad and vague (see Tolk, 2001). The definition of *Restructuring as a Covered Credit*

Event (RAACE) caused particular problems in 2000, with the default of Conseco.

CDS dealers typically do not like RAACE, which makes the cheapest-to-deliver option valuable and difficult to hedge and to price for physically settled CDS, because restructuring does not usually cause acceleration of all obligations. (Unaccelerated long-maturity debt is usually worth less than short-maturity debt.) Commercial banks, on the other hand, often like RAACE, as they are often seeking coverage for restructuring.

In May 2001, ISDA issued *modified restructuring* language in CDS contracts. This tightened the definition of restructuring, calling for multiple holders of the underlying, and for consent among 66% of them for restructuring. For physical settlement, the new ISDA contract tightens the set of deliverables by calling for a restructuring maturity limitation (RML) and a transferability requirement.

8.3. Simple Credit-Swap Spreads

We assume throughout that the credit-swap counterparties, A and B, are default-free, so as to avoid pricing the impact of their default, which can be treated by considering the correlations among default risks of the counterparties and the underlying, as in Chapter 10.

For this section, we assume that the contingent payment amount specified in the credit swap is the difference $100 - Y(\tau)$ between the face value and the market value $Y(\tau)$ of the underlying note at the credit event time τ. We begin with the simplest case in which the underlying note issued by C is a floating-rate note. We explain the pricing in stages, adding complications as we go.

8.3.1. Credit-Swap Spreads: Starter Case

Our assumptions for this starter case are as follows:

1. The underlying floating-rate note issued by C is initially at par, that is, has an initial market value equal to the notional, say 100, of the credit swap.
2. It is costless to short the underlying note issued by C. We relax this assumption in the next section.
3. There are no transactions costs, such as bid-ask spreads, in cash markets for the default-free or the underlying note issued by party C.
4. There exists a default-free floating-rate note, whose floating coupon rate at date t is denoted R_t. The coupon payments on the underlying note issued by C are contractually specified to be $R_t + S$, for a fixed spread S. In practice, floating-rate-note spreads are usually relative to LIBOR, or some other benchmark floating rate that need not be

a pure default-free rate. There is no difficulty for our analysis if the pure default-free floating rate R_t and the reference rate, say LIBOR, differ by a constant. One should bear in mind that the short-term government yield is not a pure default-free interest rate, because of repo specials (as we discuss shortly) as well as the "moneyness" and tax advantages of many government securities. A better benchmark is the general collateral rate (GCR) for the tenor of the reference floating rate, which is close to default-free and has typically been close to LIBOR, with a slowly varying spread to LIBOR, in U.S. markets. For example, suppose the note issued by C is at a spread of 100 basis points to LIBOR, which in turn is at a spread to the general collateral rate. While varying over time, suppose this spread is about 5 basis points. Then, for our purposes, an approximation of the spread of the underlying note issued by C to the default-free floating rate would be 105 basis points.

5. The termination payment given a credit event is made at the immediately following coupon date on the underlying note. If not, there is a question of accrued interest, which is messy and perhaps not terribly interesting, but which can be accommodated by standard time-value calculations, as shown later.

6. The credit swap is settled, if terminated by the stated credit event, by the physical delivery of the underlying note in exchange for cash in the amount of its face value. We suppose that no substitutions are allowed. In practice, there is an effective cheapest-to-deliver option associated with the right of the buyer of protection to deliver any of a contractually specified range of obligations of the underlying name, as discussed earlier.

7. Tax effects can be ignored. If not, the calculations to follow apply after tax, using the tax rate of investors who are indifferent to purchasing the default swap at its market price.

With these assumptions in place, one can "price" the credit swap at origination, that is, compute the at-market credit-swap spread U of Figure 8.1, by the following arbitrage argument, based on a synthesis of party B's cash flows on the credit swap. One can short the underlying par note issued by C for an initial cash receivable of 100, invest this 100 in a par default-free floating-rate note, and hold this portfolio through maturity or the stated credit event, whichever is earlier. In the meantime, one pays the coupons on the underlying note issued by C and receives the coupons on the default-free floating-rate note. The net paid is the spread S over the default-free floating rate of the par note of C. This synthetic default swap, under its ideal assumptions, is illustrated in Figure 8.2.

If the credit event occurs before maturity, one liquidates the portfolio at

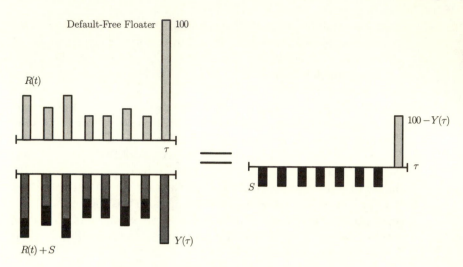

Figure 8.2.   *Synthetic credit swap cash flows.*

the coupon date immediately after the event time, collecting the difference $100 - Y(\tau)$ between the market value of the default-free floating-rate note (which is 100 on any coupon date) and the market value $Y(\tau)$ of the C-issued note. Combining the above cash flows with those received on the credit swap by the seller of protection results in a net constant annuity cash flow of $U - S$, until maturity or termination. We must therefore have $U = S$ if there is no arbitrage for the buyer or seller of protection and no other costs.

8.3.2. Repo Specials and Transaction Costs

An important common violation of the assumptions in the previous starter case is the ability to freely shortsell the underlying note issued by C. This transaction is normally conducted via a repurchase agreement, or *repo*. As illustrated in Figure 8.3, we can view a repo as a collateralized loan by Jane to Dick. The collateral is a specific bond (or other asset). The agreement requires Dick to repurchase the bond after the term T of the repo, for a price that is quoted in terms of the repo rate R. In order to short the bond, Jane could, upon receiving it from Dick as collateral, sell it, as illustrated in Figure 8.4. At the term of the repo, Jane would need to buy the note in the market in order to return the collateral to Dick.

For cases in which a particular bond is difficult to obtain as collateral, the associated repo rate R may be below the typical or general collateral rate, raising the costs of shorting. Called a *repo special*, this may raise the price of

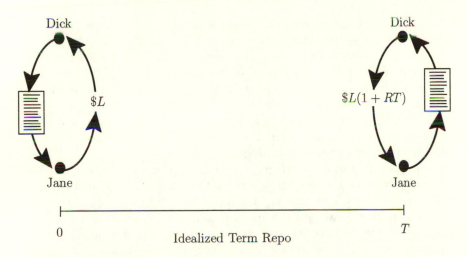

Figure 8.3. *A repurchase agreement as a collateralized loan at repo rate R, term T.*

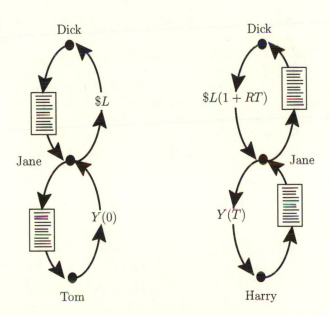

Figure 8.4. *Shorting by reverse repo and sale.*

the underlying bond, which now offers the prospect of cheap borrowing in addition to its directly promised cash flows (see, e.g., Duffie, 1996).

In synthesizing a default swap, repo specials raise the effective default-swap spread above the yield spread on the underlying bond. Moreover, one may expend resources in arranging the repo (especially if the note issued by C is rare or otherwise difficult to obtain). In addition, particularly with risky floating-rate notes, there may be a substantial bid-ask spread in the market for the underlying note at initiation of the repo (when one sells) and at termination (when one buys).

Suppose that one can arrange a term reverse repo collateralized by the underlying note issued by C, with maturity equal to the maturity date of the credit swap. The term repo special is the difference Z between the general collateral rate and the specific collateral rate for the underlying note for that term. In order to short the underlying note, one would then effectively pay an extra annuity Z, and the synthetic default-swap spread would be approximately $S + Z$. Because the term repo does not necessarily terminate at the credit event, this is not an exact arbitrage-based spread. However, because the probability of a credit event well before maturity is typically small, and term repo specials are often small, the difference may not be large in practice.[2]

For the synthesis of the position of the seller of protection in the credit swap, one purchases the note issued by C and places it into a term repo in order to capture the term repo special. In practice, long-term repos are difficult to arrange, and the shorter risks changes in the repo special or even a *short squeeze* under which the provider of the underlying note refuses to renew the repurchase agreement and the note cannot be obtained from another source. Failure to deliver the underlying asset can result in penalties, including lost repo interest or even a *buy-in*, under which the collateral note must be purchased in the market, sometimes at a significant cost to the shorter.

If there are transaction costs in the cash market for the underlying note, then the credit-swap broker-dealer may incur risk from uncovered credit-swap positions or transaction costs or some of each, and may charge an additional premium. With two-sided market making and diversification, it is not clear how quickly these costs and risks build up over a portfolio of positions. We do not consider these effects directly here. In practice, for illiquid entities, the credit-swap spread can vary substantially from the par

---

[2] If the term repo rate applies to the credit-swap maturity, then $S + Z$ is a lower bound on the theoretical credit-swap premium. It has been noted to the authors that in France, perhaps among other jurisdictions, term repos apparently terminate at maturity *or default of the collateral*, whichever is first. This makes the default-swap spread $U = S + Z$ theoretically correct under our other assumptions.

floating-rate spread, according to discussions with traders. Evidence of this is provided during our discussion of asset swaps at the end of this chapter.

We emphasize the difference between a transaction cost and a repo special. The former simply widens the bid-ask spread on a default swap, increasing the default-swap spread quoted by a broker-dealer who sells a credit swap and reducing the quoted default swap when a broker-dealer is asked by a customer to buy a default swap from the customer. A repo special, however, is not itself a transaction cost, but rather can be thought of as an extra source of income on the underlying note issued by C, effectively changing its spread relative to the default-free rate. The existence of substantial specials, which raise the cost of providing the default swap, do not necessarily increase the bid-ask spread. For example, in synthesizing a short position in a default swap, one can place the associated long position in the underlying note issued by C into a repo position and profit from the repo special.

In summary, under our assumptions to this point, a dealer can broker a default swap (i.e., take the position of party A) at a spread of approximately $S + Z$, with a bid-ask spread of K, where (1) S is the par floating-rate spread on the underlying; (2) Z is the term repo special on par floating-rate notes issued by C or otherwise the annuitized price (before transaction costs) of maintaining a short position in the underlying note to the termination of the credit swap; and (3) K reflects any annuitized transaction costs (e.g., cash-market bid-ask spreads) for hedging, any risk premium for unhedged portions of the risk (which would apply in imperfect capital markets), overhead, and a dealer margin.

There have apparently been cases in which liquidity in a credit swap has been sufficient to allow some traders to quote term repo rates for the underlying collateral by reference to the credit-swap spread!

8.3.3. Payment of Accrued Credit-Swap Premium

Some credit swaps specify that the buyer of protection must, at default, pay the credit-swap premium that has accrued since the last coupon date. For example, with a credit-swap spread of 300 basis points and default one-third of the way though the current semiannual, say, coupon period, the buyer of protection would receive face value less recovery value of the underlying, less one-third of the semiannual annuity payment, which is 0.5% of the underlying face value.

For reasonably small default probabilities and intercoupon periods, the expected difference in time between the credit event and the previous coupon date is just slightly less than one-half, in expectation, of the length of an intercoupon period, assuming that the default risk is not concentrated at a coupon date. Thus, for purposes of pricing in all but extreme cases, one can think of the credit swap as equivalent to payment at default of face value less recovery value less one-half of the regular default-swap premium payment. This assumes that the obligation to pay the coupon does not itself force default, which would reduce the correction associated with the accrued swap premium.

In a setting of constant risk-neutral default intensity λ^*, one estimates a reduction in the at-market credit-swap spread for accrued premium— below that spread S appropriate without the accrued-premium feature— of approximately $\lambda^* S / 2n$, where n is the number of coupons per year of the underlying bond. For a pure default swap, S is smaller than λ^* because of partial recovery, so this correction is smaller than $(\lambda^*)^2 / 2n$, which is negligible for small λ^*. For example, with semiannual credit-swap coupon intervals and $\lambda^* = 200$ basis points, we have a correction of under 1 basis point for this accrued premium effect. This would be a high estimate of the effect of accrual of the CDS rate if the default risk is concentrated on coupon dates when there is no accrued premium.

8.3.4. Accrued Interest on the Underlying Note

For purposes of the synthetic credit swap illustrated in Figure 8.2, there is also a question of the accrued interest payment on the default-free floating-rate note. The typical credit swap specifies payment of the difference between the face value *without* accrued interest and the market value of the underlying note. The synthetic credit-swap portfolio pictured in Figure 8.2 (long default-free floater, short defaultable floater), however, is worth face value *plus* accrued interest on the default-free note less recovery on the underlying defaultable note. If the credit event involves default of the underlying note, then the previous arbitrage argument is not quite right.

Consider, for example, a 1-year default swap with semiannual coupons. Suppose the LIBOR rate is 8%. Assuming that default arrives at an intensity that is not high and is not expected to change significantly between coupon dates, we expect roughly half of the coupon to be accrued during a coupon period within which default occurs, ignoring default that is instigated by the coupon payment itself. The expected value of the accrued interest at default on the default-free note in our example is approximately 2% of face value. Suppose the risk-neutral intensity of the credit event is 4%. Then there is a reduction in market value of the credit swap to the buyer of protection of roughly 8 basis points of face value and therefore a reduction of the at-market credit-swap spread of roughly 8 basis points.

More generally, consider a credit swap with relatively small and constant default probabilities, and suppose a relatively flat term structure of default-free rates. The reduction in the at-market credit-swap spread for the accrued-interest effect, below the par floating rate spread plus effective repo special, is approximately $\lambda^* r / 2n$, where λ^* is the risk-neutral intensity of the credit event, r is the default-free interest rate, and n is the number of coupons per year of the underlying bond. Of course, one could work out the effect more precisely with a term-structure model, as noted later.

8.3.5. If the Underlying Is a Fixed-Rate Note?

If the underlying note issued by entity C is a fixed-rate note, one can again resort to the assumption that its recovery of face value at default is the same as that of a par floater of the same seniority. (This is reasonable from a strictly legalistic interpretation if the credit event is bankruptcy.) In this case, we would once again have a default-swap spread of $S + Z$, where S is the par floating-rate spread and Z is the effective term repo special. If there is no reference par floating-rate note, however, then one must again "back it out" from other market prices. It is known that the credit spreads on par fixed-rate and par floating-rate notes of the same credit quality are approximately equal (Duffie and Liu, 2001).[3] Thus, if the only reference spread is a par fixed spread F, then it would be reasonably safe to use F in place of S in estimating the default-swap spread.

For example, Figure 8.5 shows a close relationship between the CDS rate and par fixed-coupon yield spreads for the same credit quality.[4] Some of the difference appearing in Figure 8.5 between the default-swap spread and the par fixed-coupon yield spread is in fact the accrued-interest effect discussed earlier.

It is sometimes said that if the underlying is a fixed-rate bond, then the reference par floating-rate spread may be taken to be the asset-swap spread. The usefulness of this assumption is questionable in many cases and is considered in the last section of this chapter.

8.4. Model-Based CDS Rates

Instead of pricing a CDS in terms of other traded instruments, one can price it directly using an intensity-based model, with the concepts introduced in

---

[3] The floating-rate spread is known theoretically to be slightly higher with the typical upward-sloping term structure, but the difference is typically on the order of 1 basis point or less on a 5-year note per 100 basis points of yield spread to the default-free rate. See Duffie and Liu (2001) for details.

[4] This figure is based on an illustrative correlated multifactor CIR model of default-free short rates and default arrival intensities. The short-rate model is a three-factor CIR model calibrated to recent behavior in the term structure of LIBOR swap rates. The risk-neutral default-arrival intensity model is set for an initial arrival intensity of 200 basis points, with 100% initial volatility in intensity, mean-reverting in risk-neutral expectation at 25% per year to 200 basis points until default. For details, see Duffie (1998a). The results depend on the degree of correlation, mean reversion, and volatility among short rates and default arrival intensities.

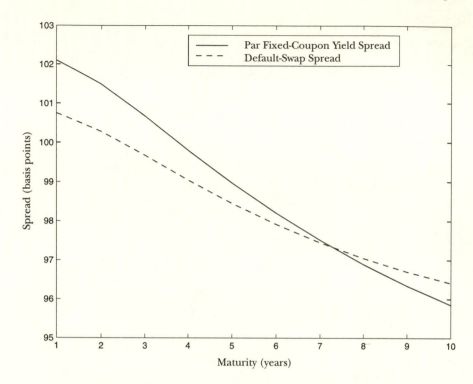

Figure 8.5. *Term structures of bond and default-swap spreads.*

Chapter 5. This section outlines this direct approach, beginning with the case of a constant risk-neutral default intensity.

8.4.1. The Case of Constant Intensity

We begin by supposing that default occurs at a risk-neutral constant intensity λ^*. We let $a_i(\lambda^*)$ be the market value at time 0 of receiving one unit of account at the ith coupon date $T(i)$ in the event that default is after that date and nothing otherwise. We have

$$a_i(\lambda^*) = e^{-[\lambda^* + y(i)]T(i)}, \tag{8.1}$$

where $T(i)$ is the maturity of the ith coupon date and $y(i)$ is the continuously compounding default-free yield to the ith coupon date, so that $\delta[0, T(i)] = e^{-y(i)T(i)}$. Likewise, under these assumptions, the market value of receiving one unit of account at $T(i)$ if default occurs between $T(i-1)$ and $T(i)$ is

$$b_i(\lambda^*) = e^{-y(i)T(i)}(e^{-\lambda^* T(i-1)} - e^{-\lambda^* T(i)}). \tag{8.2}$$

The price of an annuity of one unit of account paid at each coupon date until default or maturity $T = T(n)$, whichever comes first, is

$$A(\lambda^*, T) = a_1(\lambda^*) + \cdots + a_n(\lambda^*). \tag{8.3}$$

The value of a payment of one unit of account at the first coupon date after default, provided the default date is before the maturity date $T = T(n)$, is

$$B(\lambda^*, T) = b_1(\lambda^*) + \cdots + b_n(\lambda^*). \tag{8.4}$$

We suppose that the loss of face value at default has a risk-neutral expectation of L. Then, given the CDS maturity date T and CDS rate U, and given the default-risk-free term structure, we can compute the market value $V(\lambda^*, L, T, U)$ of the default swap, per unit of notional, as

$$V(\lambda^*, L, T, U) = B(\lambda^*, T)L - A(\lambda^*, T)U. \tag{8.5}$$

The at-market default swap spread $U(\lambda^*, T, L)$ is obtained by solving the equation $V(\lambda^*, L, T, U) = 0$ for U, leaving the model-based CDS rate

$$U(\lambda^*, T, L) = \frac{B(\lambda^*, T)L}{A(\lambda^*, T)}. \tag{8.6}$$

For more accuracy, one can easily account for the difference in time between the credit event and the subsequent coupon date. At small default intensities, this difference is just slightly more than one-half of the inter-coupon period of the credit swap, ignoring any concentration of default probabilities at the underlying coupon dates, so this effect can be treated analytically in a direct manner. Alternatively, a simple approximate adjustment can be made by noting that the effect is equivalent to the accrued-interest effect in adjusting the par floating-rate spread to the credit-swap spread. As noted previously, this causes an increase in the implied default-swap spread on the order of $\lambda^* r/2n$.

Estimates of the risk-neutral expected loss L of face value at default and the risk-neutral default intensity λ^* can be obtained from the prices of bonds or notes issued by the same entity C, from risk-free rates, and from recovery data for bonds or notes of the same seniority, as discussed in Chapter 6. However, the effects of liquidity on bond prices is difficult to disentangle from the effect of credit risk.

For example, suppose that some, possibly different, floating-rate note issued by the same entity C sells at a price of $\hat{P}$, has a maturity of $\hat{T}$, and has a spread of $\hat{S}$. Suppose the expected default loss, relative to face value, is $\hat{L}$.

Under these assumptions, by purchase of a risk-free floater and shorting a floating-rate note issued by C (with no repo specials), we have a portfolio with a market value of

$$1 - \hat{P} = B(\lambda^*, \hat{T})\hat{L} - A(\lambda^*, \hat{T})\hat{S}. \qquad (8.7)$$

This equation can be solved for the implied risk-neutral intensity λ^*.

Provided the reference prices of notes used for this purpose are near par, there is a certain robustness here associated with uncertainty about recovery, as an upward bias in L results in a downward bias in λ^*, and these errors (for small λ^*) approximately cancel each other when estimating the mark-to-market value $V(\lambda^*, L, T, U)$ of the default swap. For this robustness, it is better to use a reference note of approximately the same maturity as that of the default swap. Ideally, the note underlying the default swap has an available price quotation.

If the note issued by C that is chosen for price reference is a fixed-rate note, with price $\hat{P}$, coupon rate $\hat{c}$, expected loss at default relative to face value of $\hat{L}$, and maturity $\hat{T}$, then we would use the relationship

$$\hat{P} = A(\lambda^*, \hat{T})\hat{c} + B(\lambda^*, \hat{T})(1 - \hat{L}) + \delta(0, \hat{T})e^{-\hat{T}\lambda^*}, \qquad (8.8)$$

in order to estimate the risk-neutral intensity λ^*.

As with the case of coupon yield spreads discussed in Chapter 5, the effects on CDS rates of varying λ^* and L are more or less offsetting. (That is, if one overestimates L by a factor of 2, then for a given reference coupon rate, one will underestimate λ^* by a factor of roughly 2, using even a crude term-structure model, and the implied par-coupon spread will be relatively unaffected, meaning that the default-swap spread is also relatively unaffected.)

If there are multiple reference notes with maturities similar to that of the underlying default swap, then one could, for example, average their implied intensities, or discard outliers and then average, or use nonlinear least-squares fitting, or conduct some similar pragmatic estimation procedure. There may, however, be important institutional differences among different types of obligations that affect relative recovery. For example, in negotiated workouts, issuers may choose the investor group that they wish to favor, for public-relations purposes or other reasons. For sovereign debt, Chapter 6 discusses several distinctions among various types of obligations that could have an important effect on their relative recoveries at default.

Default swaps are a benchmark for credit pricing. For example, it is sometimes the case that the at-market default-swap quote U^* is available, and one wishes to estimate the implied risk-neutral intensity λ^*. This is obtained by solving $U(\lambda^*, T, L) = U^*$ for λ^*. As suggested above, the modeled result depends more or less linearly on the modeling assumption for the expected fractional loss at default. Sensitivity analysis is suggested if the objective is to apply the intensity estimate λ^* to price an issue that has substantially different cash flow features than the reference default swap.

8.4.2. The Term Structure of Forward Default Rates

If the reference credit pricing information is for maturities different than that of the credit swap, it may be advisable to estimate the term structure of risk-neutral forward default rates. Risk-neutral forward default rates coincide with risk-neutral intensities when the latter are deterministic. Otherwise, for the distinction, refer to Chapter 3. For example, suppose that the risk-neutral forward default rate between coupon dates $T(i-1)$ and $T(i)$ is $f^*(i)$. In this case, assuming risk-neutral independence of default risk and other risks, and given the term structure $f^* = (f^*(1), \ldots, f^*(n))$ of risk-neutral forward default rates, we have (assuming equal intercoupon time intervals) the extensions of (8.1) and 8.2) given by

$$a_i(f^*) = e^{-[H(i)+y(i)]T(i)}, \tag{8.9}$$

where $H(i) = \left[f^*(1) + \cdots + f^*(i) \right]/i$, and

$$b_i(f^*) = e^{-y(i)T(i)}(e^{-H(i-1)T(i-1)} - e^{-H(i)T(i)}). \tag{8.10}$$

With these changes in place, all of our previous results apply. As there is a well-established dependence of credit spreads on maturity, it is wise to consider this dependence when the reference credit price information is based on a significantly different duration of instrument than the note underlying the credit swap. When information regarding the shape of the term structure of risk-neutral forward default rates for the reference entity C is critical but not available, it may be pragmatic to assume that the shape is that of comparable issuers. For example, one might use the shape implied by Bloomberg par yield spreads for firms of the same credit rating and then scale the implied default rates to match the pricing available for the reference entity. This is ad hoc, and subject to the modeler's judgment.

A more sophisticated approach would be to build a term-structure model for a stochastically varying risk-neutral default-intensity process λ^*, as outlined in Chapter 5. Default-swap pricing, however, is reasonably robust to the model of intensities, calibrated to given spread correlations and volatilities, as was demonstrated for the case of bond yield spreads in Chapter 5.

If the notes used for pricing reference are on special in the repo market, an estimate of the "hidden" term repo specialness Z should be included in the above calculations, as an add-on to the floating-rate spread $\hat{S}$ or the fixed-rate coupon c, when estimating the implied risk-neutral forward default rate f^*.

Suppose, for simplicity, "instant" payment at default, rather than payment at the subsequent coupon date as assumed above. The factor $b_i(f^*)$ is then replaced by

$$b_i^*(f^*) = e^{-[y(i-1)+H(i-1)]T(i-1)}k_i(f^*(i)), \qquad (8.11)$$

where

$$k_i(f^*(i)) = \frac{f^*(i)}{f^*(i)+\varphi(i)}\left(1 - e^{-[f^*(i)+\varphi(i)][T(i)-T(i-1)]}\right) \qquad (8.12)$$

is the price at time $T(i-1)$, conditional on survival to that date, of a claim that pays one unit of account at the default time, provided the default time is before $T(i)$, and where $\varphi(i)$ is the instantaneous default-free forward interest rate, assumed constant between $T(i-1)$ and $T(i)$. This can be checked by noting that the risk-neutral probability density of the time to default, given survival to $T(i-1)$, is $e^{-f^*(i)u}f^*(i)$ over the interval $[T(i-1), T(i)]$. For reasonably short intercoupon periods, low default probabilities and small interest rates, the impact of assuming instant recovery rather than recovery at the subsequent coupon date is relatively small.

8.5. The Role of Asset Swaps

An asset swap is a derivative security that can be viewed, in its simplest version, as a portfolio consisting of a fixed-rate note and an interest-rate swap of the same notional amount that pays fixed and receives floating, say LIBOR, to the stated maturity of the underlying fixed-rate note. At the origination of the asset swap, the fixed rate of the interest-swap component is chosen so that the market value of the asset swap is equal to the face value of the underlying note. We can also view the interest rate swap as one that pays fixed-rate coupons at a rate equal to the coupon rate C on the underlying fixed-rate swap and receives floating-rate coupons at a rate equal to LIBOR plus some fixed spread, say, S. This spread S is called the *asset-swap spread*.

Before considering default, one might view an asset swap as a synthetic par-value floating-rate note. The net coupons of the interest-rate swap are normally exchanged through maturity, however, even if the underlying note defaults and its coupon payments are thereby discontinued. Thus, as illustrated in Figure 8.6, with default risk an asset swap is not equivalent to a par floating-rate note because the event of default leaves the tail end of an interest-rate swap in place. Thus, the asset-swap spread S need not be the

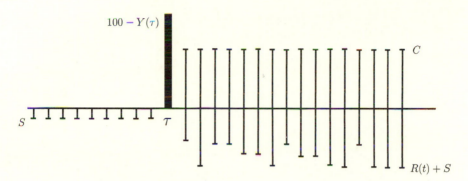

Figure 8.6. *Failed attempt to synthesize a credit swap from an asset swap.*

same as the par floating-rate spread of the same credit quality, as we shall see shortly in a numerical example.

The markets for many fixed-rate notes are sometimes less liquid than the markets for the associated asset swaps. Thus, asset-swap spreads, because they are closely related to CDS rates, are often used as benchmarks for CDS pricing. As we have explained, because an asset swap involves an interest-rate swap after default, the asset-swap spread need not be an accurate proxy for the CDS rate, especially if the underlying fixed-rate note is trading at a severe premium or discount to par. The asset-swap spread and the term structure of default-free rates can, however, be used together to obtain an implied par floating-rate spread, from which the default-swap spread can be estimated.

Figure 8.7 illustrates that the asset-swap spread is sometimes an unreliable proxy for the default-swap spread. The figure shows the divergence between the term structures of asset-swap spreads for premium (coupon rate 400 basis points over the par rate), par, and discount (coupon rate 400 basis points under the par rate) bonds. Of course, by definition, the asset-swap spread for a par underlying note is the same as the fixed-coupon par spread, which we have already suggested as a reasonable proxy for the floating-rate spread.[5] All three illustrated bonds have the same CDS rate, assuming equal recovery at default, but clearly have rather different asset-swap spreads.

Recently, there has emerged a variant of the asset swap called the *clean asset swap,* with the same features as the former except that the embedded interest swap has a contractual termination at the time of default of the underlying fixed-rate note. The clean asset swap, ignoring the default risk of the

---

[5] This figure is based on the same multifactor CIR defaultable term-structure model used for illustration in Chapter 5.

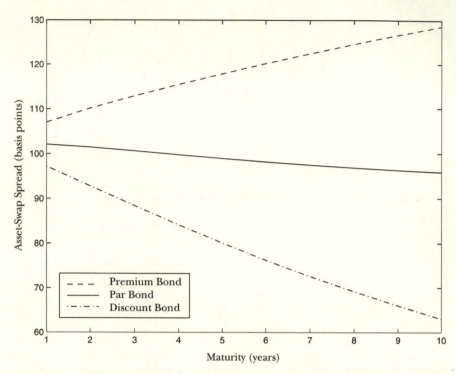

Figure 8.7. *Term structures of asset-swap spreads. The premium-bond coupon rate is 400 basis points above par and the discount-bond coupon rate is 400 basis points below par.*

Table 8.1. *Asset-Swap Spreads versus Default-Swap Rates for Selected Names, January 25, 2002*

Company	Default swap	Asset swap
IBM	33	0
J. P. Morgan/Chase	38	15
Ford Motor Credit	190	160
Merrill Lynch	52	15

Source: Bank of America.

asset-swap provider, is essentially a par floating-rate note for purposes of estimating the CDS rate.

In practice, it is not unusual for certain asset-swap spreads to be substantially tighter than credit default swap rates on the same underlying debt. For example, Table 8.1 shows spreads for asset swaps and default swaps in January 2002 for a selection of issuers. It was noted by a market participant that on February 6, 2002, hedging demand by banks and convertible-bond hedge funds drove the spread between default swaps and asset swaps on Ford Motor Credit for a short time during the day to over 75 basis points before narrowing to 35 basis points by the next day.

As of March 20, 2001, certain 5-year convertible bonds issued by Tyco and by Enron (both rated Baa1 by Moody's) had asset-swap spreads of 70–80 basis points, according to J. P. Morgan, whereas the same bonds had CDS rates of roughly 130 basis points and 170 basis points, respectively. Market news sources indicated that these bonds had been bought by convertible hedge funds, which were willing to pay large CDS rates in order to buy protection against the default risk in order to focus on a perceived "cheapness" of the convertible's equity volatility, following a strategy considered in Chapter 9.

9

Optional Credit Pricing

THIS CHAPTER REVIEWS the pricing of optional credit products, such as spread options and option-embedded corporate bonds, including callable and convertible debt. While the basic conceptual pricing issues treated here are rather similar to those for credit products without embedded option that were presented in Chapters 5–8, there are some important new practical considerations. Of U.S. corporate bonds, the number that are callable is roughly twice the number of those that are noncallable, according to the bond history data base provided by FISD, Inc. In order to use callable debt prices as a reference for measuring credit risk and for pricing other credit-sensitive instruments such as default swaps, however, one must "strip out" the optionality of the bond. In order to do so, one must have a callable-debt pricing model in which the volatility of the underlying bond price is linked to the volatility of interest rates as well as the volatility induced by changes in credit quality. The techniques introduced in this chapter allow for this. Likewise, many banks offer their corporate clients irrevocable lines of credit at fixed spreads over reference rates, such as LIBOR. Such lines of credit are essentially spread options.

A convertible bond provides the investor with an option to convert the bond into a given number of shares of equity for each unit of face value. Convertible debt is normally also callable by the issuer, which raises some relatively complex valuation issues, given that options are held by both the issuer and the investor and given the sometimes puzzling laxity with which issuers appear to exercise their call options, a question addressed in this chapter.

9.1. Spread Options

As our first and simplest illustration of the valuation of optional credit products, we consider the pricing of spread options, a type of credit derivative that conveys the right to put (sell) a given corporate or sovereign bond at a

194

given spread over a reference yield. An irrevocable line of credit at a given spread can also be viewed as a spread option, for it gives an issuer the right, in effect, to sell its own debt at a fixed spread over a reference instrument, such as LIBOR. There is a distinction, however, in that, upon exercising the option to use a line of credit, the borrower's credit risk may be increased, whereas the exercise by another investor of a spread option does not generally change the credit quality of the underlying bond.

Here, we treat options to sell debt at a given spread over a fixed-rate default-free reference, but options to sell debt at a given spread to a reference swap rate or a floating rate, such as LIBOR, could be priced with a similar model.

9.1.1. Pricing Framework

For a simple pricing example, we suppose that the underlying corporate or sovereign bond pays semiannual coupons, is noncallable, and matures at a given date T_m. The bond's price at time t is quoted in terms of its current yield spread S_t over a reference note of semiannual coupons and of the same maturity. The credit-spread derivative to be priced is an option to sell the defaultable bond at a contractually stipulated spread $\underline{S}$ over the reference yield Z_T at a stated exercise date T. If the actual market spread, S_T at time T, is less than the strike spread $\underline{S}$, then the spread option expires as worthless. If the actual market spread S_T at T exceeds $\underline{S}$, however, then the buyer of protection receives the difference between the price at a spread $\underline{S}$ and the price at the actual spread S_T, which is

$$P(\underline{S} + Z_T, T) - P(S_T + Z_T, T),　\qquad (9.1)$$

where $P(y, t)$ is the price of the underlying bond at time t, if calculated as though default-free with a yield of y.

Such options are, historically, among the earliest OTC credit derivatives, having been sold in the early 1990s on Argentinian Brady bonds, among other sovereign debt. The payoff formula given by (9.1) implies that cash settlement of the option is equivalent to the delivery of the underlying defaultable bond by the buyer of protection in return for a payment by the seller of protection of what its price would be, $P(\underline{S} + Z_T, T)$, if it were to trade instead at the strike spread $\underline{S}$.

As credit spreads underlying credit derivatives are usually relatively volatile, or may jump, the issuer of the credit derivative may wish to incorporate a cap on the degree of protection, as illustrated in Figure 9.1. For example, if, at any time t before expiration, the market spread S_t is greater than or equal to a given spread cap $\overline{S} > \underline{S}$, then the credit derivative would immediately pay

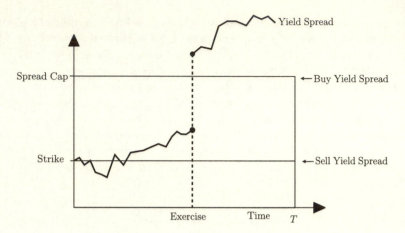

Figure 9.1.   *Capped spread option.*

$$P(\underline{S} + Z_t, t) - P(\overline{S} + Z_t, t).$$

In effect, then, the credit derivative insures an owner of the corporate bond against increases in spread above the strike rate $\underline{S}$ up to a maximum of $\overline{S}$. With this cap, at time $U = \min\left(T, \min\{t : S_t \geq \overline{S}\}\right)$, the spread option pays the amount

$$X = \max\{P(\underline{S} + Z_U, U) - P(\min(S_U, \overline{S}) + Z_U, U), 0\}, \qquad (9.2)$$

and therefore has a price at time 0 of

$$V = E_0^*\left(e^{\int_0^U -r(s)\,ds} X\right), \qquad (9.3)$$

where E_0^* denotes risk-neutral expectation, and r_t is the default-free short rate at time t. Our objective is to calculate, for given parameters, the spread-option price V. The reference yield Z_t need not be that associated with the default-free short rate r_t in order for (9.3) to apply. For example, Z_t could be the LIBOR swap rate for the same maturity.

We have assumed for simplicity that the seller of protection is itself default-free. Otherwise, one would simply discount the payoff of the spread option at the default-adjusted short rate corresponding to the seller of protection, in place of the default-free short rate $r(s)$ in (9.3).

For simplicity, we assume that the default risk of the bond underlying the spread option is captured by a risk-neutral default-intensity process λ^* and by a given fractional loss L in market value at default.

In order to value this credit derivative, one requires the following as inputs to a pricing model: (1) the coupon and maturity structure of the default-free and defaultable bonds; (2) the parameters $(\underline{S}, \overline{S}, T)$ of the spread-option contract; (3) the fractional default loss L coefficient; (4) the risk-neutral behavior of the reference yield process Z and the default-free short-rate process r; (5) the risk-neutral intensity process λ^*; and (6) the price behavior of the underlying bond *after* default. The postdefault bond price behavior is only relevant if, upon default, the spread cap $\overline{S}$ is not exceeded. For the examples that we present, however, the spread passes through the cap $\overline{S}$ at default, so postdefault price behavior plays no role.

For our numerical example, we take a two-factor risk-neutral affine state process X of the CIR type (B) reviewed in Section 7.2.1. The state variables X_{1t} and X_{2t} satisfy

$$dX_{it} = \kappa_{it}(\theta_{it} - X_{it})\, dt + \sigma_{it}\sqrt{X_{it}}\, dB_{it}^*, \qquad (9.4)$$

where κ_{it}, θ_{it}, and σ_{it} are deterministic, but possibly time-dependent, coefficients, while B_1^* and B_2^* are risk-neutrally independent standard Brownian motions. We take the short-rate process $r_t = X_{1t}$, and the short-spread process $s_t = \lambda_t^* L = \alpha X_{1t} + X_{2t}$, for a parameter α that allows for correlation between interest rates and credit spreads. The reference yield Z_t will be that of a default-free bond (associated with the default-free short rate r_t), of the same maturity as the underlying bond.

The initial state vector $X(0)$ and the coefficients $(\alpha, \kappa, \theta, \sigma)$ are chosen to match given discount functions for default-free and corporate debt, initial default-free and defaultable yield volatility curves, and a given initial correlation between the yield on the reference default-free bond and the yield spread of the defaultable bond. By *initial* vol curves and correlation, we mean the instantaneous volatility at time zero of forward rates, by maturity, and the instantaneous correlation at time zero between the yield Z_t on the reference default-free note and the yield spread S_t on the defaultable bond.[1]

9.1.2. Illustrative Numerical Example

We consider variations from the following base-case assumptions:

- The underlying defaultable note and the default-free reference note are 5-year par noncallable bonds paying semiannual coupons, with

---

[1] By Ito's lemma, both Z and S are Ito processes, other than at coupon dates and default. We can therefore write $dZ_t = \mu_Z(t)\, dt + \sigma_Z(t)\, dB_t^*$ and $dS_t = \mu_S(t)\, dt + \sigma_S(t)\, dB_t^*$. The initial volatility of Z is $\|\sigma_Z(0)\|/Z_0$. The initial volatility of S is $\|\sigma_S(0)\|/S_0$, and the initial instantaneous correlation between S and Z is $\sigma_Z(0) \cdot \sigma_S(0)/(\|\sigma_S(0)\| \, \|\sigma_Z(0)\|)$. For our parameterization, these are easy numerical calculations, using the Ricatti equations for zero-coupon yields given in Appendix A.

(annualized) coupon rates of 9 and 7%, respectively. Thus, the initial spread S_0 is 200 basis points.

- The spread option has a strike of $\underline{S} = 200$ basis points (i.e., at the money), with maximum protection at a spread cap of $\overline{S} = 500$ basis points and an expiration time of $T = 1$ year.
- The fraction L of market value lost at default is a constant 50%.

The parameter functions κ, θ, and σ and the initial state vector $X(0)$ are set so that: (1) the default-free and defaultable bonds are priced at par, and both forward-rate curves are horizontal; (2) the initial yield volatility on the reference default-free note is 15%; (3) the initial instantaneous correlation between the defaultable bond's yield spread S_t and the default-free reference yield Z_t is zero[2]; and (4) the shape of the default-free forward-rate volatility curve is conventional and does not play a significant role in the pricing of the spread option. The forward-rate spread volatility is a scaling of this same yield volatility curve, chosen so as to attain an initial yield-spread volatility of 40%.

Given the number of parameter functions and initial conditions, there are more degrees of freedom than necessary to meet all of these criteria. We have verified that our pricing of the spread option is not particularly sensitive to reasonable variation within the class of parameters that meet these criteria.

9.1.3. Numerical Option Valuation Algorithm

Our pricing calculations are based on a finite-difference solution of the partial differential equation associated with (9.3), by an alternating-direction implicit (Crank-Nicholson) method that has been found to be quite robust for this purpose. The method is equally suitable for pricing American versions of spread options and other American credit derivatives, as it is based on backward induction. Each lattice point illustrated in Figure 9.2 represents, at the jth time period, a pair of underlying state variables. The algorithm is roughly as follows.

At each state node in the state lattice illustrated in Figure 9.2 and at each discrete time $j - 1$, the value of the spread option is computed as the present value of the prices at each node at the subsequent time j, weighted by their respective risk-neutral probabilities as approximated by the finite-difference method and discounted at the short rate. An extra *default node* is included, which captures the value of the derivative conditional on default between the current and subsequent time.

---

[2] This does not imply that the short rate r and the short spread s are risk-neutrally independent.

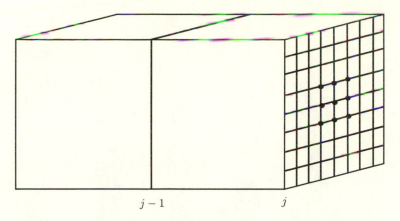

$j - 1$ j

Figure 9.2.   *Lattice-based solution method for two-factor derivative pricing.*

With an American feature, our algorithm is easily adjusted by inserting an exercise-or-not step that replaces the node-contingent present value of the next-period derivative value with the exercise value at that node, if the latter is larger.

At conventional default recovery rates our spread cap $\overline{S}$ is active at default, so our pricing is relatively insensitive to the recovery distribution, given the risk-neutral mean loss at default. This insensitivity would not apply to far-out-of-the-money, uncapped spread options.

9.1.4. Results

At the base case for our illustrative example, the spread option has a market value of approximately 2.1% of the face value of the defaultable bond.[3] Figure 9.3 shows the dependence of the spread-option price, per $100 of face value of the corporate bond, on the recovery rate $1 - L$. With higher recovery at default, the credit derivative is more expensive, for we have fixed the initial yield spread S_0 at the base-case assumption of 200 basis points, implying that the risk-neutral probability of default increases with the recovery rate as we recalibrate the model to maintain the given market spread of 200 basis points. Indeed, then, one can distinguish the separate roles of the risk-neutral default intensity λ^* and the fractional-loss rate L with price information on derivatives that depend nonlinearly on the underlying defaultable bond.

---

[3] We are especially grateful for research assistance in producing these results from Michael Boulware of Susquehanna Investment Group. Additional assistance was provided by Arthur Mezhlumian of Goldman, Sachs and Company. Boulware and Mezhlumian were Ph.D. students at Stanford University when these calculations were done.

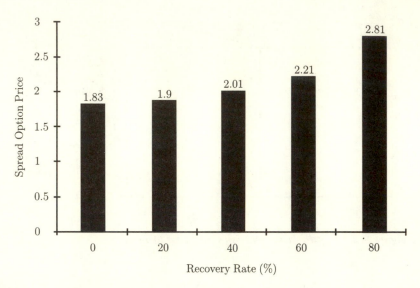

Figure 9.3. *Impact of recovery rate on the credit derivative price, measured in percent of face value. (Source: Duffie and Singleton, 1999.)*

The shape of the term structure of volatility of default-free interest rates has a relatively small impact on the price of the spread option, within typical ranges of parameters. Additional comparative statics show that

- Increasing the spread cap $\overline{S}$ from the base case of 500 up to 900 basis points, holding all else the same, increases the price of the yield-spread option from 2.1 to 2.7% of the underlying face value of debt protected.
- Increasing the strike spread $\underline{S}$ from 200 to 300 basis points reduces the spread option price to 0.7% of face value.
- Increasing the yield-spread volatility from the base case of 40% up to a volatility of 65% increases the price to 2.9% of face value, as shown in Figure 9.4. One can see that this at-the-money spread option price is roughly linear in spread volatility.
- Increasing, from 0 to 0.4, the initial correlation of yield-spread changes with default-free yield changes reduces the yield-spread option price, but only slightly, to 2.0% of face value.
- Extending the expiration date T from 1 to 4 years increases the yield-spread option price to 3.8% of face value.
- Within conventional ranges, the yield-spread option price is relatively insensitive to the default-free yield volatility. For example, as one changes the initial yield volatility of the underlying default-free note

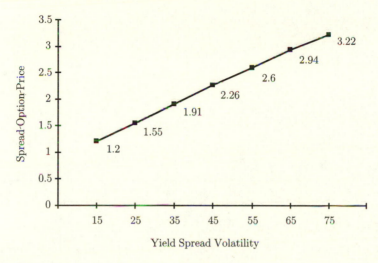

Figure 9.4. *Impact of yield-spread volatility on spread option price, measured in percent of face value.*

from 5 to 25%, the price of the yield-spread option is not affected, up to two significant figures.

In practice, it could easily be the case that some of the spread, and some of the spread volatility, is not directly due to credit risk but rather to liquidity effects of various types. We next consider the pricing implications of supposing that the underlying bond is priced at a short rate that is adjusted for both default risk and illiquidity, of the form $r + \lambda^* L + \ell$, where ℓ represents an illiquidity premium, which can be thought of as a risk-neutral expected rate of fractional loss owing to illiquidity. We suppose that the total adjustment to the short rate, $\lambda^* L + \ell$, is of the same multifactor CIR type considered above and that a constant fraction $\ell / (\lambda^* L + \ell)$ of the short spread is due to illiquidity. As we vary this fraction, we can see in Figure 9.5 how the theoretical price of the yield-spread option is lowered by the associated reduction in the likelihood of a default event, holding the behavior of spreads before default constant. Comparison with the base case, in which spreads are associated entirely with default risk, allows us to see how much of the cost of protection is associated with insurance against outright default, relative to the cost of protection against increases in spread owing to events other than default.

9.2. Callable and Convertible Corporate Debt

We now turn to the valuation of option-embedded corporate bonds. The setting is somewhat more involved than that of a credit derivative, for the

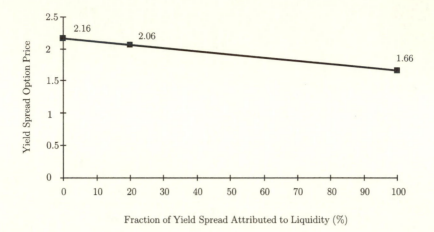

Figure 9.5. *Impact of illiquidity of bond on spread option price, measured in percent of face value.*

capital structure of the issuer may play a significant role. For example, if the issuer itself retains an option to call the bond, various considerations regarding the issuer's capital structure, tax shields, management incentives, and private information may come into play.

For convertible bonds, credit risk and equity risk play connected roles because the option investor may convert the bond into a specified number of shares of equity. Obviously, one prefers a model that accounts for the link between credit risk and equity risk. An intensity-based default model in which the risk-neutral default intensity is linked to the equity price can be convenient.

Convertible bond issuers usually retain the right to call the bond, under certain restrictions, which makes for an interesting analysis of the optionality on each side of the convertible bond contract, as we see later in this chapter. Both of these American options (the issuer's call option and the bond investor's convert option) are treated here by a lattice-based (finite-difference) computational method, extending the method used earlier in the chapter to price spread options.

9.2.1. Capital Structure

As we discussed in Chapter 5, a traditional corporate-debt pricing approach, going back to Black and Scholes (1973) and Merton (1974), treats corporate debt as a derivative security whose payoff depends on the total assets of the firm. In this sense, with a capital structure consisting only of equity and a single zero-coupon bond, the payoff of the bond may be viewed as a function of the assets available at the bond's maturity date, as shown in Figure 9.6.

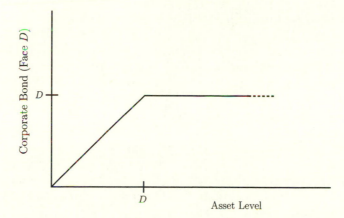

Figure 9.6.   *Corporate bond payoff as a derivative on total firm assets.*

For a bond of this type, with log-normally distributed assets and a normally distributed short-term interest-rate process, Shimko et al. (1993) provide an explicit solution for any zero-coupon noncallable corporate bond price that reflects the asset risk (and therefore the credit risk of the bond), interest-rate risk, and the correlation between the two. In Chapter 6, we discussed a variant in which default occurs at the first time at which assets fall to a given default boundary, such as the face value of debt.

Those pricing corporate debt for day-to-day business purposes, however, have often been reluctant to treat the credit risk of a corporate bond by directly modeling the capital structure of the issuer because capital structures are often complicated, including bonds of different types and maturities, with covenants, call features, convertibility options, prioritization, and many other complexities that are expensive to model. Instead, many popular industry models for callable or convertible corporate debt pricing ignore some of these complex features of a typical firm's capital structure and do not treat debt as a derivative on the underlying firm's asset process.

One conventional approach for pricing corporate bond options and callable corporate debt has been to use the same term-structure model that one uses to price default-free bond options, changing only the initial conditions of the term structure of interest rates in order to match the term structure of yields that is presumed to apply to bonds of the quality of the issuer. This can be misleading, however, for the volatility associated with random fluctuations in the credit risk of the issuer is not properly captured in such a model. An option's value is sensitive to volatility in both interest rates and credit quality, as well as their correlation. One can compensate, in certain cases, by an adjustment to the volatility parameters of the underlying term-structure model, taking the approach of a default-adjusted short-rate model, explained in Chapter 6. Moreover, for certain bonds, randomness associated with uncertain recovery in the event of default has an effect on option pricing that might not be captured by a default-free model, even if that model is recalibrated to correctly capture the predefault behavior of the issuer's credit spreads. For example, a put option struck at a low price, such as $0.50 per $1.00 of face value, would be worth significantly more for a bond with highly uncertain recovery than for a bond with relatively certain recovery of the same mean (or same risk-neutral mean). However, an issuer offering puttable bonds with a put price struck at half the face value of the bond would not normally be expected to be in a position to perform on the option. This complexity may not be critical for conventional callable bonds or convertible bonds, as the embedded options are not typically in the money after default.

We begin with a discussion of callable debt. In practice, most callable bonds are contractually restricted from being called before a stipulated *first-call date*. For example, a 10-no-call-2 is a 10-year bond whose first allowable call date is 2 years from issuance. Market imperfections lead corporations to exercise call options differently than would be specified by a standard *rational-exercise* American option pricing model. Assuming rational exercise as an illustrative starting point, however, we quickly review a traditional callable-bond pricing algorithm. Such an algorithm in a form that is simplified for the purpose of this introductory discussion is illustrated in Figure 9.7. The underlying 3-year annual-coupon bond pays 8% of its face value (100) at the end of each year, until default or maturity. At the end of 3 years, assuming survival, the bond may be redeemed for 108. At each node of the decision tree shown in Figure 9.7, the current default-adjusted short rate of the issuer, in percent, is circled. We recall from Chapter 6 that the default-adjusted short rate is the default-free short rate plus the risk-neutral mean rate of loss owing to default. (One may also add an illiquidity loss rate.) For this simple illustrative example, changes in the default-adjusted short rate constitute the only source of risk other than default. One could build multifactor models for the default-adjusted short rate, as in Chapter 7, with pricing based on the same principles.

The default-adjusted short rate is assumed to move up or down, once a year, with equal risk-neutral probabilities of 0.5, to the levels indicated at the nodes of the figure at the following year. At each decision node, the bond is worth the minimum of the call price, assumed to be 100, and the discounted risk-neutral expected present value of the price at the subsequent year. The step of taking the minimum of these two values of the bond, "dead or alive," arises from our assumption, until further elaboration, that the issuer always exercises the call option so as to minimize the market value of the liability. For example, at the node marked with a default-adjusted short rate of 4% at the end of year 2, the issuer may call immediately after

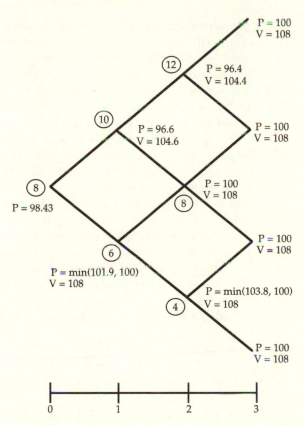

Figure 9.7. *Backward recursive valuation of an 8% annual-coupon bond, callable at face value.*

the coupon payment, and by doing so extinguish the debt with a payment to the bond investor of the call price, 100. Alternatively, the issuer may allow the bond to remain alive to maturity or default. If the bond is not called, the market value of the liability, according the default-adjusted short rate model of Chapter 6, is $(1 + 0.04)^{-1} \times 108 = 103.8$. This is simply the price of a defaultable 1-year zero-coupon bond claiming 108, at a default-adjusted short rate of 4%. At this node in the decision tree, the issuer would therefore, in this simple model, choose to call the bond for the lesser amount of 100, leaving the market value at this node, after the 8% coupon is paid, of $P = \min(103.8, 100) = 100$. The value with the coupon is $V = P + 8 = 108$, as shown. Moving backward in time through the tree, recursively filling in the prices in this manner, node by node, one has the initial market value of 98.43 for the callable bond. A careful reader who has not previously studied callable-bond pricing should perform the calculations necessary to verify this initial price, so as to ease the transition to more realistic pricing algorithms that follow in this chapter.

A direct *rational-pricing* approach such as this, although it can be elaborated with a more complex multifactor default-adjusted short-rate model and with detailed contractual limits on calling, can be misleading. In practice, market imperfections and the presence of other liabilities on issuers's balance sheets may lead issuers to call their debt in a manner that is more complex than would be suggested by a simple rational option pricing model, such as that in Figure 9.7, which assumes that the bond is called by the issuer whenever there is no contractual restriction against calling and whenever, if not called, the price would be higher than the call strike price.

Indeed, corporations have several motives that influence the exercise of a bond option, beyond the present value of cash flows generated by that particular bond. For example, tax shields sometimes provide an incentive to delay the calling of a bond beyond the point suggested by a model that treats only before-tax cash flows. The impact of calling on the pricing of other corporate securities, in light of their joint default risk and perceptions of the issuer's future prospects that are signaled by calling, can either accelerate or delay optimal calling.

In addition, the cost of raising new capital in order to replace the cash used to call a corporate bond can be expensive in imperfect markets, as explained in Chapter 2, which also causes delays in calling debt. For example, a cash-constrained firm may not find it optimal to call and give up 100 in cash in exchange for eliminating a liability that is currently worth more than 100 to bond investors.

9.2.2. Default and Equity Derivative Pricing

In order to allow for pricing algorithms in which the equity price is a guide to credit risk, we begin to consider equity-derivative pricing in settings for which the risk of default by the underlying firm may play a significant role, as for the case of callable and convertible debt, or warrants, on relatively risky firms.

When using an intensity-based defaultable-bond pricing model, it may be reasonable to model the risk-neutral default intensity λ_t^* as a function of the equity price of the issuer, S_t, as in Figure 9.8. This assumes, in effect, that the equity price is sufficient information to judge credit quality. This is particularly convenient for convertible debt, given the link between credit risk and equity conversion value.

If the issuer's capital structure changes significantly owing to other maturing debt during the life of the target bond, one may also wish to allow the risk-neutral default intensity λ_t^* to depend on calendar time t, so that a

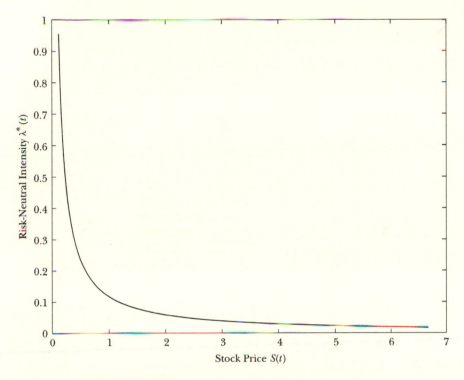

Figure 9.8. *Risk-neutral default intensity $\lambda_t^* = 0.12/S_t$.*

given equity price S_t signifies less credit risk once a significant liability has been met.

Figure 9.8 illustrates two natural boundary properties. First, the risk-neutral default intensity λ_t^* goes to 0 as the current equity price S_t goes to $+\infty$. Second, the risk-neutral default intensity goes to $+\infty$ as the equity price goes to 0. Other than conforming to these boundary properties, the particular functional form that is illustrated in Figure 9.8, $\lambda_t^* = \gamma/S_t$ for some constant parameter $\gamma > 0$, is rather arbitrary and chosen only for its convenience. After specifying the other elements of the model, as we do shortly, one could vary γ or add a constant to this functional form for λ_t^* in order to calibrate the model to a given yield spread or yield-spread volatility.

Figure 9.9 shows a typical equity-derivative pricing model. For each up-down branch in the binomial tree shown for the equity price, the price $C(S, t)$ of the equity derivative is indicated at time t, at a generic node in the underlying binomial equity tree at which the current underlying equity price is S. Before consideration of credit risk, as in the classical binomial derivative pricing model, we have the backward-recursive pricing algorithm given by

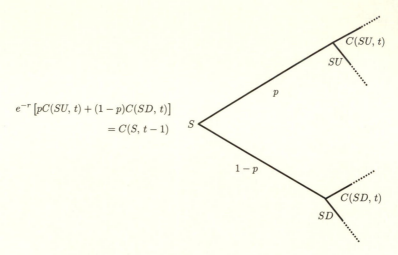

Figure 9.9.   *Binomial-tree algorithm: equity derivative.*

$$C(S, t-1) = e^{-r}\left[pC(SU, t) + (1-p)C(SD, t)\right],\qquad(9.5)$$

where p is the risk-neutral probability of an upward equity gross return of U, and $1-p$ is the complementary probability of a downward equity return of D. The up and down returns, U and D, are calibrated so that the risk-neutral mean total rate of return on equity (as for any asset) is the risk-free rate r, meaning that we restrict the parameters r, U, D, and p of the model so that

$$e^r = pU + (1-p)D.\qquad(9.6)$$

As usual, backward induction from the terminal nodes of the tree, where the derivative payoff is known, determines the initial equity-derivative price.

Figure 9.10 shows how to incorporate the event of default by the firm into the equity-derivative pricing model. The risk-neutral default intensity λ_t^* is assumed, in this example, to depend only on the level S_t of the stock price, and is assumed to remain constant during each time period. For short time periods, the assumption of constant default intensity during each period approximates a risk-neutral default intensity that continually fluctuates with equity price changes.

The default recovery of the target derivative security, such as a convertible bond, is assumed to be some fixed amount M. At each node in the valuation tree shown in Figure 9.10, one sees in addition to the usual up-return and down-return branches that appear in the classical binomial-tree valuation model of Figure 9.9, a third branch for default, with the risk-neutral

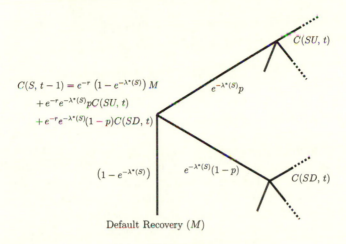

$$C(S, t-1) = e^{-r}\left(1 - e^{-\lambda^*(S)}\right)M$$
$$+ e^{-r}e^{-\lambda^*(S)}pC(SU, t)$$
$$+ e^{-r}e^{-\lambda^*(S)}(1-p)C(SD, t)$$

$C(SU, t)$

$e^{-\lambda^*(S)}p$

$\left(1 - e^{-\lambda^*(S)}\right)$ $e^{-\lambda^*(S)}(1-p)$ $C(SD, t)$

Default Recovery (M)

Figure 9.10.   *Equity derivative algorithm with default and recovery.*

one-period default probability $1 - e^{-\lambda^*(S)}$. This means that the up-return and down-return branches have probabilities $e^{-\lambda^*(S)}p$ and $e^{-\lambda^*(S)}(1-p)$, respectively, after factoring in the one-period risk-neutral probability $e^{-\lambda^*(S)}$ of survival. These three branch probabilities are designed for time periods of length 1. The up and down equity returns, U and D, should again be calibrated so that the risk-neutral net mean rate of return on the equity is again the risk-free rate. As opposed to (9.6), this implies a calibration of the parameters so that for periods of length 1,

$$e^r = e^{-\lambda^*(S)}pU + e^{-\lambda^*(S)}(1-p)D + (1 - e^{-\lambda^*(S)})\hat{S}, \qquad (9.7)$$

where $\hat{S}$ is the recovery value of equity at default. One would take $\hat{S} = 0$ if one adopts the conventional assumption of absolute priority, under which equity investors must give up any claims in the event of default. Once having calibrated the parameters to satisfy (9.7), the derivative pricing algorithm is then used to calculate the derivative price:

$$C(S, t-1) = e^{-[r+\lambda^*(S)]}[pC(SU, t) + (1-p)C(SD, t)]$$
$$+ e^{-r}(1 - e^{-\lambda^*(S)})M. \qquad (9.8)$$

For shorter time periods of length Δ, which can be chosen for a given level of accuracy relative to a continuous-time model, the default branch has risk-neutral probability $1 - e^{-\lambda^*(S)\Delta}$, which is approximately $\lambda^*(S)\Delta$, while the up-return, U, and down-return, D, branches have correspondingly adjusted probabilities. The one-period default-free discount factor is $e^{-r\Delta}$.

If the default-free short rate r also fluctuates randomly, one can accordingly add branches to the tree.

9.2.3. Convertible Debt as an Equity Derivative

A typical convertible bond is a callable bond that also includes an option for the investor to convert the bond into a given number of shares of equity. It is, however, not accurate to treat a convertible bond as a portfolio consisting of a callable bond and an equity call option, for the issuer's decision to call the bond reflects the opportunity of the issuer to time the call decision so as to minimize the total market value of the liability, including the effects of the convert option. Both the call and the convert options are American, at least within given contractually permitted time windows.

An *exchangeable bond,* a variant of a traditional convertible bond, can be exchanged by the bond investor for a given number of shares of another firm. Exchangeable bonds and traditional convertible bonds share many considerations in their pricing, especially in the often encountered cases in which the exchangeable bond can be exchanged for shares of a firm that is linked to the issuing firm. For example, the issuer of an exchangeable bond may have significant holdings of the underlying equity, and may exploit the exchangeable bond as a vehicle for "gently" disposing of some exposure to that equity holding. Most convertible bonds are also puttable by the investor for equity, although this optionality usually plays a minor role in the pricing, and we shall ignore it.

Figure 9.11 shows the payoff at maturity of a simple convertible bond as a function of the underlying equity price at the maturity date T of the bond. For example, if the bond can be converted into k shares of equity at the investor's discretion, then, assuming no default, the maturity value of the bond is the maximum of its face value D and kS_T, where S_T is the equity price at maturity and k is the number of shares of stock granted for each bond at conversion. In the event of default, however, the bond is worth some recovery amount M. If it is assumed that there are no violations of absolute priority at default, default occurs precisely when the price S_T of equity is zero, as indicated in Figure 9.11.

9.2.4. Call-Forcing Conversion

Prior to maturity, at each time t, both the issuer and the bond investor make decisions as to whether to call or to convert, respectively, as indicated in Figure 9.12. If the underlying equity is not paying dividends, then the bond investor should not exercise the American call option early. The justifying better-alive-than-dead theory for the usual American equity option applies here as well, despite the complications introduced by default risk and the

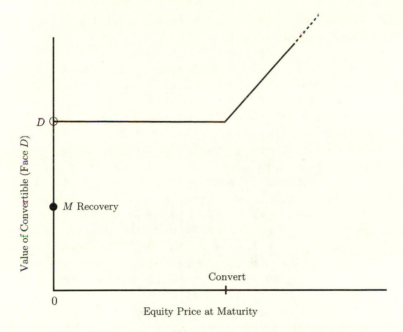

Figure 9.11. *Convertible bond as a derivative on equity.*

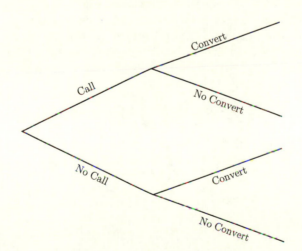

Figure 9.12. *Call and convert options.*

fact that the convert option is embedded into a callable bond. Indeed, the investor should, if possible, delay converting even if there are dividends, provided that the dividend payout rate is sufficiently small.

Let us suppose, for the sake of a simple discussion of the timing of the call and convert options embedded in the convertible bond, that there are indeed no significant equity dividends before maturity. The issuer is aware of the value to the investor of delaying conversion and that such delay increases the market value of the liability to the issuer, for the same reason that an American option is worth more alive than dead. In perfect markets, provided that the total market value of this convertible bond liability is in excess of the contractual call price (and provided that one is within the contractually stipulated time window for calling), the issuer would call the bond in order to extinguish the time value of the American equity option. In practice, this need not fully extinguish the value of the convert option, for the standard convertible bond contract allows the bond investor 30 days after the call announcement to decide whether to convert the bond to equity or to accept the call price, as illustrated in Figure 9.13.

Figure 9.13 shows two scenarios. In the conversion scenario, by 30 days after the call announcement, the price path of the equity conversion value kS_t of the bond has arrived at a point above the call price. The bond investor (if rational) would therefore exercise the right to convert. The alternative scenario illustrated is one for which the conversion value is below the call price, in which case the bond investor would rationally accept the call price. In effect, therefore, calling the bond effectively grants investors a 30-day American equity option that is struck at the call price divided by the number

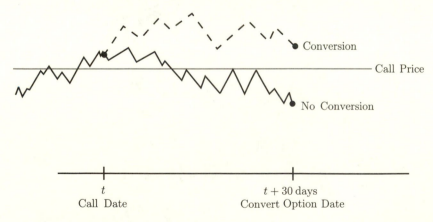

Figure 9.13. *Scenarios for conversion value up to 30 days after a call.*

of shares, k, of stock accorded at conversion to each bond. As pointed out by Ingersoll (1977), this implies that a rational issuer, even in perfect markets, would not announce a decision to call as soon as the market value of the convertible bond is above the convert value kS_t, but rather would wait until the market value is sufficiently above the convert value to minimize the all-in market value to the bond investor, including the effect of the extra 30-day convert option effectively granted to the bond investor at the call announcement.

The amount by which the convertible bond price is optimally allowed to exceed the call price is sometimes called a *safety premium*. If the convert option is far out of the money, the issuer may nevertheless call the bond, for example, because of a significant decline in interest rates. In such a scenario, however, the safety premium would be small, and the call would optimally occur at a bond price that is close to the contractual call price. Likewise, if the convert option is far into the money, then the 30-day option is likely to be exercised, so the additional option to accept the call price after 30 days is not particularly valuable, and the safety premium would again be small. It is for near-the-money scenarios and significant equity volatility that the safety premium could induce a notable delay in the issuer's call.

9.2.5. Evidence of Delayed Calls

Figure 9.14, compiled from the results of Ederington et al. (1997), provides evidence that issuers of convertible bonds have often ignored the opportunity to force bond investors to exercise their American conversion options as quickly as possible. The horizontal axis indicates the excess conversion value, the percentage amount by which the current conversion value kS_t, of k shares of stock, exceeds the bond's current contractual call price $\overline{C}_t$. (For some corporate callable bonds, the call price adjusts with calendar time.) The height of each vertical bar is the fraction, marked in percent, of cases in which a bond was called within 6 months of the time at which the indicated excess conversion value was reached. Even at relatively large excess conversion values, it appears that issuers have frequently neglected the opportunity to force conversion. Asquith (1995), however, provides some support for the hypothesis that issuers have nevertheless not acted suboptimally by these delays. As Ingersoll (1977) pointed out, the effect of the 30-day extra equity option held after any call implies that some degree of excess conversion value is to be expected in some cases. It should be noted, moreover, that extremely large excess conversion values are associated with relatively less time value in the American option because the convert options are typically so far in the money that the bonds are approximately equivalent to equity.

An additional reason that has been proposed for the late exercise of

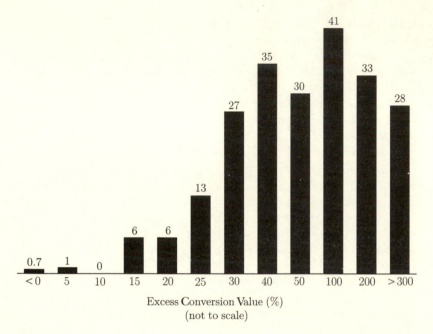

Figure 9.14. *Fractions, in percent, of convertible bonds called within 6 months of the time at which the indicated excess conversion value was reached (based on results from Ederington et al., 1997).*

a call by the issuer that could force conversion is the effect of asymmetric information held by the issuer about its own future prospects. As this story goes, the issuer may wish to convince bond investors that it has weak future prospects in order to induce investors to convert quickly, and thus force convertible bond investors to share in the anticipated price decline. Ederington et al. (1997) and Ederington and Goh (2000), as well as earlier studies that they cite, find little empirical support for this signaling story. Ederington et al. (1997) do, however, find support for the hypothesis that issuers delay exercising their call options so as to maintain the value of tax shields embedded in the convertible bonds, which can only be realized if the bond is allowed to continue to pay coupons that, subject to tax rules, are deductible from earnings as an interest expense.

The same study by Ederington et al. (1997) also indicates some support for the fact that issuers are more likely to delay calls to the extent that the underlying stock is paying dividends. Indeed, if bond issuers are of the opinion that bond investors are unaware of the benefits of early conversion in the presence of large dividends (which reduce the expected rate of growth of the stock price), then issuers may delay calling in order to take advantage of the opportunity to exploit this perceived benefit to issuers of delayed conversion.

9.3. A Simple Convertible Bond Pricing Model

We now present a simple two-factor pricing model for convertible bonds, with some numerical results illustrating the impact of "slow" call-forcing conversion and the interplay of credit risk, callability, and convertibility through the influence of random changes in both equity prices and interest-rate changes.

9.3.1. Background Modeling

Traditional academic models of convertible bond pricing, such as Brennan and Schwartz (1977, 1980) and Nyborg (1996), have taken the underlying risk factor to be the market value of the issuing firm's assets. This approach incorporates a structural model of default, which is assumed to occur whenever the firm's assets are insufficient to make coupon or principal payments on the bond. This approach also explicitly treats the effect of the dilution of equity caused by conversion. At conversion, the number of shares of equity outstanding is increased by the number of shares received by converting bond investors. In effect, each share of equity becomes, at conversion, a claim to a smaller fraction of the total market value of equity. Prior to conversion, equity investors are aware of the risk of dilution at conversion, and this effect is priced into the current shares, and thus into the initial price of the convertible bonds, as in standard models of warrant pricing such as found in Galai and Schneller (1978).

While the valuation of convertible bonds using the total asset value of the issuer as the underlying risk factor is convenient for cases in which the issuing firm has a simple balance sheet with only one or two outstanding liabilities, practical considerations may suggest a direct treatment of convertible debt as an equity derivative. Indeed, at investment banks, convertible bonds are typically traded and hedged by the equity-derivatives desk, despite the separate presence of a corporate bond desk. As we shall see by example, the most significant risk factor for a typical convertible bond is the equity price (which also captures default risk). Interest-rate risk is usually a secondary consideration. The trading and risk management of convertible bond positions are perhaps most naturally integrated with the management of portfolios of more standard equity derivatives, such as call and put options. In any case, convertible bond pricing models used in industry practice, such as those of Goldman Sachs (1994) and Tsiveriotas and Fernandes (1998), more often rely on the equity price as the key underlying risk factor. As in our model, explained later, such industry models take the short-term interest rate as the second risk factor. One may prefer a multifactor term-structure model, as in Chapter 7, in order to more accurately capture the effects of changes in the term structure of interest rates on the valuation of the options embedded in the convertible bond. Taking equity as the underlying security also forces one to deal with the effects of dilution by approximate methods.

9.3.2. Convertible Bond Model Setup

Our simple illustrative model of convertible bond pricing is, in effect, based on the algorithm illustrated in Figure 9.10, with some enhancements to allow for calls that are not based on the perfect-market assumption of minimizing the market value of the bond, assuming instead that the issuer does not react instantly to the opportunity to call and thereby reduce the market value of the liability. Instead, the issuer is assumed to call with a probability that is larger when the value of calling is larger, in a sense that we explain shortly.

Our model supposes that the stock-price process S has a constant volatility of $\sigma = 0.25$ until the time of default, at which point the equity price is assumed to jump to zero, as would be the case with absolute priority. Without loss of generality for this model, we take the initial stock price to be $S_0 = 1$.

The default-risk-free short-term interest-rate process r is assumed to be, risk-neutrally, a CIR process, with risk-neutral mean-reversion $\kappa = 0.3$, an initial condition r_0 equal to the long-run risk-neutral mean of $\theta = 0.1$, and a CIR volatility parameter $\sigma_r = 0.23$. This implies an extremely high initial level of interest-rate volatility of 73%, in a proportional sense. We chose such a high base-case level of interest-rate volatility in order to capture at least some role for interest-rate risk in the convertible bond price. At more common lower levels of interest-rate volatility, the call and convert options are far more influenced by equity risk than by interest-rate risk.

Default is assumed to occur at a risk-neutral intensity of $\lambda_t^* = \gamma/S_t$, for a constant parameter $\gamma > 0$, which is taken to be 0.12 at the base case and gives the natural dependence on equity price illustrated in Figure 9.8. Before default, the stock price S_t therefore satisfies

$$dS_t = (r_t + \lambda_t^*)S_t \, dt + S_t\sigma \, dB_t^*, \tag{9.9}$$

where B^* is a risk-neutral standard Brownian motion. One notes that the risk-neutral predefault growth rate of the stock price $r_t + \lambda_t^*$ is elevated from the usual equity-derivative risk-neutral mean rate of return, r_t, by the risk-neutral mean loss rate due to default, λ_t^*. This is the continuous-time version of the risk-neutral rate-of-return restriction of the binomial model (9.7). The loss of equity at default is 100% of its market value, as we have assumed absolute priority. This stock price model (9.9) thus correctly reflects the total risk-neutral mean rate of return of r_t, once one allows for the effects of default.

We assume that investors in convertible bonds recover a deterministic fraction of 50% of the face value of the bond at default. Because the optional features of the bond are effective only when the bond is not in default, the probability distribution of the recovery plays no serious role in the convertible bond's value, beyond its risk-neutral mean.

Our parameters for r, λ^*, and recovery imply a 5-year straight-debt (i.e., noncallable, nonconvertible, coupon bond) par yield spread of 468 basis points over the default-free 5-year yield that is associated with the CIR interest-rate model.

The convertible bond to be priced has a maturity of 5 years, pays semi-annual coupons, and is callable at a price of $\overline{C} = 101$, plus accrued coupon income. The convertible bond is call protected (the issuer may not call) for 1 year. That is, this bond is a 5-no-call-1. Each bond can be converted, at the discretion of bond investors, to 0.7 shares of stock at any time up to and including maturity. We ignore dilution effects here, as well as the effect of the 30-day safety premium, assuming that bond investors must choose to receive the call price or to convert as soon as the bond is called. Bond investors are assumed to exercise this convert option rationally.

From the issuer's standpoint, however, rather than assuming rational exercise, we suppose that the (risk-neutral) probability of a call depends on the excess of the convertible bond's current price C_t over the value if called, which is $\max(kS_t, \overline{C})$, the larger of the conversion value and the call price. That is, the likelihood of a call at time t is assumed to depend on

$$Y_t = \frac{C_t}{\max(kS_t, \overline{C})} - 1. \tag{9.10}$$

When $Y_t \leq 0$, there is no incentive to call the bond, for it is trading in the market at a price that is lower than the cost of calling it. To the extent that $Y_t > 0$, the issuer has an incentive to call that increases with Y_t, and would call instantly in a perfect-market setting whenever $Y_t > 0$.

We pick a simple and somewhat arbitrary parameterization of this dependence of the risk-neutral call probability on the excess relative value Y_t. The risk-neutral intensity of a call is assumed to be zero whenever $Y_t < 0$ and otherwise to be $-pY(t)$ for some *call speed parameter* p that is set to 20 (annualized) for our base case. At this choice for the speed parameter p, for example, if the bond is trading at a price that exceeds its called value by 10% ($Y_t = 0.1$), the bond would be called with approximately 20% risk-neutral probability within 1 month.

At these base-case parameters, the risk-neutral probability of conversion before maturity turns out to be 0.58. The base-case risk-neutral probability of a call before conversion is 0.83. All conversions before maturity are forced by calling because the stock pays no dividends before maturity and the bond investor converts rationally, thus keeping the American conversion option alive as long as possible in order to maximize the market value of the convertible bond.

9.3.3. Pricing Algorithm

The convertible bond price is now solved by a backward recursion from the maturity date, in a manner analogous to the algorithm of Figure 9.10, but incorporating the exercise of the call and conversion options and using a more sophisticated finite-difference method for each valuation step, based on a two-dimensional lattice for the stock price S_t and the interest rate r_t.

At each time t, we first calculate the risk-neutral expected discounted present value of the claim to the convertible bond at the next time period, $t + \Delta$. If it is assumed that it has not defaulted by time t, the convertible bond price, before considering the opportunity to call, is

$$C_b(S_t, r_t, t) = e^{-[r(t)+\lambda^*(t)]\Delta} E_t^*[C(S_{t+\Delta}, r_{t+\Delta}, t + \Delta)]$$
$$+ (1 - e^{\lambda^*(t)\Delta}) e^{-r(t)\Delta}M, \qquad (9.11)$$

where E_t^* denotes risk-neutral expectation at time t, recalling that M is the assumed default recovery, 50% of the bond's face value. We use a conventional Crank-Nicholson alternating directions algorithm for this expected-present-value computation,[4] based on the two-dimensional lattice illustrated in Figure 9.2 for S_t and r_t. This is the same lattice-based finite-difference algorithm used earlier in the chapter to price spread options, although in that case the coordinate axes had different interpretations.

The options to call and to convert are then introduced into the algorithm in order to obtain the value at time t of

$$C(S_t, r_t, t) = g(t) + e^{-pY(t)\Delta} C_b(S_t, r_t, t)$$
$$+ (1 - e^{-pY(t)\Delta}) \max(kS_t, \overline{C}), \qquad (9.12)$$

where $g(t)$ is the coupon paid (if any) at time t. The second term of (9.12) is the risk-neutral probability of no call between t and $t + \Delta$ multiplied by the market value $C_b(S_t, r_t, t)$, from (9.11), of the bond if left uncalled for at least one more period. The final term of (9.12) is the risk-neutral

---

[4] We are grateful to Nicolae Gârleanu for writing the code and performing the following numerical calculations.

probability of a call multiplied by the value if called, which is the larger of the conversion value kS_t and the call price $\overline{C}$. (We assume that the call would occur instantly if it occurs at all, an approximation that is accurate for short Δ.) It should be emphasized that an incentive to call can arise from both a large conversion value kS_t and a small default-free short rate $r(t)$, which raises the uncalled price $C_b(S_t, r_t, t)$ and motivates the issuer, as with any callable bond, to issue new debt at a lower effective interest expense. Indeed, a higher equity price S_t implies both a higher conversion value kS_t as well as a larger value $C_b(S_t, r_t, t)$ of an uncalled bond because of a reduction in the risk-neutral default intensity, $\lambda_t^* = \gamma/S_t$, and an increase in the moneyness of the conversion option.

At our base-case parameters, in order for the convertible bond to trade at par, it must offer coupons that are roughly 150 basis points above the risk-free rate. This is of course far less than the straight bond par yield spread of 468 basis points. In order to gain some sense of the importance of a volatile intensity process, we could consider a parallel model without a link between credit quality and yield spread having constant risk-neutral default intensity chosen for the same straight bond yield spread of 468 basis points. For the comparison model, the spread demanded on the par convertible bond goes down from our base-case (stock-price-dependent intensity) spread of 150 basis points to only 74 basis points.

9.3.4. Convertible Bond Hedging Strategies

As we pointed out earlier, a convertible bond is, roughly speaking, an equity derivative. Much of its value, as distinct from that of a callable non-convertible bond that is otherwise the same, is the value of the option to convert. As opposed to the usual case of an equity derivative, however, hedging strategies should account for both credit risk and interest-rate risk.

Figure 9.15 shows the initial convertible bond price for our illustrative example as a function of the initial equity price, holding all other parameters constant. For sufficiently high stock prices, the likelihood of conversion is large, and the convertible bond trades at roughly its conversion value, $0.7S_t$. For sufficiently low stock prices, the risk-neutral intensity of default, as illustrated earlier in Figure 9.8, is large, and the convertible bond trades at close to its default recovery value, $M = 0.5$.

Figure 9.16 shows the joint effect of the stock price and time. The accordion-like effect of changing calendar time is simply the result of semi-annual coupon payments. (The price shown is the actual price, not the price net of accrued interest.)

In Figure 9.17, the same effects are apparent, but more exaggerated by recalibrating the model with the parameter γ determining the intensity process $\lambda_t^* = \gamma/S_t$ for initial straight bond yield spreads of 100 basis points

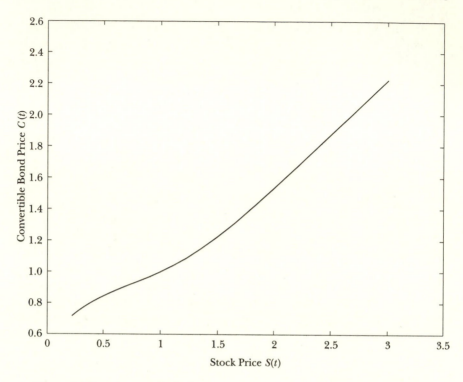

Figure 9.15. *Convertible bond price versus stock price: base-case parameters.*

and 1,000 basis points, respectively, holding the base-case equity price at $S_0 = 1.0$. The relatively high-quality issuer, with a spread of 100 basis points, has a convertible bond price that responds to equity price changes more or less in the manner of an equity call option, except at extremely low equity prices, at which the convertible bond price finally responds dramatically to the high risk-neutral likelihood of default accompanied by the 50% recovery of face value. One notes the relatively convex response of the convertible bond price to the equity price for stock prices that are at the money or in the money and the relatively concave response to stock prices when the convert option is far out of the money. This suggests a rather different hedging strategy and sensitivity to equity volatility for high-quality versus low-quality convertible debt.

A classical *delta hedge* of the convertible bond would be a short position in the underlying equity equal in magnitude to the sensitivity of the convertible bond price to a "small" change in the equity price. This sensitivity is measured as the slope (first derivative) of the convertible bond price function shown in Figure 9.15 or Figure 9.17. A delta hedge, however, misses

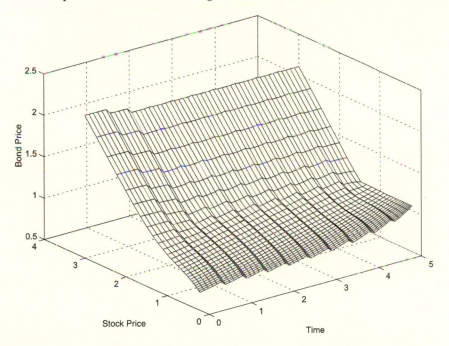

Figure 9.16. *Bond price dependence on stock price and time: base-case parameters.*

the effect of both large changes in the equity price, which could include default, and of unexpected changes in the volatility of the underlying stock.

As for volatility hedges, we have assumed a constant volatility σ (before default), but in practice volatility is stochastic, and recent and more sophisticated stochastic-volatility models, such as those cited in Appendix A, incorporate volatility as a factor to be hedged. For the classical constant-volatility (Black-Scholes) equity-option model, volatility is hedged by adopting opposite-signed positions in another equity option of the same sensitivity to volatility. This is sometimes called *vega* hedging. In such conventional cases, the sensitivity of an option to the volatility of the underlying is positive for convex option pricing functions and negative for concave option pricing functions, as a consequence of Jensen's inequality. For convertible bonds, however, as one can see in Figure 9.17, the pricing function switches in behavior from convex for at-the-money and in-the-money cases to concave for out-of-the money cases. Thus, a volatility hedge with another equity option, say a simple call or put on the underlying, might have to be dramatically adjusted as the conversion option moves into and out of the money.

A key difference between typical convertible bond hedging and the text-book strategy for hedging a standard equity option is the potential for de-

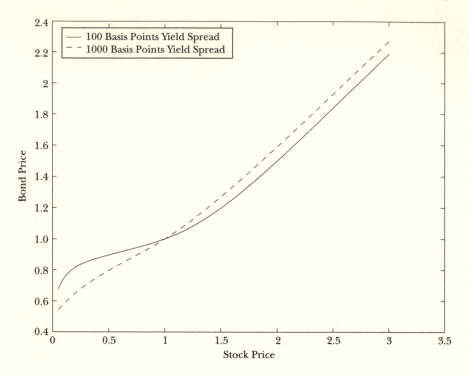

Figure 9.17.   *Convertible bond prices as a function of the underlying stock price for a high-quality issuer (100 basis points spread) and low-quality issuer (1,000 basis points spread).*

fault and an associated downward jump in the equity price. In our theoretical model, the risk to a convertible bond investor of equity price changes, including the effect of default, can be hedged with a hedge portfolio containing appropriate combinations of simple put or call options or options in combination with positions in the underlying stock. For example, one can solve two equations for the two unknown hedging positions that immunize the bond investor from both small predefault equity price changes as well as the large equity price change that could occur at any time owing to default. For example, let the two hedging instruments have market values of $G(S_t, t)$ and $H(S_t, t)$, suppressing from our notation the dependence of prices on the short rate r_t in order to address the key hedging issues. Our hedging position sizes, g_t and h_t, respectively, are chosen so that

$$-C_S(S_t, t) = g_t\, G_S(S_t, t) + h_t H_S(S_t, t) \qquad (9.13)$$

$$M - C(S_t, t) = g_t\,[G(S_t, t) - G(0, t)] + h_t\,[H(S_t, t) - H(0, t)]. \qquad (9.14)$$

The first equation provides immunization to random equity returns prior to default. The second equation immunizes against default, exploiting our absolute-priority assumption that the equity price is known to be zero at default, and the assumed recovery value M for the convertible bond. These linear equations can be solved for g_t and h_t provided that the associated coefficient matrix is of full rank. One can similarly extend the hedging portfolio with protection against interest-rate risk, for example, with an appropriately sized interest-rate swap.

Perhaps the most important reason that hedges based on this form of portfolio delta matching are not fully effective in practice is uncertainty in the default recoveries of both the underlying equity (violations of absolute priority) and particularly of the convertible bond. Instead, hedgers of convertible bonds, such as hedge funds that specialize in exploiting perceived cases of underpricing of convertible bonds, typically obtain some direct form of default protection, such as a default swap, as explained in Chapter 8, in combination with an interest-rate swap that hedges most of the interest-rate risk. Both interest-rate and default risk are in some cases partially hedged with a single position in an asset swap.[5]

In general, the common objective of convertible bond arbitrageurs is to strip the convertible bond of both default risk and interest-rate risk, to the degree possible with simple and relatively static hedges, and to retain the effect of a position in call options on the underlying equity. Conventional wisdom, yet to be validated in published studies of which we are aware, is that call options "stripped from" convertible bonds in this manner have been available at attractive risk-adjusted expected rates of return, relative to standard exchange-traded call options. Following this suggested strategy, the final component of an arbitrageur's strategy is to write call options on the underlying equity and "capture" the perceived mispricing of the equity option embedded in the convertible bond.

9.3.5. Exposure to Equity Volatility

If we were to move from the base case of 25% equity volatility ($\sigma = 0.25$) to 50% equity volatility, the convert option would be more valuable, and in order to issue the bond at par, the coupon rate of the convertible bond would actually be 100 basis points below the default-free yield of the same maturity. This comparison is slightly misleading, however, for raising the equity volatility to 50% also increases the volatility of the risk-neutral default

---

[5] A recent variant of the asset swap designed for use by convertible bond arbitrageurs is the *floored asset swap,* which gives the counterparty providing the hedge, often an investment bank, an additional option to put the associated interest-rate swap back to the convertible bond arbitrageur.

intensity, $\lambda_t^* = \gamma/S_t$. (The volatility of λ^* is equal to the equity volatility σ in this model, given the assumption that $\log \lambda_t^*$ is linear in $\log S_t$.) Increasing the volatility of λ_t^* through this increase in σ would therefore also reduce the implied yield spread of this issuer's straight debt, based on the analysis in Chapter 5. If we were to increase the equity volatility to 50% and simultaneously reduce the risk-neutral default-intensity parameter γ so that the straight debt yield spread remains at 468 basis points, then the par coupon rate on the convertible debt would be reduced to roughly 150 basis points below the default-free yield.

9.3.6. The Issuer's Propensity to Call

Figure 9.18 shows the effect of adjusting the call-speed parameter p on the risk-neutral likelihood of a call within one coupon period (vertical axis) as a function of the ratio $C_t/\max(kS_t, \underline{C})$ (shown on the horizontal axis) of the current convertible bond price to the value of the bond if called. The case

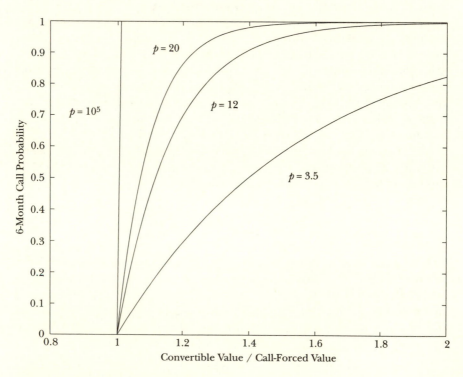

Figure 9.18. *Risk-neutral likelihood of a call for call-speed parameters $p = 3.5$ (slow); $p = 12$; $p = 20$ (base case); and $p = 10^5$ (rational).*

of $p = 10^5$ corresponds to essentially instant forced conversion when the convertible bond price is at least as high as call-forced value. The case of slow calling ($p = 3.5$) corresponds to an assumption that the convertible bond is called with only 50% risk-neutral probability within 6 months when the current convertible bond price is 40% higher than the value if called.

It is not clear whether there should be a significant market risk premium for delayed-call risk that would drive a wedge between actual and risk-neutral call probabilities, given the underlying risk factors. Without consideration of such a risk premium, one might be able to estimate the call-speed parameter p from historical data, along the lines of the logit model of Ederington et al. (1997) (who use the excess conversion value, as opposed to the excess of the convertible bond price over the forced-conversion value, as the basis for estimating the likelihood of a call).

It would be potentially more realistic to introduce a *burnout factor*, reflecting the reduced tendency of the issuer to call given a history of not calling during lengthy prior periods of excess conversion value. This might approximate the role of missing model features that determine the actual incentives to delay calls. A burnout factor would, however, introduce a path dependency, or additional state variable, which we avoid here for simplicity.

The impact of the various call-speed assumptions of Figure 9.18 on the initial price of the convertible bond are shown in Figure 9.19, as a premium over par, in percent. For example, raising the issuer's assumed speed parameter p from the slowest that we considered ($p = 3.5$) to the fastest considered ($p = 10^5$) reduces the price of the convertible bond by more than 7%.

9.3.7. Duration and Convexity

Figure 9.20 compares the price responses of three different types of debt—straight bonds, callable nonconvertible bonds, and callable convertible bonds—to parallel shifts of the term structure of interest rates. For this calculation, we have simplified the model by assuming deterministic default-free interest rates. The response of the price of straight debt to shifts in the risk-free yield curve is roughly linear and slightly convex, along the lines of the usual textbook explanations of bond duration and convexity. For example, the 5-year straight bond, whose price graph is marked with circles, apparently has a duration of roughly 3.5 years, because its price increases from par to approximately 7% more than par with a downward parallel shift in the yield curve of 200 basis points. The positive convexity of a straight bond implies that this response accelerates with increasingly large downward shifts of the yield curve and decelerates with increasingly large upward shifts of the yield curve (an attractive property from the viewpoint of risk management). The fact that the underlying straight debt is defaultable does

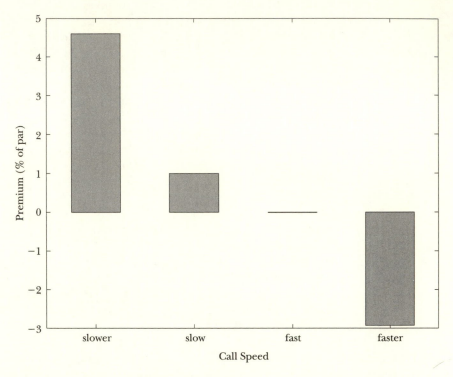

Figure 9.19   *Bond price premium under various call-speed parameters: slower:* $p =$ *3.5; slow:* $p = 12$; *fast:* $p = 20$ *(base case); faster:* $p = 10^5$ *(rational).*

not have a significant effect on its duration or convexity in this example, although introduction of correlation between default risk and interest-rate risk, along the lines of the empirical results of Chapter 7, would cause some degree of interaction between interest-rate risk and credit risk, which could have a measurable effect on duration and convexity in some cases.

The callable nonconvertible bond price, whose graph is marked with asterisks in Figure 9.20, displays the conventional negative convexity (concavity) of most callable debt, in that the bond price increases with reductions in the yield curve, but these price increases decelerate with successively larger reductions in interest rates because the issuer is increasingly likely to call in the debt in order to take advantage of the opportunity to extinguish a liability whose market value is increasingly large relative to its call price. For example, the issuer could redeem the current bond by issuing a new bond of the same face value whose coupons are smaller. The price declines of the callable bond with increasing interest rates are more severe than the increases in prices with declining rates.

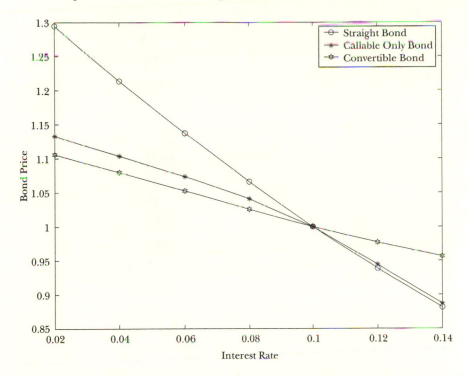

Figure 9.20. *Effects of a shift in the yield curve (deterministic rates).*

The response of the convertible bond price to shifts in the yield curve, plotted with stars in Figure 9.20, shows relatively little convexity, positive or negative, because both the issuer and the bond investor hold options. It should be emphasized once again that while one traditionally thinks of the convert option as an equity option and the call option as an interest-rate option, each of these options affects the market value of the bond in a manner that reflects changes in both interest rates and equity prices. The duration of the convertible bond is less than that of the either straight debt or callable nonconvertible debt.

The numerical results for this example reinforce the notion that a convertible bond, while sensitive to interest rates, is usually more aptly treated as an equity derivative than as an interest-rate derivative at conventional parameters. Obviously, however, if the convert option is extremely far out of the money, the equity-derivative component is small. Although convertible bonds are not normally issued with convert options that are relatively out of the money, the option may fall out of the money over time if the stock price declines dramatically, and in this case the convertible bond would begin to be priced similarly to callable nonconvertible debt.

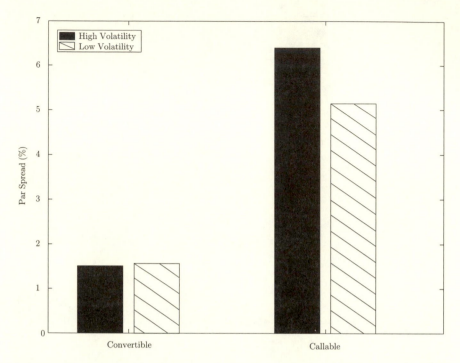

Figure 9.21. *Par spreads: left bars, high interest-rate volatility (base case); right bars, low interest-rate volatility (25 % of base-case volatility).*

Figure 9.21 confirms the intuition that convertible bonds are relatively insensitive to interest-rate volatility, because both the issuer and the bond investor hold an effective option on the value of the bond versus the conversion value. The darker bars in the figure show, for both the convertible and the callable (nonconvertible) bonds, the par coupon rate associated with the large base-case interest-rate volatility. The lighter bars show, for each bond, the par coupon rates associated with a smaller interest-rate volatility parameter σ_r, which is 25% of its base-case level. The impact on the par coupon rate of the convertible bond is negligible. However, its impact on the callable nonconvertible bond's par coupon rate is more substantial because the optionality is all on the side of the issuer.

10

Correlated Defaults

THIS CHAPTER PRESENTS models, empirical methods, and simulation algorithms for correlated default times. Empirically reasonable models of correlated defaults are central to the credit risk-management and pricing systems of major financial institutions. In subsequent chapters, we apply correlated default models to the valuation of instruments subject to joint default risk, such as collateralized debt obligations, and to the measurement of credit risk for portfolios of OTC positions.

10.1. Alternative Approaches to Correlation

The degree of correlation of default risk for a given list of n entities can be captured by various measures that depend on the joint probability distribution of their respective default times $\tau_1, \ldots, \tau_n$. These entities could be the obligors underlying a collateralized debt obligation or a set of over-the-counter broker-dealer counterparties. As one possible measure of correlation, Figure 10.1 illustrates estimates of the correlation of the indicator variables for 1-year default between a randomly chosen pair of firms within a given sector for each of a range of sectors. (The default indicator for a particular firm has an outcome of 1 in the event of default within 1 year and 0 otherwise.) The correlation estimates in Figure 10.1 are "bootstrapped" from historical data.[1]

Other measures of correlation of default risk include correlations between the default times $\tau_1, \ldots, \tau_n$ themselves or correlations in the changes in the conditional default probabilities over time.

---

[1] One may imagine that, for a given sector, a starting time and a pair of firms active at that time are chosen at random. The indicators for default over the subsequent year for each of the two firms is determined. This provides one observation. Across all such choices of starting times and pairs of firms, one has a data set of observed pairs of default indicators. The sample correlation of these data is an estimate of the default-indicator correlation.

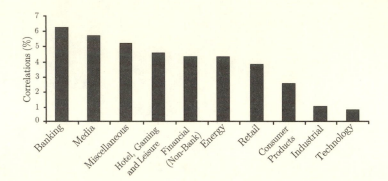

Figure 10.1. *Estimates of incidence-of-default correlations for pairs of speculative-grade firms within an industry. (Source: Moody's.)*

Among the most popular approaches to modeling correlated default are:

- *CreditMetrics,* a method by which ratings transitions for multiple entities can be simulated with the correlation induced by underlying correlated *drivers,* such as asset returns.
- *Doubly stochastic correlated default-intensity processes,* an approach to modeling multientity default risk in which correlation is captured through correlated changes in the default intensities of the entities.
- *Copulas,* devices that allow entity-by-entity default models to be linked with auxiliary correlating variables.
- *Intensity-based models of default with joint credit events* that can cause multiple issuers to default simultaneously. The simplest example is the multivariate exponential model of default times, which has constant default intensities.

We review these approaches, providing some critical commentary on their relative advantages and disadvantages.

10.2. CreditMetrics Correlated Defaults

The CreditMetrics approach to correlated default assumes that the credit rating of an entity is the basic measure of its default risk. CreditMetrics provides a framework for simulated correlated changes in the credit ratings of a given set of entities, as illustrated in Figure 10.2, which shows sample paths for the ratings of three different entities.[2]

---

[2] Lando (1998) considered correlation within the framework of finite-state continuous-time Markov chains for each entity's rating. For example, with two entities and three ratings,

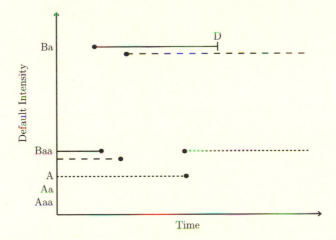

Figure 10.2.   *Correlated ratings-based default intensity for three issuers.*

In order to simulate the change in rating of a given counterparty in this framework, an underlying driving variable X, such as the *asset return* of the entity, is simulated. A normal distribution for the asset return X is a typical assumption, as, for example, in the corporate debt pricing models of Black and Scholes (1973) and Merton (1974), as reviewed in Section 5.4. These debt pricing models assume default when assets are insufficient to meet liabilities, so it is natural to use asset returns as a driver for the change in credit rating.

The range of outcomes of the driving variable X is divided into intervals, one for each rating, as illustrated in Figure 10.3. For each current rating of a firm, these intervals are chosen with the property that the probability that the driver X has an outcome in the interval associated with a given rating is equal to a separately specified probability for transition into that rating. These specified ratings-transition probabilities are sometimes based on historical transition frequencies, as explained in Chapter 4. CreditMetrics, however, does not require the use of average historical ratings-transition frequencies.

By simulating the drivers $X_1, \ldots, X_n$ of n different entities with correlation and assigning the new ratings for each entity according to the outcomes, one obtains correlated ratings changes, as illustrated for two firms, i and j, in Figure 10.4, which shows the assignment of new credit ratings to

A, B, and C, the states are {AA, AB, AC, BA, BB, BC, CA, CB, CC}, where, e.g., AB is the state for which entity 1 is currently in rating A and entity 2 is in rating B. This leads, however, to an exponential growth in the size of the state space as the number of entities and ratings grows.

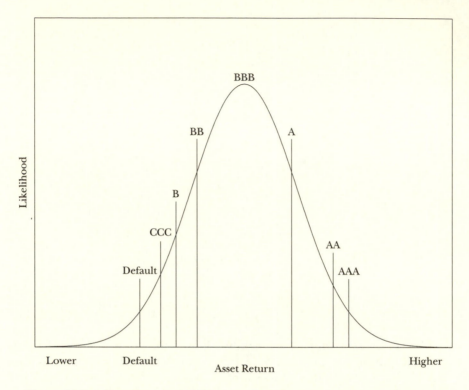

Figure 10.3. *Transition probabilities of a BBB firm from asset-return likelihood.*

a pair of firms based on the outcomes of their asset returns. CreditMetrics prescribes a joint normal distribution for the drivers, which allows for simple simulation methods. For example, suppose $X_1, \ldots, X_n$ is joint normal with a covariance matrix Σ (of n rows and n columns). The Cholesky decomposition of Σ is a certain matrix C of the same number of rows and columns, with the property that $CC^\top = \Sigma$. By simulating independent standard normal (zero mean, unit variance) variables $Z_1, \ldots, Z_n$, one can simulate the drivers with the appropriate means and covariances by letting

$$X_i = E(X_i) + C_{i1} Z_1 + \cdots + C_{in} Z_n, \tag{10.1}$$

where C_{ij} is the (i, j) element of the Cholesky matrix C.

Sources of covariance information are the volatilities and correlations of equity returns for the n firms in the case of publicly traded firms. One could also take the drivers to be the KMV (or some substitute) measures of *distance to default,* firm by firm, which is more in the spirit of the asset-return

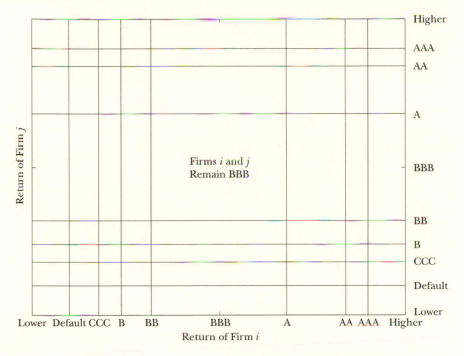

Figure 10.4. *Joint transition regions for two BBB firms.*

foundation of the CreditMetrics model. Time-series data on distances to default for pairs of firms could be used to estimate the covariance matrix Σ and calibrate the ranges in Figure 10.3.

10.3. Correlated Default Intensities

Alternatively, one can build rich and tractable models of default correlation by building correlation into the default intensities $\lambda_1, \ldots, \lambda_n$ of the various entities. From such models, one can easily simulate correlated defaults and correlated changes in default probabilities over various time horizons. The particular form of correlation explored in this section is that of the doubly stochastic model of default. This construction assumes that after conditioning on the intensity processes $\lambda_1, \ldots, \lambda_n$ of the n names, the respective default times $\tau_1, \ldots, \tau_n$ are independent and that τ_i is the first arrival time of a Poisson process with deterministic time-varying intensity process λ_i. This means that the *only* source of default correlation is covariation in default intensities. (The CreditMetrics model is a special case.) The following parametric specifications of the intensities illustrate this approach.

10.3.1. Correlated Jump-Intensity Processes

A special case of a doubly stochastic model is one with default intensities that mean revert and have randomly timed upward (adverse) jumps of random size. By allowing for the possibility of common jump times, one has a relatively simple but useful model for simulating correlated defaults and the opportunity for a relatively high degree of default time correlation. Without correlated jumps, it is difficult to obtain a high degree of correlation for relatively high-quality entities, a point made by Schönbucher (1998).

Suppose, for instance, that each default intensity, λ_i for entity i, is of the type described in Section 3.5.1, that is, mean reverting with jumps. The parameters for such an intensity model, we recall, are the mean-reversion rate κ, the level γ to which the intensity reverts between jumps, the mean arrival rate c of jumps, and the mean jump size J. The additional parameters to be chosen govern the likelihood of common jumps, which determines the degree of default correlation.

This model is particularly tractable for simulation and is a member of the family of multivariate affine jump-diffusion-intensity models, for which survival probabilities as well as moments, Laplace transforms, and Fourier transforms of default times can be computed by analytical means, as indicated in Appendix A. A more general affine model, combining both jump and diffusion risk, is considered in Chapter 11.

The fact that default-intensity jumps are upward only, rather than potentially upward or downward, is restrictive and is used to guarantee that default intensities remain nonnegative, as in theory they must. Table 10.1 shows the lists of largest favorable and adverse changes in estimated 1-year conditional default probabilities according to the proprietary model of Moody's Risk Management Services, for the month of January 2001. For this month, and for most other monthly reports, it is apparent that the significantly sized jumps are upward jumps in default probabilities.

For illustration, consider an example in which all entities' default intensities have the same parameters (κ, γ, c, J). Suppose, for simplicity, that the sizes of jumps in intensity are independent (across time and counterparties) and exponentially distributed. Suppose, further, that common

Table 10.1.   Significant Changes in Moody's Probabilities of Default, January 2001

Declines (%)		Increases (%)	
Redhook Ale Brewery	0.16	Cylink Corporation	3.82
United Natural Foods	0.18	Media 100 Inc.	9.0
Reebok International	0.18	Display Technologies	14.73
Pediatrix Medical Group	0.13	United Shipping and Technology	12.3
Winter Sports	0.12	Xerox Corporation	15.14

adverse changes in credit quality arrive according to a Poisson process with constant intensity Λ_c. At such a common event, a given entity's default intensity jumps with some probability p. With conditional probability $1 - p$, no jump occurs. Thus, an entity experiences commonly generated adverse credit shocks with mean arrival intensity $p\Lambda_c$. Conditional on common jump times, all jumps in default intensity are independent across issuers and times.

Jumps to individual default intensities that are *idiosyncratic*, meaning not instigated by the arrival of common credit events, occur at the remaining jump intensity $c - p\Lambda_c$, so that the total jump arrival intensity is c, as required by the given parameters (κ, γ, c, J) for individual default intensities. The parameters Λ_c and p are chosen to provide a given amount of correlation, within the limits imposed by the model structure. Note that as the mean jump size J goes to infinity, firms can default simultaneously at the arrival time of a common credit event, as with the multivariate exponential default-time model described at the end of this chapter.

As p approaches 0, the model converges to one of independent default times. As p converges to 1 and c converges to 0, the model approaches one of perfectly correlated jump intensities. This does *not* mean perfectly correlated default times because, in this doubly stochastic framework, conditional on the paths taken by the various default intensities, default times are independent. That is, with $p = 1$ and $c = 0$, all names have the same default intensity process λ, but conditional on the path of λ, the default times are independent.

We can obtain the limiting effect of perfectly correlated (i.e., identical) default times by taking $p = 1$ and letting $J \to \infty$.

In order to illustrate the model, we take the same parameters for individual-entity default risk ($\kappa = 0.5, \gamma = 0.001, c = 0.002, J = 5$) that were used in the one-entity model of Section 3.5.1. For correlation parameters, we take $p = 0.02$ and $\Lambda_c = 0.05$, so that the rate of arrival of idiosyncratic jumps in an entity's default intensity is $c - p\Lambda_c = 0.001$. This implies that the probability that λ_i jumps at a given time t given that λ_j jumps at t is $p\Lambda_c/c = 1\%$.

A portion of a typical sample path for the total arrival intensity of defaults for 1,000 original entities for this model is illustrated in Figure 10.5. On this sample path, a common credit shock at approximately 2.76 years instigated (at random) jumps in default intensity for a number of entities. As some of these entities default, at times indicated by the symbol X on the horizontal axis, and as the intensities of default for the surviving firms mean revert back to typical levels, the total arrival intensity for defaults drops quickly, moving back to near its pre-event levels within roughly 1 year. Duffie and Singleton (1998) provide some numerical examples of the distribution of default losses for this example.

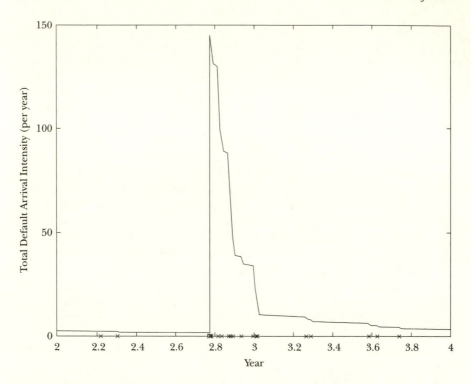

Figure 10.5. *A portion of a simulated sample path of total default arrival intensity (initially 1,000 firms). An* X *indicates a default event. A common jump in intensity occurs at year 2.76.*

10.3.2. Correlated Log-Normal Intensities

We illustrate another simple doubly stochastic correlated default model, this time with correlated log-normal default intensities. Suppose that the intensities change only once a year. (One could rework the model based on a shorter time interval, such as one quarter.) Further, for counterparty i, the default intensity λ_{it} during year $t+1$ is a log-normal model with mean reversion, in the sense that

$$\log \lambda_{i,t+1} = \kappa_i(\log \bar{\lambda}_i - \log \lambda_{i,t}) + \sigma_i \epsilon_{i,t+1},$$

where κ_i is the rate of mean reversion, $\log \bar{\lambda}_i$ is the steady-state mean level for the log-intensity, and σ_i is the volatility. The $\{\epsilon_{i,1}, \ldots, \epsilon_{i,t}\}$ are independent standard-normal random variables.

One can introduce correlation in default risk through the correlation

ρ_{ij} between ϵ_i and ϵ_j. Illustrative examples with Monte Carlo simulation of default losses are provided by Duffie and Singleton (1998).

10.4. Copula-Based Correlation Modeling

We saw in Chapter 3 that one can simulate a default time τ from its associated survival function $p(\cdot)$, which is defined by $p(t) = P(\tau \geq t)$. First, one simulates a uniformly distributed random variable U. Then, the associated default time τ satisfies $p(\tau) = U$, as illustrated earlier in Figure 3.18.

One can extend this inverse-CDF algorithm to allow for the simulation of n correlated default times $\tau_1, \ldots, \tau_n$, using what is often called the *copula method*. In order to explain this, let $p_1(\cdot), \ldots, p_n(\cdot)$ be the associated survival functions. Let $U_i = p(\tau_i)$, a random variable that, under mild regularity conditions, is uniformly distributed on $[0, 1]$. Thus, if we can simulate $U_1, \ldots, U_n$ with the correct joint probability distribution of $p_1(\tau_1), \ldots, p_n(\tau_n)$, then we can simulate $\tau_1, \ldots, \tau_n$ with the correct joint distribution as follows. First, simulate $U_1, \ldots, U_n$ and then choose $\tau_1, \ldots, \tau_n$ so that $p(\tau_i) = U_i$, as in Figure 10.6.

Rather than specifying the joint probability distribution of the default times $\tau_1, \ldots, \tau_n$ directly, the typical copula approach takes as primitives the

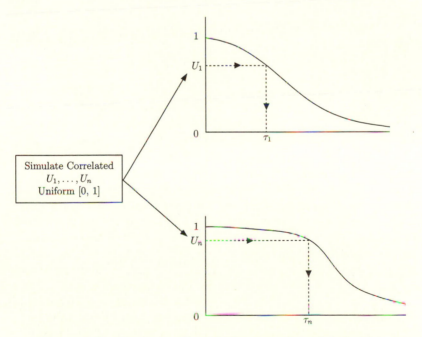

Figure 10.6. *Copula-based simulation of correlated default times.*

survival functions $p_1(\cdot), \ldots, p_n(\cdot)$ as well as the joint probability distribution of the correlated uniforms $U_1, \ldots, U_n$, which is specified by a copula function $C(\cdot)$ in n variables, defined with the property that

$$C(u_1, \ldots, u_n) = P(U_1 \le u_1, \ldots, U_n \le u_n).$$

Examples of copulas in the bivariate case include:

- Independence: $C(u, v) = uv$.
- Perfect correlation: $C(u, v) = \min(u, v)$.
- Gumbel copula:

$$C(u, v) = \exp\left[-\left[(-\ln u)^\delta(-\ln v)^\delta\right]^{1/\delta}\right].$$

- Frank copula:

$$C(u, v) = \frac{1}{\alpha} \log\left(1 + \frac{(e^{\alpha u} - 1)(e^{\alpha v} - 1)}{e^\alpha - 1}\right).$$

- Gaussian copula, with correlation ρ:

$$C(u, v) = P(N(X) \le u, N(Y) \le v),$$

where X and Y are standard joint normal with correlation ρ and $N(\cdot)$ is the standard-normal cumulative distribution function.

A popular copula in default applications is the Gaussian, perhaps because of the ease of simulating correlated Gaussians using Cholesky decompositions, as explained for the CreditMetrics model and illustrated in Figure 10.7. As for the parameterization of the survival functions $p_1, \ldots, p_n$, we are not aware of standard approaches, although it may be natural to adopt the survival functions of some given default-intensity processes $\lambda_1, \ldots, \lambda_n$ for the n respective firms. There is a question of consistency, however, between the correlations in default times implied by the copula function and the joint distribution of the default intensity processes. Schönbucher and Schubert (2001) present results incorporating copulas into an default-conditional intensity framework.

Das and Geng (2002) and Das et al. (2002) have recently explored the empirical goodness-of-fit of several combinations of individual issuer survival functions p_i and copulas C, using historical data on default probabilities (PDs) provided by Moody's. Letting PD_t devote the 1-year default probability observed at time t for a typical firm, they used the transformed

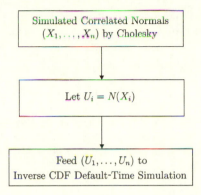

Figure 10.7. *Using correlated Gaussians to simulate correlated uniforms.*

variable $h_t \equiv -\ln(1 - PD_t)$ as their measure of default intensity,[3] and modeled h_t as either (1) a mean-reverting Gaussian process with Poisson arrival of jumps that are positive and uniformally distributed, or (2) a *switching-regime* model in which h_t is a CIR process within each regime (high-mean and low-mean regimes), and in which a two-state Markov chain governs the transitions between regimes. Both of these models capture *jumpiness* in h_t (though in somewhat different ways), a feature of the data that is discussed in more depth in Section 10.5. As for the copulas, Gaussian, Gumbel, Clayton, and Student-t specifications were examined. They concluded that Gaussian-jump/Student-t and regime-switching/Gaussian pairs of intensity/copula specifications did a good job of matching the correlation structure of their 1-year PDs. Goodness-of-fit was assessed by comparing features of the historical and model-implied correlations among the average h_t by rating class.

Two natural questions raised by the wide variety of choices of marginal distributions for intensities and copulas for determining default correlations are: (1) If we specify a plausible model for the true process generating default correlations, how well does a standard copula approach describe this truth? (2) If we use a copula approach to match the 1-year default correlations, will we be assured of matching the multiyear conditional default correlations? The answer to the latter is, of course, important in pricing and risk measurement, where positions are outstanding for multiple years.

---

[3] To motivate this calculation recall from Chapter 3 that in a model in which the intensity λ_t is an affine diffusion, the negative of the logarithm of the survival probability is an affine with respect to the factors determining λ_t. Therefore, in a one-factor model (in which the state is described by λ_t itself), h_t is perfectly correlated with λ_t, though not equal to it.

Table 10.2.   Joint Default Probabilities, in Basis Points, for First-Passage, Actual (Plain Type) versus Gaussian Copula (Bold Type) with the Same Correlation $\rho=\rho_G=0.5$

	$0 < \tau_1 \leq 1$	$1 < \tau_1 \leq 2$	$2 < \tau_1 \leq 3$	$3 < \tau_1 \leq 4$	$4 < \tau_1 \leq 5$
$0 < \tau_2 \leq 1$	(78, **168**)	(27, **79**)	(5, **31**)	(2, **15**)	(1, **9**)
$1 < \tau_2 \leq 2$	(27, **77**)	(55, **48**)	(13, **20**)	(0.05, **11**)	(2, **6**)
$2 < \tau_2 \leq 3$	(6, **31**)	(14, **20**)	(17, **10**)	(5, **5**)	(2, **3**)
$3 < \tau_2 \leq 4$	(3, **14**)	(4, **11**)	(5, **5**)	(6, **3**)	(2, **1**)
$4 < \tau_2 \leq 5$	(1, **9**)	(2, **6**)	(2, **3**)	(2, **1**)	(3, **1**)
$5 < \tau_2$	(24, **323**)	(44, **320**)	(37, **158**)	(29, **85**)	(29, **50**)

To shed some light on these issues we construct an example of two firms with correlated default times τ_1 and τ_2. We suppose that the "true" underlying model is default caused by first passages of the firms respective log-normal assets to default boundary levels. The two firms are assumed to have identical default risk. Their assets have the same volatility, $\sigma = 0.3$, and a mean growth rate of $\mu = 0.2$. The initial asset levels are both $1.5B$, where B is the default-triggering boundary. That is, τ_i is the first time t at which $A_{it} \leq B$, where A_{it} is the level of assets of firm i at time t. The asset returns of the two firms have correlation $\rho = 0.5$.[4] Both firms have the survival function $p(\cdot)$ associated with first passage, given by (3.10).

The joint distribution of the first-passage default times τ_1 and τ_2 implies some particular correct copula function, although this may be difficult to calculate and has not been used in practice. Instead, it has been more common to impose an *approximating* copula function, such as the Gaussian. There is the issue of which correlation ρ_G to use for the normal variables X_1 and X_2, which are used for purposes of simulating each uniform-$[0, 1]$ variable, $U_i = N(X_i)$, that enters the copula model, as in Figure 10.7. First, we try taking the copula correlation ρ_G to be the same as the asset-return correlation ρ. Later, we try calibrating the Gaussian copula correlation so as to match the joint probability of default in the first year. Both approaches to choosing ρ_G have been used in practice.

Table 10.2 compares the actual joint distribution of the default times τ_1 and τ_2 with that implied by the same survival function $p(\cdot)$, but with the approximating Gaussian copula, at correlation $\rho_G = \rho = 0.5$. The table shows, in each cell (i, j), the probability $P(i < \tau_1 \leq i+1, j < \tau_2 \leq j+1)$ that the default times of the two firms are in years i and j, respectively, for each of

---

[4] That is, the correlation of the Brownian motions underlying the two asset processes A_1 and A_2 is $\rho = 0.5$.

Table 10.3. *Joint Default Probabilities, in Basis Points, for First-Passage, Actual with Correlation $\rho = 0.1$ (Plain Type) versus Gaussian Copula (Bold Type) with Calibrated Correlation $\rho_G = 0.149$*

	$0 < \tau_1 \leq 1$	$1 < \tau_1 \leq 2$	$2 < \tau_1 \leq 3$	$3 < \tau_1 \leq 4$	$4 < \tau_1 \leq 5$
$0 < \tau_2 \leq 1$	(16, **16**)	(9, **5**)	(3, **1**)	(1, **1**)	(1, **0**)
$1 < \tau_2 \leq 2$	(8, **5**)	(14, **11**)	(3, **4**)	(1, **1**)	(0, **1**)
$2 < \tau_2 \leq 3$	(3, **1**)	(4, **4**)	(4, **3**)	(1, **1**)	(0, **0**)
$3 < \tau_2 \leq 4$	(1, **1**)	(1, **1**)	(1, **1**)	(1, **2**)	(0, **0**)
$4 < \tau_2 \leq 5$	(0, **0**)	(1, **1**)	(1, **0**)	(1, **0**)	(1, **0**)
$5 < \tau_2$	(38, **601**)	(57, **451**)	(43, **201**)	(33, **97**)	(32, **41**)

the first 5 years, according to the actual first-passage model and according to the approximating model based on the Gaussian copula. The actual joint default probabilities are shown in plain type; those based on the Gaussian copula are shown in bold type. All values are in basis points and estimated by Monte Carlo simulation. For example, the actual probability of joint default in the first year is 78 basis points, while the joint probability of default in the first year for the Gaussian copula–based model is 168 basis points. These estimates are approximate, owing to Monte Carlo sampling noise,[5] but sufficiently accurate for us to see that at the given asset correlation ρ the Gaussian copula does not come close to the true joint distribution of default times.

Table 10.3 shows the effect of calibrating the Gaussian-copula correlation ρ_G so that the implied probabilities of joint default in the first year from the Gaussian-copula and actual models match, for an asset-return correlation of $\rho = 0.1$. As shown, despite the calibration, the models do not match well over the entire 5-year period. In particular, the joint probability that issuer 1 defaults within 1 of the first 4 years and issuer 2 survives for at least 5 years is very poorly matched by the copula model (see the last row of Table 10.3). Table 10.4 provides the same comparison for an asset correlation of $\rho = 0.9$. In this case, the match is also poor for many cases in which issuer 2 also defaults before year 5.

We stress that because the correct first-passage survival function $p(\cdot)$ is used throughout, the two firms' default times have the correct marginal distributions in all cases. Thus, it is precisely the correlation of the default times that is not being well captured by the Gaussian copula.

---

[5] Since the setup treats the two firms symmetrically, the degree of error in the numerical results can be viewed in terms of differences in symmetric cells in Table 10.2. For example, by symmetry, $P(1 < \tau_1 \leq 2, 0 < \tau_2 \leq 1) = P(0 < \tau_1 \leq 1, 1 < \tau_2 \leq 2)$, but for approximating the Gaussian-copula model, the Monte Carlo estimate of $P(1 < \tau_1 \leq 2, 0 \leq \tau_2 < 1)$ is 79 basis points, whereas the Monte Carlo estimate of $P(0 < \tau_1 \leq 1, 1 < \tau_2 \leq 1)$ is 77 basis points.

*Table 10.4.   Joint Default Probabilities, in Basis Points, for First-Passage,
Actual with Correlation ρ = 0.9 (Plain Type) versus Gaussian
Copula (Bold Type) with Calibrated Correlation $\rho_G = 0.311$*

	$0 < \tau_1 \leq 1$	$1 < \tau_1 \leq 2$	$2 < \tau_1 \leq 3$	$3 < \tau_1 \leq 4$	$4 < \tau_1 \leq 5$
$0 < \tau_2 \leq 1$	(254, **253**)	(37, **182**)	(6, **61**)	(2, **41**)	(1, **7**)
$1 < \tau_2 \leq 2$	(37, **181**)	(189, **101**)	(24, **48**)	(6, **15**)	(2, **8**)
$2 < \tau_2 \leq 3$	(7, **61**)	(24, **48**)	(76, **9**)	(13, **7**)	(3, **6**)
$3 < \tau_2 \leq 4$	(2, **42**)	(6, **15**)	(12, **7**)	(35, **2**)	(6, **1**)
$4 < \tau_2 \leq 5$	(1, **6**)	(2, **8**)	(3, **5**)	(7, **1**)	(19, **1**)
$5 < \tau_2$	(4, **81**)	(11, **170**)	(9, **143**)	(10, **70**)	(15, **5**)

10.5. Empirical Methods

Suppose one has in mind a particular doubly stochastic model for correlated default, with intensity processes $\lambda_1, \ldots, \lambda_n$, whose behavior, including correlation effects, depends on a vector θ of parameters to be estimated. One approach to estimating θ is to use the incidence of actual historical default data, and estimate, say, a logit model that predicts default based on a vector $X_t = (X_{1t}, \ldots, X_{kt})$ of covariates, such as firm size, industry, debt ratios, GDP growth rates, and the like, as in Chapter 3. The parameters to be estimated include both the logit parameters, specifying how default intensities depend on the covariates, and the parameters that determine the random evolution of the underlying covariates. Without capturing the time-series behavior of the covariates, one cannot capture the implied behavior of the default intensities over time.

Another approach is to use historical estimates of the conditonal probability p_{it} at time t that entity i survives for 1 year. KMV and Moody's, for example, both have such historical data. Then, given the available data across all past times t and names i, one can estimate a model for the joint evolution of the default-intensity processes $\lambda_1, \ldots, \lambda_n$ that reflects the observed correlated variation over time in $p_{1t}, \ldots, p_{nt}$.

For example, one could let $X_t = (X_{1t}, \ldots, X_{kt})$ denote a state vector that captures the credit quality at time t of the given set of firms. These data can include both p_{it} as well as industry or macro data. We could then suppose that the default intensities are of the form

$$\lambda_{it} = f(X_t, \theta_i), \tag{10.2}$$

for a parameter vector θ_i to be estimated. With historical data on X_t, one can estimate the dynamics of X and the parameters determining intensities.

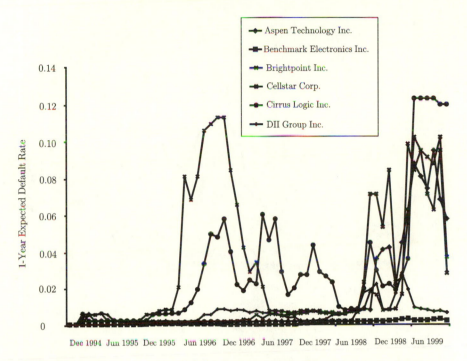

Figure 10.8. *One-year expected default rate* $-\log(p_t)$: *Moody's data for 1-year survival probability* p_t *at* t *for selected electronics firms.*

Monthly time series of data on estimated default probabilities for various firms, such as those of Moody's or KMV, could be used to estimate default-intensity volatilities and correlations. A small sample of Moody's PD data is illustrated in Figure 10.8, for selected electronics firms. A casual examination of these time series reveals a significant degree of jumpiness and mean reversion as well as correlation across firms within the sector. Figure 10.9 shows time series of sector averages. The figure also reveals some co-movement across sectors.

10.6. Default-Time Simulation Algorithms

Given stochastic intensity processes $\lambda_1, \ldots, \lambda_n$ for each entity, our objective is to simulate the associated default times $\tau_1, \ldots, \tau_n$, and the identities of the defaulter at each default time. Some of the basic algorithms, coming from the reliability literature on failure-time modeling,[6] are reviewed below

---

[6] See, e.g., the survey by Shaked and Shanthikumar (1993).

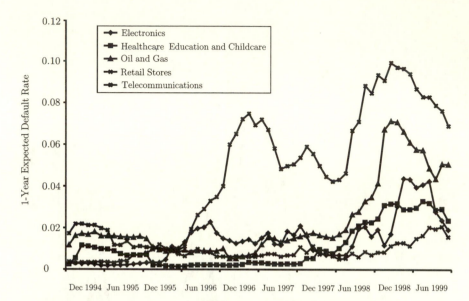

Figure 10.9. *Average of 1-year expected default rate* $-\log(p_t)$: *Moody's data for the survival probability* p_t *for averages of ten selected firms within each of five selected industries.*

and extend the default-time simulation methods for one entity illustrated in Chapter 3. In some cases, as we point out, these algorithms are computationally burdensome for general correlated multivariate diffusion models for intensities.

For simplicity, we take the doubly stochastic model, with default intensities $\lambda_1, \ldots, \lambda_n$. One can simulate the default times $\tau_1, \ldots, \tau_n$ with the correct joint distribution (including correlation) by the following basic algorithms, letting T denote the time horizon, assuming that one is interested in knowing the outcome of τ_i only if it is in the interval $(0, T)$.

10.6.1. Multicompensator Method

In the doubly stochastic setting, we can extend the compensator method for one entity to simulate all of the default times $\tau_1, \ldots, \tau_n$ that occur before some given time horizon T, as follows. It is assumed that the compensator $\Lambda_i(t) = \int_0^t \lambda_i(u)\, du$ can be simulated for each name i and time t, with the correct joint distribution. In practice, this is often done numerically, as in Chapter 3. The multicompensator algorithm is as follows:

1. Simulate n independent unit-mean exponentially distributed random variables $Z_1, \ldots, Z_n$.

2. For each i, if $\Lambda_i(T) < Z_i$, then $\tau_i > T$.
3. Otherwise, let $\tau_i = \min\{t : \Lambda_i(t) = Z_i\}$.

This algorithm is in effect the same as that for a single entity, illustrated earlier in Figure 3.19.

10.6.2. First-Defaults Simulation

The following algorithm also generates default times with the correct distribution, assuming that one needs to simulate only the first m default times out of n. If m is small relative to n, as is the case with certain first-to-default credit derivatives, this algorithm is more efficient than the complete multi-compensator algorithm of the last example.

The setting is again one of doubly stochastic default of n entities with respective intensity processes $\lambda_1, \ldots, \lambda_n$. The steps of the algorithm are as follows:

1. Simulate m independent unit-mean exponentially distributed random variables $Z_1, \ldots, Z_m$. After simulation, we relabel them so that they are ordered, in that $Z_i < Z_j$ for $i < j$.
2. For each k, let $A(k) \subset \{1, \ldots, n\}$ denote the set of surviving entities after the kth default. We start with $k = 0$ and $A(0) = \{1, \ldots, n\}$.
3. Simulate, as t gets larger and larger, for each i in $A(k)$, the compensator $\Lambda_i(t)$ until one reaches the time horizon T (in which case, stop) or until such time as one of the compensators, $\Lambda_i(t)$, reaches the level Z_{k+1}. At that time t, entity i defaults and is removed from $A(k)$ to form $A(k+1)$.
4. Increment k by 1, and go back to the previous step, unless $k = m + 1$ (in which case, stop).

Compensator-based simulation approaches are also possible, in a more complicated form, if one computes the intensities when conditioning only on the history of the default times and identities of defaulting entities. This information structure is sometimes called the *internal filtration,* and the resulting intensities in this setting are often called conditional hazard rates. The failure-time simulation is then called the *multivariate hazard construction,* proposed by Norros (1986) and Shaked and Shanthikumar (1987). The multivariate-hazard construction is preferred if the hazard rates relative to the internal filtration can be computed explicitly.

For most of our numerical results for correlated default times, we have used an algorithm based on compensator simulation. For the mean-reverting-with-jumps model, however, we have avoided the need to discretize the simulation of the compensators $\Lambda_i(t)$ in time because the paths of the intensity are piecewise deterministic and have an explicit integral between jumps. (We need only simulate their jump times and jump sizes, which in our examples have explicit distributions.)

10.6.3. Recursive Inverse-CDF Simulation

We extend the single-entity inverse-CDF default time simulation to one of doubly stochastic default of n entities with respective intensity processes $\lambda_1, \ldots, \lambda_n$. One proceeds as follows,[7] letting T_k denote the kth to occur of the default times, with I_k the identity of the kth defaulter, $A(k)$ the set of undefaulted entities after T_{k-1}, and

$$W_k = \{(T_1, I_1, Y_1), \ldots, (T_k, I_k, Y_k)\},$$

the set of conditioning variables available at time T_k, where Y_k denotes a list of any additional state variables used for computing the CDF $p(T_k, \cdot)$ of the next default time T_{k+1}. For example, in the doubly stochastic model with intensities that are functions of a Markov state variable X, we can take $Y_k = X(T_k)$. We let $\lambda^{(k)} = \sum_{i \in A(k)} \lambda_i$ denote the total intensity of default over the remaining entities and let

$$q_k(t, s) = E_t \left[\exp \left(\int_t^s -\lambda^{(k)}(s) \, ds \right) \right]. \tag{10.3}$$

We have $p(T_k, s) = q_k(T_k, s)$ for any $s > T_k$. Under technical conditions, the conditional probability given (W_{k-1}, T_k) that i is the defaulting entity at T_k is

$$g_i(k) = P(I_k = i \,|\, W_{k-1}, T_k) = \frac{\gamma_i(T_{k-1}, T_k)}{\sum_{j \in A(k)} \gamma_j(T_{k-1}, T_k)},$$

where, for each $s > T_{k-1}$,[8]

$$\gamma_i(T_{k-1}, s) = E \left[\exp \left(\int_{T_{k-1}}^s -\lambda^{(k)}(u) \, du \right) \lambda_i(s) \,\Bigg|\, W_{k-1} \right]. \tag{10.4}$$

If the state process X is affine and the intensities depend in an affine manner on X, one can compute γ_i analytically, as pointed out in Appendix A.

The steps of the default-time simulation algorithm are as follows:

1. Let $k = 1$, $T_0 = 0$, and $A_0 = \{1, \ldots, n\}$.

---

[7] We leave out technical conditions and details.
[8] For more, but not all, details, see Duffie (1998b).

2. At time T_{k-1}, simulate, by inverse-CDF simulation using $p(T_{k-1}, \cdot)$, the next-to-default time T_k.
3. If $T_k > T$ stop.
4. Simulate the identity I_k of the kth defaulter from $A(k)$, with the conditional probability of $g_i(k)$ that $I_k = i$.
5. Simulate the additional state variables Y_k, with their distribution given the conditioning variables W_{k-1}, T_k, I_k. This is computationally challenging for most stochastic intensity models.
6. Remove I_k from $A(k-1)$ to get $A(k)$, and unless $A(k)$ is empty, advance k by 1 and go back to Step 2.

10.7. Joint Default Events

Certain default events may be common to a number of counterparties. These could include severe natural catastrophes, systemic defaults or liquidity breakdowns, political events such as the acts of foreign governments, or the defaults of counterparties linked to each other through contracts or capital structure.

Allowing joint default events is a significant departure from our usual setting, for both structural models and for doubly stochastic intensity models of correlated default. With joint credit events, some of the default intensity of each entity is tied to an event at which another entity may default with some given probability. In particular, it is *not* the case that after conditioning on the paths of the different entities' intensities that default times are independent.

With joint default events in an intensity-based setting, the total default intensity of entity i at time t is

$$\lambda_{it} = p_{it} J_t + H_{it}, \tag{10.5}$$

where, at time t, J_t is the intensity for arrival of joint credit events; p_{it} is the probability that entity i defaults given a joint credit event; and H_{it} is the intensity of arrival of default from causes specific to entity i. With this model, the intensity of arrival of any kind of event is

$$H_t = J_t + H_{1t} + \cdots + H_{nt}.$$

A version of this approach is the classical multivariate-exponential distribution of failure times, reviewed later in this section, under which all individual intensities (H_i and J) and conditional default probabilities (p_i) are constants. The main advantage of the multivariate exponential model is its simplicity. Both simulation and computation of numerous statistics (moments, joint survival probabilities, and so on) are easy. For example, the impact of correlation is easily captured for first-to-default swap pricing. On the other hand, because the multivariate-exponential model has constant default intensities, it is not easily calibrated to data that bear on the term structure of default probabilities, such as bond or equity price data, or on the volatility of credit risk before default. For example, with risk-neutral bond investors, the term structure of credit yield spreads for the multivariate-exponential model of default times is literally flat because the default hazard rates are constant, whereas credit spreads often exhibit substantial slope, volatility, and correlation. (Term-structure effects could arise, however, from time variation in conditional expected recovery at default, as in Das and Tufano, 1996, or in risk premia.)

Moreover, it is somewhat unrealistic to suppose that two or more firms would default literally simultaneously, unless there is a parent subsidiary or similar contractual relationship. For example, Global Crossings defaulted in early 2002, and its affiliate, Global Crossings Asia, defaulted a few days later. While the difference between simultaneous and nearly timed default may not be critical for expected default losses or for the pricing of certain credit derivatives, it may indeed be an important distinction for measurement of the likelihood of a given sized loss within a relatively small time window. With the multivariate exponential model, to the extent that correlations in the incidence of defaults within a given year are realistically captured, the model implies an unrealistically high likelihood of joint default within a given week.

A related alternative is a contagion model, such as the static *infectious default* model of Davis and Lo (1999).

The simplest of all models of correlated credit event times is the multivariate exponential. The basic idea of this model is that all types of events, whether joint or particular to a given entity, have constant intensities. That is, with this model, each credit event has a Poisson arrival with constant intensity, but certain entities may default simultaneously by common credit events, with specified probabilities.

There are equivalent ways to specify such a model. The following is unconventional but convenient for applications to credit pricing and risk measurement.

The basic ingredients are independent credit-event-counting Poisson processes $N_1, \ldots, N_m$ with intensity parameters $\beta_1, \ldots, \beta_m$. Whenever, for any j, there is a jump in process N_j, entity i defaults provided the outcome of an independent 0-or-1 trial, with probability p_{ij} of 1, is in fact 1.

We can think of the jumps of some (or all) of the underlying Poisson processes $N_1, \ldots, N_m$ as marketwide events that could, at random, affect any of n entities. Correlation effects are determined by the underlying credit-event intensities $\beta_1, \ldots, \beta_m$ and by the impact probabilities p_{ij}.

With this model, the default intensity of entity i is constant at

$$\lambda_i = \sum_{j=1}^{m} p_{ij} \beta_j.$$

The intensity of arrival of simultaneous credit events for entities i and k is

$$\lambda_{ik} = \sum_{j=1}^{m} p_{ij} p_{kj} \beta_j.$$

Likewise, for any subset $A \subset \{1, \ldots, n\}$ of entities, the Poisson-arrival rate of a simultaneous credit event for all entities in A is

$$\lambda_A = \sum_{j=1}^{m} \beta_j \prod_{i \in A} p_{ij},$$

where $\prod_{i \in A} p_{ij}$ denotes the product of p_{ij} over all i in A.

Conditional on survival of entities i and j to the current date, the correlation between the times to the next credit events for entities i and k turns out to be[9]

$$\rho_{ik} = \frac{\lambda_{ik}}{\lambda_i + \lambda_k - \lambda_{ik}}.$$

Many other statistics regarding the joint distribution of event times can be worked out explicitly.[10]

It is useful to note that, at any time, the default-time model for the remaining (nondefaulted) entities is multivariate exponential.

An extension of the model is to assume that the underlying Poisson processes "disappear" at certain (say, Poisson) arrival times, and perhaps that others, with different parameters, "appear" at certain times. In this case, it is easy to update the model parameters with each appearance and disappearance, so that the model is piecewise-in-time multivariate exponential. Simulation in this framework is easily accomplished. First one simulates the appearance and disappearance times, which form *epochs*. Then one simulates the event times within each epoch as jointly exponentially distributed, with right censoring.

---

[9] See Barlow and Proschan (1981, p. 135, Exercise 8c). We are grateful to Josh Danziger of CIBC for bringing this convenient formula to our attention.

[10] See Barlow and Proschan (1981).

11

Collateralized Debt Obligations

THIS CHAPTER ADDRESSES the risk analysis and market valuation of collateralized debt obligations (CDOs).[1] After describing some of the economic motivations for, and institutional features of, CDOs, we turn to an extensive illustration of the effects of correlation and prioritization for the market valuation, diversity score, and risk of CDOs, in a setting of correlated default intensities.

11.1. Introduction

A CDO is an asset-backed security whose underlying collateral is typically a portfolio of bonds (corporate or sovereign) or bank loans. A CDO cash flow structure allocates interest income and principal repayments from a collateral pool of different debt instruments to a prioritized collection of CDO securities, which we shall call *tranches*. While there are many variations, a standard prioritization scheme is simple subordination: Senior CDO notes are paid before mezzanine and lower-subordinated notes are paid, with any residual cash flow paid to an equity piece. Some illustrative examples of prioritization are provided in Section 11.4.

A *cash flow* CDO is one for which the collateral portfolio is not subjected to active trading by the CDO manager, implying that the uncertainty regarding interest and principal payments to the CDO tranches is determined mainly by the number and timing of defaults of the collateral securities. A *market value* CDO is one for which the CDO tranches receive payments based essentially on the mark-to-market returns of the collateral pool, which depends on the trading performance of the CDO asset manager. In this chapter, we concentrate on cash flow CDOs, avoiding an analysis of the trading behavior of CDO managers.

---

[1] This chapter is based on Duffie and Gârleanu (2001).

A generic example of the contractual relationships involved in a CDO is shown in Figure 11.1, taken from Schorin and Weinreich (1998). The collateral manager is charged with the selection and purchase of collateral assets for the special purpose vehicle (SPV). The trustee of the CDO is responsible for monitoring the contractual provisions of the CDO. Our analysis assumes perfect adherence to these contractual provisions. The main issue that we address is the impact of the joint distribution of default risk of the underlying collateral securities on the risk and valuation of the CDO tranches. We are also interested in the efficacy of alternative computational methods and the role of *diversity scores,* a measure of the risk of the CDO collateral pool that has been used for CDO risk analysis by rating agencies.

We will see that default-time correlation has a significant impact on the market values of individual tranches. The priority of the senior tranche, by which it is effectively "short a call option" on the performance of the underlying collateral pool, causes its market value to decrease with risk-neutral default-time correlation. The value of the equity piece, which resembles a call option, increases with correlation. However, there is no clear effect of optionality for the valuation of intermediate tranches. With sufficient overcollateralization, the option "written" (to the lower tranches) dominates, but it is the other way around for sufficiently low levels of overcollateralization. Market spreads, at least for conventional mezzanine and senior tranches, are not especially sensitive to the *lumpiness* of information arrival regarding credit quality. For example, for our jump-diffusion model of default intensity, replacing the contribution of diffusion with jump risks (of various types), holding constant the degree of covariance of risk-neutral

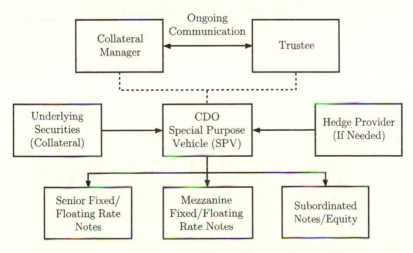

Figure 11.1. *Typical CDO contractual relationships. (Source: Morgan Stanley.)*

default intensities and the term structure of credit spreads, generates relatively small changes in pricing. Regarding alternative computational methods, we show that if (risk-neutral) diversity scores can be evaluated accurately, which is computationally simple in the framework we propose, these scores can be used to obtain good approximate market valuations for reasonably well-collateralized tranches. Currently the weakest link in the chain of CDO analysis is the limited availability of empirical data bearing on the correlation of default risk.

11.2. Some Economics of CDOs

In perfect capital markets, CDOs would serve no purpose; the costs of constructing and marketing a CDO would inhibit its creation. In practice, CDOs address some important market imperfections. First, banks and certain other financial institutions have regulatory capital requirements that make it valuable for them to securitize and sell some portion of their assets, reducing the amount of (expensive) regulatory capital that they must hold. Second, individual bonds or loans may be illiquid, leading to a reduction in their market values. Securitization and prioritization may improve liquidity and thereby raise the total market valuation of the CDO structure relative to the sum of the market values of its collateral components.

In light of these market imperfections, two broad classes of CDOs are popular: (1) balance-sheet CDOs and (2) arbitrage CDOs. The balance-sheet CDO, typically in the form of a collateralized loan obligation (CLO), is usually designed to remove loans from the balance sheets of banks, achieving capital relief and perhaps also increasing the valuation of the assets through an increase in liquidity. A synthetic balance-sheet CLO differs from a conventional balance-sheet CLO in that the bank originating the loans does not actually transfer ownership of the loans to the SPV, but instead uses credit derivatives to transfer the default risk to the SPV. The direct sale of loans to SPVs may sometimes compromise client relationships or secrecy, or can be costly because of contractual restrictions on transferring the underlying loans. Unfortunately, regulations do not always provide the same capital relief for a synthetic CLO as for an standard balance-sheet CLO (see Punjabi and Tierney, 1999).

The second basic class of CDOs is of the arbitrage type, often underwritten by an investment bank and designed to capture some fraction of the likely difference between the total cost of acquiring collateral assets in the secondary market and the value received from management fees and the sale of the associated CDO structure. Balance-sheet CDOs are normally of the cash flow type. Arbitrage CDOs may be collateralized bond obligations (CBOs), and have either cash flow or market value structures.

Among the sources of illiquidity that promote, or limit, the use of CDOs are adverse selection, trading costs, and moral hazard.

With regard to adverse selection, there may be a significant amount of private information regarding the credit quality of a junk bond or a bank loan. An investor may be concerned about being "picked off" when trading such instruments. For instance, a potentially better-informed seller has an option to trade or not at the given price. The value of this option is related to the quality of the seller's private information. Given the risk of being picked off, the buyer offers a price that, on average, is below the price at which the asset would be sold in a setting of symmetric information. This reduction in price owing to adverse selection is sometimes called a *lemon's premium* (Akerlof, 1970). In general, adverse selection cannot be eliminated by securitization of assets in a CDO, but it can be mitigated. The seller achieves a higher total valuation (for what is sold and what is retained) by designing the CDO structure so as to concentrate the majority of the risk about which there may be fear of adverse selection into small subordinate tranches. A large senior tranche, relatively immune to the effects of adverse selection, can be sold at a small lemon's premium. The issuer can retain, on average, significant fractions of smaller subordinate tranches that are more subject to adverse selection. For models supporting this design and retention behavior, see DeMarzo (1998) and DeMarzo and Duffie (1999).

For a relatively small junk bond or a single bank loan to a relatively obscure borrower, there can be a small market of potential buyers and sellers. This is not unrelated to the effects of adverse selection, but depends as well on the total size of an issue. In order to sell such an illiquid asset quickly, one may be forced to sell at the highest bid among the relatively few buyers with whom one can negotiate on short notice. Searching for such buyers can be expensive. One's negotiating position may also be poorer than it would be in an active market, and the valuation of the asset is correspondingly reduced. Potential buyers recognize that they are placing themselves at the risk of facing the same situation in the future, resulting in yet lower valuations. The net expense of bearing these costs may be reduced through securitization into relatively large homogeneous senior CDO tranches, perhaps with significant retention of smaller and less-easily-traded junior tranches.

Moral hazard, in the context of CDOs, bears on the issuer's or CDO manager's incentives to select high-quality assets for the CDO and to engage in costly enforcement of covenants and other restrictions on the behavior of obligors. By securitizing and selling a significant portion of the cash flows of the underlying assets, these incentives are diluted. Reductions in value through lack of effort are borne to some extent by investors. There may also be an opportunity for *cherry picking*, that is, for sorting assets into the issuer's own portfolio or into the SPV portfolio based on the issuer's private information. There could also be *front-running* opportunities, under which a CDO manager could trade on its own account in advance of trades on behalf of the CDO. These moral hazards act *against* the creation of CDOs, for the incentives to select and monitor assets promote greater efficiency, and higher valuation, if the issuer retains a full 100% equity interest in the asset cash flows. The opportunity to reduce other market imperfections through a CDO may, however, be sufficiently great to offset the effects of moral hazard and result in securitization, especially in light of the advantage of building and maintaining a reputation for not exploiting CDO investors. The issuer has an incentive to design the CDO in such a manner that it retains a significant portion of one or more subordinate tranches, which would be among the first to suffer losses stemming from poor monitoring, servicing, or asset selection, demonstrating to investors a degree of commitment on the part of the issuer to perform at high effort levels. Likewise, for arbitrage CDOs, a significant portion of the management fees may be subordinated to the issued tranches (see Schorin and Weinreich, 1998). In light of this commitment, investors may be willing to pay more for the tranches in which they invest, and the total valuation to the issuer is higher than would be the case for an unprioritized structure, such as a straight-equity pass-through security. Innes (1990) has a model supporting this motive for security design.

As an early example, one of a pair of CLO cash flow structures issued by NationsBank in 1997 is illustrated in Figure 11.2. A senior tranche of $2 billion in face value is followed by successively lower-subordination tranches. The ratings assigned by Fitch are also illustrated. The bulk of the underlying assets are floating-rate NationsBank loans rated BBB or BB. Any fixed-rate

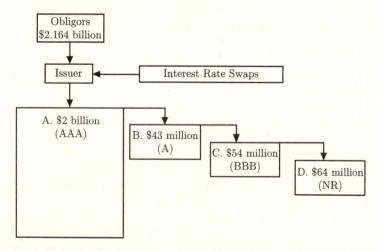

Figure 11.2.   *NationsBank 1997-1 CLO tranches. (Source: Fitch.)*

loans were significantly hedged against interest-rate risk by fixed-to-floating interest-rate swaps. As predicted by theory, the majority of the (unrated) lowest tranche was retained.

The valuation model that we describe next does not deal directly with the effects of market imperfections. It takes as given the default risk of the underlying loans and assumes that investors are symmetrically informed. While this is not perfectly realistic, it is not necessarily inconsistent with the roles of moral hazard or adverse selection in the original security design. For example, DeMarzo and Duffie (1999) demonstrate a fully separating equilibrium in which the sale price of the security or the amount retained by the seller signal the seller's privately held value-relevant information to all investors. As for moral hazard, the efforts of the issuer or manager are, to a large extent, determined by the security design and the fractions retained by the issuer. Once these are known, the default risk of the underlying debt is also determined. However, our simple valuation model does not account for the effects of many other forms of market imperfections.

11.3. Default-Risk Model

This section lays out some of the basic default modeling for the underlying collateral. First, we propose a simple model for the default risk of one obligor. Then we turn to default-risk correlation in a multi-issuer setting. Throughout, we work under risk-neutral probabilities, so that value will be given by expectations of discounted future cash flows.

11.3.1. Obligor Default Intensities

We take a doubly stochastic model of default times. As explained in Chapter 10, this means that we suppose that, conditional on the paths of their default intensities, obligors' default times are independent Poisson arrivals with those time-varying intensities. An alternative would be a model in which simultaneous defaults could be caused by certain common credit events, such as a multivariate-exponential model, as explained in Chapter 10, or in the infectious default models of Davis and Lo (1999, 2000).

Specifically, we suppose that each obligor's default time is a basic affine process, in the sense of Appendix A, meaning an intensity process λ solving a stochastic differential equation of the form

$$d\lambda(t) = \kappa [\theta - \lambda(t)] \, dt + \sigma \sqrt{\lambda(t)} \, dB(t) + \Delta J(t). \qquad (11.1)$$

Here B is a standard Brownian motion and $\Delta J(t)$ denotes the jump at time t (if one occurs) of a pure-jump process J, independent of W, whose jump sizes are independent and exponentially distributed with mean μ and whose jump times are those of an independent Poisson process with mean jump arrival rate ℓ. (Jump times and jump sizes are also independent.)[2] We call a process λ of this form (11.1) a *basic affine process with parameters* $(\kappa, \theta, \sigma, \mu, \ell)$. These parameters can be adjusted in several ways to control the manner in which default risk changes over time. For example, we can vary the mean-reversion rate κ, the long-run mean $\overline{m} = \theta + \ell\mu/\kappa$, or the relative contributions to the total variance of λ_t that are attributed to jump risk and to diffusive volatility. The long-run variance of λ_t is

$$\text{var}_\infty = \lim_t \text{var}(\lambda_t) = \frac{\sigma^2\overline{m}}{2\kappa} + \frac{\ell\mu^2}{\kappa}. \tag{11.2}$$

We can also vary the relative contributions to jump risk of the mean jump size μ and the mean jump arrival rate ℓ. A special case is the no-jump ($\ell = 0$) model of Feller (1951), which was used by Cox et al. (1985) to model interest rates. We can calculate that for any t and any $s \geq 0$,

$$E_t \left(e^{\int_t^{t+s} -\lambda_u \, du} \right) = e^{\alpha(t,s)+\beta(t,s)\lambda(t)}. \tag{11.3}$$

Explicit solutions for the coefficients $\alpha(t, s)$ and $\beta(t, s)$ are provided in Appendix A. This provides a simple, reasonably rich, and tractable model for the default-time probability distribution and how it varies at random over time as information comes into the market.

11.3.2. Multi-Issuer Default Model

In order to study the implications of changing the correlation in the default times of the various participations (collateralizing bonds or loans) of a CDO, while holding the default-risk model of each underlying obligor constant, we exploit the fact that a basic affine model can be written as the sum of independent basic affine models, provided that the parameters κ, σ, and μ governing, respectively, the mean-reversion rate, diffusive volatility, and mean jump size are common to the underlying pair of independent basic affine processes. (For a proof, see Duffie and Gârleanu, 2001.) This result allows us to maintain a fixed parsimonious and tractable one-factor Markov model for each obligor's default intensities, while varying the correlation among different obligors' default times, as explained below.

We suppose that there are N participations in the collateral pool, whose default times $\tau_1, \ldots, \tau_N$ have basic affine intensity processes $\lambda_1, \ldots, \lambda_N$,

---

[2] A technical condition that is sufficient for the existence of a strictly positive solution to (11.1) is that $\kappa\theta \geq \sigma^2/2$. We do not require it, since none of our results depends on strict positivity.

respectively. In order to introduce correlation in a simple way, we suppose that

$$\lambda_i = X_c + X_i, \tag{11.4}$$

where X_i is a basic affine process with parameters $(\kappa, \theta_i, \sigma, \mu, \ell_i)$, and X_c is a basic affine process with parameters $(\kappa, \theta_c, \sigma, \mu, \ell_c)$. These underlying state variables $X_1, \ldots, X_N, X_c$ are independent. As the sum of X_c and X_i, the default intensity λ_i is itself a one-dimensional basic affine process with parameters $(\kappa, \theta, \sigma, \mu, \ell)$, where $\theta = \theta_i + \theta_c$ and $\ell = \ell_i + \ell_c$. One may view X_c as a state process governing common aspects of economic performance in an industry, sector, or currency region and X_i as a state variable governing the idiosyncratic default risk specific to obligor i. The parameter

$$\rho = \frac{\ell_c}{\ell} \tag{11.5}$$

is the long-run fraction of jumps to a given obligor's intensity that are common to all (surviving) obligor's intensities. One can also see that ρ is the probability that λ_j jumps at time t given that λ_i jumps at time t, for any time t and any distinct i and j. We also suppose that $\theta_c = \rho\theta$.

11.3.3. Sectoral, Regional, and Global Risk

For extensions to handle multifactor risk (regional, sectoral, and other sources), one could suppose that the default time τ_i of the ith obligor has an intensity process of the form $\lambda_i = X_i + a_i Y_{c(i)} + b_i Z$, where the sector factor $Y_{c(i)}$ is common to all issuers in the sector $c(i)$, a subset of the set $\{1, \ldots, N\}$ of firms, for some number S of different sectors, where Z is common to all issuers and $\{X_1, \ldots, X_N, Y_1, \ldots, Y_S, Z\}$ are independent basic affine processes. The *factor-loading* coefficients a_i and b_i depend on the obligor.

If one does not restrict the parameters of the underlying basic affine processes, then an individual obligor's default intensity need not itself be a basic affine process, but calculations are nevertheless easy. We can use the independence of the underlying state variables to see that the conditional probability $p_i(t, s)$ at time t that issuer i survives to time s is of the form

$$p_i(t, s) = \exp\left[\alpha(s) + \beta_i(s) X_i(t) + \beta_{c(i)}(s) Y_{c(i)}(t) + \beta_Z(s) Z(t)\right], \tag{11.6}$$

where $\alpha(s) = \alpha_i(s) + \alpha_{c(i)}(s) + \alpha_Z(s)$ and all of the α and β coefficients are obtained explicitly, as explained in Appendix A, from the respective parameters of the underlying basic affine processes X_i, $Y_{c(i)}$, and Z.

Even more generally, one can adopt multifactor affine models in which the underlying state variables are not independent and interest rates are jointly determined by an underlying multifactor affine jump-diffusion model, as explained in Appendix A.

11.3.4. Recovery Risk

We suppose that, at default, any given piece of debt in the collateral pool may be sold for a fraction W of its face value whose actual and risk-neutral conditional expectation, given all the information available at any time t before default, is a constant $w \in (0, 1)$ that does not depend on t. The recovery fractions of the underlying participations are assumed to be independently distributed and independent of default times and interest rates. (Here again, we are referring to risk-neutral behavior.)

The recovered fraction W of face value is assumed to be uniformly distributed on $[0, 1]$, which is roughly representative of the empirical cross-sectional distribution of recovery of face value for senior unsecured debt, as measured by Moody's, as illustrated in Chapter 6.

11.3.5. Collateral Credit Spreads

We suppose for simplicity that changes in default intensities and changes in interest rates are (risk-neutrally) independent. An extension to treat correlated interest-rate risk is provided in Chapter 6. Combined with the above assumptions, this implies that for an issuer whose default time τ has a basic affine intensity process λ^*, a zero-coupon bond maturing at time s has an initial market value at time t of

$$v(t, s) = d(t, s)p^*(t, s) + w \int_t^s d(t, u)\pi(t, u)\, du, \qquad (11.7)$$

where $d(t, s)$ denotes the default-free zero-coupon discount from time t to time s, $p^*(t, s)$ is the risk-neutral survival probability, and

$$\pi(t, u) = -\frac{\partial}{\partial u}p^*(t, u)$$

is the (risk-neutral) probability density of the default time, evaluated at time t. The first term of (11.7) is the market value of a claim that pays 1 at maturity in the event of survival. The second term is the market value of a claim to any default recovery between times t and s.

Using this defaultable discount function $v(\cdot)$, we can value any straight coupon bond or determine par coupon rates. For example, for quarterly coupon periods, the (annualized) par coupon rate $c(t, s)$ for maturity at time s is determined at any time t by

$$1 = v(t, s) + \frac{c(t, s)}{4} \sum_{j=1}^{4(s-t)} v\left(t, t + j/4\right), \tag{11.8}$$

which is trivially solved for $c(t, s)$.

We conduct our numerical example with a constant default-free interest rate r, for which the discount $d(0, t)$ is simply e^{-rt}.

11.3.6. Diversity Scores

A key measure of collateral diversity developed by Moody's for CDO risk analysis is the diversity score. The diversity score of a given pool of participations is the number n of bonds in an idealized comparison portfolio that meet the following criteria:

- The total face value of the comparison portfolio is the same as the total face value of the collateral pool.
- The bonds of the comparison portfolio have equal face values.
- The comparison bonds are equally likely to default, and their default is independent.
- The comparison bonds are, in some sense, of the same average default probability as the participations of the collateral pool.
- The comparison portfolio has, according to some measure of risk, the same total default risk as does the collateral pool.

At least in terms of publicly available information, it is not clear how the (equal) default probability of the bonds of the comparison portfolio is determined. One method that has been discussed by Schorin and Weinreich (1998) is to assign a default probability corresponding to the weighted average rating score of the collateral pool, using rating scores such as those illustrated in Table 11.1 and weights that are proportional to face value. Given the average rating score, one can assign a default probability q to the resulting average rating. For the choice of q, Schorin and Weinreich (1998) discuss the use of the historical default frequency for that rating.

A diversity score of n and a comparison-bond default probability of q imply, using the independence assumption for the comparison portfolio, that the probability of k defaults out of the n bonds of the comparison portfolio is

$$q(k, n) = \frac{n!}{(n-k)!k!} \; q^k(1-q)^{n-k}. \tag{11.9}$$

From this binomial-expansion formula, a risk analysis of the CDO can be conducted by assuming that the performance of the collateral pool is sufficiently well approximated by the performance of the comparison portfolio. Moody's would not rely exclusively on the diversity score in rating

Table 11.1.   Rating Scores Used to Derive Weighted Average Ratings

	Moody's	Fitch	Duff and Phelps
Aaa/AAA	1	1	0.001
Aa1/AA+	10	8	0.010
Aa2/AA	20	10	0.030
Aa3/AA−	40	14	0.050
A1/A+	70	18	0.100
A2/A	120	23	0.150
A3/A−	180	36	0.200
Baa1/BBB+	260	48	0.250
Baa2/BBB	360	61	0.350
Baa3/BBB−	610	94	0.500
Ba1/BB+	940	129	0.750
Ba2/BB	1,350	165	1.000
Ba3/BB−	1,780	210	1.250
B1/B+	2,220	260	1.600
B2/B	2,720	308	2.000
B3/B−	3,490	356	2.700
CCC+	NA	463	NA
Caa/CCC	6,500	603	3.750
CCC−	NA	782	NA
<Ca/<CCC−	10,000	1,555	NA

Source: Schorin and Weinreich (1998), from Moody's Investors Service, Fitch Investors Service, and Duff and Phelps Credit Rating.

the CDO tranches. For a review of Moody's approach to rating CDOs, see Gluck and Remeza (2000).

Table 11.2 shows the diversity score that Moody's would apply to a collateral pool of equally sized bonds of different firms within the same industry. It also lists the implied probability $P(d_i \mid d_j)$ of the event d_i of default of participation i, given the event d_j of default of another, as well as the correlations $\mathrm{corr}(d_i, d_j)$ of the 0-1, survival-default, random variables associated with any two participations. The implied probability $P(d_i \mid d_j)$ and correlation $\mathrm{corr}(d_i, d_j)$ are tabulated for two levels of individual default probability ($q = 0.5$ and $q = 0.05$).

11.4. Pricing Examples

This section provides an algorithm for the pricing of CDO tranches. In the absence of any tractable alternative, we use Monte Carlo simulation of the default times. Essentially any intensity model could be substituted for the basic affine model that we have adopted here. The advantage of an

Table 11.2. Moody's Diversity Scores for Firms within an Industry

Firms in industry	Diversity score	$P(d_i \mid d_j)$ ($q = 0.5$)	($q = 0.05$)	(d_i, d_j) ($q = 0.5$)	($q = 0.05$)
1	1.00				
2	1.50	0.78	0.48	0.56	0.45
3	2.00	0.71	0.37	0.42	0.34
4	2.33	0.70	0.36	0.40	0.32
5	2.67	0.68	0.33	0.36	0.30
6	3.00	0.67	0.31	0.33	0.27
7	3.25	0.66	0.30	0.32	0.26
8	3.50	0.65	0.29	0.31	0.25
9	3.75	0.65	0.27	0.29	0.24
10	4.00	0.64	0.26	0.28	0.23
>10	Evaluated on a case-by-case basis				

Source: The assumed diversity score is that assigned by Moody's, as tabulated by Schorin and Weinreich (1998).
Note: Here, q is the default probability of an arbitrary name, while d_i is the event of default by name i. The conditional probability and default correlation calculations assume symmetry.

affine intensity model is the ability to quickly calibrate the model to the underlying participations, in terms of given default correlations, default probabilities, yield spreads, and so on, and to obtain an understanding of the role of diffusion, jumps, mean reversion, and diversification for both valuation and (when working under the actual probabilities) for various risk measures.

We study various alternative CDO cash flow structures and default-risk parameters. The basic CDO structure consists of an SPV that acquires a collateral portfolio of participations (debt instruments of various obligors) and allocates interest, principal, and default-recovery cash flows from the collateral pool to the CDO tranches, and perhaps to the asset manager, as described later.

11.4.1. Collateral

There are N participations in the collateral pool. Each participation pays quarterly cash flows to the SPV at its coupon rate until maturity or default. At default, a participation is sold for its recovery value, and the proceeds from the sale are also made available to the SPV. In order to be precise, let $A(k) \subset \{1, \ldots, N\}$ denote the set of surviving participations at the kth coupon period. The total interest income in coupon period k is then

$$W(k) = \sum_{i \in A(k)} M_i \frac{C_i}{n}, \tag{11.10}$$

where M_i is the face value of participation i and C_i is the coupon rate on participation i. If $B(k)$ denotes the set of participations defaulting between coupon periods $k-1$ and k [those in $A(k-1)$ but not in $A(k)$], the total total cash flow in period k is

$$Z(k) = W(k) + \sum_{i \in B(k)} (M_i - L_i), \qquad (11.11)$$

where L_i is the loss of face value at the default of participation i.

For our example, the initial pool of collateral available to the CDO structure consists of $N = 100$ participations that are straight quarterly coupon 10-year par bonds of equal face value. Without loss of generality, we take the face value of each bond to be 1.

In order to simplify the simultaneous discussion of risk analysis and pricing, we assume from this point that the actual and risk-neutral default risk models are identical. In particular, $\lambda_i = \lambda_i^*$. This is unrealistic, but keeps the discussion simple.

Table 11.3 shows four alternative sets of parameters for the default intensity $\lambda_i = X_c + X_i$ of each individual participation. We initiate X_c and X_i at their long-run means, $\theta_c + \ell_c \mu / \kappa$ and $\theta_i + \ell_i \mu / \kappa$, respectively. This implies an initial condition (and long-run mean) for each obligor's default intensity of 5.33%. Our base-case default-risk model is defined by parameter set 1 and by letting $\rho = 0.5$ determine the degree of diversification.

The three other parameter sets shown in Table 11.3 are designed to illustrate the effects of replacing some or all of the diffusive volatility with jump volatility and the effect of reducing the mean jump size or increasing the mean jump arrival frequency ℓ. All of the parameter sets have the same long-run mean intensity $\theta + \mu \ell / \kappa$. The parameters θ, σ, ℓ, and μ are adjusted so as to maintain essentially the same term structure of survival probabilities illustrated in Figure 11.3. (As all parameter sets have the same κ parameter, this is a rather straightforward numerical exercise, using (11.3) for default probabilities.) This in turn implies essentially the same term structure of zero-coupon yields. Table 11.3 provides, for each parameter set, the 10-

Table 11.3. Risk-Neutral Default Parameter Sets

Set	κ	θ	σ	ℓ	μ	Spread (basis points)	var_∞ (%)
1	0.6	0.0200	0.141	0.2000	0.1000	254	0.42
2	0.6	0.0156	0.000	0.2000	0.1132	254	0.43
3	0.6	0.0373	0.141	0.0384	0.2500	253	0.49
4	0.6	0.0005	0.141	0.5280	0.0600	254	0.41

year par-coupon spreads and the long-run variance of $\lambda_i(t)$. In order to illustrate the qualitative differences between parameter sets, Figure 11.4 shows sample paths of new 10-year par spreads for two issuers, one with the base-case parameters (set 1), the other with pure jump intensity ($\sigma = 0$, set 2), calibrated to the same initial spread curve.

Letting d_i denote the event of default by the ith participation, Table 11.4 shows, for each parameter set and each of three levels of the correlation parameter ρ, the unconditional probability of default $P(d_i)$ and the conditional probability $P(d_i \mid d_j)$ of default by one participation given default by another. Table 11.4 also shows the diversity score of the collateral pool that is implied by matching the variance of the total loss of principal of the collateral portfolio to that of a comparison portfolio of bonds of the same individual default probabilities. This calculation is based on the analytical methods described in Section 11.5.

For our basic examples, we suppose first that any cash in the SPV reserve account is invested at the default-free short rate. We later consider investment of SPV free cash flows in additional risky participations.

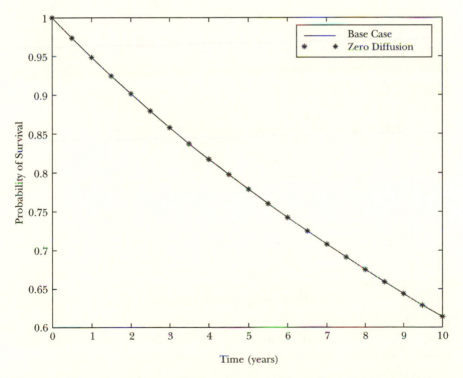

Figure 11.3. *Term structures of survival probabilities, with and without diffusion.*

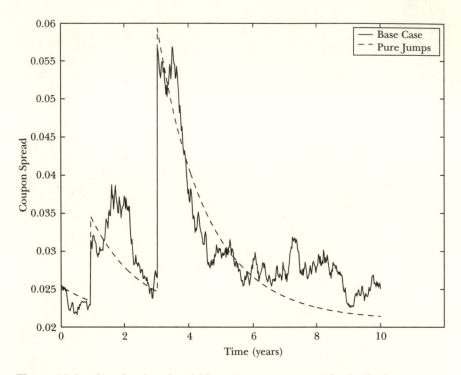

Figure 11.4. *Simulated paths of 10-year par-coupon spreads, for the base-case parameters and for the pure jump intensity parameters.*

Table 11.4. *Conditional Probabilities of Default and Diversity Scores*

		$\rho = 0.1$		$\rho = 0.5$		$\rho = 0.9$	
Set	$P(d_i)$	$P(d_i \mid d_j)$	Diversity	$P(d_i \mid d_j)$	Diversity	$P(d_i \mid d_j)$	Diversity
1	0.386	0.393	58.5	0.420	21.8	0.449	13.2
2	0.386	0.393	59.1	0.420	22.2	0.447	13.5
3	0.386	0.392	63.3	0.414	25.2	0.437	15.8
4	0.386	0.393	56.7	0.423	20.5	0.454	12.4

11.4.2. Sinking-Fund Tranches

We consider a CDO structure that pays SPV cash flows to a prioritized sequence of sinking-fund bonds, as well as a junior subordinate residual tranche, as follows.

In general, a sinking-fund bond with n coupon periods per year has some remaining principal $F(k)$ at coupon period k, some annualized coupon rate c, and a scheduled interest payment at coupon period k of $F(k)c/n$. In the event that the actual interest paid, $Y(k)$, is less than the scheduled interest payment, any difference $F(k)c/n - Y(k)$ is accrued at the bond's own coupon rate c so as to generate an accrued unpaid interest at period k of $U(k)$, where $U(0) = 0$ and

$$U(k) = \left(1 + \frac{c}{n}\right) U(k-1) + \frac{c}{n} F(k) - Y(k).$$

There may also be some prepayment of principal, $D(k)$ in period k, and some contractual unpaid reduction in principal, $J(k)$ in period k, in order to prioritize payments in light of the default and recovery history of the collateral pool. By contract, we have $D(k) + J(k) \le F(k-1)$, so that the remaining principal at quarter k is

$$F(k) = F(k-1) - D(k) - J(k). \tag{11.12}$$

At maturity, coupon period number K, any unpaid accrued interest and unpaid principal, $U(K)$ and $F(K)$, respectively, are paid to the extent provided in the CDO contract. (A shortfall does not constitute default as long as the contractual prioritization scheme is maintained.) The total actual payment in any coupon period k is $Y(k) + D(k)$. (As a practical matter, Moody's may assign a default rating to a CDO tranche even if it meets its contractual payments, if the investors' losses from default in the underlying collateral pool are sufficiently severe.)

The par-coupon rate on a given sinking-fund bond is the scheduled coupon rate c with the property that the initial market value of the bond is equal to its initial face value $F(0)$. We illustrate our initial valuation results in terms of the par-coupon spreads of the respective tranches, which are the excess of the par-coupon rates of the tranches over the default-free par-coupon rate.

11.4.3. Prioritization Schemes

We experiment with the relative sizes and prioritization of two CDO bond tranches: (1) a 10-year senior sinking-fund bond with some initial principal $F_1(0) = P_1$, and (2) a 10-year mezzanine sinking-fund bond with initial principal $F_2(0) = P_2$. The residual junior tranche receives any cash flow remaining at the end of the 10-year structure. As the base-case coupon rates on the senior and mezzanine CDO tranches are, by design, par rates, the base-case initial market value of the residual tranche is $P_3 = 100 - P_1 - P_2$.

At the kth coupon period, tranche j has a face value of $F_j(k)$ and an accrued unpaid interest $U_j(k)$ calculated at its own coupon rate c_j. Any excess cash flows from the collateral pool (interest income and default recoveries) are deposited in a reserve account. To begin, we suppose that the reserve account earns interest at the default-free one-period interest rate, denoted $r(k)$ at the kth coupon date. At maturity, coupon period K, any remaining funds in the reserve account, after payments at quarter K to the two tranches, are paid to the subordinated residual tranche. (Later, we investigate the effects of investing the reserve account in additional participations that are added to the collateral pool.) We neglect any management fees.

We investigate valuation for two prioritization schemes, which we now describe. Given the definition of the sinking funds in the previous subsection, in order to completely specify cash flows to all tranches, it is enough to define the actual interest payments, $Y_1(k)$ and $Y_2(k)$, for the senior and mezzanine sinking funds, respectively; any payments of principal, $D_1(k)$ and $D_2(k)$; and any contractual reductions in principal, $J_1(k)$ and $J_2(k)$.

We examine the pricing implications of two priority schemes, *uniform* and *fast*. Under our uniform prioritization scheme, the interest $W(k)$ collected from the surviving participations is allocated in priority order, with the senior tranche getting

$$Y_1(k) = \min\left[U_1(k), W(k)\right]$$

and the mezzanine getting

$$Y_2(k) = \min\left[U_2(k), W(k) - Y_1(k)\right].$$

The available reserve $R(k)$, before payments at period k, is thus defined by

$$R(k) = \left[1 + \frac{r(k)}{4}\right][R(k-1) - Y_1(k-1) - Y_2(k-1)] + Z(k), \qquad (11.13)$$

recalling that $Z(k)$ is the total cash flow from the participations in period k.

Unpaid reductions in principal from default losses occur in reverse priority order, so that the junior residual tranche suffers the reduction

$$J_3(k) = \min[F_3(k-1), H(k)],$$

where

$$H(k) = \max\left\{\sum_{i \in B(k)} L_i - [W(k) - Y_1(k) - Y_2(k)], 0\right\}$$

is the total of default losses since the previous coupon date, less collected and undistributed interest income. Then the mezzanine and senior tranches are successively reduced in principal by

$$J_2(k) = \min[F_2(k-1), H(k) - J_3(k)]$$

$$J_1(k) = \min[F_1(k-1), H(k) - J_3(k) - J_2(k)],$$

respectively. Under uniform prioritization, there are no early payments of principal, so $D_1(k) = D_2(k) = 0$ for $k < K$. At maturity, the remaining reserve is paid in priority order, and principal and accrued interest are treated identically, so that, without loss of generality, for purposes of valuation we take $Y_1(K) = Y_2(K) = 0$,

$$D_1(K) = \min[F_1(K) + U_1(K), R(K)],$$

and

$$D_2(K) = \min[F_2(K) + U_2(K), R(K) - D_1(K)].$$

The residual tranche finally collects

$$D_3(K) = R(K) - Y_1(K) - D_1(K) - Y_2(K) - D_2(K).$$

For our alternative fast prioritization scheme, the senior tranche is allocated interest and principal payments as quickly as possible until maturity or until its remaining principal is reduced to zero, whichever is first. Until the senior tranche is paid in full, the mezzanine tranche accrues unpaid interest at its coupon rate. Then the mezzanine tranche is paid interest and principal as quickly as possible until maturity or until retired. Finally, any remaining cash flows are allocated to the residual tranche. Specifically, in coupon period k, the senior tranche is allocated the interest payment

$$Y_1(k) = \min[U_1(k), Z(k)]$$

and the principal payment

$$D_1(k) = \min[F_1(k-1), Z(k) - Y_1(k)],$$

where the total cash $Z(k)$ generated by the collateral pool is again defined by (11.11). The mezzanine receives the interest payments

$$Y_2(k) = \min[U_2(k), Z(k) - Y_1(k) - D_1(k)]$$

and principal payments

$$D_2(k) = \min[F_2(k-1), Z(k) - Y_1(k) - D_1(k) - Y_2(k)].$$

Finally, any residual cash flows are paid to the junior subordinated tranche. For this scheme, there are no contractual reductions in principal $[J_i(k) = 0]$.

In practice, there are many other types of prioritization schemes. For example, during the life of a CDO, failure to meet certain contractual over-collateralization ratios in many cases triggers a shift to some version of fast prioritization. For our examples, the CDO yield spreads for uniform and fast prioritization would provide upper and lower bounds, respectively, on the senior spreads that would apply if one were to add such a feature to the uniform prioritization scheme that we have illustrated.

11.4.4. Simulation Methodology

Our computational approach consists of simulating piecewise linear approximations of the paths of X_c and $X_1, \ldots, X_N$, for time intervals of some relatively short fixed length Δt. (We have taken an interval Δt of 1 week.) Defaults during one of these intervals are simulated at the corresponding discretization of the total arrival intensity $\Lambda(t) = \sum_i \lambda_i(t) 1_{A(i,t)}$, where $A(i, t)$ is the event that issuer i has not defaulted by t. With the arrival of some default, the identity of the defaulter is drawn at random, with the probability that i is selected as the defaulter given by the discretization approximation of $\lambda_i(t) 1_{A(i,t)} / \Lambda(t)$. The probability that more than one default occurs during one time step is very small, hence ignored. Based on experimentation, we chose to simulate 10,000 independent scenarios. The basis for this and other multi-obligor default-time simulation approaches is discussed Chapter 10.

11.4.5. Results for Par CDO Spreads

Table 11.5 shows the estimated par coupon spreads, in basis points, of the senior (s_1) and mezzanine (s_2) CDO tranches for the four-parameter sets, for various levels of overcollateralization and for our two prioritization schemes. In order to illustrate the accuracy of the simulation methodology, estimates of the standard deviation of these estimated spreads that are due to Monte Carlo noise are shown in parentheses. Tables 11.6 and 11.7 show estimated par spreads for the case of low ($\rho = 0.1$) and high ($\rho = 0.9$) default correlation. In all of these examples, the risk-free rate is constant at 6%, and there are no management fees.

Figure 11.5 illustrates the impacts on the market values of the three tranches of a given CDO structure of changing the correlation parameter ρ. The base-case CDO structures used for this illustration are determined by uniform prioritization of senior and mezzanine tranches whose coupon

Table 11.5. Par Coupon Spreads of Senior
(S_1) and Mezzanine (S_2) CDO Tranches ($\rho = 0.5$)

| | Principal | | Spread (basis points) | | | |
| | | | Uniform | | Fast | |
Set	P_1	P_2	s_1	s_2	s_1	s_2
1	92.5	5	18.7 (1)	636 (16)	13.5 (0.4)	292 (1.6)
2	92.5	5	17.9 (1)	589 (15)	13.5 (0.5)	270 (1.6)
3	92.5	5	15.3 (1)	574 (14)	11.2 (0.5)	220 (1.5)
4	92.5	5	19.1 (1)	681 (17)	12.7 (0.4)	329 (1.6)
1	80	10	1.64 (0.1)	67.4 (2.2)	0.92 (0.1)	38.9 (0.6)
2	80	10	1.69 (0.1)	66.3 (2.2)	0.94 (0.1)	39.5 (0.6)
3	80	10	2.08 (0.2)	51.6 (2.0)	1.70 (0.2)	32.4 (0.6)
4	80	10	1.15 (0.1)	68.1 (2.0)	1.70 (0.2)	32.4 (0.6)

Table 11.6. Par Coupon Spreads for Low Default Correlation ($\rho = 0.1$)

| | Principal | | Spread (basis points) | | | |
| | | | Uniform | | Fast | |
Set	P_1	P_2	s_1	s_2	s_1	s_2
1	92.5	5	6.7	487	2.7	122
2	92.5	5	6.7	492	2.9	117
3	92.5	5	6.3	473	2.5	102
4	92.5	5	7.0	507	2.7	137
1	80	10	0.27	17.6	0.13	7.28
2	80	10	0.31	17.5	0.15	7.92
3	80	10	0.45	14.9	0.40	6.89
4	80	10	0.16	19.0	0.05	6.69

rates are at par for the base-case parameter set 1 and correlation $\rho = 0.5$. For example, suppose this correlation parameter is moved from the base case of $\rho = 0.5$ to the case of $\rho = 0.9$. Figure 11.5, which treats the case ($P_1 = 92.5$) of relatively little subordination available to the senior tranche, shows that this loss in diversification reduces the market value of the senior tranche from 92.5 to about 91.9. The market value of the residual tranche, which benefits from volatility in the manner of a call option, increases in market value from 2.5 to approximately 3.2, a dramatic relative change. While a precise statement of convexity is complicated by the timing of the prioritization effects, this effect is along the lines of Jensen's inequality,

Table 11.7. *Par Spreads for High Default Correlation ($\rho = 0.9$)*

			Spread (basis points)			
	Principal		Uniform		Fast	
Set	P_1	P_2	s_1	s_2	s_1	s_2
1	92.5	5	30.7	778	23.9	420
2	92.5	5	29.5	687	23.7	397
3	92.5	5	25.3	684	20.6	325
4	92.5	5	32.1	896	23.1	479
1	80	10	3.17	113	1.87	68.8
2	80	10	3.28	112	1.95	70.0
3	80	10	4.03	90	3.27	60.4
4	80	10	2.52	117	1.06	65.4

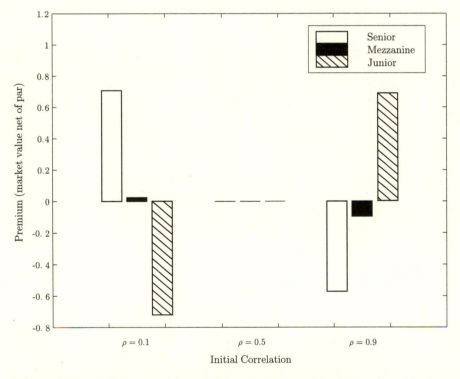

Figure 11.5. *Impact on market values of correlation with uniform prioritization (parameter set 1) for low overcollateralization ($P_1 = 92.5$).*

as an increase in correlation also increases the (risk-neutral) variance of the total loss of principal. These opposing reactions to diversification of the senior and junior tranches also show that the residual tranche may offer some benefits to certain investors as a default-risk-volatility hedge for the senior tranche.

The mezzanine tranche absorbs the net effect of the impacts of correlation changes on the market values of the senior and junior residual tranches (in this example resulting in a decline in market value of the mezzanine from 5.0 to approximately 4.9). This must be the case, given that the total market value of the collateral portfolio is not affected by the correlation of default risk. We can compare these effects with the impact of correlation on the par spreads of the senior and mezzanine tranches that are shown in Tables 11.5, 11.6, and 11.7. As we see, the mezzanine par spreads can be dramatically influenced by correlation, given the relatively small size of the mezzanine principal. Moreover, experimenting with various mezzanine overcollateralization values shows that the effect is ambiguous: Increasing default correlation may *raise or lower* mezzanine spreads.

An indication of the impact of fast prioritization on senior and mezzanine spreads is found in Figures 11.17 and 11.18.

11.4.6. Risky Reinvestment

We also illustrate how one can implement a contractual provision that recoveries on defaulted participations and excess collected interest are to be invested in collateral of comparable quality to that of the original pool. This method can also be used to allow for collateral assets that mature before the termination of the CDO.

The default intensity of each new collateral asset is of the type given by (11.4), where X_i is initialized at the time of the purchase at the initial base-case level (long-run mean). Par spreads are computed for these bonds. Figures 11.6 and 11.7 show the effect of changing from safe to risky reinvestment. Given the *short-option aspect* of the senior tranche, it becomes less valuable when reinvestment becomes risky. It is interesting to note that the mezzanine tranche benefits from the increased variance in this case.

11.5. Default Loss Analytics

Here, exploiting the symmetry assumptions of our special example, analytical results are provided for the probability distribution for the number of defaulting participations and the total of default losses of principal, including the effects of random recovery.

The key is an ability to compute explicitly the probability of survival of all participations in any chosen subgroup of obligors. However, given the

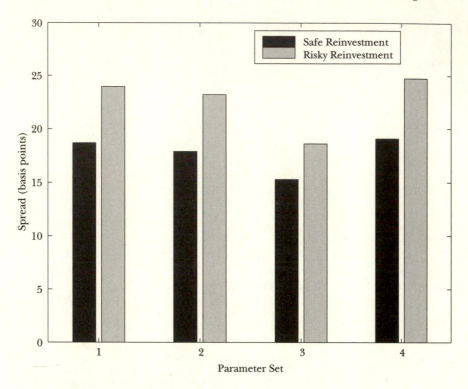

Figure 11.6. *Senior-tranche spreads in the uniform prioritization and risky reinvestment schemes* ($P_1 = 92.5$, $P_2 = 5$).

large number of combinations of subgroups to be considered, these explicit probabilities must be evaluated with extremely high numerical accuracy.

For a given time horizon T, let d_j denote the event that obligor j defaults by T. That is, $d_j = \{\tau_j < T\}$ and $d_j^c = \{\tau_j \geq T\}$ is the complementary event of survival. We let M denote the number of defaults. Assuming *shuffling symmetry* (invariance under permutation of names) in the unconditional joint distribution of default times,

$$P(M = k) = \binom{N}{k} P(d_1 \cap \cdots \cap d_k \cap d_{k+1}^c \cap \cdots \cap d_N^c),$$

where

$$\binom{N}{k} = N! / [(N-k)!k!].$$

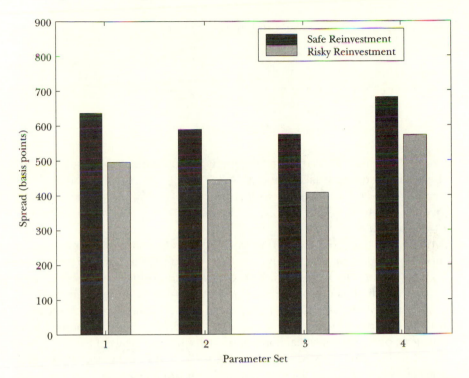

Figure 11.7. *Mezzanine-tranche spreads in the uniform prioritization and risky reinvestment schemes* ($P_1 = 92.5$, $P_2 = 5$).

This extends the traditional binomial-expansion formula (Gluck and Remeza, 2000) to allow for correlation. Let

$$q(k, N) = P(d_1 \cap \cdots \cap d_k \cap d^c_{k+1} \cap \cdots \cap d^c_N).$$

The probability $p_j = P(d_1 \cup \cdots \cup d_j)$ that at least one of the first j names defaults by T is computed later; for now, we take this calculation as given. This leaves

$$q(k, N) = \sum_{j=1}^{N} (-1)^{(j+k+N+1)} \binom{k}{N-j} p_j, \qquad (11.14)$$

using the convention that $\binom{m}{l} = 0$ if $l < 0$ or $m < 1$. A proof of (11.14) is provided in Duffie and Gârleanu (2001). Using the fact that, in this setting, the intensity of the first-to-arrive $\tau^{(j)} = \min(\tau_1, \ldots, \tau_j)$ of the stopping times

$\tau_1, \ldots, \tau_j$ is $\lambda_1 + \cdots + \lambda_j$, and using the independence of $X_1, \ldots, X_N, X_c$, we have

$$p_j = 1 - P(\tau^{(j)} > T) = 1 - E\left[\exp\left(-\int_0^T \sum_{i=1}^{j} \lambda_i(t)\, dt\right)\right] \qquad (11.15)$$

$$= 1 - e^{\alpha_c(T) + \beta_c(T)X_c(0) + j\alpha_i(T) + j\beta_i(T)X_i(0)}, \qquad (11.16)$$

where $\alpha_c(T)$ and $\beta_c(T)$ are given explicitly in Appendix A as the solutions of the ordinary differential equations (A.32) and (A.33) for the case $n = -\kappa$, $p = \sigma^2$, $q = -j$, $\ell = \ell_c$, and $m = \kappa\theta_c$; while $\alpha_i(T)$ and $\beta_i(T)$ are the explicitly given solutions of (A.32) and (A.33) for the case $n = -\kappa$, $p = \sigma^2$, $q = -1$, $\ell = \ell_i$, and $m = \kappa\theta_i$.

It is not hard to see how one would generalize so as to accommodate more than one type of intensity—that is, how to treat a case with several internally symmetric pools. Introducing each such group, however, increases by one the dimensions of the array p and the summation. Given the relatively lengthy computation required to obtain adequate accuracy for even two subgroups of issuers, one may prefer simulation as a method of calculating p_j, over this analytical approach, with multiple types of issuers.

Based on this analytical method, Figure 11.8 shows the probability $q(k, 100)$ of k defaults within 10 years out of the original group of 100 issuers for parameter set 1 for a correlation-determining parameter ρ that is high (0.9) or low (0.1). Figure 11.9 shows the corresponding low-correlation and high-correlation probability $q(k, 100)$ of k defaults out of 100 for the no-diffusion case, parameter set 2. Figures 11.10 and 11.11 compare the probability $q(k, 100)$ of k defaults for all four parameter sets. The low-correlation distributions are rather more similar across the various parameter sets than are the high-correlation distributions, with intuition along the lines of the central limit theorem, under which independence leads to an approximately normal distribution for the fraction of defaulting names, for a large number of names.

One can also compute analytically the likelihood of a total loss of principal of a given amount x. This is done by adding up, over k, the probability $q(k, 100)$ of k defaults multiplied by the probability that the total loss of principal from k defaults is at least x. For the latter, we do not use the actual distribution of the total fractional loss of principal of a given number k of defaulting participations. Instead, for ease of computation, we substitute with a central-limit approximation for the distribution of the sum of k independent uniform-$[0, 1]$ random variables, which is merely the distribution of a normally distributed variable with the same mean and variance. We are interested in this calculation for moderate to high levels of x, corresponding, for example, to estimating the probability of failure to meet

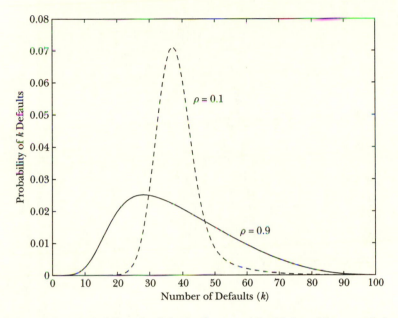

Figure 11.8. *Probability of k defaults (base case) for high and low correlation.*

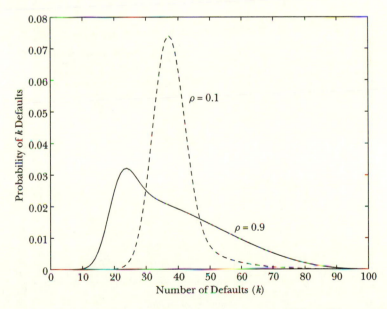

Figure 11.9. *Probability of k defaults (parameter set 2) for high and low correlation.*

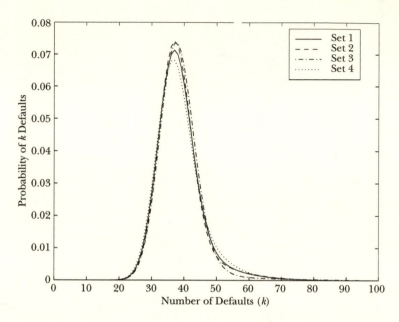

Figure 11.10. *Probability of k defaults (all parameter sets) with low correlation*
(ρ = 0.1).

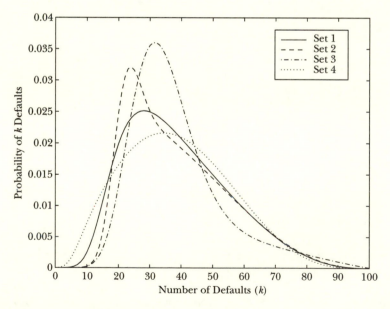

Figure 11.11. *Probability of k defaults (all parameter sets) with high correlation*
(ρ = 0.9).

an overcollateralization target. We have verified that, even for relatively few defaults, this central-limit approximation is adequate for our purposes. A sample of the resulting loss distributions is illustrated in Figure 11.12.

One can also analytically compute the variance of total loss of principal, whence diversity scores, as tabulated for our example in Table 11.4. A description of the computation of diversity score of a general pool of collateral, not necessarily with symmetric default risk, can be found in Section 11.6. Given a (risk-neutral) diversity score of n, one can then estimate CDO yield spreads by a much simpler algorithm, which approximates by substituting the comparison portfolio of n independently defaulting participations for the actual collateral portfolio. The default times can be simulated independently directly from the explicit unconditional default-time distribution for each obligor, rather than by use of a much more arduous simulation of the intensity processes. The diversity-based algorithm is roughly as follows:

1. Simulate a draw from the explicit distribution of the number M of defaults of the comparison portfolio of n bonds, with probability $q(k, n)$ of k defaults obtained from (11.14).

2. For each of the M comparison-portfolio defaults, simulate the cor-

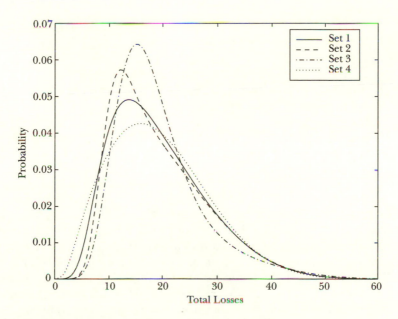

Figure 11.12. *Probability density of total losses of principal through default (parameter set 1) with high correlation.*

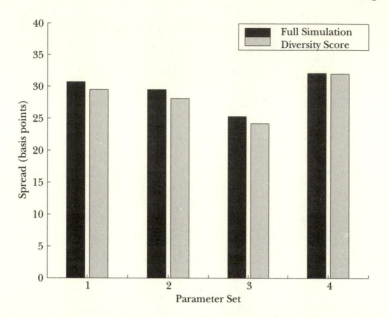

Figure 11.13. *Senior-tranche spreads and diversity-based approximate spreads, with high correlation ($\rho = 0.9$) and low subordination ($P_1 = 92.5$).*

responding default times independently, using the explicit default-time distribution of each participation, given by $P(\tau_j > t) = E(e^{-\int_0^t \lambda_j(s)\,ds})$.

3. Simulate M fractional losses of principal.
4. Allocate cash flows to the CDO tranches, period by period, according to the contractual prioritization scheme.
5. Discount the cash flows of each CDO tranche to present value at risk-free rates.
6. For each tranche, average the discounted cash flows over many independently generated scenarios.

A comparison of the resulting diversity-score-based approximation of CDO spreads with those computed earlier are provided, for certain cases, in Figures 11.13 and 11.14. For well-collateralized tranches, the diversity-based estimates of spreads are reasonably accurate, at least relative to the uncertainty that one would have, in any case, regarding the actual degree of diversification in the collateral pool. For highly subordinated tranches and moderate or high default correlation, the diversity-based spreads can be rather inaccurate, as can be seen from Figure 11.15 and Table 11.8.

Figure 11.16 shows the likelihood of a total loss of principal of at least 24.3% of the original face value as we vary the correlation-determining parameter ρ. This computation is based on the same analytical method

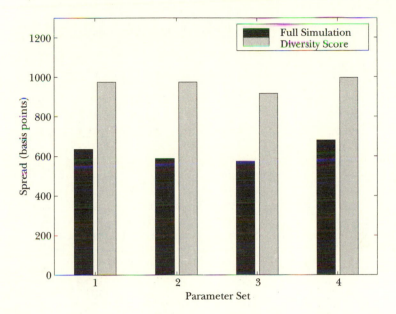

Figure 11.14. *Mezzanine-tranche spreads and diversity-based approximate spreads, with moderate correlation ($\rho = 0.5$) and low subordination ($P_1 = 92.5$, $P_2 = 5$).*

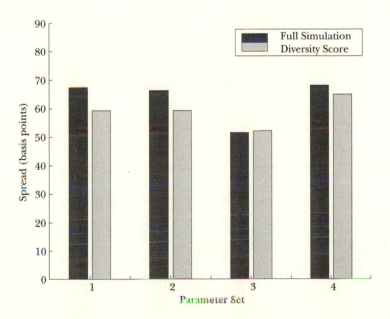

Figure 11.15. *Mezzanine-tranche spreads and diversity-based approximate spreads, with moderate correlation ($\rho = 0.5$) and high subordination ($P_1 = 80$, $P_2 = 10$).*

Table 11.8.   Par Spreads Obtained from Simulation Based on Diversity Scores

Set	Correlation ρ	Diversity score	Principal P_1	P_2	Uniform s_1	s_2	Fast s_1	s_2
1	0.1	59	92.5	5	6.58	604.0	0.99	150
1	0.5	22	92.5	5	17.2	973.6	8.14	340
1	0.9	13	92.5	5	29.5	1172	19.1	452
1	0.1	59	80	10	0.01	14.5	0.00	1.05
1	0.5	22	80	10	0.57	59.3	0.04	18.0
1	0.9	13	80	10	2.15	116	0.77	51.2
2	0.1	59	92.5	5	6.58	604.0	0.99	150
2	0.5	22	92.5	5	17.2	973.6	8.14	340
2	0.9	14	92.5	5	28.1	1148	17.7	442
2	0.1	59	80	10	0.01	14.5	0.00	1.05
2	0.5	22	80	10	0.57	59.3	0.04	18.0
2	0.9	14	80	10	1.93	108.8	0.68	47.5
3	0.1	63	92.5	5	6.19	585	0.78	140
3	0.5	25	92.5	5	15.6	916	7.04	313
3	0.9	16	92.5	5	24.2	1107	14.2	405
3	0.1	63	80	10	0.02	12.5	0.00	0.81
3	0.5	25	80	10	0.43	52.2	0.05	15.5
3	0.9	16	80	10	1.34	90.3	0.44	36.4
4	0.1	57	92.5	5	6.76	605	1.04	153
4	0.5	21	92.5	5	18.6	996	9.46	367
4	0.9	12	92.5	5	32.0	1203	21.3	474
4	0.1	57	80	10	0.02	14.5	0.00	1.14
4	0.5	21	80	10	0.68	65.0	0.11	22.0
4	0.9	12	80	10	2.71	126.8	1.25	56.5

used to produce Figure 11.12. It is also illustrative of a calculation of the probability of failing to meet an overcollateralization target.

11.6. Computation of Diversity Scores

This section contains methods for calculation of diversity scores, and can be skipped by readers not interested in the underlying computational issues.

We define the diversity score S associated with a "target" portfolio of bonds of total principal F to be the number of identically and independently defaulting bonds, each with principal F/S, whose total default losses have the same variance as the target-portfolio default losses. The computation of the diversity score S entails computation of the variance of losses on the target portfolio of N bonds.

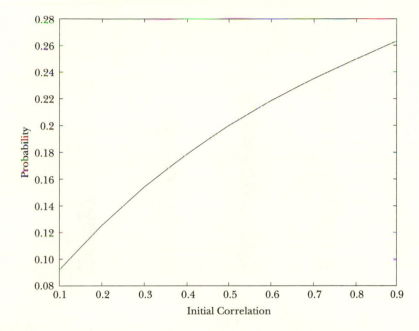

Figure 11.16. *Likelihood of total default losses of at least 24.3% of principal within 10 years.*

Perhaps because of the goal of simplicity, any interest-rate effects on losses have been ignored in the calculation of diversity, and we shall do so here as well, although such effects could be tractably incorporated, for example, by the discounting of losses. (With correlation between interest rates and default losses, the meaningfulness of direct discounting is questionable.) It is also problematic that lost-coupon effects are not considered separately in diversity scores. These effects, which could be particularly important for high-premium bonds, can also be captured along the lines of the following calculations. Finally, diversity scores do not account directly for the replacement of defaulted collateral or new investment in defaultable securities during the life of a product, except insofar as covenants or ratings requirements stipulate a minimum diversity score that is to be maintained for the current collateral portfolio for the life of the CDO structure. This might argue for a short-horizon, say 1-year, diversity score, even for long-maturity collateral, which can also be accommodated in our calculations.

With d_i denoting the indicator (0-or-1 random variable) of the event that participation i defaults by a given time T and L_i being the random loss of principal when this event occurs, the definition of the variance of a

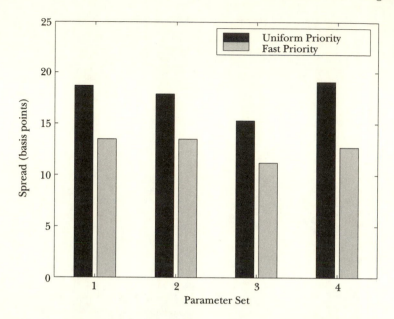

Figure 11.17.   *Senior-tranche spreads in the uniform and fast prioritization schemes* $(P_1 = 92.5, P_2 = 5)$.

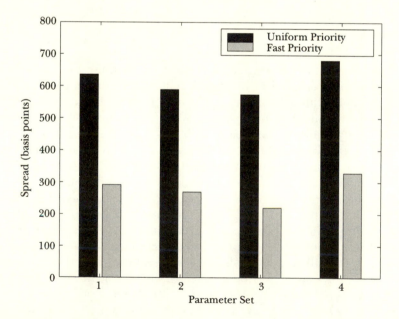

Figure 11.18.   *Mezzanine-tranche spreads in the uniform and fast prioritization schemes* $(P_1 = 92.5, P_2 = 5)$.

random variable implies that

$$\text{var}\left(\sum_{i=1}^{N} L_i d_i\right) = E\left[\left(\sum_{i=1}^{N} L_i d_i\right)^2\right] - \left[E\left(\sum_{i=1}^{N} L_i d_i\right)\right]^2$$

$$= \sum_{i=1}^{N} E\left(L_i^2\right) E\left(d_i^2\right) + \sum_{i \neq j} E\left(L_i L_j\right) E\left(d_i d_j\right)$$

$$- \sum_{i=1}^{N} [E\left(L_i\right)]^2 [E\left(d_i\right)]^2. \tag{11.17}$$

Given an affine intensity model, one can compute all the terms in (11.17). In the symmetric case, letting $p_{(1)}$ denote the marginal probability of default of a bond and $p_{(2)}$ the joint probability of default of any two bonds, the above reduces to

$$\text{var}\left(\sum_{i=1}^{N} L_i d_i\right) = N p_{(1)} E\left(L_i^2\right) + N(N-1) p_{(2)} [E\left(L_i\right)]^2$$

$$- N^2 p_{(1)}^2 \left(E\left[L_i\right]\right)^2.$$

Equating this variance of the original pool to that of the comparison pool yields

$$\frac{N}{S}\left(p_{(1)} E\left[L_i^2\right] - p_{(1)}^2 \left(E\left[L_i\right]\right)^2\right)$$

$$= p_{(1)} E\left[L_i^2\right] + (N-1) p_{(2)} \left(E\left[L_i\right]\right)^2 - N p_{(1)}^2 \left(E\left[L_i\right]\right)^2. \tag{11.18}$$

Solving this equation for the diversity score S, one gets

$$S = \frac{N\left(p_{(1)} E\left[L_i^2\right] - p_{(1)}^2 \left(E\left[L_i\right]\right)^2\right)}{p_{(1)} E\left[L_i^2\right] + (N-1) p_{(2)} \left(E\left[L_i\right]\right)^2 - N p_{(1)}^2 \left(E\left[L_i\right]\right)^2}.$$

To end the computation, one uses the identities

$$p_{(1)} = p_1$$

$$p_{(2)} = 2p_1 - p_2,$$

where p_1 and p_2 are computed according to (11.15) and one uses the fact that $E\left[L_i^2\right] = \frac{1}{3}$ and $\left(E\left[L_i\right]\right)^2 = \frac{1}{4}$, assuming losses are uniformly distributed on [0,1]. (Other assumptions on the distribution of L_i, even allowing for correlation here, can be accommodated.)

More generally, suppose that $\lambda_i(t) = b_i \cdot X(t)$ and $\lambda_j(t) = b_j \cdot X(t)$, where X is a multivariate affine process of the general type considered in Appendix A, and b_i and b_j are coefficient vectors. Even in the absence of symmetry, for any times $t(i)$ and $t(j)$, assuming without loss of generality that $t(i) \leq t(j)$, the probability of default by i before $t(i)$ and of j before $t(j)$ is

$$
E\left(d_i d_j\right) = 1 - E\left[e^{-\int_0^{t(i)} \lambda_i(u)\, du}\right] - E\left[e^{-\int_0^{t(j)} \lambda_j(u)\, du}\right]
$$

$$
+ E\left[e^{-\int_0^{t(j)} b(t) \cdot X(t)\, du}\right], \tag{11.19}
$$

where $b(t) = b_i + b_j$ for $t < t(i)$ and $b(t) = b_j$ for $t(i) \leq t \leq t(j)$. Each of the terms in (11.19) is analytically explicit in an affine setting, as can be gathered from Appendix A. Beginning with (11.19), the covariance of default losses between any pair of participations, during any pair of respective time windows, can be calculated; from that the total variance of default losses on a portfolio can be determined, and finally the diversity score S can be computed. With lack of symmetry in the original collateral pool, however, one must take a stand on the definition of an "average" default to be applied to each of the S independently defaulting issues of the comparison portfolio. We do not address that issue here. A pragmatic decision could be based on further investigation, perhaps accompanied by additional empirical work.

12

Over-the-Counter Default Risk and Valuation

THIS CHAPTER TREATS the default risk of over-the-counter (OTC) positions, with a particular focus on swaps, by far the largest source of OTC derivatives exposure. We begin with a discussion of exposure measurement, motivated by the central role in risk-management practice of exposure limits on positions with a given counterparty. Then we turn to the implications of exposure for the market valuation of default risk on an individual position, such as an interest-rate swap, and on a family of positions with a given counterparty covered by netting under a master swap agreement.

12.1. Exposure

Roughly speaking, the exposure on an OTC position is the amount that would be lost on that position in the event of default by the counterparty, assuming no recovery. For example, assuming that there is no collateral or other offsetting positions with the counterparty, the exposure on a purchased currency option is its market value. For the sake of consistency with practice and for ease of calculation, we follow the usual market convention that exposures are based on default-free market values, even though the actual counterparty may have credit risk. That is, for the stand-alone currency option mentioned earlier, we would measure an exposure of 100 if the default-risk-free market value is 100, even though the actual market value, because of the counterparty's credit risk, might be smaller, such as 98.

Some positions, such as swaps and forwards, can, depending on market conditions, have negative market values (meaning that the market value to one's counterparty is positive). In the case of a negative market value, the exposure is zero because default by the counterparty would, under the standard settlement procedures of the International Swaps and Derivatives Association (ISDA), result in immediate settlement at market value and,

285

thus, zero loss. In general, at a given time t, for an uncollateralized position with a market value of Y_t, the exposure is $\max(0, Y_t)$.

For a collateralized position, the exposure is the loss given default, assuming no recovery, after accounting for collateral. For instance, with a market value of Y_t and collateral worth C_t, the exposure is $\max(0, Y_t - C_t)$. If, for example, a currency option with a default-free market value of 100 is collateralized by Treasury bills worth 95, then the exposure is 5.

The exposure to a counterparty on a portfolio of positions covered under the same master ISDA agreement is based on the total market value of those positions, net of any collateral. For example, if one has purchased from the counterparty a currency option with a market value of 100 and sold a forward contract with a current market value of -40 (i.e., a positive value for the counterparty of 40), then (ignoring collateral) the exposure is $100 - 40 = 60$.

Bilateral netting, the ISDA standard, has been endorsed by the Group of Thirty (G30) report on derivatives practices and principles, by the Bank for International Settlements (BIS), and by the Derivatives Policy Group (DPG), among others. The extent to which netting is legally enforceable, however, is an outstanding issue in some jurisdictions, and one may wish to measure exposure under the assumption that netting is enforceable with some given probability. For example, assuming enforceability of netting with a probability of 50%, the exposure in the last example of an option worth 100 and a forward worth -40, is, in expected terms, $0.5 \times 100 + 0.5 \times (100 - 40) = 80$. From this point on, however, we will assume for simplicity that netting is fully enforceable.

In general, if a master agreement covers positions with market values of $Y_{1t}, Y_{2t}, \ldots, Y_{nt}$, then the exposure at time t is $\max(0, Y_{1t} + Y_{2t} + \cdots + Y_{nt} - C_t)$, where C_t is the market value of collateral.

There is a definitional issue of whether third-party credit derivatives are considered when calculating exposure or considered separately when applying exposure limits. For example, with an exposure of 200 before consideration of credit derivatives and a credit derivative paying 150 in the event of default by the counterparty, the net effective exposure is 50, provided the seller of protection on the credit derivative is itself default-free.

12.1.1. Potential Exposure

In deciding whether to grant (or seek) additional OTC positions with a given counterparty, it is common to measure *potential exposure*, often in the form of a confidence limit on the future exposures of the portfolio covered by the master agreement. A typical confidence level is 95%. The potential exposure is usually measured on a lifetime-maximum basis. That is, a potential exposure of 200 on a 95%-confidence basis means that there is some future time t such that the 95% confidence limit on exposure at that time is 200, while at every other time the 95% confidence limit on exposure is less than 200. It would not be unreasonable to base exposure limits on expected exposures rather than confidence limits on exposures.

Typically, OTC broker-dealers assign limits on the potential exposure to each counterparty, based on the credit quality of the counterparty. For this purpose, internal credit ratings, often corresponding to those of major rating agencies, are normally used to classify credit quality.

If one's policy limit for potential exposure to a given counterparty is, say, 500, then any new position that increases total potential exposure to that counterparty above 500 would not be allowed without a waiver of the policy limit, unless there are offsetting credit derivatives. Usually, no consideration is given to uncertain future changes in the composition of a portfolio, ow- ing, for instance, to possible offsetting trades or hedges. Changing market conditions, for example, prices and volatilities, can on their own cause ex- posure limits to be breached. The point at which a reduction in exposure is required and the level to which it must be adjusted are policy issues. One could, for example, preclude new positions with a given counterparty that would bring potential exposure above a given limit, say 500, and also have a requirement that, in the event that market conditions bring potential ex- posure above some higher limit, say 600, then offsetting positions or credit derivatives must be obtained that reduce potential exposure below the lower limit of 500.

There is no particular theory under which potential exposure, mea- sured and applied in the same way to all master-swap agreements, is opti- mal. For example, the exposure of a floating-rate loan will remain relatively near its potential exosure at all times before maturity. The exposure on an interest-rate swap, however, is unlikely to be near its originally measured lifetime-maximum 95% confidence limit on any given date. Thus, when granting access to credit in the form of limits on potential exposure, a po- tential exposure limit of $100 million on a floating-rate loan means some- thing quite different than a potential exposure limit of $100 million on an interest-rate swap.

Even on fully collateralized positions, there is potential exposure as- sociated with changes in the market value of the collateral relative to the market value of the position. For this reason, a *haircut* is normally applied to each collateral type, based largely on the market volatility and liquidity of typical collateral of that general type. For example, one bank might assign a single haircut of, say, 75%, for all publicly traded U.S. equities, whereas U.S. Treasury bonds might receive a haircut of, say, 95%. (Even Treasury bonds are subject to market risk, because of their exposure, roughly pro- portional to duration, to interest-rate risk.) For an exposure to some given counterparty of X_t at time t, measured before consideration of collateral, the counterparty in this example would be required to post any combination of equities and U.S. government bonds, with current market values of U_t and V_t, respectively, such that $0.75 U_t + 0.95 V_t \geq X_t$. In practice, new collateral is requested whenever the market value of previously posted collateral, after adjusting for a haircut, drops below some threshold, relative to the market value of the position. The net effective exposure at time $t + 1$ in the above example, for instance, before recollateralization, is $\max(X_{t+1} - 0.75 U_t R_U(t+1) - 0.95 V_t R_V(t+1), 0)$, where $R_U(t+1)$ and $R_V(t+1)$ are the market returns on the equities and notes posted at the previous date. Allowing for a potential lag in time necessary to post additional collateral, and for emergencies associated with settlement, even fully collateralized positions are in fact subject to some net effective exposure, and certain large commercial banks measure the associated credit risk and its market value.

Some banks consider, as well, the possibility of a failure of enforceability of netting provisions in certain jurisdictions, which can create additional effective exposures. According to bank call reports, as analyzed by the Office of the Comptroller of the Currency (a U.S. bank regulator), the net effective exposure reduced through netting increased from roughly 45% in 1996 to over 60% in 2000. This means that the exposure to a randomly chosen counterparty in 2000 was, on average, approximately 50% larger assuming a failure of netting enforceability than it would be assuming full enforceability.

12.1.2. BIS Capital Add-Ons for Exposure

BIS coordinates capital standards for regulated banks. In determining minimum capital requirements under these guidelines, banks add current exposure and a measure of incremental potential future exposure to arrive at a total credit-equivalent amount of exposure. These total exposures for each counterparty are then weighted according to a factor based on the credit category of the counterparty, in order to arrive at the total associated regulatory capital requirements.

In order to compute the potential future exposure on a given contract, the notional amount[1] of the underlying contract is multiplied by a *credit conversion factor* (examples of which are shown in Table 12.1) that depends on the remaining life of, and type of, the contract. The degree of uncertainty of changes in exposure is not considered, except as reflected in these factors.

The April 1993 proposal of the Basle Committee recognized netting for calculating current exposure, but it did not do so for potential future

---

[1] An *effective notional amount* is used for certain cases in which leverage or the time structure of the position played a role in exposure.

Table 12.1.   BIS Add-Ons for Potential Exposure

Residual maturity	Interest rate	Exchange rate, gold	Equity	Metals	Other commodities
< 1 year	0.0	1.0	6.0	7.0	10.0
1–5 years	0.5	5.0	8.0	7.0	12.0
> 5 years	1.5	7.5	10.0	8.0	15.0

exposure. The banking industry responded with a proposal for a reduction in the add-on factor. In April 1995, after extensive comments from financial institutions, the Basle Committee settled on the following formula for add-ons in light of netting:

$$A_{\text{Net}} = 0.4 \times A_{\text{Gross}} + 0.6 \times \text{NGR} \times A_{\text{Gross}}, \tag{12.1}$$

where A_{Gross} is the sum of the individual add-on amounts (calculated by multiplying the notional principal amount by the appropriate add-on factor in Table 12.1) of all transactions that are subject to enforceable netting agreements with the counterparty, and NGR is the ratio of the net replacement cost to the gross replacement cost for transactions subject to legally enforceable netting agreements.[2] The factor NGR in (12.1) is zero only if all derivative positions have negative mark-to-market value from the viewpoint of the financial institution measuring its risk exposure (which is unlikely for dealer banks making two-way markets). Some individuals, for example, Heldring (1997), have argued that this modified formula continues to overstate the risks of dealer banks.

12.1.3. Interest-Rate Swaps

Interest-rate swaps account for, by far, the largest notional quantity of OTC derivatives exposure, representing over $50 trillion of notional positions according to BIS statistics for 2001. We will therefore devote significant attention to modeling the exposure and valuation of default risk for interest-rate swaps.

We first review the terms of a plain-vanilla interest-rate swap, ignoring the possibility of default. Later, we bring in default risk. Litzenberger (1992) provides a general discussion of the institutional features of swap markets that are relevant in a discussion of credit risk. Smith et al. (1988) and Marshall (1993) give overviews of the workings of swap markets. Cossin and Pirotte (1996) provide some empirical analyses.

---

[2] See Basle Committed on Banking Supervision and IOSCO (1995).

Plain-vanilla interest-rate swaps are OTC contracts between two counter-parties specifying the periodic exchange of fixed-coupon payments by one counterparty in return for floating-rate payments by the other. The inter-coupon period is often one-quarter or one-half year. The floating rates are contractually set at the LIBOR rate of the relevant coupon period. For example, if the swap's coupon period is one quarter, the floating rate r_{k-1} set at quarter $k-1$ and paid at quarter k for 3-month loans is the floating-rate payment on the swap.

For illustration, consider a quarterly coupon floating-for-fixed swap maturing in n quarters. As depicted in Figure 12.1, this swap is a commitment to pay at each future quarter $k \leq n$ the previous quarter's short rate r_{k-1} in return for a fixed payment of $s(n)$, the n-quarter swap rate. That is, at quarter k one pays a fraction $r_{k-1}/4$ of the notional principal underlying the swap and receives a fraction $s(n)/4$. To be precise, one actually pays the difference $[s(n) - r_{k-1}]/4$, if positive, and otherwise receives $[r_{k-1} - s(n)]/4$.

At the origination of a plain-vanilla swap, the swap rate $s(n)$ is chosen so that the swap is *at market,* meaning that it has an initial market value of zero. Ignoring credit risk for the moment, this implies that the swap rate $s(n)$ is the par-coupon rate on default-free n-quarter fixed-rate loans. That is, $s(n)$ is the coupon rate at which a fixed-rate quarterly dividend bond maturing in n quarters would sell at its face value. In order to see this, consider the exchange of a floating-rate bond for a par-coupon fixed-rate bond of the same principal. A floating-rate bond always sells at par, at

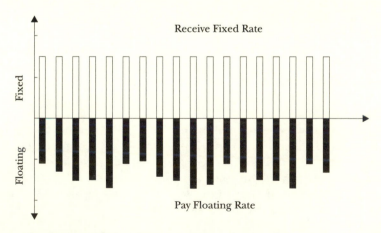

Figure 12.1. *A floating-for-fixed interest-rate swap.*

issue or immediately after the payment of any of its coupons.[3] Because the principal payments on the two bonds are precisely offsetting, the exchange of the floating-rate and fixed-rate bonds is a synthetic swap, as depicted in Figure 12.2. Since both bonds sell initially at par, this bond exchange is an at-market swap. To repeat, we have so far ignored credit risk.

The exposure on an interest-rate swap is substantially smaller than that of a loan or bond with the same coupon rate, face value, and maturity. First, there is no exposure to the loss of the notional principal because the exchange of these principal amounts on the two sides of the swap is avoided by the terms of the swap contract. There is only coupon risk. Moreover, not even the full amounts of the coupons are at risk. The swap contract does not obligate the fixed-rate payer to pay the fixed-rate coupons regardless of the floating-rate payer's performance. Rather, at each coupon date, there is an exchange only of the *difference* between the fixed-rate payment and the floating-rate payment. If one counterparty fails to perform at any time, there is no further obligation for either counterparty to continue to make coupon payments. Instead, independent quotations are obtained for the market value of the swap, and the counterparty that is *in the money* (i.e., for whom the swap has positive market value) is immediately owed this market value by the other counterparty, regardless of who defaulted. Failure to settle on these terms may result in legal action designed to recover this obligation. Moody's Investors Service (1994) discusses the legal status of swaps in bankruptcy.

12.1.4. Midmarket Revaluation of Swaps

After the inception of a swap, market interest rates move, causing a mark-to-market profit or loss on the swap, changing the exposure. In order to calculate the change in the market value of the swap between any two dates (before adjusting for credit risk), it is enough to calculate the change in the market values of the fixed-rate and floating-rate bonds that are, in effect, being exchanged. To the fixed-rate receiver, the change in market value of the swap is the change in value of the fixed-rate bond less the change in value of the floating-rate bond. (Again, this is before all considerations of default risk.)

At each new coupon date, the floating-rate bond is equivalent to a new floating-rate bond and so has a market value equal to its face value after

---

[3] All of the floating-rate payments could be made by investing the notional principal, say, P, currently at the short rate and rolling the investment into a one-quarter loan at every quarterly coupon date. After each first quarter, one has $P(1 + r_{k-1}/4)$, from which one makes the floating-rate payment $r_{k-1}/4$, and reinvests the principal P at the new short rate r_k. Continuing to roll over the investment at the short rate, making all quarterly floating-rate payments when due, one is left with the notional principal at maturity.

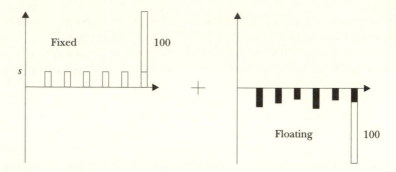

Figure 12.2. *Synthetic swap: exchange of floating- and fixed-rate bonds.*

its coupon has been paid. For any other date t, one knows that at the next coupon date, the floating-rate bond will have a market value V equal to its face value plus the amount of the coupon payment, which is already known at date t, since the coupon payments are set at the previous coupon date. Thus, the market value of the floating-rate bond at date t is equal to the market value of a loan whose maturity is the next coupon date and whose principal is a known fixed amount V. We can therefore calculate the price of the floating-rate bond directly from the current short-term market interest rate for the maturity of the next coupon date. Later, we discuss relevant information sources for this short-term interest rate.

The market value at any date t of the fixed-rate bond can be computed by a standard discounted–cash flow calculation from the current term structure of interest rates. A reasonable source for these new interest rates is the new term structure of at-market swap rates for high-quality counterparties, for these reflect the current market interest rates at which the fair market values of new high-quality fixed-rate bonds are determined. These new swap rates are reported at all times from major vendors of financial data and are normally based on dealer quotes. If the data are bid and ask rates, it is common to use the midpoint of the bid and ask rates for this purpose. While a detailed theoretical analysis could raise some issues about the use of the precise midpoint, this is reasonable, and in any case the bid-ask spread is extremely narrow, shrinking in the late 1990s to a few basis points for conventional swaps, given the exceptional size and liquidity of this market. For shorter maturities, at which swap rates are not quoted, LIBOR rates are a reasonable proxy for the purpose of midmarket valuation. We shall have more to say about this when raising the question of default risk. For numerous reasons, one should *not* use the term structure of interest rates associated with government bonds. In the United States, for example, government bond yields are "contaminated" by state tax exemptions for Treasury coupon payments; the occasionally severe scarcity of Treasuries in repo markets, which implies special repo-rate advantages; and the superior liquidity and margin or collateral service values of Treasuries.

One may reconstruct the term structure of interest rates from futures prices in the LIBOR or Eurodollar futures markets, although Cox et al. (1981) pointed out that interest-rate futures prices can be converted into the corresponding term structure of interest rates only after corrections for the resettlement feature of futures contracts. These corrections are model-based and depend on volatility (Grinblatt and Jegadeesh, 1996). Futures rates are nevertheless a natural source of information, provided the appropriate adjustments are made.

In order to determine discount factors from market yields for the discounted–cash flow calculation mentioned above, statistical curve-fitting methods are normally used, for example, the method proposed by Fisher et al. (1994).

The market LIBOR rates used for purposes of setting the contractual swap floating-rate payments at each coupon date are obtained from a poll of rates offered on short-term loans by major high-quality banks to high-quality borrowers (roughly, those with AA credit ratings). As such, the floating-rate payments on the swap are not default-free rates, *even if both swap counterparties are themselves default-free.* LIBOR short-term rates are often significantly higher than Treasury rates of the same maturity. The spread between the two has often been more than 100 basis points. As a result, at-market swap rates are, maturity by maturity, sometimes significantly higher than the similar-maturity Treasury rates. This may raise some concern about the source of discount rates used to mark swaps to market, *even if both swap counterparties are default-free.* As we have noted, Treasury rates are themselves unreliable for this purpose. Whether midmarket swap rates are reliable in this case is a somewhat subtle matter. Duffie and Singleton (1997) show that, under reasonable conditions, midmarket swap rates are effectively the bond yields that would apply to a hypothetical issuer whose credit quality will remain of short-term LIBOR (roughly AA) quality for the life of the swap.[4] This hypothetical issuer is sometimes said to be of *refreshed LIBOR quality.* It is difficult to obtain true market long-term discount rates that are not at all contaminated by default risk, tax effects, or institutional factors. However, the incidence of default on short-term obligations by AA quality borrowers is exceptionally small.

12.1.5. Expected Swap Exposures

The expected exposure on an OTC position is just that, the expectation of the exposure at some future time t. With a single uncollateralized position

---

[4] See Collin-Dufresne and Solnik (2001) for an analysis of initial LIBOR–quality versus refreshed AA–quality yields.

of market value Y_t, the expectation of the exposure at time t is $E[\max(0, Y_t)]$. The expected exposure can be used for the purpose of measuring and limiting credit exposure, in the same manner as a confidence limit on exposure. For an at-market interest-rate swap, the mean exposure is near zero at origination because the fixed rate is set for zero initial market value. The mean exposure first grows over time, then shrinks to zero as maturity approaches because fewer and fewer exchanges of coupons remain. With a currency swap, the counterparties exchange coupon payments in different currencies, which can be specified as fixed or floating. Some currency swaps call for an exchange of notional amounts of the two different currencies at maturity. The potential for changes in the relative values of the currencies before maturity thus implies substantially higher mean exposure, at typical currency volatilities, than an interest-rate swap of the same notional amount. Increasingly, currency swaps do not call for an exchange of the notional principal amounts of each currency.

We computed, and illustrate in Figure 12.3, the *expected exposure* on a 10-year, at-the-money semiannual coupon plain-vanilla interest-rate swap, according to a standard multifactor term-structure model.[5] Figure 12.3 shows a distinction between the actual expected exposure and the risk-neutral expected exposure. Actual expected exposures are appropriate when judging the actual expected loss in the event of default, whereas pricing is done on the basis of risk-neutral probabilities.

For an illustrative example, we computed actual and risk-neutral expected exposures for the lifetime of a 10-year plain-vanilla interest-rate swap in a three-factor affine model of interest rates, estimated using the daily time series of U.S.-dollar LIBOR and swap rates and swaption prices over the sample period of January 1, 1992, to December 31, 1997 (1,516 daily observations). We used a version of the affine model[6] in which there is one stochastic-volatility process driving the volatilities of all three factors. The other two factors are Gaussian after conditioning on the time path of the stochastic volatility.[7] Our calculations of expected exposures are done using state variables implied by swap rates and swaption prices as of the first date of the sample, January 1, 1992.

We see that the exposures under the actual and risk-neutral measures are notably different. Indeed, at their peaks, approximately 3 years from inception, the actual expected exposure is roughly three times the risk-neutral counterpart. The difference between the two is, to a large degree,

---

[5] This section draws from Singleton and Umantsev (2002) and uses their (approximate) analytic approach to pricing swaptions in order to compute expected exposures.

[6] This is the $A_1(3)$ variant of a three-factor affine model, as estimated by Singleton and Umantsev (2002).

[7] The parameters of these models were estimated by the method of maximum likelihood (Appendix B), holding the parameters fixed over the sample period. In this manner, we use the entire sample period to "pin down" the distributional properties of swap rates.

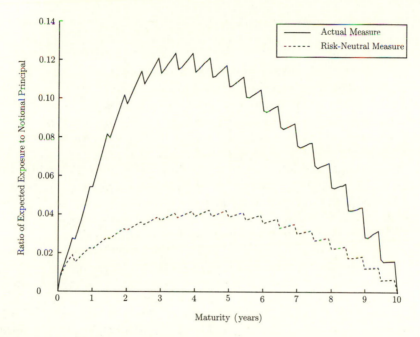

Figure 12.3. *Expected exposures for a 10-year interest-rate swap for a three-factor affine model under the actual (solid line) and risk-neutral (dotted line) probabilities.*

caused by the fact that the estimated risk-neutral mean reversion is much smaller than the estimated actual mean reversion.

In practice, some (if not most) swap broker-dealers use risk-neutral exposure measures, because they have already calibrated risk-neutral term-structure models for pricing interest-rate derivatives.

12.2. OTC Credit Risk Value Adjustments

When making markets or marking to market OTC positions, normal practice among broker-dealers is to adjust "midmarket" values with credit adjustments and possibly administrative cost adjustments. One could also contemplate adjustments for illiquidity. Here, we consider only adjustments for credit risk. A midmarket value is the value that would apply if both counterparties are of relatively high quality, say AA rated, and is usually measured as the average of the bid and ask prices.[8] It has become increasingly the norm that midmarket quotes are also based on the assumption of collateralization,

---

[8] In practice, the midmarket price is measured as the price associated with the average of the bid and ask rates, in the case of swaps, or the average of the bid and ask implied volatilities, in the case of options.

so valuations are essentially default-free, except to the extent of the risks of collateral insufficiency and of a failure of enforceability of netting in the event of default.

For a credit risk adjustment relative to a midmarket value, a theoretically consistent approach is to compute the market value of credit risk of the actual position, *net* of the market value of credit risk for a hypothetical midmarket set of counterparties. In practice, participants sometimes ignore the value of the credit risk for midmarket counterparties, since it is usually negligible.

For example, consider a yen-dollar currency option with midmarket valuation of 100 that includes a market value of 1 for default risk. Suppose the counterparty credit risk implies a market value of default risk of 3. Then the credit risk adjustment is a downward adjustment of $3 - 1 = 2$ from midmarket, leaving an adjusted price of 98.

The midmarket valuations of swaps are based on hypothetical counterparties of roughly AA quality. At the inception of a swap, the expected exposures to each counterparty, while not identical, are similar, so the effects of default risk are close to offsetting even without collateralization, as we shall see in the numerical examples to follow. This may not be the case for currency swaps that have an exchange of notional principals at maturity, for which expected exposures can be substantial. Swap exposures may grow considerably after inception.

12.2.1. One-Sided Default Risk

We begin with the simplest case, in which there is but a single time at which there is an exchange between the counterparties. This is effectively the case of an OTC forward contract on an asset with price process S for delivery at some time T at a fixed forward price F. The net payment due from the counterparty is therefore $S_T - F$.

We suppose that the counterparty paying $S_T - F$ is defaultable, whereas the receiver is default-free. The opposite case can be treated symmetrically; the case of two-sided default risk is covered in the next section. The exposure at delivery is thus $\max(S_T - F, 0)$, the same as that of an option on the underlying asset struck at F.

For simplicity, we also suppose that the underlying price process S and the default risk are (risk-neutrally) independent. This is also relaxed later in the chapter.

We let L be the fraction of the exposure that is lost at default, and D be the indicator for default, which is 1 in the event of default and 0 in the event of no default. The total default loss is then $LD(S_T - F)^+$, and the market value of the default loss is

$$V = E^* \left[e^{-\int_0^T r(s)\, ds} LD(S_T - F)^+ \right], \tag{12.2}$$

where r is the default-free short rate. Assuming that DL is independent, risk-neutrally, of S_T and the default-free short rate r, we have

$$V = E^*(DL)E^* \left[e^{-\int_0^T r(s)\, ds} (S_T - F)^+ \right] = E^*(DL)Y, \tag{12.3}$$

where

$$Y = E^* \left[e^{-\int_0^T r(s)\, ds} (S_T - F)^+ \right]$$

is the price of a default-free option struck at F on the underlying, for exercise on the delivery date T. We may view $E^*(DL)$ as the risk-neutral mean loss rate, that is, the risk-neutral expected fraction of the exposure that will be lost owing to default. For reference, DPG minimum 1-year mean loss rates (actual, not risk-neutral) for swaps and forwards are shown in Table 12.2. For pricing, one would use risk-neutral mean loss rates, which can be estimated from credit spreads. For example, the price of a loan of the same credit quality, under the same recovery and independence assumptions, is

$$d(0, T) = E^* \left[e^{-\int_0^T r(s)\, ds} (1 - DL) \right]$$

$$= [1 - E^*(DL)]E^* \left[e^{-\int_0^T r(s)\, ds} \right]$$

$$= [1 - E^*(DL)]\delta(0, T),$$

where $\delta(0, T)$ is the price of a default-free loan of the same maturity. Thus, one can estimate the risk-neutral mean loss rate as

$$E^*(DL) = \frac{\delta(0, T) - d(0, T)}{\delta(0, T)}, \tag{12.4}$$

Table 12.2.   DPG Mean Default Loss Rates

	Credit rating		
	AA	A	BBB
Swaps	0.001	0.006	0.020
F/X forwards	0.001	0.001	0.002

from credit spreads of the same quality. The same idea applies when credit risk and interest-rate risk are correlated, and the calculations can be obtained from the methods explained in Chapters 5 and 6.

Likewise, consider a swap, say a plain-vanilla interest-rate swap, receiving fixed coupons at rate F and paying floating rates at coupon dates $t(1), \ldots,$ $t(n)$. We suppose for illustration that only the fixed-rate payer is defaultable. Later, we consider the case of two-sided credit risk.

The swap is assumed to be the only position with the counterparty and has a midmarket value of $S_{t(i)}$ at coupon date $t(i)$. We suppose that, in the event of default by the counterparty at date $t(i)$, the receiver loses some fraction, say L, of the exposure $X_{t(i)} = \max(S_{t(i)}, 0)$. If D_i denotes the indicator for default between $t(i-1)$ and $t(i)$ (with outcome 1 in the event of default between these dates and 0 otherwise), then the total initial market value of default losses is

$$V = E^* \left[\sum_{i=1}^{n} e^{-\int_0^{t(i)} r(s)\, ds} D_i L X_{t(i)} \right]. \tag{12.5}$$

Assuming (risk-neutral) independence between $D_i L$ and $\{r, S\}$, we have

$$V = \sum_{i=1}^{n} E^*(L D_i) E^* \left[e^{-\int_0^{t(i)} r(s)\, ds} X_{t(i)} \right] \tag{12.6}$$

$$= \sum_i k_i f_i, \tag{12.7}$$

where $k_i = E^*(D_i L)$ is the risk-neutral mean loss rate for the ith coupon period and

$$f_i = E^* \left[e^{-\int_0^{t(i)} r(s)\, ds} \max(0, S_{t(i)}) \right] \tag{12.8}$$

is the default-free price of a swaption, specifically an option to enter as a fixed-rate receiver into a swap at time $t(i)$ at fixed rate F, for maturity $t(n)$. Under these simplifying assumptions, we may view the total market value of default losses on a swap as the market value of a portfolio of swaptions. This approach to valuing the default risk of a swap is based on Sorenson and Bollier (1994). Provided L and D_i are independent (risk-neutrally), we can further obtain $E^*(D_i L) = \ell^* p_i^*$, where $\ell^* = E^*(L)$ is the risk-neutral mean fractional loss of exposure given default, and p_i^* is the risk-neutral probability of default after coupon date $t(i-1)$ and by coupon date $t(i)$. For example, with default between dates $t(i-1)$ and $t(i)$ at a constant risk-neutral intensity of λ^*, we have $p_i^* = e^{-\lambda^* t(i-1)} - e^{-\lambda^* t(i)}$. The resulting swap credit risk adjustment to market value is illustrated in Figure 12.4.

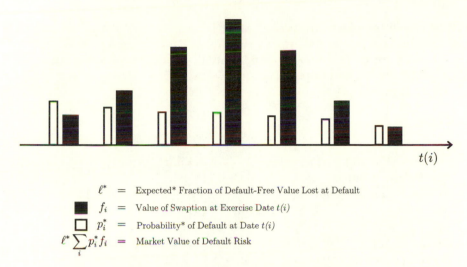

$$t(i)$$

ℓ^*	$=$	Expected* Fraction of Default-Free Value Lost at Default
■ f_i	$=$	Value of Swaption at Exercise Date $t(i)$
☐ p_i^*	$=$	Probability* of Default at Date $t(i)$
$\ell^* \sum_i p_i^* f_i$	$=$	Market Value of Default Risk

Figure 12.4.   Valuing credit risk on a swap.

12.2.2. Adjustment with Netting and Collateral

The credit risk adjustment for the valuation of default losses on a set of positions covered by a master agreement with netting, in the case of one-sided default risk only, is computed by the same formula (12.5) used for stand-alone swaps, except of course that the exposure $X_{t(i)}$ at the ith payment date is the total market value of all positions, after considering all enforceable netting and collateral. If the enforceability of netting is uncertain, this can also be captured within a model.

The following proposition from Duffie and Huang (1996) states that, when ignoring one's own credit risk, the market value of a portfolio with a netting provision is always higher than that of the same portfolio without a netting provision. This captures the market value of the industry practice of placing, if possible, swaps of offsetting default risk in a portfolio with netting provisions (see, e.g., Ruml, 1992). Of course, swap diversification is also a useful means of credit risk mitigation, independently of its impact on market values. In a similar spirit, Cooper and Mello (1991) show that a bank that already owns a claim on a counterparty can afford to offer a more competitive rate to the same counterparty on a forward contract for hedging purposes.

Proposition. *Let V^a, V^b, and V^{ab} be, respectively, the credit risk adjustments of stand-alone position a, stand-alone position b, and the combined positions a and b, assuming netting, from the viewpoint of the market value to a counterparty that is default-free. Then $V^{ab} \leq V^a + V^b$.*

The proof is simply an application of Jensen's inequality, using the fact that the exposure function $f(\cdot)$, defined by $f(x) = \max(0, x)$, is convex. The same proposition holds, more generally, under two-sided default risk, provided that the counterparty is always of relatively lower credit risk, as demonstrated by Duffie and Huang (1996).

12.2.3. Two-Sided Default Risk

A general method for computing credit risk adjustments when both counterparties are defaultable is as follows. One first calculates the market value V_B of default losses to counterparty A that are caused by any default of counterparty B that occurs before the default of A. (If counterparty A defaults first, then, under standard master agreements, there is no default loss to A caused by the default of B because all contracts are settled at the time of the default by A.) The same algorithm can be used to calculate the market value V_A of losses to counterparty B through any default by counterparty A that occurs

---

Table 12.3.   Monte Carlo Valuation Algorithm for Credit-Risk Adjustment

1. Initialize at zero the cumulative discounted loss Z to A caused by default by B.
2. Initiate a new independently simulated scenario, unless a sufficiently large number of independently simulated scenarios have already been generated. If a sufficient number of scenarios have been simulated, go to step 7.
3. Simulate, date by date, whether B defaults and whether A defaults. If neither defaults, or if A defaults before B, return to step 2. Otherwise, record the time t that B defaulted before A.
4. Simulate, for this scenario, the net exposure X_t of counterparty A to default by counterparty B, after discounting to time zero at the path of short-term interest rates up to time t. That is, X_t is the discounted amount (based on the default-free market value of the position) that would be lost from default by B with no recovery, with all applicable netting agreements in force and net of all collateral. The enforceability of netting can also be simulated if uncertain.
5. Simulate the fraction L of the exposure X_t that is lost given default by B.
6. Increment the cumulative discounted default loss Z by the scenario result LX_t, and return to step 2.
7. A sufficient number of scenarios have been simulated, so divide the cumulative discounted loss Z over all scenarios by the number of scenarios. This average is an estimate of the risk-neutral discounted expected loss, which is the market value V_B of default losses to counterparty A caused by the first default of counterparty B.
8. Similarly, estimate the market value V_A of default losses to counterparty B owing to first default by counterparty A. The difference $V_B - V_A$ is the credit-risk adjustment for counterparty A, which can be positive or negative.

---

before default by B. The difference $V_B - V_A$ is the net market value of the default losses to party A.

An algorithm for computing the credit risk adjustment can be based on Monte Carlo simulation methods that are now commonly available. An illustrative example is presented in Table 12.3. This algorithm considers the default risk of both counterparties, general types of OTC positions including loans and derivatives, as well as netting and collateral agreements. The algorithm allows for correlations among the default risks of the counterparties and market prices and interest rates. All simulation described here is based on risk-neutral models, the same models used for derivative pricing. For illustrative purposes, the algorithm is described in simple terms, and not in a complete and computationally efficient manner. Typically, some thousands or tens of thousands of scenarios are used, depending on the technique, in order to capture the effect of the law of large numbers, under which the average of the scenario results comes arbitrarily close to the risk-neutral expectation. We emphasize that, in each simulated scenario, it is critical to keep track of which counterparty, if any, defaults first. This is true whether or not the counterparties' defaults are correlated.

12.2.4. Example: Ten-Year Swap Adjustments

As an example, we illustrate the pricing of credit risk for a 10-year interest-rate swap, with an at-market fixed rate. Using the same three-factor affine term-structure model whose actual and risk-neutral expected exposures are shown in Figure 12.3, we show in Figure 12.5 the initial price $f(t)$ of a swaption, an option to enter into a receive-fixed swap in t years, for t ranging between 0 and 10 years. The underlying swap is of maturity $10 - t$ years, with a fixed rate, in all cases, that is the initial at-market 10-year swap rate.[9] Figure 12.5 also shows the market values of the associated strip of payer swaptions.

In Table 12.4, we show the calculation of the two-sided credit risk adjustment for parties of equal credit quality. We have assumed for illustration that both the fixed-rate payer and the fixed-rate receiver have the same risk-neutral constant default intensity $\lambda_p^* = \lambda_r^* = 0.01$. For example, at a 50% risk-neutral expected fractional loss in face value at default, these intensities correspond to bond credit spreads of approximately 50 basis points. The figures in Table 12.4 are calculated as follows.

The net credit adjustment for the market value of the swap to the receiver is the present value of cash flows lost owing to default by the payer,

---

[9] The initial state vector Y_t is set to the vector $(3.1181, -19.9433, -447.2830)'$, which implies 2-year and 10-year swap rates that are at their long-run mean values (6.65 and 7.60%, respectively), and a 6-month-into-2-year swaption volatility that is at its long-run mean (16.54%). We are grateful to Len Umantsev for providing these customized calculations.

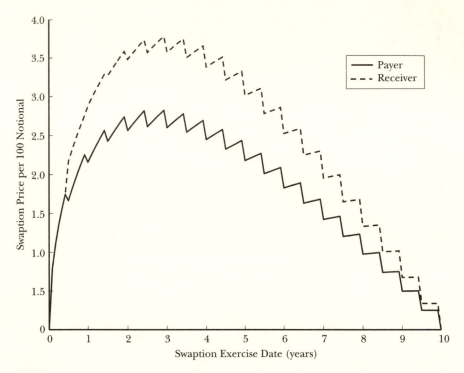

Figure 12.5. *In t for 10 − t swaption prices, for a notional of 100, both payer and receiver, for a range of times t between 0 and 10 years, on an underlying 10-year interest-rate swap, to receive the fixed rate, in all cases, that is the initial at-market 10-year swap rate, for a three-factor affine model with one stochastic-volatility factor.*

provided that the payer defaults before the receiver, minus the present value of the payer's cash flows lost owing to default by the receiver, provided that the receiver defaults before the payer. Thus, a key intermediate calculation is the risk-neutral probability that the payer defaults before the receiver and that this happens during a particular coupon period. (We also want the corresponding calculation for first default by the receiver during a particular coupon period.) Because we have assumed constant risk-neutral default intensities, these first-default probabilities are easily calculated as follows.

The time at which the receiver defaults first has a risk-neutral probability density of $e^{-(\lambda_r^* + \lambda_p^*)t}\lambda_r^*$. This is intuitive, for $e^{-\lambda_r^* t}e^{-\lambda_p^* t} = e^{-(\lambda_r^* + \lambda_p^*)t}$ is the probability that both survive to time t, and, conditional on joint survival, $\lambda_r^* dt$ is the "probability" that the receiver defaults during the "small time interval" $[t, t + dt]$. For each coupon date $t(i)$, we integrate this first-default density from $t(i - 1)$ to $t(i)$ in order to obtain the risk-neutral probabil-

Table 12.4. **Example Computation of Market Values of**
Credit Risk Owing to First Default by Payer and by Receiver,
at Equal Risk-Neutral Default Intensities of 100 Basis Points

$t(i)$	$X_p(i)$	$X_r(i)$	$L_r^*(i)$	$L_p^*(i)$	$X_r(i)L_p^*(i)$	$X_p(i)L_r^*(i)$
0.5	1.67	2.17	0.00249	0.00249	0.00539	0.00414
1.0	2.16	2.88	0.00246	0.00246	0.00709	0.00532
1.5	2.43	3.27	0.00244	0.00244	0.00797	0.00592
2.0	2.56	3.48	0.00241	0.00241	0.00840	0.00619
$\vdots$	$\vdots$	$\vdots$	$\vdots$	$\vdots$	$\vdots$	$\vdots$
9.5	0.25	0.34	0.00208	0.00208	0.00070	0.00052
Total					0.10796	0.07906

Note: Here $t(i)$ is the ith coupon date, $L_p^*(i)$ is the fraction of default-free market value of the swap lost owing to first default by the payer during the ith coupon period, $X_r(i)$ is the market value of the exposure to the receiver at the ith coupon date, which is the market value of an option to enter the same swap at date $t(i)$ as a receiver.

ity $p_{rp}^*(i)$ that the receiver defaults first, and defaults during this coupon period. These first-default calculations are easily extended to settings with correlated affine default-intensity processes (see Duffie, 1998b).

We multiply this first-default probability $p_{rp}^*(i)$ by the assumed risk-neutral expected fraction 0.5 of the market value of the (default-free) payer swaption lost, as of the time of the first coupon date after default. We then obtain $L_r^*(i)$, the risk-neutral expected fraction lost owing to the event that the receiver defaults first, and that this event occurs during the ith coupon period. Multiplying $L_r^*(i)$ by the market value $X_p(i)$ of the payer swaption value for exercise at date $t(i)$ leaves the market value $L_r^*(i)X_p(i)$ of default losses to the payer associated with default by the receiver during the ith coupon period, as shown in the last column of Table 12.4. Across all coupon periods, these market values total 0.07906. The results of the same calculation from the viewpoint of losses to the receiver owing to first default by the payer are also shown in Table 12.4, and total 0.10796. The net credit adjustment on the swap, relative to a default-free swap, is a reduction in the market value to the fixed-rate receiver of 0.0289 per 100 notional, or roughly 3 basis points of notional value. When reflected by an adjustment to the swap rate so as to compensate the receiver, this implies an upward adjustment in the default-free 10-year swap rate, 7.6%, of approximately 0.4 basis points. Because we have assumed that the risk-neutral default intensities of the payer and the receiver are the same and deterministic, this adjustment is due entirely to asymmetry in the time profile of the market values, $X_p(i)$ and $X_r(i)$, of exposures to the payer and to the receiver that are shown in Figure 12.5. The receiver's exposures are generally larger in this sense, even though the swap is at market.

Table 12.5 considers the same example, adjusted only by supposing that the fixed-rate receiver is default-free. In this case, the default risk to which the receiver is exposed implies a reduction in market value to the receiver of approximately 0.11 per 100 notional, for an implied compensating increase in the 10-year swap rate of roughly 1.5 basis points. The primary source of this adjustment in this case is that the payer has a debt credit spread that is roughly 50 basis points higher than that of the receiver.

12.3. Additional Swap Credit Adjustments

We now illustrate some additional credit risk adjustments to interest-rate swap rates, using an alternative method developed by Duffie and Huang (1996).[10] In particular, we are interested in the quantitative relationship between the term swap-rate spread that counterparties with different credit qualities face in the fixed-for-floating swap market (against the same counterparty), compared with the yield spreads at which they issue corporate bonds. Because we allow the default risk and the underlying interest rate risk to be correlated, the Sorensen-Bollier method used in Section 12.2.4 cannot be employed. Instead, our computations are based on partial differential equations (PDE) for the market value of a swap, which consider the impact of a change in effective credit quality as the swap moves in and out of the money to the receiver. When the swap has positive market value to the receiver, the payer's default risk is relevant, and conversely.

12.3.1. Setup

For our illustrative example, we consider a plain-vanilla swap with semi-annual exchanges of fixed-rate payments for floating-rate payments on a constant notional amount. We assume that counterparty A pays the 6-month LIBOR rate and that counterparty B pays a fixed rate. For at-market swaps, we consider the impact of a change in the credit quality of counterparty B on the fixed swap rate.

Counterparty A to the swap is assumed to have a risk-neutral default intensity process λ^* and, at default, a risk-neutral expected fractional loss ℓ^* of market value given default. Thus, $s_t^A = \lambda_t^* \ell^*$ is the risk-neutral mean rate of loss of market value. Similarly, counterparty B has some risk-neutral mean loss–rate process s^B, possibly different.

---

[10] For other approaches, see Solnik (1990), Cooper and Mello (1991), Sundaresan (1991), Rendleman (1992), Abken (1993), Hull and White (1995), Li (1995), Jarrow and Turnbull (1997), and Huge and Lando (1999).

Table 12.5. **Example Computation of Market Values of Credit Risk Owing to Default by Payer for a Default-Free Receiver**

$t(i)$	$X_p(i)$	$X_r(i)$	$L_r^*(i)$	$L_p^*(i)$	$X_r(i)L_p^*(i)$	$X_p(i)L_r^*(i)$
0.5	1.67	2.17	0	0.00249	0.00540	0
1.0	2.16	2.88	0	0.00248	0.00714	0
1.5	2.43	3.27	0	0.00247	0.00807	0
2.0	2.56	3.48	0	0.00246	0.00855	0
$\vdots$	$\vdots$	$\vdots$	$\vdots$	$\vdots$	$\vdots$	$\vdots$
9.5	0.25	0.34	0	0.00228	0.00077	0
Total					0.1121	0

The default risk–adjusted short-rate process of counterparty A is $\rho_t = r_t + s_t^A$, where r_t is the default-free short rate. For our base case, we assume that the credit quality of counterparty A is such that its default-adjusted short rate ρ_t is always that associated with borrowers of the quality associated with the LIBOR floating rate. We also assume that the spread $s^B - s^A$ between the mean loss rates of counterparties B and A depends only on the current short-term LIBOR short rate ρ_t, which allows us, for simplicity, to stay within a simple one-factor setting. Finally, for illustrative purposes, the short-term LIBOR rate ρ_t is modeled as a CIR process, in that

$$d\rho_t = \kappa(\theta - \rho_t)\,dt + \sigma\sqrt{\rho_t}\,dB_t^*, \tag{12.9}$$

where κ, θ, and σ are positive constants and B^* is a risk-neutral standard Brownian motion. For our base-case analysis, we suppose that $\kappa = 0.4$, $\theta = 0.1$, and $\sigma = 0.06$. These parameters are not empirical estimates, but they are not atypical (see Chen and Scott, 1993, Pearson and Sun, 1994, or Duffie and Singleton, 1997). This one-factor default-adjusted LIBOR-quality interest-rate model is less realistic than the three-factor affine model of the example in Section 12.2.4, but simplifies the PDE-based calculations used here to treat a variety of types of credit adjustments.

12.3.2. Base-Case Results

Figure 12.6 shows credit risk adjustments to at-market 5-year coupon swap rates, at typical interest-rate volatility. These and subsequent calculations are from Duffie and Huang (1996). We assume that counterparty B has a mean loss–rate process s^B that is always 100 basis points higher than that of counterparty A, implying that bond yields for B are 100 basis points above

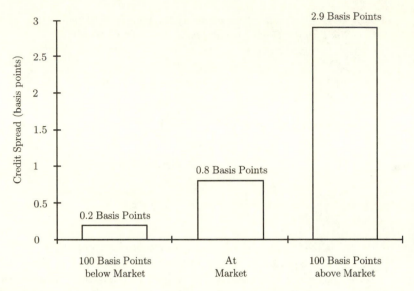

Figure 12.6. *Credit spread on a plain-vanilla swap rate, for a fixed-rate payer whose yield spreads are 100 basis points over LIBOR swap rates.*

those for A. If one assumes a risk-neutral mean fractional loss at default of $\ell^* = 50\%$[11] for both counterparties, the 100 basis points difference in yields translates into an annual risk-neutral default probability for counterparty B that is roughly 2% more than that of counterparty A.

The initial LIBOR rate is set at $\rho_0 = 10.18\%$. The results are not sensitive to ρ_0 within reasonable ranges. The at-market swap-rate credit adjustment shown in Figure 12.6 for this base case is approximately 0.8 basis points. This correction is roughly linear in the underlying swap-rate volatility.

Figure 12.6 shows that the netting of fixed against floating payments in interest-rate swaps significantly reduces the impact of default risk on swap rates relative to bond yields.[12] These results are roughly consistent

---

[11] The fractional recovery rate of swaps is likely to be somewhat different from that of bonds, even for like firms, although we are not aware of many data on this issue.

[12] There are significant numerical differences between our results and those of Sorenson and Bollier (1994), who estimate that the swap credit spread on a plain-vanilla interest-rate swap between AAA and BBB parties should be about 10 basis points. Our model, applied to a standard term-structure setup with typical parameters, and assuming a bond yield spread of 100 basis points between the two counterparties, implies a swap credit spread of less than 1 basis point. Sorenson and Bollier (1994) also indicated that, for the same two counterparties, the swap credit spread can vary 10–15 basis points as the yield curve goes from steep to inverted.

with subsequent calculations by Jarrow and Turnbull (1997) and Huge and Lando (1999).

12.3.3. Off-Market Swap-Rate Credit Spreads

If, after the initiation of a swap, interest rates decline, then the fixed-rate receiver has greater exposure. We capture this effect by considering an interest-rate swap whose fixed rate is 100 basis points higher than the at-market rate. Our setup is otherwise identical to the one considered above. As shown in Figure 12.6 for our base-case parameters, a swap credit spread of 2.9 basis points would compensate the floating-rate payer for bearing the risk of a fixed-rate payer with a bond yield spread of 100 basis points. The swap credit spread becomes 0.2 basis points if the swap is off the market against the LIBOR party by 100 basis points, while everything else remains the same.

12.3.4. Dependence of Default Risk on LIBOR Rate

We now allow for dependence of the default risk on the underlying interest rates. Specifically, for one example, we assume that B's loss-rate increases by 40 basis points for each 100 basis-point decline in LIBOR, after re-calibrating the model so that B's bond yield spread remains at 100 basis points over LIBOR. As B is paying fixed and receiving LIBOR, we expect a large correction in the swap rate owing to credit risk, for it is precisely when the swap is in the money to A that B's default risk increases. Indeed, the credit risk correction in the swap rate is roughly doubled. When the exposure to B of changes in LIBOR is reversed, the credit risk correction in the swap rate is roughly cut in two.

12.3.5. Asynchronous Swap Payments

We have so far assumed that the fixed-rate payment dates match the floating-rate payment dates. Some swaps, however, involve a fixed-rate payment once (or twice) a year, but a floating-rate payment four times a year. (We call these coupon swaps 4-for-1 [or 4-for-2].) Compared with the case of matched payment dates, the precedence of the floating-rate payments over the fixed-rate payments increases the exposure of the floating-rate payer and generally results in a larger swap credit spread when the floating-rate payer has the higher credit quality. To illustrate this effect, we consider a 4-for-1 swap, for which the floating-rate payer exchanges four quarterly payments of the 3-month LIBOR rate against a year-end fixed-rate payment by the other party,

Our results show that the impact of the yield curve on swap credit spread is rather small (less than 2 basis points as the difference between the 5-year LIBOR rate and the short LIBOR rate varies by 650 basis points).

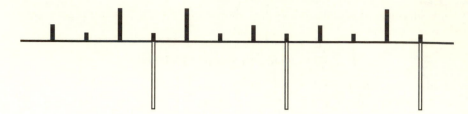

Figure 12.7.   *Asynchronous swap payments on a 4-for-1 swap.*

as illustrated in Figure 12.7. The 4-for-1 swap has a credit spread of approximately 4.4 basis points. This higher credit spread reflects the floating-rate payer's additional exposure to default risk by the fixed-rate payer, for example at the point in time at which three quarterly payments by the LIBOR party have been made, while the offsetting annual fixed-rate payment is yet to be made.

These results are consistent with the practice of some investment banks that, as floating-rate payers, request that their floating-rate payments be placed in escrow, compounded, and paid on the fixed-rate payment dates. Our credit-spread calculation for 4-for-1 swaps implies that this practice increases the value of the swap to the floating-rate payer by over 3 basis points, in terms of the swap rate, in addition to mitigating the credit risk.

12.3.6. The Impact of the Slope of the Yield Curve

We show in Figure 12.8 how the swap credit spread can depend on the slope of the yield curve. We vary the initial LIBOR rate ρ_0 and the long-term mean θ of the CIR model (12.9), holding the swap rate for a LIBOR-quality fixed-rate payer constant. Our setup is otherwise the same as that underlying Figure 12.6. Intuitively, we expect that, as the yield curve becomes less upward sloping, the risk-neutral expected exposure of the floating-rate payer should increase, since the (risk-neutral) median sample path of the market value of the swap becomes more upward sloping. This in turn causes the swap credit spread to increase. This is confirmed by the results shown in Figure 12.8.

12.3.7. Term Structure of Credit Spreads

In practice and in theory,[13] the term structure of yield spreads for medium- and high-quality issuers is often viewed as upward sloping. For low-quality issuers, this may or may not also be true; the empirical evidence is not yet

---

[13] See, e.g., Johnson (1967), Merton (1974), Pitts and Selby (1983), and Helwege and Turner (1999).

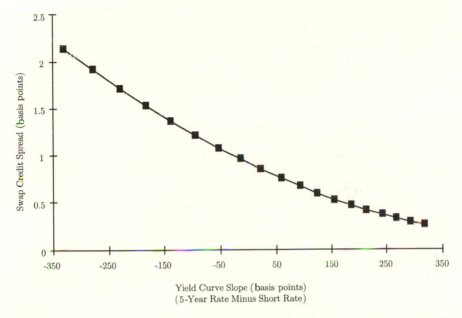

Figure 12.8. *Slope of yield curve and credit spread for 5-year swaps. (Source: Duffie and Huang, 1996.)*

clear (see Helwege and Turner, 1999, He et al., 2000, and Chapter 5). We now assume that the default-spread asymmetry $s_t^B - s_t^A$ is linearly increasing in time and that the model is otherwise the same as that underlying the results of Figure 12.6. Calibrating so that there remains a spread of 100 basis points between the two counterparties in their 5-year zero-coupon bond yields, the swap credit spread is 0.84 basis points, roughly the same as for the base case.

12.3.8. When Both Counterparties Are Risky

We consider the possibility that both parties have a positive default spread against the LIBOR rate. We assume that the effective instantaneous discount rates of the "LIBOR party" and the other fixed-rate-paying party are, respectively, 100 and 200 basis points higher than the spot LIBOR rate, while keeping the model otherwise the same as that underlying the results of Figure 12.6. The spread of one counterparty's bonds over the other's is kept at 100 basis points. We have computed the swap credit spread to be 0.95 basis points, close to the swap credit spread of the base case illustrated in Figure 12.6, which is otherwise identical.

12.3.9. The Impact of Netting

As indicated in Section 12.2.2, netting among swaps in a swap portfolio influences the value of the portfolio. We now use a simple example to illustrate the effect of a master-swap agreement with netting on the valuation of swap portfolios and the setting of swap rates.

Suppose that counterparty A, the party with higher credit quality, is about to enter into a swap contract, called the *new swap*, with counterparty B. If the new swap is not to be netted with an existing swap portfolio, then its term rate should be set so that its market value is zero at initiation. If, however, the new swap is to be netted with some existing swap portfolio between the two parties, then counterparty A may set a slightly lower rate for counterparty B because, for any given promised payment, the marginal value of the new swap with netting is higher than it is without netting. The amount of discount depends on the extent to which the credit exposure of the new swap offsets that of the existing swap portfolio. In practice, since swap rates are negotiated in the OTC market, there is a bargaining issue as to the fraction of the netting benefit to the high-quality counterparty that is shared with the low-quality counterparty.

To illustrate this effect, we consider the following example. The setup for the new swap is the same as that underlying the results of Figure 12.6, except that there is a previous swap in place and a master-swap agreement with full netting provisions. The terms of the previous swap are the same as those of the new swap, except that, under the previous swap, counterparty A pays fixed and counterparty B pays floating. The notional amount of the previous swap is a multiple k of that of the new swap. We can think of k as a hedge ratio of the old swap against the new. If $k = 1$, there is perfect hedging, since there is no net cash flow on the combined swap portfolio. We take the case of a constant bond yield spread, $s^B - s^A$, of 100 basis points.

The fixed-coupon rate $C(k)$ of the new swap depends on the extent to which the payments of the old and new swaps offset each other, that is, the hedge coefficient k. If $k \leq 0$, the payoffs of the new swap and those of the old swap are perfectly positively correlated, leaving no impact for hedging. That is, $C(k) = C(0)$ for $k \leq 0$. For $0 < k < 1$, the payoff of the old swap partially offsets that of the new swap, with the greatest offset occurring at $k = 1$. Consequently, the term rate $C(k)$ of the new swap is smaller than $C(0)$ and decreases with increasing k up to $k = 1$. For $k \geq 1$, the cash flows of the new swap are more than fully offset by the previous swap, and there are no additional marginal value benefits as k increases above 1. That is, $C(k) = C(1)$ for $k \geq 1$. This is illustrated in Figure 12.9. The linear dependence on k for $0 < k < 1$, shown in Figure 12.9, is demonstrated in Duffie and Huang (1996).

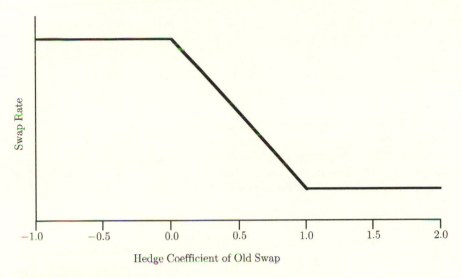

Figure 12.9. *Impact of netting on credit spread for swaps. (Source: Duffie and Huang, 1996.)*

We provide the numerical result for one example. For an initial short rate of $\rho_0 = 10.18\%$, we have

$$C(0) = 10.30\%, \quad C(1) = 10.28\%,$$

for a maximum impact of netting on swap rates of 1.8 basis points, which is, not surprisingly, about twice the credit spread indicated for the base case. These calculations assume that the benefits of netting are fully priced into the new swap. That is, the benefits to the high-quality counterparty are entirely reflected in the rate offered to the low-quality counterparty.

The netting effect of a master-swap agreement should be quantitatively more significant for other forms of contracts, such as certain foreign-exchange swaps or forwards, with larger credit-risk exposure.

12.4. Credit Spreads on Currency Swaps

Those currency swaps that involve an exchange of notionals in different currencies are typically subject to significantly more exposure to default than are interest-rate swaps. In this section, we calculate the impact of default risks on such currency-swap rates.

We use dollar and yen to denote, respectively, the units of the domestic and foreign currencies. Suppose that counterparties A and B are engaged in a fixed-for-fixed foreign-currency swap. The principal amounts of domestic currency (in dollars) and foreign currency (in yen) are P_d and P_f, respectively. Counterparty A exchanges a fixed coupon payment of $\frac{1}{2}c_d P_d$ dollars for a fixed coupon payment of $\frac{1}{2}c_f P_f$ yen with counterparty B, semiannually until maturity at time T, where c_d and c_f are the respective constant coupon rates. At maturity, counterparty A exchanges P_d dollars for P_f yen with counterparty B.

Since the volatility of the market value of the above fixed-for-fixed currency swap depends mostly on the volatility of the currency exchange rate, we simplify by taking constant domestic and foreign interest rates, r_d and r_f, respectively. The exchange rate q_t, which is the market value (in dollars) of 1 yen at time t, is taken to be log-normal. That is,

$$dq_t = (r_d - r_f)q_t \, dt + \sigma_q q_t \, dB_t^*, \qquad (12.10)$$

where σ_q is the constant exchange-rate volatility and B^* is a risk-neutral Brownian motion. The drift term $(r_d - r_f)q_t$ in (12.10) ensures that the gain process associated with rolling over 1 yen in short-term riskless lending, discounted by the domestic interest rate, is a risk-neutral martingale, as required by no-arbitrage theory.

Consistent with common practice, we assume for our example that P_d dollars have the same initial market value as P_f yen; that is, $P_d = q_0 P_f$. Second, we assume that the domestic and foreign interest rates are equal; that is, $r_d = r_f$. Third, we assume that the default spread s^A of counterparty A is a constant. Finally, we assume that the default-spread asymmetry $s^B - s^A$ is a constant c. These assumptions are made for analytical tractability and should not heavily influence the numerical relationship between the swap credit spread and the default-spread asymmetry $s^B - s^A$, which depends essentially on the exchange-rate volatility.

One way to estimate the impact of default risk on currency-swap rates is to apply a finite-difference numerical pricing solution, as used for interest-rate swaps, taking q as the state variable. It is also possible, however, to get an explicit expression for the first derivative of the swap-rate adjustment for credit risk with respect to the difference $s_t^B - s_t^A$ in the risk-neutral mean loss rates of the two counterparties. Figure 12.10 shows that the resulting first-order approximation provides sufficient accuracy for most practical applications. The advantage of this approximation method is that it can be computed relatively quickly for purposes of real-time quotation. For example, with

$$\sigma_q = 15\%, \quad R^A = 6\%, \quad T = 5 \text{ years}, \quad \text{and} \quad c_d = c_f = 5\%,$$

Duffie and Huang (1996) found that a linear approximation to the swap rate credit risk adjustment of $0.087c$, where c is the yield spread between

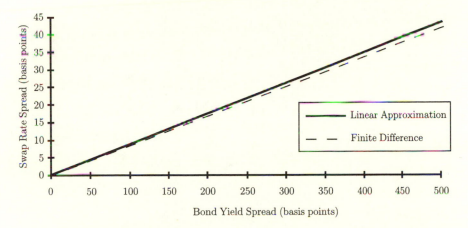

Figure 12.10. *Credit spread for currency swap by bond yield asymmetry. (Source: Duffie and Huang, 1996.)*

the two counterparties. At a constant credit-spread difference between the two counterparties of $c = 100$ basis points, the currency-swap credit spread is therefore about 8.7 basis points.

As with interest-rate swaps, a major determinant of currency-swap credit adjustments is market volatility. For our currency-swap example, doubling the volatility parameter σ_q from 15 to 30% increases the currency-swap-rate credit adjustment from approximately 8.7 basis points to approximately 17.2 basis points, as illustrated in Figure 12.11. These estimates are roughly consistent with those obtained by Hull and White (1995).

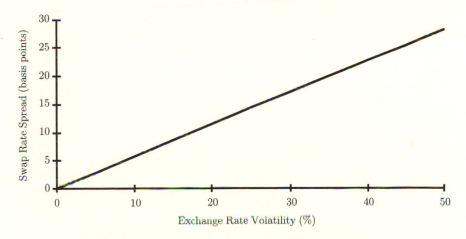

Figure 12.11. *Credit spread for currency swaps by volatility.*

13
Integrated Market and Credit Risk Measurement

THE INTEGRATION OF the risks of credit-sensitive instruments into portfolio market risk measures, such as value at risk (VaR), leads one to consider both default as well as changes in market valuation owing to predefault fluctuations in credit quality. One methodology for achieving this integration is roughly as follows:

- Catalog the sensitivities of all positions to fluctuations in market value owing to (1) changes in underlying marketwide risk factors (e.g., prices, rates, market credit spreads, and volatilities); and (2) counterparty-specific fluctuations in credit quality.
- Applying a risk model for changes in marketwide risk factors and counterparty-specific credit quality, estimate the overall risk of all positions, allowing for correlation.

Given the limited data that would typically bear on a risk model for counterparty credit quality, one does not expect precise results. Moreover, even reasonable differences in formulating a credit-risk model may imply substantial differences in overall portfolio risk estimates. In comparing several basic, commercialized credit-risk measurement systems, Lopez and Saidenberg (1999), Crouhy et al. (2000), and Gordy (2000), among others, have shown that they share similar conceptual foundations and provide similar quantitative assessments of credit risk over short horizons for a range of plausible parameterizations. Finger (2000), however, argues that more significant differences across these models emerge when examining risks over multiperiod horizons in an analysis of collateralized debt obligations. Further, many of the "stripped down" versions of commercial systems compared in these studies restrict, in counterfactual ways, the dynamic properties of credit spreads and changes in credit quality (see, e.g., Kiesel et al., 2000). These observations do not imply that the use of such basic risk-measurement

314

systems is pointless. Surely these models allow one to make more reasonable judgments about capital sufficiency and risk allocation than would be possible without such a model. They do, however, underscore the need for richer models within which one can judge the sensitivity of measures of credit risk to many of the assumptions currently used in practice.

We proceed to discuss some of the practical issues that arise in specifying each of the model ingredients outlined above. This is followed by a series of examples of risk measurement for portfolios of option and loan positions. For the purpose of this discussion, we take a generic object for risk evaluation to be a collection consisting of all positions with a given counterparty that are captured under one netting agreement.

13.1. Market Risk Factors

A common general approach is to model the market risk of a portfolio of financial positions in terms of a list $X = (X_1, \ldots, X_n)$ of n marketwide risk factors, such as prices, rates, volatilities, and so on. How should we specify the probability distributions of these factors? Of particular concern is the question of how stochastic volatility and infrequent jumps in asset returns affect the shapes of the probability distributions of returns. We focus on stochastic volatility and jumps, because the use of time-series models for returns that incorporate these features is a natural first step in extending the basic normal model to capture the widely documented *fat-tailed* and *skewed* characteristics of asset-return distributions. Moreover, stochastic volatility and jumps play central roles in industry implementations of security pricing models.

13.1.1. Preliminaries

In discussing the shapes of return distributions and the effects of changing shapes on measures of risk, we focus on *skewness* and *kurtosis*. The skewness of a random variable r is defined as

$$\frac{E\left([r - E(r)]^3\right)}{\sigma^3}, \tag{13.1}$$

where σ is the standard deviation. (All of these moments are assumed to exist.) Skewness is thus a measure of the degree to which positive deviations from the mean of the random variable are larger than negative deviations from the mean, as measured by the expected third power of these deviations. If one holds long positions (exposure to declining prices), then negative skewness is a source of concern as it implies that large negative returns are more likely, in the sense of skewness, than large positive returns. Figure 13.1 illustrates probability densities associated with

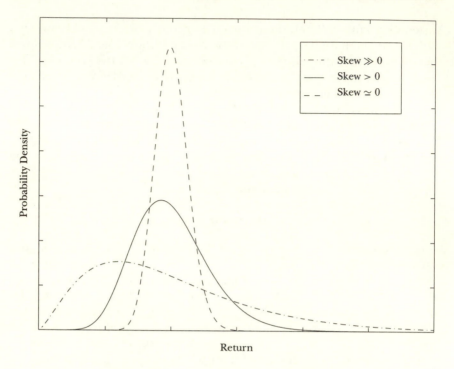

Figure 13.1. *Positively skewed distributions.*

various degrees of positive skewness. Normally distributed returns have zero skewness.

A second important feature of a probability distribution is the degree to which it is *thick* (*fat*) or *thin tailed*. A fat-tailed distribution is one for which large positive and negative outcomes (sometimes called *outliers*) are more likely than for a relatively thin-tailed distribution, such as the normal distribution. Kurtosis, a standard measure of tail fatness, is defined as

$$\frac{E\left([r - E(r)]^4\right)}{\sigma^4}. \tag{13.2}$$

The kurtosis of a normally distributed random variable is 3, so distributions with kurtoses larger than 3 are said to exhibit *excess* kurtosis. A fat-tailed probability density, one associated with excess kurtosis, is shown in Figure 13.2, along with a normal density.

In order to develop some intuition for the extent to which market variables are skewed or fat-tailed, Table 13.1 presents sample means, standard deviations, skewnesses, and kurtoses for various markets and instruments around the world. As an illustrative fixed-income instrument, we

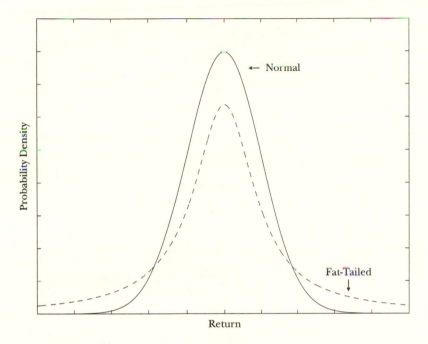

Figure 13.2. *Normal and fat-tailed return distributions.*

chose 5-year interest-rate swaps because data were available for a wider range of countries than was the case for intermediate-term government bonds. These instruments are defaultable, of course, and also reflect implicitly the sovereign risks associated with the currencies in which they were issued. The raw data for the equity and swap daily returns, in terms of local currencies, are for the period 1990–1996. For some of the series, especially the Asian swap data, only shorter sample periods were available. The *return* on a swap (which actually has a zero initial market value) is actually defined as the return on the fixed-rate bond underlying the swap.

Table 13.1 displays the sample mean (μ), standard deviation (σ), skewness (Skew), and kurtosis (Kurt) of each return for the respective sample periods. All of the equity returns exhibited substantial excess kurtosis. Hong Kong equity returns had the largest kurtosis, owing in part to the political turmoil surrounding the return of Hong Kong to Chinese control. Additionally, daily equity returns in developed markets tended to be negatively skewed, while several Asian markets exhibited positive skewness.

In the case of swaps, the European currency crisis of 1992 and the consequent large interventions by monetary authorities is partially responsible for the large estimated kurtoses. In particular, substantial increases in short-term rates by the central bank of Sweden in 1992, designed to defend its

Table 13.1. Sample Unconditional Moments of 1-Day Holding Period Returns for Various Markets and Countries

Equity returns (daily)

Moments	Austria	Canada	France	Germany	Hong Kong	Japan	Spain	Sweden	United Kingdom	United States
μ	0.051	0.042	0.060	0.055	0.101	−0.003	0.049	0.081	0.056	0.061
σ	0.854	0.556	0.936	0.998	1.431	1.169	0.967	1.104	0.752	0.734
Skew	−0.308	−0.360	−0.298	−1.227	−2.236	0.609	−0.306	0.325	0.140	−0.346
Kurt	6.636	5.166	6.694	22.423	37.163	11.250	10.339	10.163	6.235	7.213

Swap holding-period returns (daily)

Moments	Austria	Canada	France	Germany	Hong Kong	Japan	Spain	Sweden	United Kingdom	United States
μ	0.054	0.035	0.039	0.028	0.037	0.025	0.054	0.051	0.041	0.033
σ	0.392	0.420	0.257	0.205	0.355	0.217	0.343	0.451	0.291	0.278
Skew	−0.651	−0.317	0.161	−0.176	−0.294	−0.450	−0.339	2.670	0.851	−0.092
Kurt	10.797	5.325	8.128	6.205	11.526	8.541	11.704	52.070	13.280	5.420

Corporate yield spreads (monthly)

Moments	Long AA	Long A	Long BAA	Med AA	Med A	Med BAA
μ	91.2	114.4	176.3	71.5	100.9	146.8
σ	17.8	19.6	30.1	16.5	22.2	39.1
Skew	1.02	1.54	0.64	0.94	1.29	1.53
Kurt	4.45	5.89	4.43	3.93	5.04	5.37

Sources: Goldman Sachs and Lehman Brothers.

currency against "speculative attacks," are reflected in a kurtosis estimate of 52 for Swedish kroner swap returns.

Finally, the last panel of Table 13.1 shows the corresponding moments of monthly changes in spreads for our series of yields on noncallable U.S. corporate bonds, constructed from the Lehman Brothers data base over the period April 1987 through December 1994. All of the spread changes exhibit some positive skewness and moderate excess kurtosis for this sample period. Positively skewed spread changes contribute to negatively skewed bond returns, fixing the underlying government yields.

In summary, most returns on securities exhibit excess kurtosis (fat tails), and many exhibit significant negative or positive skewness, suggesting that, whatever the econometric model of returns adopted, it should allow for nonnormal marginal return distributions.

13.1.2. Modeling Return Distributions

Though risk measurement is often discussed as if financial institutions are implementing models in which returns are independently and identically distributed over time, most financial institutions consider return distributions that accommodate stochastic volatility. The most widely used formulation of stochastic volatility is the discrete-time generalized autoregressive conditional heteroskedasticity (GARCH) model proposed by Bollerslev (1986),[1] which has returns $r_1, r_2, \ldots$ in successive periods described by

$$r_t = \mu + \sigma_{t-1}\epsilon_t, \tag{13.3}$$

$$\sigma_{t-1}^2 = \omega + \alpha(r_{t-1} - \mu)^2 + \beta\sigma_{t-2}^2, \tag{13.4}$$

with standard normal (zero-mean, unit-variance) shocks $\epsilon_1, \epsilon_2, \ldots$ that are independent (and therefore uncorrelated). The coefficients ω, α, and γ, to be estimated, are nonnegative. For risk measurement, the mean parameter μ in (13.3) is often set to zero.

It is not unusual in practice for risk managers to use a variant of (13.4) with $\mu = 0$, $\omega = 0$, and $\alpha = (1 - \beta)$, and with a finite *look-back* horizon. This variant of the GARCH model has commonly been referred to as the *rolling historical* volatility model (see, e.g., Litterman and Winkelmann, 1998), and gives a conditional-variance estimator at time t of

$$\hat{\sigma}_{t,\beta}^2 = (1 - \beta) \sum_{j=0}^{T} \beta^j r_{t-j}^2, \tag{13.5}$$

---

[1] For specifics and generalizations, as well as a review of models with autoregressive conditional heteroskedasticity in finance, see Bollerslev et al. (1992).

where T is the look-back horizon. The geometric weighting in (13.5) mitigates the sensitivity of equally weighted, rolling histories to outliers. J. P. Morgan introduced RiskMetrics with a volatility model similar to (13.5) (Phelan, 1995), using a rolling history of 100 days and a decay factor of $\beta = 0.96$.

A potential limitation of the GARCH model is that the impact of the current return r_t on the new volatility σ_{t+1}^2 is quadratic. Consequently, a day of exceptionally large absolute returns may cause *overshooting* when forecasting volatility. Such an overshooting dies out over time at the decay rate $\beta + \alpha$. Thus, with any reasonable degree of persistence, a jump caused by a market crash, for example, could imply a sustained overestimate of volatility.

With the GARCH model, the quadratic nature of the dependence of σ_t^2 on past returns also implies that return shocks are symmetric in their effect on volatility. Large positive or negative returns of equal absolute magnitude have the same effect on volatility. For many markets, however, and in particular many equity markets, it has long been recognized that positive and negative returns have asymmetric effects on volatility. Large negative returns are viewed as having a larger effect than correspondingly large positive returns. Historical volatility measures, including GARCH models, do not capture this asymmetry.

The normally distributed innovation ϵ_t in the GARCH model implies that the conditional distribution of one-period returns is also normal, an assumption that is counter to the empirical evidence. We therefore also examine the MIX-GARCH variant of the GARCH model, which replaces the assumption that ϵ_t in (13.4) is normal with the assumption that ϵ_t has a mixture of normal distributions. Specifically, ϵ_t is, with some given mixture probability p, drawn from a normal distribution with standard deviation γ_1, and with the complementary probability $1 - p$ is drawn from a normal distribution with standard deviation γ_2. The mixing probability p and the standard deviations γ_1 and γ_2 are chosen so that $p\gamma_1^2 + (1-p)\gamma_2^2 = 1$, maintaining the property that ϵ_t has a variance of 1. When calibrated to the kurtoses of most return series, one typically has p near 1 and γ_2^2 significantly larger than γ_1^2, so that, in most of the mixing outcomes, ϵ_t has the smaller variance γ_1, but with some small probability $1 - p$, one has the more volatile conditional return variance. One may view this, in effect, as an occasional jump event, increasing the kurtosis of the distribution of returns. With zero means for each of the underlying normal distributions that are mixed, ϵ_t remains symmetrically distributed and hence has zero skewness, as illustrated in Figure 13.2 for fat-tailed distributions.

Neither of these variants of the GARCH model have "true" stochastic volatility, in the sense that the only source of uncertainty for the volatility σ_t for these models is the return itself. The volatility does not have a separate source of uncertainty. There is evidence, however, that the level of volatility does change randomly, even after controlling for the impact of returns. Indeed, financial institutions often treat volatility as a separate risk factor. Letting P_t denote the price of a risky asset, one widely studied stochastic-volatility model has

$$\frac{dP(t)}{P(t)} = \mu \, dt + \sigma(t) \, dB_P(t) + dJ(t), \tag{13.6}$$

$$d\sigma^2(t) = [\alpha - \kappa\sigma^2(t)] \, dt + \eta\sigma(t) \, dB_\sigma(t), \tag{13.7}$$

where J is a pure-jump process to be described shortly, and B_P and B_σ are standard Brownian motions that may be correlated, according to a parameter $\rho = \text{corr} \, [B_P(t), B_\sigma(t)]$. The stochastic *instantaneous variance* in this model, $\sigma^2(t)$, is a CIR process, mean reverting to a long-run mean of α/κ. A negative correlation parameter ρ induces negative skewness in the distributions of discretely sampled returns.

The jump process J in (13.6) has jumps at Poisson arrivals, independent of B_P and B_σ, with constant arrival intensity φ. The amplitude of the jumps to the logarithm of the price is an independently and identically distributed $N(-\delta^2/2, \delta^2)$ process, and is independent of the jump times, B_P, and B_σ. This stochastic-volatility jump-diffusion model allows us to explore the impact of stochastic volatility and jumps on the shapes of portfolio-return distributions.

Table 13.2 shows estimated parameters of the three models, GARCH, GARCH with mixture-of-normals returns (MIX-GARCH), and stochastic-volatility jump diffusion (SVJD). The data are Standard & Poor's 500 equity

Table 13.2. Estimates of the Parameters of the Reference Models Using the Standard & Poor's Equity Index

Model	Parameter estimates				
	μ	ω	α	β	γ_1
GARCH	0.057	0.013	0.070	0.918	NA
	(0.012)	(0.002)	(0.002)	(0.004)	
MIX-GARCH	0.057	0.009	0.053	0.938	0.835
	(0.011)	(0.002)	(0.004)	(0.006)	(0.009)

Model	Parameter estimates						
	μ	α	κ	η	ρ	φ	δ
SVJD	0.057	0.009	0.013	0.068	−0.330	0.019	0.019
	(0.011)	(0.002)	(0.003)	(0.015)	(0.085)	(0.011)	(0.0005)

Note: Standard errors of the estimates are given in parentheses.

index returns sampled daily from January 1, 1980, through December 31, 1996.[2] For the MIX-GARCH model, the estimate of γ_2 is 1.93, implying that the mixture-of-normals return model may be viewed as drawing high-variance normal returns rarely and low-variance normal returns frequently.

The degree of persistence in volatility is captured in the GARCH and MIX-GARCH models from the fact that $E_t(\sigma_{t+1}^2) = (\alpha + \beta)\sigma_t^2$. For these models, we have estimates of the persistence parameter $\alpha + \beta$ of 0.988 and 0.991, respectively. Similarly, the low estimate of κ for the SVJD model implies highly persistent volatility. (For $\kappa = 0$, there is no mean reversion.) These findings are consistent with previous studies that show high persistence in equity-return volatility.

13.1.3. Shapes of Return Distributions

When assessing market risk with parametric models for returns, such as those we have just reviewed, it is important to consider the effects of stochastic volatility and jumps on the shapes of the tails of return distributions over various time horizons that could be considered for risk-management applications. In order to consider these effects, we computed the conditional skewnesses and kurtoses of returns for various holding periods.[3] In this case, we are computing the third and fourth moments of the conditional distributions of returns, and these moments vary with market conditions. That these moments do indeed change over time is suggested by the rolling sample moments shown in Figure 13.3, computed using Standard & Poor's 500 returns, with the rolling variance estimator $\hat{\sigma}_{t,\beta}^2$ of (13.5), with the decay factor $\beta = 0.98$, and look-back horizon of $T = 100$ days. Figure 13.3 shows notable periods of volatility clustering (quiet and turbulent times), with associated changes in rolling kurtosis and skewness statistics. Large upward spikes in volatility are often accompanied by large increases in kurtosis.

The term structure of conditional skewness for the SVJD model is displayed in Figure 13.4. (The term structures of skewness for the GARCH and the MIX-GARCH models are perfectly flat at zero by assumption.) For comparison, we have also included the skewness implied by a *pure jump-diffusion* (PJD) model, identical to the SVJD model except that the volatility

---

[2] The GARCH parameters were estimated by the method of maximum likelihood. For the MIX-GARCH model, we used the residuals from the GARCH model and calibrated the mixture-of-normals distribution so as to match the sample variance and kurtosis of these residuals. Finally, the parameters for the SVJD model are taken from Andersen et al. (2002, Table 6), who estimated their model using the same data and sample period. For an alternative approach to estimating the SVJD moel, using time series of option prices, see Pan (2002).

[3] Formulas for these moments in the SVJD and PJD models are presented in Das and Sundaram (1999), where the implications of these models for the shapes of option-implied volatility smiles are investigated. The term structures of kurtosis for the GARCH and MIX-GARCH models were computed by Monte Carlo simulation.

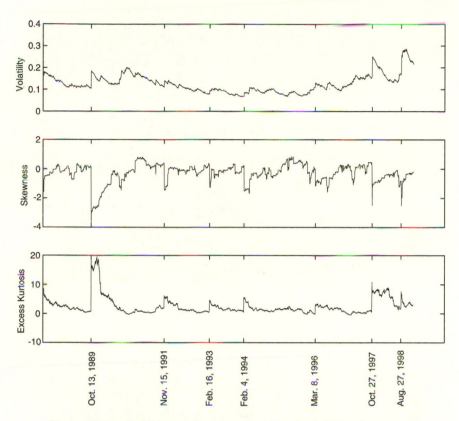

Figure 13.3. *Rolling-sample moments of Standard & Poor's returns.*

σ_t^2 is constant. In general, the SVJD model has two sources of conditional skewness: (1) stochastic volatility combined with correlation ρ between the Brownian motions driving returns and stochastic volatility, and (2) the jump component, if we allow for a nonzero mean jump amplitude (a negative mean implies negative skewness). Skewness is, roughly speaking, increasing in ρ. For negative skewness, we would want $\rho < 0$, ignoring the skewness effects of jumps. In the absence of the jump component ($\delta = 0$), for short time horizons, skewness is small, shrinking to zero as the time horizon goes to zero. This is a consequence of the return shock being approximately normal for short holding periods. This point is formalized in Das and Sundaram (1999), who also show that, in the absence of jumps, as the holding period goes to infinity, skewness converges to zero. The version of the SVJD model examined subsequently, taken from Andersen et al. (2002), sets the mean jump size to zero so only the first source of negative skewness is operative.

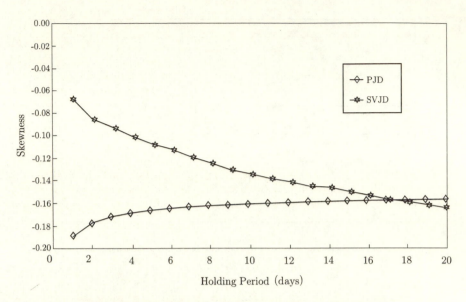

Figure 13.4. *Term structures of skewness at 14% volatility.*

The SVJD and PJD models, at typical parameter estimates for Standard & Poor's 500 returns, both imply negatively skewed returns over short holding periods, although in both cases the fitted magnitudes are smaller than their historical counterparts. Furthermore, as the length of the holding period is increased, these two models have notably different patterns. The PJD model has negative mean jump sizes, implying negative return skewness over short holding periods. This skewness diminishes toward zero as the holding period is increased. In contrast, the estimated negative skewness for the SVJD model starts near zero (consistent with the preceding discussion) and then increases with the length of the holding period.

The term structures of conditional kurtoses implied by these continuous-time models are displayed in Figure 13.5. For the PJD model, kurtosis is positive at short horizons, and converges to the normal kurtosis of 3 as the holding period goes to infinity (as a result of the Central Limit Theorem). At the estimated parameter values, the jump effect is strong over horizons of a few days, but after about two weeks little excess kurtosis remains.

The MIX-GARCH model displays more conditional kurtosis than any of the other models considered. The effect is much like that of the PJD model, which can also be viewed as a mixture-of-normals model, but with constant conditional variance. Because of the persistent volatility of the MIX-GARCH model, with a draw from the high-volatility normal distribution, the effect

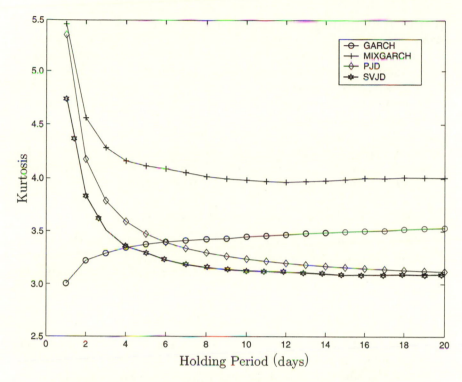

Figure 13.5. *Term structures of kurtosis at 14% volatility.*

on kurtosis persists for several periods, as one is, in effect, also mixing distributions over time with different variances, an additional source of excess kurtosis for the MIX-GARCH model.

Stochastic volatility models, with or without jumps, also have the effect of mixing normal return shocks of different variances. For small returns, because the stochastic volatility state variable $\sigma^2(t)$ is moving continuously in time, the degree of mixing is small, and little excess kurtosis is induced by this effect. As the holding period increases, there is more scope for significant random changes in $\sigma^2(t)$, so the impact of mixing on kurtosis is larger. This is exhibited in Figure 13.5 for the GARCH model. We expect that the conditional kurtosis in the GARCH model is small over short horizons, because the one-period return shocks are normal. As the holding period is increased, this model implies positive excess kurtosis, but the degree of excess kurtosis generated by the GARCH is small for the investment horizons examined.

Finally, the jump component of the SVJD model is evidently at work over horizons of 1 or 2 days, inducing substantial excess kurtosis in equity returns. As in model PJD, the effects of the jump component on kurtosis dissipates quite quickly, leading to kurtoses closer to three over horizons beyond a few days. This pattern suggests that, as in the GARCH model, stochastic volatility is contributing little to excess kurtosis in the SVJD model.

A practical conclusion to be drawn from these examples is that it is likely to be important to incorporate a jumplike component to return distributions if one wishes to capture the degree of excess kurtosis for short holding periods that one sees in many historical time series of returns. The GARCH model is inadequate to this task, unless one allows, as we have here, for fat-tailed return shocks, for example, with a mixture-of-normals distribution, in order to reflect the historical degree of excess kurtosis.

13.2. Delta-Gamma for Derivatives with Jumps

In the light of our preceding discussion of the role of fat tails in returns, we next briefly explore the potential sensitivity of methods such as delta-gamma approximations for estimating the risk of derivative positions, such as options, to the presence of jumps.

13.2.1. Delta Measures of Derivatives Risk

We consider a derivative whose price at a given time is $f(y)$ if the underlying asset price level is y. Assuming that the derivative pricing function $f(\cdot)$ is differentiable, the *delta* (Δ) of this derivative is the slope $f'(y)$ of the graph of f at the current underlying price y, as depicted in Figure 13.6 for the case of the Black-Scholes pricing formula $f(\cdot)$ for a European put option.

For small changes in the underlying price, we know from calculus that a reasonably accurate measure of the change in market value of a derivative price is obtained from the usual first-order approximation:

$$f(y+x) = f(y) + f'(y)x + \epsilon(1), \tag{13.8}$$

where $\epsilon(1)$ is the first-order approximation error, illustrated in Figure 13.6. Thus, for small changes in the underlying price y, we could approximate the change in market value of a derivative by that of a fixed position in the underlying whose size is the delta of the derivative. For spot or forward positions in the underlying, the delta approach is fully accurate, because the associated price function f is linear in the underlying.

The delta approximation illustrated in Figure 13.6 is the foundation of delta hedging. A position in the underlying asset whose size is *minus* the delta of the derivative is a hedge of changes in price of the derivative, if continually reset as delta changes, and if the underlying price does not jump.

The estimation of value at risk (VaR) or other tail-risk measures, however, is a rather difficult test for the delta approximation, which is designed

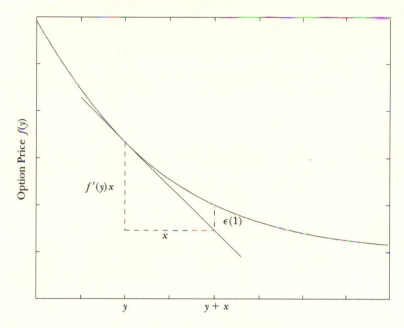

Figure 13.6.   *The delta (first-order) approximation.*

to treat only small changes in the underlying prices. It is of course the *large* price changes that are of most concern when measuring VaR and other measures of the risk of extreme loss.

For a given level of volatility, delta-based approximations are accurate only over short periods of time, and even then are not satisfactory if the underlying index may jump dramatically and unexpectedly (see Estrella, 1994, and Page and Costas, 1996). One can see from the convexity of option-pricing functions such as that illustrated in Figure 13.6 that the delta approach over-estimates the loss on a long-option position associated with any change in the underlying price. (If one had sold the option, one would underestimate losses by the delta approach.)

The delta approach allows us to approximate the VaR of a stand-alone derivative position as the VaR of the underlying asset multiplied by the delta of the derivative.[4] Figure 13.7 shows, as predicted, that the probability density function for the put price at a time horizon of 2 weeks, shown as a solid line, has a left tail that is everywhere to the right of the density function for a delta-equivalent position in the underlying. The option is

---

[4] It may be more accurate to expand the first-order approximation at points other than the current price x. We use the forward price of the underlying at the VaR time horizon for these calculations, but the difference is negligible.

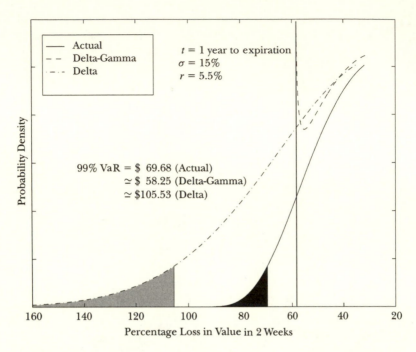

Figure 13.7.   *Two-week loss on 20% out-of-money put (normal returns).*

a European put worth $100, expiring in 1 year, and struck 20% out of the money. We assume that the price process of the underlying is log-normal with a volatility of 15%. The short rate and the expected rate of return on the underlying are assumed to be 5.5%.[5] As illustrated, the 2-week VaR (at 99% confidence) of the put is $69.68, but is estimated by the delta approach to have a VaR of $105.53 (representing a loss of more than the full price of the option, which is possible because the delta-approximating portfolio is a short position in the underlying.) Figure 13.8 shows the same VaR estimates for a short position in the same put option.

Figure 13.9 illustrates the same calculations shown in Figure 13.7, with one change: The returns model is a jump diffusion, with an expected frequency φ of two jumps a year, and return jumps that have a standard deviation of ν of 5%. The total annualized volatility of daily returns, σ is kept at 15%. The VaR of the put has gone up from $69.68 to $74.09. The delta approximation is roughly as poor as it was for the benchmark-normal return model. For these calculations, we are using the correct theoretical

---

[5] The short rate and expected rate of return have negligible effects on the results for this and other examples to follow.

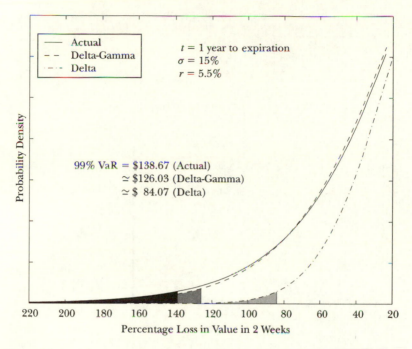

Figure 13.8. *Two-week loss on short 20% out-of-money put (normal returns).*

option-pricing formula, the correct delta, and the correct probability distribution for the underlying price.[6] (We could also have done these calculations with the Black-Scholes option prices and deltas, which is incorrect.)

13.2.2 Beyond Delta to Gamma

A common resort when the first-order (i.e., delta) approximation of a derivative revaluation is not sufficiently accurate is to move on to a second-order approximation. For smooth f, we have

$$f(y + x) = f(y) + f'(y)x + \tfrac{1}{2}f''(y)x^2 + \epsilon(2), \qquad (13.9)$$

---

[6] One can condition on the number k of jumps, compute the variance of the normally distributed total return over 1 year conditional on k jumps, use the Black-Scholes price for this case, weight by the probability of p_k of k jumps, and add up for k ranging from 1 to a number chosen for reasonable accuracy, say ten jumps. For the probability distribution, one again conditions on the number of jumps, and adds up the k-conditional densities for the underlying return over a 1-year period, and averages these densities with p_k weights. The resulting density is a weighted sum of exponentials of quadratics.

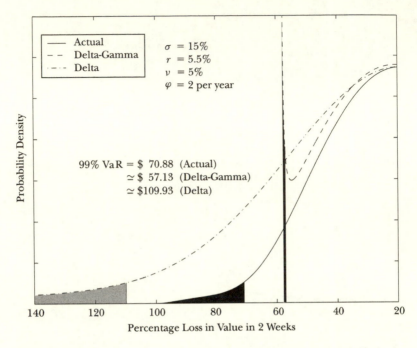

Figure 13.9.   *Two-week loss on 20% out-of-money put (jump-diffusion).*

where the second-order error $\epsilon(2)$ is smaller, for sufficiently small x, than the first-order error, as illustrated by a comparison of Figures 13.10 and 13.6.

For options, with underlying index y, we say that $f''(y)$ is the gamma (Γ) of the option. In the setting of the standard log-normal model, both the delta and the gamma of a European option are known explicitly (as found, e.g., in Cox and Rubinstein, 1985), so it is easy to apply the second-order[7] approximation (13.9) in order to get more accuracy in measuring risk exposure.

For VaR calculations for benchmark-normal returns and plain-vanilla options, gamma methods are often "optimistic" for long option positions because the approximating parabola can sometimes be well above the Black-Scholes price, as shown in Figure 13.10. Gamma-based VaR estimates therefore often underestimate the actual VaR of options portfolios. We can see

---

[7] One might think that even higher-order accuracy can be achieved, and this is in principle correct as one adds successively higher-order terms (see Estrella et al., 1994). On the other hand, the approximation error need not go to zero (see Estrella, 1994).

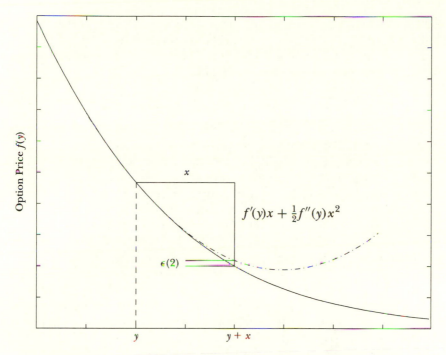

Figure 13.10. *Delta-gamma hedging, second-order approximation.*

this in the previous two figures. Indeed the gamma-based density approximations[8] have a distorted estimation of the tail density, corresponding to the *turn-back point* of the approximating parabola, as shown in Figure 13.9.

The variance $\mathrm{var}[f(y + x)]$ of the revaluation of a derivative whose underlying is $y + x$, where x is the unexpected change, is approximated from (13.9), using the formula for the variance of a sum, as

$$V_f(y) = f'(y)^2 \mathrm{var}(x) + \tfrac{1}{4} f''(y)^2 \mathrm{var}(x^2)$$

$$+ f'(y) f''(y) \, \mathrm{cov}(x, x^2). \tag{13.10}$$

For log-normal or normal x, these moments are known explicitly, providing a simple estimate of the risk of a position. This calculation is relatively accurate in the above settings for typical parameters. One may then approximate the VaR at the 99% confidence level as $2.33\sqrt{V_f(y)}$, taking the 0.99 critical value 2.33 for the standard normal density as an estimate of the

---

[8] This can be calculated by the same method outlined for the delta case.

0.99 critical value of the normalized density of the actual derivative position. The accuracy of this approximation declines with the magnitude of gamma, with deviations from the benchmark-normal returns model, with increasing volatility, and with increasing time horizon.

13.3. Integration of Market and Credit Risk

Our objective now is to review the integration of market risks owing to changes in underlying market prices and interest rates with risks owing to the changes in credit quality, including default, of specific counterparties.

We let y denote a sufficient statistic for the credit quality of a generic counterparty, such as the default intensity, the credit rating, or the credit spread of the counterparty's debt. Specific examples will follow when we discuss computational algorithms. We let $p(y, T)$ denote the probability of survival to the VaR time horizon T, say 1 or 2 weeks. For example, in an intensity or credit-rating-based model with constant default intensity $\lambda(y)$, $p(y, T) \simeq e^{-\lambda(y)T}$, where T is the time horizon.

We let $C(x, y)$ denote the current market value of the object portfolio, assuming default has yet to occur, including the effects of netting and collateral, at the current vector x of marketwide factors and at the current vector y of the counterparty credit risk factors. For a short-horizon risk measure, such as a 2-week VaR, we will, for notational simplicity, ignore the time value of the portfolio and let $C(X_T, Y_T)$ denote the survival-contingent market value of the same portfolio at the risk horizon at the new risk factors X_T and Y_T. If we assume that a fraction L, possibly random, of initial market value is lost at default and let D_T be the default indicator (0 in the case of survival to T, and 1 in the case of default), the change in market value at the VaR time horizon T is

$$V = C(X_T, Y_T)(1 - D_T) + D_T(1 - L)C(x, y) - C(x, y). \quad (13.11)$$

The first term in (13.11) is the valuation associated with survival at the new risk factors X_T and Y_T; the second is the valuation associated with default; the third term nets out the current valuation.

A basic algorithm for capturing credit risk within a market-risk measurement system can be explained in terms of a Monte Carlo simulation. (We later consider numerical methods other than Monte Carlo.) The Monte Carlo steps are:

1. Simulate the default indicator D_T to have outcome 0 with probability $p(y, T)$ and outcome 1 with probability $1 - p(y, T)$.
2. If the outcome of D_T is 1, simulate the loss-given-default factor L.
3. If the outcome of D_T is 0, simulate X_T and Y_T.
4. Evaluate the change V in market value from (13.11).

This Monte Carlo procedure would apply to each of the portfolios of positions with the given N counterparties. The resulting changes in market values $V_1, \ldots, V_N$ of the N counterparty portfolios would be aggregated to obtain the total change in value, $V = V_1 + \cdots + V_N$, for that scenario. The simulation should incorporate the effects of correlation across the default indicators $D_{1T}, \ldots, D_{NT}$ of the N object portfolios and of correlation in the risk factors X_T and $Y_{1T}, \ldots, Y_{NT}$, where Y_{iT} is the credit risk factor for the ith counterparty. Many such scenarios, independently generated with the same algorithm, would then give the random sample from which the VaR and other risk measures can be estimated.

Figure 13.11 illustrates this algorithm for the case in which actual and risk-neutral default probabilities are captured in terms of actual and risk-neutral default intensities, λ and λ^*, respectively. The market value $C(X_T, \lambda_T^*)$ at the risk horizon T is approximated in this implementation with the gamma-delta approximation. The actual survival probability is denoted by $p(\lambda_0, T)$. On the other hand, for pricing, we use the risk-neutral intensity λ^*. This means that we need to simulate, *under the actual probability measure*, the outcome of the risk-neutral intensity λ_T^* in order to revalue the position at the risk horizon date T. For settings in which λ^* is expressed as a function of the underlying credit risk state vector Y_t, this is accomplished by simulating Y_T under the actual measure and then evaluating λ_T^* and $C(X_T, \lambda_T^*)$.

Executing this Monte Carlo algorithm in a timely manner can, for large portfolios, be computationally intensive. Among the especially challenging problems are:

- Even given a reasonable credit risk model for each counterparty, it is difficult to capture the effects of correlation across counterparties. In particular, there is an issue of whether to build in the effects of correlation associated with major marketwide credit events through joint default events (causing possibly simultaneous defaults) or merely through correlated changes in the credit-risk factors $Y_1, \ldots, Y_N$ that determine the respective default likelihoods of the counter-

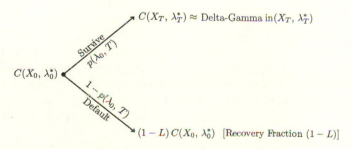

Figure 13.11. *Revaluation step with credit risk.*

parties. Over short time horizons, model differences along these lines can make significant relative differences in estimated credit risk, as we shall see by example.

- For portfolios with netting, or for positions such as swaps with two-sided default risk, estimating the sensitivity of the total position value $C(x, y)$ to the risk factors x and y can be computationally demanding. For example, a given change in market prices can increase the exposure associated with one of the underlying cash flows and reduce the exposure associated with a different cash flow at a different maturity. Because of netting, the total marginal effect of these two changes in exposure is *not* necessarily the sum of the marginal effects of each alone.

13.4. Examples of VaR with Credit Risk

We present a series of examples of VaR with credit risk for portfolios of options or loans. Our objectives are to illustrate the implementation of a simple integrated model of market and credit risk and to obtain a sense of which are the key risk factors for extreme loss on loan portfolios, versus that for option portfolios, over relatively short time horizons.

We assume that there are N counterparties. For measuring the market interest-rate risk underlying the loan portfolio, we suppose that the term structure of interest rates is determined by a two-factor affine model, with a short rate $r_t = R[X(t)] = \bar{r} + X_1(t) + X_2(t)$, where $\bar{r}$ is a constant and X_1 and X_2 are, risk-neutrally, independent CIR processes. This is case (B) of the two-factor affine models of Section 7.2.1.

Our basic model of default allows for common default events that, as discussed in Section 10.7, arrive according to some actual intensity process λ^C. At the arrival of a common credit event, all counterparties are exposed to immediate default, independently, each with probability p. Each counterparty i is also subject to idiosyncratic default events, specific to that counterparty only, arriving according to an intensity process λ_i^I. At the arrival of such an i-specific event, i defaults with probability 1. The total intensity for the arrival of default by counterparty i is thus $\lambda_i = \lambda_i^I + p\lambda^C$. All of $\lambda_1^I, \ldots, \lambda_N^I$ and λ^C are assumed to be independent and, conditional on $\lambda_1^I, \ldots, \lambda_N^I$, and λ^C, all of the event arrival times, and the survival events at common event times, are independent. We parameterize these processes so that each counterparty default-intensity process λ_i is a CIR process with some mean-reversion parameter κ, long-run mean $\bar{\lambda}$, and volatility parameter σ. This can be done if λ_i^I and λ^C are CIR processes with the same mean-reversion and volatility parameters, as explained in Chapter 11.

Because our discussion would otherwise become rather complicated, we suppose throughout that the actual and risk-neutral default probabilities are identical. This would not be the case in practice.

Default correlation is induced in this model through both the common state variable λ^C contributing to every counterparty's intensity and the arrival of common credit events, which can cause defaults to occur simultaneously. For example, with $N = 100$ initial counterparties and a probability $p = 0.1$ of default at the arrival of a common credit event, the expected number of simultaneously defaulting counterparties at the arrival of this event is $pN = 10$, until the first default time. Between the first and second default times, the expected number of defaults given the arrival of such an event is $p \times (N - 1) = 9.9$, and so on. Variation in the common-event arrival intensity λ^C over time is also a source of correlation in the market values of the surviving positions. Because of these common credit events, this is not a doubly stochastic default model.

We suppose that, at default, a given fraction L, possibly random, of the market value of a counterparty's position is lost. Credit risks are assumed to be independent of the underlying interest rate or price risks. The numerical algorithm that we use to provide example risk estimates is the analytic Fourier-transform method of Duffie and Pan (2001). This method also applies to cases with jumps in market risk factors as well as to cases with correlation between default intensities and market risk factors. These analytical methods are based on the approximation of the change in value V of (13.11) given by

$$\hat{V} = C_{\Delta,\Gamma}(X_T, Y_T) - D_T LC(X_0, Y_0) - C(X_0, Y_0), \qquad (13.12)$$

where $C_{\Delta,\Gamma}(X_T, Y_T)$ is the delta-gamma approximation of the actual market value, taking simple jump-diffusion approximations for X_T and Y_T. With this, and using a simple model for the distribution of L, Duffie and Pan (2001) obtain the explicit characteristic function for the approximate loss $\hat{V}$. Then, standard Fourier-inversion methods provide a quick estimate of VaR at any confidence level. These approximations are remarkably accurate for our applications, as we shall see for two examples, one a loan portfolio and the other an options portfolio.

13.4.1. Example: Loan Portfolio VaR with Credit Risk

We first consider an illustrative estimate of the VaR for a portfolio of 1-year loans of equal principal, say 1, to each of the N counterparties. The market risk factors X_T are those determining the term structure of interest rates. For a borrower i that survives to time T (starting from time 0), the market value of its loan is

$$C(X_T, \lambda_T^*) = E_T^* \left[\exp\left(-\int_T^1 \left(R[X(t)] + \bar{L}\lambda_i^*(t) \right) dt \right) \middle| X_T, \lambda_T^* \right], \quad (13.13)$$

where $\bar{L}$ is the risk-neutral mean of the fractional loss of market value of the loan at default. (This default-adjusted short-rate model for valuing loans is described in Chapter 6.) The state process X underlying the interest-rate model is assumed to be independent of the risk-neutral default-intensity processes.

In this example, we fix the model parameters for the risk-free short-rate model to be those reported in Duffie and Singleton (1997) and set the initial levels of X_1 and X_2 to their respective long-run means. We take $L = \bar{L} = 0.5$. (Any reasonable parameters would suffice for our illustration.) Because of the CIR assumptions, we have

$$C(X_T, \lambda_T^*) = \exp\left[a + b_1 X_1(T) + b_2 X_2(T) + c\lambda_i^*(T) \right], \quad (13.14)$$

where the coefficients a, b_1, b_2, and c are determined explicitly, as usual, for a multifactor CIR setting, as explained in Chapter 6.

The CIR default-intensity process $\lambda_i = \lambda_i^*$ of borrower i is assumed to have a mean-reversion rate of $\kappa = 0.25$, a long-run mean of $\bar{\lambda} = \bar{\lambda}^I + p\bar{\lambda}^C = 0.03$, and a volatility parameter σ set so that, initiating λ_i at the long-run mean $\bar{\lambda}$, the initial instantaneous volatility of λ_i is 100%. Default intensities are initiated at their long-run means by letting $\lambda_i^I(0) = \bar{\lambda}^I$ and $\lambda^C(0) = \bar{\lambda}^C$, the long-run means of these underlying CIR processes. For simplicity, all of these parameters are assumed to be the same under actual probabilities as under risk-neutral probabilities.

Keeping κ, $\bar{\lambda}$, and σ fixed, two cases with different degrees of correlation are considered. For the high-correlation case, we take $p = 0.8$ and $\bar{\lambda}^I/\bar{\lambda} = 20\%$. For the low-correlation case, we take $p = 0.2$ and $\bar{\lambda}^I/\bar{\lambda} = 80\%$. The high-correlation case includes significant exposure to common credit events and also has significant correlation through correlated changes in intensities before default, relative to the low-correlation case. We emphasize that each individual issuer's default risk, both unconditionally and conditional on the information available at any fixed time t before default, is the same for the high- and the low-correlation cases.

The VaR, as a percentage of the initial portfolio market value, is shown in Table 13.3 for a portfolio of $N = 320$ borrowers. As opposed to the case of the options portfolio considered later, there is a substantive contribution of credit risk to VaR, if one examines sufficiently far out into the tail of the distribution. For example, for both the high- and the low-correlation case, the percentage VaR increases significantly from the 0.2 to the 0.1% level. This difference can be ascribed to the likelihood of a marketwide credit

Table 13.3.   Total 2-Week VaR for a Loan Portfolio

Probability (%)	High correlation		Low correlation		No credit risk	
	Analytical	Simulation	Analytical	Simulation	Analytical	Simulation
0.1	38.53	38.62 (0.17)	8.49	8.50 (0.16)	0.64	0.65 (0.00)
0.2	0.87	0.87 (0.01)	0.77	0.77 (0.00)	0.59	0.59 (0.00)
0.3	0.79	0.79 (0.00)	0.70	0.70 (0.00)	0.55	0.55 (0.00)
0.4	0.74	0.74 (0.00)	0.65	0.65 (0.00)	0.52	0.52 (0.00)
0.5	0.70	0.70 (0.00)	0.62	0.62 (0.00)	0.50	0.50 (0.00)
0.6	0.67	0.67 (0.00)	0.60	0.60 (0.00)	0.49	0.49 (0.00)
0.7	0.65	0.65 (0.00)	0.58	0.58 (0.00)	0.47	0.47 (0.00)
0.8	0.63	0.63 (0.00)	0.56	0.56 (0.00)	0.46	0.46 (0.00)
0.9	0.61	0.61 (0.00)	0.54	0.54 (0.00)	0.45	0.45 (0.00)
1.0	0.60	0.60 (0.00)	0.53	0.53 (0.00)	0.44	0.44 (0.00)
2.0	0.49	0.49 (0.00)	0.43	0.43 (0.00)	0.36	0.36 (0.00)
3.0	0.43	0.43 (0.00)	0.38	0.38 (0.00)	0.31	0.31 (0.00)
4.0	0.38	0.38 (0.00)	0.34	0.33 (0.00)	0.28	0.28 (0.00)
5.0	0.34	0.34 (0.00)	0.30	0.30 (0.00)	0.25	0.25 (0.00)

Source: Duffie and Pan (2001).

Note: The sample standard errors (in parentheses) are calculated using ten simulated sub-samples of 500,000 scenarios each. The VaR estimate based on simulation is the sample mean of the ten subsample estimates.

event before the VaR horizon T, which is 0.12% for $\lambda^C = 0.03$, indeed lying between 0.1 and 0.2%. The simulation results are also provided from Duffie and Pan (2001) and do not suffer from the approximation (13.12) of (13.11), showing that this approximation is not at all severe.

Figure 13.12 shows the impact on the VaR of increasing the number N of borrowers, considering alternative portfolios with 32, 320, or 1,600 borrowers. We also compare the VaR for a comparison model with no common credit events. Specifically, in the parallel model, there is a common factor $p\lambda^C$ of intensities as before, but conditional on the intensities $\lambda_1^I, \ldots, \lambda_N^I$, and λ^C, all default times are independent. The intensity processes for this comparison model have the same joint distribution (same individual default risk model and same correlation among default intensities) as for our original model, but there are no common default-generating events.

From Figure 13.12a, we see that the marketwide credit event hits these portfolios, with different numbers of borrowers, with a probability of approximately 0.2% within the 2-week time horizon. One can show that the initial arrival intensity of such a marketwide credit event is $\lambda_0^C = 0.06$, which corresponds to the arrival of a common credit event with probability 0.23% over the 2-week horizon. It is also interesting to see the behavior of the VaR as one changes the confidence level. There is a visible "platform" in the case

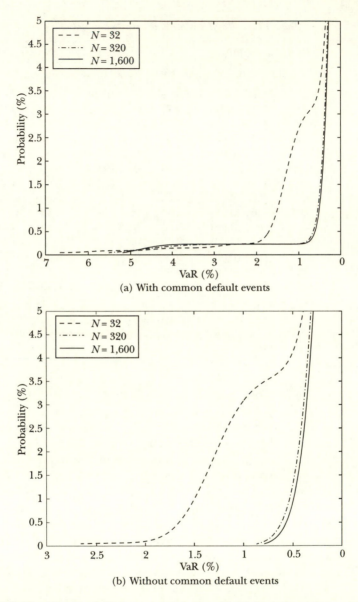

(a) With common default events

(b) Without common default events

Figure 13.12. *Two-week VaR as a percentage of initial market value, varying N, for a portfolio of N 1-year loans. Default intensities are CIR with $\bar{\lambda} = 3\%$, $\kappa = 0.25$, and initial volatility of 100%. Intensities are correlated, with 20% contributed by a common credit-event intensity. For case (a), each firm defaults with probability 10%. For case (b), intensities have the same joint distribution as for case (a). (Source: Duffie and Pan, 2001.)*

of $N = 32$ borrowers, whose diversification benefit is limited relative to the case of $N = 320$ or $N = 1,600$.

Figure 13.13 shows the effect of increasing the volatility of interest rates, at both the 2-week and 16-week VaR time horizons. Figure 13.14 shows the effect of increasing the correlation of default risk, in two ways: (1) through the likelihood p of default by a given borrower at a common credit event, and (2) through correlation in the intensity processes. In both cases, the individual credit quality is held constant. Overall, these suggest that the presence of joint credit events may significantly increase VaR, holding the joint distribution of default-intensity processes fixed.

13.4.2. Example: Options Portfolio with Credit Risk

As a second example, we examine the VaR for a portfolio of at-the-money options on the equity indices of thirty-two countries. For the volatility and pairwise correlations among the thirty-two markets, we use the RiskMetrics data base on November 20, 1998. The thirty-two countries and their respective volatilities are shown in Table 13.4. Figure 13.15 shows the eigenvalues of the covariance matrix, which partially demonstrates the degree of diversification offered by our option portfolio. The ratio of the largest eigenvalue to the sum of all of the eigenvalues is a measure of the degree to which the market risk in these thirty-two equity indices can be concentrated into a single risk factor, the first principal component. We suppose a total of $N = 320$ counterparties, each holding an option on one of the thirty-two equity indices. Default risk is modeled in the same manner as for the previous example of a loan portfolio and is assumed to be independent of the underlying equity risk (in both the actual and risk-neutral sense). The options are of European style and all have an initial time to exercise of 1 year.

We let $X(t) = [X_1(t), \ldots, X_{32}(t)]$ denote the joint-log-normal prices at time t of the underlying thirty-two indices, and for this calculation we assume deterministic rates, so as to apply Black-Scholes pricing. Given no default by the corresponding counterparty up to the VaR time horizon T, the market value at time T of the option expiring at time S is

$$C_i(X_T, \lambda_T) = f_i(X_T, S - T)E_T^* \left[\exp \left(-\bar{L} \int_T^S \lambda_i(t)\, dt \right) \Big| \lambda_i^*(T) \right]$$

$$= f_i(X_T, S - T)e^{\bar{\alpha}(S-T)+\bar{\beta}(S-T)\lambda_i^*(T)},$$

where $\bar{L} = E(L_i)$ is the mean fractional loss of market value at default and $f_i(X_T, S - T)$ is the Black-Scholes option pricing formula for the at-the-money option on index i, with time $S - T$ to expiration, in the absence

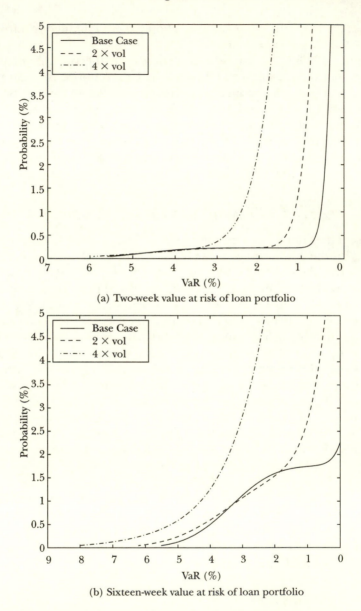

(a) Two-week value at risk of loan portfolio

(b) Sixteen-week value at risk of loan portfolio

Figure 13.13. *Varying the volatility of the default-free short rate, the percentage VaR for a portfolio of 320 loans. Default intensities are CIR with long-run mean $\bar{\lambda} = 3\%$, mean-reversion rate $\kappa = 0.25$, and initial volatility of 100%. Intensities are 20% common. At a common credit event, each borrower defaults with 10% probability. (Source: Duffie and Pan, 2001.)*

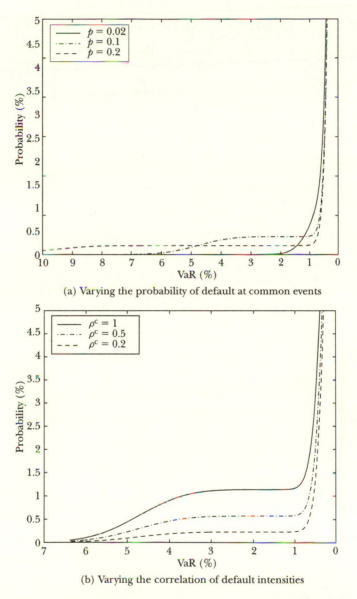

(a) Varying the probability of default at common events

(b) Varying the correlation of default intensities

Figure 13.14. *Two-week VaR as a percentage of initial market value, varying (a) the probability p of default conditional on a common credit event, and (b) the fraction ρ^c of each borrower's default intensity that is common, for a portfolio of 320 1-year loans. For case (a), ρ^c is fixed at 20%, whereas for case (b), p is fixed at 10%. Default intensities are CIR with $\bar{\lambda} = 3\%$, $\kappa = 0.25$, and an initial volatility of 100%. (Source: Duffie and Pan, 2001.)*

Table 13.4.   Equity Indices of Thirty-Two Countries with Respective Volatilities

ARS	58%	EMB	37%	ITL	43%	PHP	50%
ATS	34%	ESP	43%	JPY	36%	PTE	36%
AUD	16%	FIM	47%	KRW	49%	SEK	44%
BEF	27%	FRF	36%	MXN	47%	SGD	41%
CAD	27%	GBP	29%	MYR	66%	THB	59%
CHF	38%	HKD	45%	NLG	39%	TWD	29%
DEM	40%	IDR	56%	NOK	38%	USD	25%
DKK	29%	IEP	31%	NZD	22%	ZAR	31%

Source: RiskMetrics, November 20, 1998.

Note: The three-letter codes are the SWIFT currency code, except for EMB, which represents J. P. Morgan's Emerging Markets Bond Index Plus.

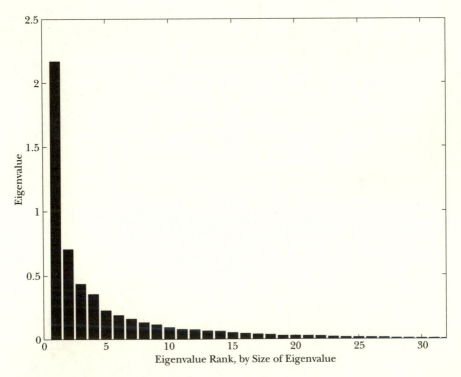

Figure 13.15.   *Eigenvalues of the variance-covariance matrix of thirty-two equity indices. (Data source: RiskMetrics, November 20, 1998.)*

Table 13.5.   Total 2-Week VaR for an Options Portfolio

Prob-ability (%)	High correlation		Low correlation		No credit risk	
	Analytical	Simulation	Analytical	Simulation	Analytical	Simulation
0.1	45.88	45.58 (0.14)	44.38	44.33 (0.11)	44.32	44.28 (0.13)
0.2	43.05	42.98 (0.11)	42.19	42.17 (0.09)	42.14	42.08 (0.13)
0.3	41.42	41.37 (0.09)	40.79	40.78 (0.06)	40.74	40.69 (0.12)
0.4	40.24	40.21 (0.07)	39.73	39.70 (0.06)	39.69	39.64 (0.13)
0.5	39.30	39.30 (0.06)	38.88	38.84 (0.06)	38.84	38.80 (0.12)
0.6	38.52	38.51 (0.04)	38.15	38.13 (0.07)	38.11	38.10 (0.10)
0.7	37.84	37.84 (0.05)	37.51	37.49 (0.07)	37.48	37.46 (0.10)
0.8	37.24	37.23 (0.07)	36.95	36.93 (0.05)	36.91	36.90 (0.11)
0.9	36.71	36.67 (0.06)	36.44	36.42 (0.05)	36.40	36.39 (0.10)
1.0	36.22	36.18 (0.07)	35.97	35.95 (0.05)	35.94	35.93 (0.10)
2.0	32.75	32.76 (0.05)	32.61	32.59 (0.03)	32.58	32.57 (0.08)
3.0	30.48	30.49 (0.05)	30.38	30.37 (0.04)	30.35	30.34 (0.06)
4.0	28.72	28.74 (0.05)	28.65	28.64 (0.03)	28.63	28.62 (0.06)
5.0	27.27	27.29 (0.05)	27.21	27.20 (0.03)	27.19	27.19 (0.05)

Source: Duffie and Pan (2001).

Note: The sample standard errors (in parentheses) are calculated using ten simulated subsamples of 500,000 independent scenarios each. The VaR estimate, based on simulation, is the sample mean of the ten subsamples.

of credit risk. The coefficients $\bar{\alpha}(S - T)$ and $\bar{\beta}(S - T)$ for the CIR intensity model are provided in Appendix A. (This defaultable option pricing formula $C_i(X_T, \lambda_T)$ is a special case of that in Duffie and Singleton, 1999.) The high- and low-correlation cases are those of the loan example.

The percentage VaR is shown for various cases in Table 13.5. Figure 13.16 compares the sensitivity of the risk of the option portfolio to the mean default intensity of counterparties to the analogous effect on the loan portfolio of the previous example. Clearly, at the 2-week VaR horizon, the risk of the option portfolio owing to variation of the underlying equity indices dominates the effect of credit risk. Even at the 16-week VaR horizon, as shown by Figure 13.17, the relative contribution of credit risk to the VaR of the option portfolio is small.

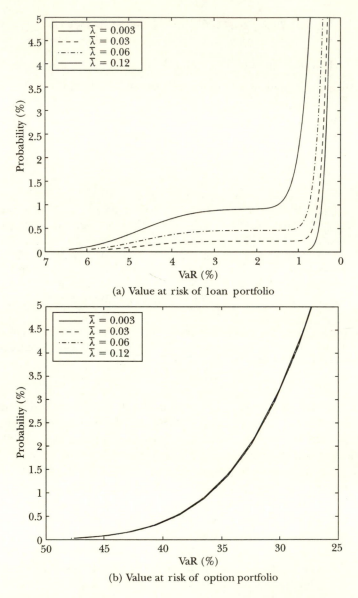

(a) Value at risk of loan portfolio

(b) Value at risk of option portfolio

Figure 13.16. *Two-week VaR as a percentage of initial market value, varying the initial (equal to long-run mean) default intensity* $\bar{\lambda}$, *for a portfolio of 320 loans, and for a portfolio of 320 at-the-money options on thirty-two equity indices (covariances from RiskMetrics, November 20, 1998). Default intensities are CIR, initiated at* $\bar{\lambda}$, *with mean reversion 0.25, and initial volatility of 100%; 20% of intensities are common. At a common credit event, each counterparty defaults with probability 10%. (Source: Duffie and Pan, 2001.)*

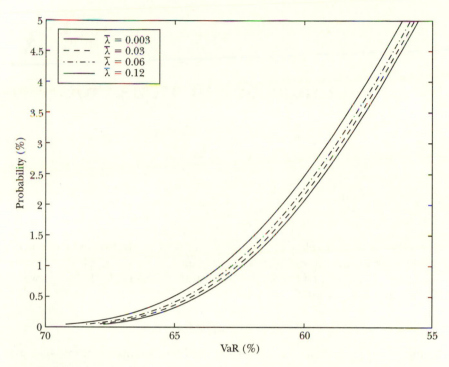

Figure 13.17. *VaR at 16 weeks as a percentage of initial market value, varying the initial (equal to long-run mean) default intensity $\bar{\lambda}$, for a portfolio of 320 at-the-money options on thirty-two equity indices (covariances from RiskMetrics). Default intensities are CIR, initiated at $\bar{\lambda}$, with mean reversion 0.25, and initial volatility of 100%; 20% of intensities are common. At a common credit event, each counterparty defaults with probability 10%. (Source: Duffie and Pan, 2001.)*

A

Introduction to Affine Processes

THIS APPENDIX IS a relatively nontechnical survey of affine Markov processes, which summarizes some of the advantages we exploit for several financial applications that appear in this volume. Duffie et al. (2003a) provide technical foundations, which are omitted here.

A.1. Introduction

In modeling prices and sources of risk in financial applications that are based on a state vector X_t, a useful assumption is that the state process X is *affine*. Roughly speaking, an affine process is a jump-diffusion process for which the drift vector, the *instantaneous* covariance matrix, and the jump-arrival intensities all have affine (constant-plus-linear) dependence on the current state vector X_t.

Prominent among affine processes in the term-structure literature are the Gaussian and square-root diffusion models of Vasicek (1977) and Cox et al. (1985), respectively. A general multivariate class of affine jump diffusion models was introduced by Duffie and Kan (1996) for term-structure modeling. For option pricing, there is a substantial literature that builds on the particular affine stochastic-volatility model for currency and equity prices proposed by Heston (1993).

Affine processes allow for wide variety of features, such as stochastic volatility, jumps, and correlations among the elements of the state vector. Using three-dimensional affine models, for example, Dai and Singleton (2000) found that both time-varying conditional variances and negatively correlated state variables are essential ingredients for explaining the historical behavior of term structures of U.S. interest rates.

For option-pricing applications, Heston (1993), Bakshi et al. (1997), and Bates (1997) brought successively more general affine models to bear in order to allow for stochastic volatility and jumps, while maintaining the simple property that the logarithm of the characteristic function of the state vector X_T at a future date T, conditional on information at date t, is affine with respect to the current state vector X_t. This is a powerful source of tractability for option pricing and risk-measurement applications. Affine models allow for generality while maintaining this analytical tractability. For example, jumps in returns and in volatility may be simultaneous, or may have correlated stochastic arrival intensities. These jumps may be correlated because the jump sizes are correlated, or because of correlation in jump times, or both, as illustrated by Duffie et al. (2000).

The remainder of this appendix is organized as follows. Section 2 reviews the class of affine jump diffusions and shows how to compute some relevant transforms and how to invert them. Section 3 presents some applications. Additional sections contain various technical results and extensions.

A.2. Analytical Solutions in Affine Settings

We begin with the idea of a Markov process X, which lives in a state space D. For example, if $D = \mathbb{R}$, then the outcome of X_t is a real number. If $D = \mathbb{R}^d_+$ for some positive integer d, then the outcome of X_t is a nonnegative d-dimensional vector.

By *Markov*, we mean that for any function $g : D \to \mathbb{R}$ satisfying technical conditions, and for any fixed times t and $s > t$, we have

$$E_t[g(X_s)] = f(X_t), \tag{A.1}$$

for some function $f : D \to \mathbb{R}$, where E_t denotes expectation conditional on *all* information available at time t. This means that the conditional distribution at time t of X_s, given all available information, depends only on the current state X_t. This Markov property holds, for example, if X is real valued and satisfies a stochastic differential equation of the form

$$dX_t = \mu(X_t)\, dt + \sigma(X_t)\, dB_t, \tag{A.2}$$

where B is a standard Brownian motion and μ and σ satisfy technical conditions.

Extending, for any *discount-rate function* $R : D \to \mathbb{R}$ (again, limited only by technical conditions), if X is a Markov process in D then

$$E_t\left[\exp\left(\int_t^s -R(X_u)\, du\right) g(X_s)\right] = F(X_t), \tag{A.3}$$

for some function $F : D \to \mathbb{R}$.

In general, a function is affine if it is constant plus linear. For example, if D is taken as some subset of $\mathbb{R}^d$, an affine function $h : D \to \mathbb{R}$ is defined by some scalar a and some vector b in $\mathbb{R}^d$ so that, for all x, we have

$$h(x) = a + b \cdot x = a + b_1 x_1 + \cdots + b_d x_d.$$

Roughly speaking, an affine process is a Markov process that is defined by the following convenient property: Whenever, in (A.3), the discount rate R is of the affine form $R(x) = \rho_0 + \rho_1 \cdot x$ and the payoff function g is of the exponential-affine form $g(x) = e^{a+b \cdot x}$, then (under technical conditions) the solution $F(X_t)$ of (A.3) is also of the exponential-affine form. That is, under technical conditions, we have, as shown by Duffie et al. (2000),

$$E_t \left[\exp \left(\int_t^s -[\rho_0 + \rho_1 \cdot X(u)] \, du \right) e^{a+b \cdot X(s)} \right] = e^{\alpha(t)+\beta(t) \cdot X(t)}, \quad \text{(A.4)}$$

for some coefficients $\alpha(t)$ and $\beta_1(t), \ldots, \beta_d(t)$ that depend only on s and t. We show later how to calculate these coefficients. The calculation (A.4) arises in many financial applications, some of which are reviewed shortly. An obvious example is discounted expected cash flow.

A simple example of an affine process is a process X solving the stochastic differential equation (A.2) for which both $\mu(x)$ and $\sigma(x)^2$ are affine in x. This includes the Gaussian case, for which σ is constant (e.g., the Vasicek model for interest rates), as well as the CIR (square-root) diffusion model of Feller (1951), under which

$$dX_t = \kappa(\bar{x} - X_t) \, dt + \bar{\sigma}\sqrt{X_t} \, dB_t, \quad \text{(A.5)}$$

for some constant positive parameters[1] $\bar{\sigma}, \kappa$, and $\bar{x}$. The parameter $\bar{x}$ is called a *long-run mean,* and the parameter κ is called the *mean-reversion rate.* Indeed for (A.5), the mean of X_t converges from any initial condition to $\bar{x}$ at the rate κ as t goes to infinity. The square-root process is sometimes called a *Feller diffusion,* or a CIR process, or simply a *square-root diffusion.*

For the Gaussian case, often called an *Ornstein-Uhlenbeck process,* or a *Vasicek process* in financial applications, we would take the state space D to be the real numbers. For the Feller diffusion, we would take D to be the nonnegative real numbers.

A large class of d-dimensional affine processes are of the *jump-diffusion* form

$$dX_t = \mu(X_t) \, dt + \sigma(X_t) \, dB_t + dJ_t,$$

---

[1] The solution X of (A.5) will never reach zero from a strictly positive initial condition if $\kappa\bar{x} > \bar{\sigma}^2/2$, which is sometimes called the Feller condition.

where B is a standard Brownian motion in $\mathbb{R}^d$ and J is a pure-jump process, with technical details in Section A.4. For example, in the one-dimensional case, J could be a *compound Poisson* process, which means that J jumps at Poisson-arrival times and that the successive jump sizes are independent of the jump times and independently and identically distributed, with J independent of the Brownian motion B. Between jump times, X would solve a stochastic differential equation of the form (A.2). One can also allow the jump arrival intensity to depend (in an affine manner) on the current state X_t.

An example of a one-dimensional affine jump diffusion that is often used for applications is a *basic affine process*, meaning a nonnegative affine process X satisfying

$$dX_t = \kappa(\bar{x} - X_t)\,dt + \bar{\sigma}\sqrt{X_t}\,dB_t + dJ_t, \tag{A.6}$$

where J is a compound Poisson process, independent of B, with exponential jump sizes. The Poisson-arrival intensity $\bar{\lambda}$ of jumps and the mean γ of the jump sizes completes the list $(\kappa, \bar{x}, \bar{\sigma}, \bar{\lambda}, \gamma)$ of parameters of a basic affine process. Special cases of the basic affine model are the mean-reverting-with-jumps model of Chapter 3 (for $\bar{\sigma} = 0$), and the CIR (square-root) diffusion of Feller (1951) (for $\bar{\lambda} = 0$). The basic affine process is especially tractable, in that the coefficients $\alpha(t)$ and $\beta(t)$ of (A.4) are known explicitly. These coefficients are provided in Section A.5.

As for examples of multidimensional affine processes, it suffices for now to give two illustrative cases.

A.2.1. Multivariate Example: Independent Coordinates

The first multivariate example is an affine process X of the form $X_t = (X_{1t}, \ldots, X_{dt})$, for which the coordinate processes $X_1, \ldots, X_d$ are independent one-dimensional affine processes. The independence assumption implies that we can break the calculation (A.4) down as a product of terms of the same form as (A.4), but for the one-dimensional coordinate processes. For example, independence of X_1 and X_2 implies that

$$E_t\left(e^{b_1 X_1(s) + b_2 X_2(s)}\right) = E_t\left(e^{b_1 X_1(s)}\right) E_t\left(e^{b_2 X_2(s)}\right),$$

and more generally that

$$E_t\left(e^{\int_t^s -\rho_1 X_1(u)\,du}e^{b_1 X_1(s) + b_2 X_2(s)}\right) = E_t\left(e^{\int_t^s -\rho_1 X_1(u)\,du}e^{b_1 X_1(s)}\right) E_t\left(e^{b_2 X_2(s)}\right),$$

and so on. Each of these expressions can then be solved using (A.4) for the univariate case. If each coordinate process X_i is a basic affine process, we then have closed-form solutions for the coefficients $\alpha(t)$ and $\beta_1(t), \ldots, \beta_d(t)$ in (A.4).

A.2.2. Multivariate Example: The Heston Model

One important two-dimensional affine model is the Heston model for asset returns with stochastic volatility. Here, we suppose that the price process U of an asset satisfies

$$dU_t = U_t(a + bV_t)\, dt + U_t\sqrt{V_t}\, dB_{1t}, \qquad (A.7)$$

where a and b are constants and V is a stochastic-volatility process, which is a Feller (CIR) diffusion satisfying

$$dV_t = \kappa(\bar{v} - V_t)\, dt + \bar{\sigma}\sqrt{V_t}\, dZ_t, \qquad (A.8)$$

where $Z = \rho B_1 + \sqrt{1 - \rho^2}\, B_2$ is a standard Brownian motion that is constructed as a linear combination of independent standard Brownian motions B_1 and B_2. The correlation coefficient ρ generates what is known as *volatility asymmetry* and is usually negative for major market stock indices. Option implied-volatility *smile curves* are, roughly speaking, rotated clockwise into *smirks* as ρ becomes negative. Letting $Y = \log U$, a calculation based on Itô's formula (see, e.g., Pan, 2002) implies that the two-dimensional affine process $X = (Y, V)'$ satisfies (A.8) and

$$dY_t = \left[a + \left(b - \tfrac{1}{2}\right)V_t\right] dt + \sqrt{V_t}\, dB_{1t}. \qquad (A.9)$$

While V is, on its own, a one-dimensional affine process (i.e., a Feller diffusion), we can also treat the pair $(Y, V)'$ as a two-dimensional affine process with the state space $D = \mathbb{R} \times \mathbb{R}_+$ (consisting of pairs of real numbers of the form (y, v), where v is a nonnegative). This leads to valuable tools for option pricing, as shown by Heston. This model and extensions allowing for jumps are also useful for the statistical analysis of stock returns from time-series data on underlying asset returns and option prices, as we explore later in this appendix.

In general, the form $e^{\alpha(t)+\beta(t)\cdot X(t)}$ of the solution to (A.4) and the fact that it is easy to calculate $\alpha(t)$ and $\beta(t)$ imply that affine processes are analytically tractable for many applications. This tractability, combined with the rich variety of alternative types of stochastic behavior that can be built into affine processes, through mean reversion, stochastic volatility, and jumps, make them ideal models for fitting data and for generating useful and tractable examples of bond prices, default probabilities, stock returns, option prices, and many other applications.

A.2.3. The Riccati Equations

Now, in order to calculate the coefficients $\alpha(t)$ and $\beta(t)$ that define the solution of (A.4), which is crucial in many applications, it turns out that there is an ordinary differential equation (ODE), called a *generalized Riccati equation*, describing the dependence of these coefficients on calendar time t, of the form

$$\frac{d\beta(t)}{dt} = \mathcal{B}(\beta_t) \tag{A.10}$$

$$\frac{d\alpha(t)}{dt} = \mathcal{A}(\beta_t), \tag{A.11}$$

where $\mathcal{B}(\beta_t)$ and $\mathcal{A}(\beta_t)$ depend explicitly on β_t and are specified for a large class of affine processes in Section A.4. The boundary conditions are obtained by taking $t = s$ in (A.4), so that

$$\beta(s) = b \qquad \text{and} \qquad \alpha(s) = 0. \tag{A.12}$$

In some cases, the solution of this ODE is known explicitly. This is true, for example, for Heston's model, for Gaussian models, and for basic affine processes, including the Feller square-root diffusion as a special case whose explicit solutions are provided in Section A.5. A special case is the bond price formula of Cox et al. (1985).

For cases in which the solution to the generalized Riccati equation (A.10) and (A.11) is not known explicitly, it has become routine to solve these ODEs by simple numerical procedures such as Runge-Kutta, which are sufficiently fast for most practical applications.

A.2.4. Transforms of Affine Processes

In this section, we review several types of transforms of affine processes that frequently arise in applications.

First, for a one-dimensional affine process, we consider the Laplace transform $\varphi(\cdot)$, whenever well defined at some real number u by

$$\varphi(u) = E_t\left(e^{-uX(s)}\right). \tag{A.13}$$

We sometimes call $\varphi(\cdot)$ the moment-generating function of $X(s)$, for it has the convenient property that, if its successive derivatives

$$\varphi'(0), \varphi''(0), \varphi'''(0), \dots, \varphi^{(m)}(0)$$

up to some order m are well defined, then they provide us with the respective moments

$$\varphi^{(k)}(0) = E_t[X(s)^k].$$

From (A.4), we know that $\varphi(u) = e^{\alpha(t)+\beta(t)X(t)}$, for coefficients $\alpha(t)$ and $\beta(t)$ obtained from the generalized Riccati equation (A.10). We can calculate the dependence of $\alpha(t)$ and $\beta(t)$ on the boundary condition $\beta(s) = u$, writing $\alpha(t, u)$ and $\beta(t, u)$ to show this dependence explicitly. Then, by the chain rule for differentiation, we have

$$\varphi'(0) = e^{\alpha(t,0)+\beta(t,0)X(0)}[\alpha_u(t, 0) + \beta_u(t, 0)X(0)],$$

where β_u denotes the partial derivative of β with respect to its boundary condition u. Successively higher-order derivatives can be computed by repeated differentiation. Pan (2002) provides an efficient recursive algorithm for higher-order moments, even in certain multivariate cases.

For the multivariate case, the transform at $u \in \mathbb{R}^d$ is defined by

$$\varphi(u) = E\left(e^{-u \cdot X(t)}\right) = e^{\alpha(t,u)+\beta(t,u)\cdot X(0)}, \tag{A.14}$$

and provides covariance and other cross moments, again by differentiation.

Having an explicit term structure of such moments as variances, covariances, skewness, kurtosis, and so on, as the time horizon s varies, allows one to analytically calibrate models to data or to formulate them in light of empirical regularities, as shown by Das and Sundaram (1999). For example, method-of-moments statistical estimation in a time-series setting can also be based on the conditional moment-generating function (A.13).

Analogously to the Laplace transform, the characteristic function $\psi(\cdot)$ of $X(s)$, in the one-dimensional case, is defined at any real number u by

$$\psi(u) = E\left(e^{iuX(s)}\right), \tag{A.15}$$

where i is the imaginary number that is sometimes called $\sqrt{-1}$. The characteristic function is often called a Fourier transform. From (A.4), taking $b = iu$ and $\rho_i = 0$, we have

$$\psi(u) = e^{\alpha(0,iu)+\beta(0,iu)X(0)},$$

where, again, the dependence of the coefficients $\alpha(t, iu)$ and $\beta(t, iu)$ on the terminal boundary condition $\beta(s, iu) = iu$ is shown explicitly. We also note that these coefficients $\alpha(t, iu)$ and $\beta(t, iu)$ are complex numbers, but that the same ODE (A.10) determines them in any case, under technical conditions provided by Duffie et al. (2003a).

The probability distribution of $X(s)$ can be recovered from its characteristic function by the Lévy inversion formula, according to which (under technical regularity conditions),

$$P(X(s) \leq y) = \frac{\psi(0)}{2} - \frac{1}{\pi} \int_0^\infty \frac{\text{Im}\left[\psi(u)e^{-iuy}\right]}{u} \, du, \qquad (A.16)$$

where Im(c) denotes the imaginary part of any complex number c.

The integral in (A.16) is typically calculated by a numerical method such as quadrature, which is rapid. In a few cases, such as the Ornstein-Uhlenbeck (Gaussian) model and the Feller diffusion (noncentral χ^2), the probability distribution is known explicitly. More generally, knowledge of ψ is equivalent to knowledge of the transition distribution function of X, which is useful in the statistical estimation of the parameters of X, as in Singleton (2001) and in many other applications involving the transition densities of affine processes. As we shall see, option prices are quickly obtained from the characteristic function.

A.3. Some Applications

This section reviews a few of the applications that take particular advantage of affine models. The applications cover term-structure modeling, correlated default analytics, credit-spread modeling, and option pricing.

A.3.1. Term-Structure Models

A large literature on the term structure of default-free bond yields presumes that there is an affine process X underlying interest-rate movements.

Assuming that the instantaneous default-free short-term interest rate r_t is given by $r_t = \rho_0 + \rho_1 \cdot X_t$ and that X is an affine process under risk-neutral probabilities, Duffie and Kan (1996) used (A.4) to characterize the price at time t of a zero-coupon bond maturing at time $s > t$, which is defined by

$$d(t, s) = E_t^*\left(e^{\int_t^s -r(u)\,du} \right), \qquad (A.17)$$

where E^* denotes risk-neutral expectation. From (A.4), this discount is of the exponential-affine form $d(t, s) = e^{\alpha(t) + \beta(t) \cdot X(t)}$. This means that yields to maturity and forward rates are also affine in X_t and allows for tractable calibration and analysis of time-series data, as in Dai and Singleton (2000). As will be explained further on in this appendix, this also implies that zero-coupon bond option prices, and therefore cap prices, can be obtained explicitly, up to an inversion of the Fourier transform ψ associated with X. This point was emphasized by Chen and Scott (1995) for the case of a multivariate affine model with independent coordinate processes that are Feller diffusions.

A.3.2. Default Intensities and Probabilities

Recently, considerable attention has been focused on extending term-structure models to allow for the possibility of default, in order to price corporate and sovereign bonds and other credit-sensitive instruments.[2]

If default is at the first arrival of a Poisson process with some constant intensity $\bar{\lambda}$, then the initial probability of no default by s is $p(s) = e^{-\bar{\lambda}s}$. Extending, if default occurs at a deterministic but time-varying Poisson-arrival intensity $\lambda(t)$ at each time t, we find that the probability $p(t, s)$ of no default before time s, in the event of no default by t, is

$$p(t, s) = e^{\int_t^s -\lambda(u)\,du}. \tag{A.18}$$

Extending finally to the case of randomly varying default arrival intensity, we suppose that the arrival of default is at a stochastic intensity $\lambda_t = \Lambda(X_t)$, where X is a Markov process. We adopt the conventional *doubly stochastic* model, under which, conditional on the entire path of the underlying state process X, default is at a Poisson arrival with conditionally deterministic time-varying intensity $\Lambda(X_t)$. If we apply the law of iterated expectations as well as (A.18), this implies that the conditional survival probability $p(t, s)$, in the event of no default by time t and conditional on all information at time t, is

$$p(t, s) = E_t\left[\exp\left(-\int_t^s \Lambda(X_u)\,du\right)\right]. \tag{A.19}$$

Now, if X is an affine process and $\Lambda(\cdot)$ is affine, then we can apply (A.4) to get a solution of the form $p(t, s) = e^{\alpha(t,s)+\beta(t,s)\cdot X(t)}$, where the dependence of the coefficients $\alpha(t, s)$ and $\beta(t, s)$ on the time horizon s is shown explicitly. We can also differentiate with respect to s, in many cases explicitly, to get the conditional probability density $\pi(t, s)$ of the default time at horizon s as $\pi(t, s) = p(t, s)[-\alpha_s(t, s) - \beta_s(t, s) \cdot X(t)]$.

A.3.3. Correlated Default

Extending, we suppose that defaults by n given names are at respective arrival intensities $\Lambda_1(X_t), \ldots, \Lambda_n(X_t)$. Here, X_t could include industry or

---

[2] See, e.g., Jarrow et al. (1997) and Duffie and Singleton (1999).

economywide business cycle variables, or market yield spread factors, or other sources of correlation. We suppose that the only source of default correlation is through the common dependence of these intensities on the underlying state vector X_t. Specifically, we again adopt a doubly stochastic model in which, conditional on the entire path of the state process X, the default times of the n entities are independent, and Poisson arrival of default is governed by deterministic intensities $\Lambda_1(X_t), \ldots, \Lambda_n(X_t)$. This implies that the first time $\tau = \min(\tau_1, \ldots, \tau_n)$ of any default has an intensity $\Lambda(X_t) = \Lambda_1(X_t) + \cdots + \Lambda_n(X_t)$ and that the first-to-default time distribution is again given by (A.19).

If $\Lambda_i(X_t)$ is affine in X_t for each i, then so is the first-to-default intensity $\Lambda(\cdot)$, and if the state process X is also an affine process, we can again exploit the solution form $p(0, s) = e^{\alpha(0,s) + \beta(0,s) \cdot X(0)}$ for the probability of no default by time s.

For any given time horizons $s_1, \ldots, s_n$ for the n respective entities, $P(\tau_1 > s_1, \ldots, \tau_n > s_n)$ can be shown to be of the same exponential-affine form, as explored further in Duffie (1998b) and Duffie and Gârleanu (2001).

A.3.4. Defaultable Term-Structure Models

We can extend the results for term-structure models for default-probability calculations to treat the term structure of discounts for credit risky bonds. The affine modeling approach is tailor-made for this application.

For this purpose, we take the short-rate process r to be of the form $r_t = R(X_t)$ for some state process X that is Markov under given risk-neutral probabilities. Likewise, we suppose that the risk-neutral arrival of default is doubly stochastic with a risk-neutral intensity process λ^* of the state-dependent form $\lambda_t^* = \Lambda^*(X_t)$. We suppose, to begin simply, that there is no recovery at default. Then, from results in Lando (1998), the price of a defaultable zero-coupon bond maturing at s is

$$d(t, s) = E_t^* \left[e^{\int_t^s -[r(u) + \lambda^*(u)] \, du} \right], \tag{A.20}$$

in the event that the bond has not defaulted by time t.

If both the short-rate process and the risk-neutral intensity process are affine with respect to the state process X, and if X is affine under the given risk-neutral probabilities, then $d(t, s)$ is of the exponential affine form obtained by applying (A.4) to (A.20).

Extending, we suppose, upon default, that the bond investor recovers a constant fraction w of the face value of the bond. Then, from results in Lando (1998), the price at time t of a yet-to-default zero-coupon bond with maturity s is given, under technical conditions, by

$$d(t, s) = d_0(t, s) + \int_t^s k(t, u)\, du, \tag{A.21}$$

where

$$k(t, u) = w E_t^* \left[\lambda^*(u) e^{\int_t^u -[r(v) + \lambda^*(v)]\, dv} \right]. \tag{A.22}$$

The first term $d_0(t, s)$ in (A.21) is the value at time t of a claim that pays 1 unit of account contingent on survival to maturity s. We may view $k(t, u)\, du$ as the price at time t of a claim that pays the recovery w if default occurs in the infinitesimal "interval" $(u, t + du)$. Thus the second term in (A.21) is the present value of any proceeds from default before s.

In order to treat calculations such as (A.22) in an affine setting, Duffie et al. (2000) extend the solution (A.4) to cases in which the boundary condition is of the form $e^{b \cdot X(s)} c \cdot X(s)$, allowing a *linear payoff* factor. They show that, under technical conditions,

$$E_t^* \left[e^{\int_t^s -[\rho_0 + \rho_1 \cdot X(u)]\, du} e^{b \cdot X(s)} c \cdot X(s) \right] = e^{\alpha(t,s) + \beta(t,s) \cdot X(t)} \Gamma(t) \cdot X(t), \tag{A.23}$$

where $\Gamma(t)$ is another coefficient vector that can be calculated by solving a related ODE. With this, $k(t, u)$ in (A.22) is easily computed in an affine setting.

In summary, if both r_t and λ_t^* are affine with respect to X_t and if X is, risk-neutrally, an affine process, then there is a closed form solution for $k(t, u)$, and we can therefore calculate the defaultable discount $d(t, s)$ from (A.21) after an easy numerical integration of $k(t, u)$.

Duffie and Singleton (1999) avoid some of the complexity in (A.21) by noting that if the loss in market value at default is treated as a given fraction ℓ of the market value of the bond just before default, then the zero-coupon defaultable bond price is

$$d(t, s) = E_t^* \left[e^{\int_t^s -[r(u) + \ell \lambda^*(u)]\, du} \right], \tag{A.24}$$

which is solved explicitly by (A.4) in the affine setting, where the *default-adjusted short rate* $r(t) + \ell \lambda^*(t)$ depends in an affine manner on the state vector X_t.

A.3.5. Option Pricing

In an influential paper in the option-pricing literature, Heston (1993) showed that the risk-neutral exercise probabilities appearing in the call option pricing formulas for bonds, currencies, and equities can be computed by Fourier inversion of the conditional characteristic function, which he provided in closed form for his particular affine, stochastic-volatility model (A.8) and (A.9). Building on this insight,[3] a variety of option pricing models have been developed for settings in which the state process X that determines returns, interest rates, and volatility, possibly with jumps in each, is described by a multivariate affine process.

In order to illustrate Heston's method for option pricing with stochastic volatility, we assume for simplicity that the short rate r is a constant. This means that the price of a European call option struck at K on the asset with price process U and expiration at time s is

$$
\begin{aligned}
C(K, s) &= e^{-rs} E^* [(U_s - K)^+] \\
&= e^{-rs} E^*(U_s 1_A) - e^{-rs} E^*(K 1_A) \\
&= U_0 \tilde{P}(A) - Ke^{-rs} P^*(A), \qquad (A.25)
\end{aligned}
$$

where A is the event $\{U_s > K\}$ of exercise, $P^*(A)$ denotes its risk-neutral probability, and $\tilde{P}(A)$ denotes its probability under the *asset-numeraire measure* $\tilde{P}$, which is a probability measure under which all asset prices are martingales after normalizing by the price U_t of the underlying asset. Indeed, the classical Black-Scholes formula can be viewed in this form (A.25).

A particular risk-neutral measure P^* is not uniquely determined by the underlying model of asset returns, given the presence of stochastic volatility. If we suppose, however, that the risk-neutral behavior of the volatility process is of the same form as (A.8), albeit with different risk-neutral than actual coefficients, this will also be the case under the asset-numeraire measure $\tilde{P}$, and the joint model (Y, V) for returns and volatility remains affine under all of the relevant probability measures, P, P^*, and $\tilde{P}$.

Now, because of the affine behavior of the state process $X = (Y, U)$ under the risk-neutral probability P^*, we have an explicit solution for the risk-neutral characteristic function ψ^*, defined by $\psi^*(u) = E^* \left(e^{iuY(s)} \right)$. Likewise, we have an explicit solution for the characteristic function $\tilde{\psi}(\cdot)$ under the asset-numeraire measure $\tilde{P}$. The risk-neutral exercise probability,

$$
P^*(A) = P^*(Y_s \le -\log K),
$$

can thus be calculated from (A.16) applied to $\psi^*(\cdot)$. Likewise, $\tilde{P}(A)$ can be

---

[3] Among the many recent papers examining option prices for the case of state variables following affine processes are Chen and Scott (1993), Bates (1996), Scott (1996, 1997), Bakshi et al. (1997), Chernov and Ghysels (1998), Bakshi and Madan (2000), Duffie et al. (2000), and Pan (2002).

calculated from (A.16) applied to $\tilde{\psi}(\cdot)$. Thus, the option price $C(K, s)$ can be calculated analytically from (A.25), for any expiration date s and strike price K.

This option pricing methodology extends to general multidimensional affine processes with much richer dynamic interrelations among the state variables and much richer jump distributions. This approach also leads directly to pricing formulas for plain-vanilla options on currencies, quanto options (such as an option on a common stock or bond struck in a different currency), options on zero-coupon bonds, as well as caps, floors, spread options, chooser options, and other related derivatives. Furthermore, one can price payoffs of the form $(b \cdot X_T - c)^+$ and $(e^{a \cdot X_T} b \cdot X_T - c)^+$ by exploiting (A.23), allowing treatment of Asian options. Details can be found in Duffie et al. (2000).

A.4. Generalized Riccati Equations

This section contains some technical material, including mathematical definitions and the generalized Riccati equation (A.10), that was omitted earlier.

We fix $(\Omega, \mathcal{F}, \mathcal{P})$, a complete probability space, and $(\mathcal{F}_t)_{0 \leq t < \infty}$, a filtration of sub-$\sigma$-fields of $\mathcal{F}$ satisfying the usual technical conditions (see Protter, 1990).

Focusing solely on a certain class of affine processes, we suppose that X is a strong Markov process in some state space D, a subset of $\mathbb{R}^d$, uniquely solving the stochastic differential equation

$$X_t = X_0 + \int_0^t \mu(X_s) \, ds + \int_0^t \sigma(X_s) \, dW_s + J_t, \qquad (A.26)$$

where W is an $(\mathcal{F}_t)$-adapted standard Brownian motion in $\mathbb{R}^d$; $\mu : D \to \mathbb{R}^d$, $\sigma : D \to \mathbb{R}^{d \times d}$, where D is a subset of $\mathbb{R}^d$ to be defined; J is a pure-jump process whose jump-counting process N has a stochastic intensity $\{\lambda(X_t) : t \geq 0\}$, for some $\lambda : D \to [0, \infty)$, and whose jump-size distribution is ν, a probability distribution on $\mathbb{R}^d$. Duffie et al. (2000, 2003a) consider more general jump behavior, including Lévy jump measures.

We can equally well characterize the behavior of X in terms of the infinitesimal generator[4] $\mathcal{D}$ of its transition semigroup, defined by

$$\mathcal{D}f(x) = f_x(x, t)\mu(x) + \tfrac{1}{2}\text{tr}\left[f_{xx}(x)\sigma(x)\sigma(x)^\top\right]$$

$$+ \lambda(x) \int_{\mathbb{R}^d} \left[f(x + z) - f(x)\right] d\nu(z), \qquad (A.27)$$

---

[4] The generator $\mathcal{D}$ is defined by the property that, for any f in its domain, $\{f(X_t) - \int_0^t \mathcal{D}f(X_s) \, ds : t \geq 0\}$ is a martingale. See Ethier and Kurtz (1986) for details.

for sufficiently regular $f : D \to \mathbb{R}$, where $\sigma(x)^\top$ denotes the transpose of $\sigma(x)$.

We fix a discount-rate function $R : D \to \mathbb{R}$. The functions μ, $\sigma\sigma^\top$, λ, and R are assumed to be affine and determined by coefficients (K, H, l, ρ) according to:

$\mu(x) = K_0 + K_1 x$,   for $K = (K_0, K_1) \in \mathbb{R}^d \times \mathbb{R}^{d \times d}$.

$(\sigma(x)\sigma(x)^\top)_{ij} = (H_0)_{ij} + (H_1)_{ij} \cdot x$,   for $H = (H_0, H_1) \in \mathbb{R}^{d \times d} \times \mathbb{R}^{d \times d \times d}$.

$\lambda(x) = l_0 + l_1 \cdot x$,   for $l = (l_0, l_1) \in \mathbb{R} \times \mathbb{R}^d$.

$R(x) = \rho_0 + \rho_1 \cdot x$,   for $\rho = (\rho_0, \rho_1) \in \mathbb{R} \times \mathbb{R}^d$.

For $c \in \mathbb{C}^n$, the set of n-tuples of complex numbers, we let $\theta(c) = \int_{\mathbb{R}^n} \exp(c \cdot z) \, d\nu(z)$ whenever the integral is well defined. This *jump transform* θ determines the jump size distribution.

The *coefficients* (K, H, l, θ) of X completely determine its distribution, given an initial condition $X(0)$. A *characteristic* $\chi = (K, H, l, \theta, \rho)$ captures both the distribution of X as well as the effects of any discounting, and determines a transform $\psi^\chi : \mathbb{C}^n \times D \times \mathbb{R}_+ \times \mathbb{R}_+ \to \mathbb{C}$ of X_T conditional on $\mathcal{F}_t$, when well defined at $t \leq T$, by

$$\psi^\chi(u, X_t, t, T) = E^\chi \left[\exp\left[-\int_t^T R(X_s) \, ds \right] e^{u \cdot X_T} \,\bigg|\, \mathcal{F}_t \right], \quad \text{(A.28)}$$

where E^χ denotes expectation under the distribution of X determined by χ. Here, ψ^χ differs from the familiar (conditional) characteristic function of the distribution of X_T because of the discounting at rate $R(X_t)$.

The key to our applications is that, as shown in Duffie et al. (2000),

$$\psi^\chi(u, x, t, T) = e^{\alpha(t) + \beta(t) \cdot x}, \quad \text{(A.29)}$$

where β and α satisfy the complex-valued ODEs[5]

$$\frac{d\beta(t)}{dt} = \rho_1 - K_1^\top \beta(t) - \tfrac{1}{2}\beta(t)^\top H_1 \beta(t) - l_1 \left(\theta[\beta(t)] - 1\right) \quad \text{(A.30)}$$

$$\frac{d\alpha(t)}{dt} = \rho_0 - K_0 \cdot \beta(t) - \tfrac{1}{2}\beta(t)^\top H_0 \beta(t) - l_0 \left(\theta[\beta(t)] - 1\right), \quad \text{(A.31)}$$

with boundary conditions $\beta(T) = u$ and $\alpha(T) = 0$. The ODE (A.30)–(A.31) is easily conjectured from an application of Ito's formula to the candidate form (A.29) of ψ^χ. In order to apply our results, we would have to compute

---

[5] Here, $c^\top H_1 c$ denotes the vector in $\mathbb{C}^n$ with kth element $\sum_{i,j} c_i (H_1)_{ijk} c_j$.

solutions α and β to these ODEs. In some applications, for example, the basic affine process in Section A.5, explicit solutions can be found. In other cases, solutions would be found numerically, for example, by a Runge-Kutta method. This suggests a practical advantage of choosing a jump distribution ν with an explicitly known or easily computed jump size transform $\theta(\cdot)$.

A.5. Solution for the Basic Affine Model

This section summarizes some results from Duffie and Gârleanu (2001) for the solutions β and α to (A.30) and (A.31) for the basic affine model X of (A.6).

These Riccati equations reduce in this special case to the form

$$\frac{d\beta_t}{dt} = -n\beta_t - \tfrac{1}{2}p\beta_t^2 - q, \tag{A.32}$$

$$\frac{d\alpha_t}{dt} = -m\beta_t - \ell\frac{\bar{\mu}\beta_t}{1 - \bar{\mu}\beta_t}, \tag{A.33}$$

for some constant coefficients n, p, q, m, ℓ, and $\bar{\mu}$, with boundary conditions $\alpha_s = u$ and $\beta_s = v$.

For example, the expectation

$$E_t\left[e^{\int_t^s qX(z)\,dz} e^{v+uX(s)}\right] = e^{\bar{\alpha}(s-t)+\bar{\beta}(s-t)X(t)}, \tag{A.34}$$

has explicit solutions for $\bar{\alpha}(s)$ and $\bar{\beta}(s)$ given below. The case (11.3) is obtained as the special case with $u = v = 0$, $n = -\kappa$, $p = \sigma^2$, $q = -1$, and $m = \kappa\theta$. In general, solutions are given by

$$\bar{\beta}(s) = \frac{1 + a_1 e^{b_1 s}}{c_1 + d_1 e^{b_1 s}} \tag{A.35}$$

$$\bar{\alpha}(s) = v + \frac{m(a_1 c_1 - d_1)}{b_1 c_1 d_1}\log\frac{c_1 + d_1 e^{b_1 s}}{c_1 + d_1} + \frac{m}{c_1}s \tag{A.36}$$

$$+ \frac{\ell(a_2 c_2 - d_2)}{b_2 c_2 d_2}\log\frac{c_2 + d_2 e^{b_2 s}}{c_2 + d_2} + \left(\frac{\ell}{c_2} - \ell\right)s,$$

where

$$c_1 = \frac{-n + \sqrt{n^2 - 2pq}}{2q}$$

$$d_1 = (1 - c_1 u)\frac{n + pu + \sqrt{(n + pu)^2 - p(pu^2 + 2nu + 2q)}}{2nu + pu^2 + 2q}$$

$$a_1 = (d_1 + c_1)u - 1$$

$$b_1 = \frac{d_1(n + 2qc_1) + a_1(nc_1 + p)}{a_1 c_1 - d_1}$$

$$a_2 = \frac{d_1}{c_1}$$

$$b_2 = b_1$$

$$c_2 = 1 - \frac{\bar{\mu}}{c_1}$$

$$d_2 = \frac{d_1 - \bar{\mu} a_1}{c_1}.$$

A.6. Intensities for Stopping Times

This section provides some technical background and extensions for affine default probability and bond valuation models. A probability space $(\Omega, \mathcal{F}, P)$ and filtration $\{\mathcal{F}_t : t \geq 0\}$ satisfying the usual conditions are fixed. For details, see Protter (1990).

A counting process is an increasing (right-continuous) adapted process taking the values $0, 1, 2, \ldots$ in succession. A counting process Y has an intensity η (a nonnegative, predictable process with $\int_0^t \eta_s \, ds < \infty$ for all t) if a local martingale M is defined by $M_t = Y_t - \int_0^t \eta_s \, ds$. We will say that a stopping time τ has an intensity process η if τ is the first jump time of a counting process with intensity η. (This definition is not used uniformly in the literature.) For a given Markov process X valued in some state space D, a counting process Y is doubly stochastic, driven by X with intensity λ, if, conditional on X, the counting process Y is a Poisson process with deterministic intensity $\{\lambda_t : t \geq 0\}$, for $\lambda_t = \Lambda(X_t)$, where $\Lambda : D \to [0, \infty)$. For the associated first jump time τ of Y, this implies by the law of iterated expectations that, on the event that $\tau > t$, for any $s > t$ we have

$$P(\tau > s \mid \mathcal{F}_t) = E\left[\exp\left(\int_t^s -\lambda_u \, du\right) \Big| \mathcal{F}_t\right]. \tag{A.37}$$

For stopping times $\tau_1, \ldots, \tau_N$ with respective intensities $\lambda_1, \ldots, \lambda_N$, the corresponding multivariate counting process $Y = (Y_1, \ldots, Y_N)$ is said to be doubly stochastic driven by X if, for each i, Y_i is doubly stochastic driven by X and if, conditional on the path of X, the processes $Y_1, \ldots, Y_N$ are independent. In this case, the stopping time $\tau = \min(\tau_1, \ldots, \tau_N)$ has intensity process $\lambda = \lambda_1 + \cdots + \lambda_N$ and (A.37) applies.

B
Econometrics of Affine Term-Structure Models

THIS APPENDIX BRIEFLY outlines the estimation strategy that we used for the examples in the text that were estimated with historical data.

We know from Appendix A that, in affine term-structure models, the functional relation between a vector c_t of yields used in estimation and the state vector X_t is $c_t = g(X_t; \psi)$ for a differentiable function $g(\cdot)$ that is easily computed, where ψ is the vector of parameters determining the model. At a given parameter vector ψ, the model-implied state vector X_t^{ψ} is defined by

$$X_t^{\psi} = g(\cdot; \psi)^{-1}(c_t), \tag{B.1}$$

assuming invertibility (which is not an issue in our applications). If ψ is the true parameter vector for the model, then $X_t^{\psi} = X_t$.

From this point, we let $f(X \mid Z; \psi)$ denote the conditional density of some random vector X given some random vector Z, under the assumption that the model's parameter vector is ψ (and assuming that this density exists). We likewise use $f(X; \psi)$ for the unconditional density. If we let $c = (c_1, \ldots, c_T)$ denote the sequence of observed vectors of yields to be used in estimation, standard change-of-variable arguments lead to the likelihood function (joint density of the data)

$$f(c; \psi) = \prod_{t=1}^{T} f(X_t^{\psi} \mid X_{t-1}^{\psi}; \psi) \frac{1}{|\det Dg(X_t^{\psi}; \psi)|}, \tag{B.2}$$

where, for affine term-structure models, the Jacobian Dg can be easily computed. The challenge in estimating affine term-structure models is that the transition density $f(X_t \mid X_{t-1}; \psi)$ of an affine process X is not generally known in closed form, apart from special cases, such as Gaussian and independent square-root diffusions. Following Duffie et al. (2003b), we proceed using a simple approximation of the likelihood function that leads to reliable estimates in a large subclass of affine models.

To illustrate their basic idea, we consider the bivariate affine diffusion, the hybrid model (C) of Section 7.2, with $X_t' = (X_{1t}, X_{2t})$, where

$$dX_{1t} = (a_1 - K_{11}X_{1t}) \, dt + \sqrt{X_{1t}} \, dB_{1t}, \tag{B.3}$$

$$dX_{2t} = (a_2 - K_{21}X_{1t} + K_{22}X_{2t}) \, dt + \sqrt{1 + \beta X_{1t}} \, dB_{2t}, \tag{B.4}$$

where $B = (B_1, B_2)'$ is a standard two-dimensional Brownian motion. We are interested in computing the transition density of X_{t+1} given X_t implied by the parameters of (B.3) and (B.4), where time is measured relative to the sampling interval of the available data.

Consider the conditional density $f(X_t \mid X_{t-h})$, for some $h > 0$. The particular structure of this model, which has no feedback from X_2 to X_1, implies that

$$f(X_{1t} \mid X_{t-h}) = f(X_{1t} \mid X_{1,t-h}) \tag{B.5}$$

and therefore from Bayes's rule that

$$f(X_t \mid X_{t-h}) = f(X_{1t} \mid X_{1,t-h}) \times f(X_{2t} \mid X_{1t}, X_{t-h}). \tag{B.6}$$

The structure of (B.3) as a one-factor CIR model is such that the distribution of X_{1t} given $X_{1,t-h}$ is noncentral χ^2 with known parameters (Feller, 1951). No approximation for its conditional density function is necessary. Thus, we can calculate $f(X_t \mid X_{t-h})$ from (B.6) once we can compute $f(X_{2t} \mid X_{1t}, X_{t-h})$.

Now, the conditional density of X_{2t}, given X_{t-h} *and the entire path of* X_1 *between dates* $t - h$ *and* t, is joint normal. In particular, the distribution of X_{2t} given $X_{2,t-h}$ and $\{X_{1s}, s \in [t - h, t]\}$ is normal with mean μ_t and variance σ_t^2, where

$$\mu_t = e^{-K_{22}h} \left[\int_{t-h}^t e^{K_{22}s} (a_2 - K_{11}X_{1s}) \, ds + X_{2,t-h} \right] \tag{B.7}$$

$$\sigma_t^2 = e^{-K_{22}h} \left[\int_{t-h}^t e^{2K_{22}s} (1 + \beta X_{1s}) \, ds \right]. \tag{B.8}$$

This is an implication of the observations that, conditional on the path of X_1, the form of (B.4) implies that X_2 is a diffusion with a drift that is linear in X_{2t} and a volatility process that is a conditionally deterministic function of time.

We are actually interested in calculating $f(X_{2t} \mid X_{1t}, X_{t-h})$, which does not have this normal distribution because the conditioning information does not include the path of X_1 between dates $t - h$ and t. For small h, however, we approximate the former by the latter. That is, we use the approximation

$$f(X_{2t} \mid X_{1t}, X_{t-h}) \simeq f_N(X_{2t}; \mu_t, \sigma_t^2), \tag{B.9}$$

where $f_N(\,\cdot\,; \bar{\mu}, \bar{\sigma}^2)$ denotes the normal density with mean $\bar{\mu}$ and variance $\bar{\sigma}^2$. Furthermore, we approximate the moments μ_t and σ_t^2 by $\tilde{\mu}_t$ and $\tilde{\sigma}_t^2$, respectively, where

$$\tilde{\mu}_t = e^{-K_{22}h} \left[\int_{t-h}^{t} e^{K_{22}s} \left[a_2 - K_{11}\ell(X_{1t}, X_{1,t-h}, s) \right] ds + X_{2,t-h} \right] \tag{B.10}$$

$$\tilde{\sigma}_t^2 = e^{-K_{22}h} \left[\int_{t-h}^{t} e^{2K_{22}s} \left[1 + \beta\ell(X_{1t}, X_{1,t-h}, s) \right] ds \right], \tag{B.11}$$

and where $\ell(X_{1t}, X_{1,t-h}, s)$ is a deterministic scheme for interpolating between $X_{1,t-h}$ and X_{1t}. One simple version of ℓ (that we use in our numerical examples) is the linear interpolation

$$\ell(X_{1t}, X_{1,t-h}, s)X_{1s} = X_{1,t-h} + s(X_{1t} - X_{1,t-h}). \tag{B.12}$$

We can now combine this approximation with the known noncentral χ^2 transition density for X_1 to give us an approximation of $f(X_t \mid X_{t-h})$. That is, approximate $f(X_t \mid X_{t-h})$ with

$$\tilde{f}(X_t \mid X_{t-h}) = f(X_{1t} \mid X_{1,t-h}) \times f_N(X_{2t}; \mu_t, \sigma_t^2). \tag{B.13}$$

In some cases, choosing h to be the sampling interval of the data leads to reliable parameter estimates, and no further steps are required to implement an approximate maximum likelihood estimator. This was the case for the examples considered in this book.

For cases in which it is desirable to choose a discretization interval h smaller than the sampling interval of the data, Duffie et al. (2003b) propose the following. Each sampling interval $[t, t + 1]$ is divided into n subintervals, say, of equal length $h = 1/n$, and the density function of the data is expressed, using the law of iterated expectations, as

$$f(X_{t+1} \mid X_t; \psi) = E \left[f(X_{t+1} \mid X_{t+1-h}; \psi) \mid X_t; \psi \right], \tag{B.14}$$

where $E[\,\cdot \mid X_t; \psi]$ means the conditional expectation given X_t, under the model with parameter vector ψ. A similar idea was exploited previously by Pedersen (1995) and Brandt and Santa-Clara (2001) in constructing a simulated maximum likelihood estimator for general diffusion models. Though their estimator and the one we use both start from (B.14), the subsequent calculations are different. Most importantly, we exploit the affine structure of X to approximate $f(X_{t+1} \mid X_{t+1-h})$.

Therefore, choosing h so that the preceding approximation scheme is reliable for $f(X_{t+1} \mid X_{t+1-h})$, we can compute (B.14) by Monte Carlo integration. Specifically, we factor $f(X_{t+1-h} \mid X_t)$ as

$$f(X_{t+1-h} \mid X_t) = f(X_{t+1-h} \mid X_{t+1-2h}) \times f(X_{t+1-2h} \mid X_{t+1-3h}) \times$$
$$\cdots \times f(X_{t+1-(n-1)h} \mid X_t). \qquad \text{(B.15)}$$

For the kth draw of X_{t+1-h}, say X_{t+1-h}^k, each factor $f(X_{t+1-jh} \mid X_{t+1-(j+1)h})$ is replaced with the approximate density $\tilde{f}(X_{t+1-jh} \mid X_{t+1-(j+1)h})$. Then, starting with the initial value X_t, one can sequentially draw X_{t+1-jh}, for each integer j between $n-1$ and 1, from the approximate densities, with the previous draw used as the conditioning variable in the current draw, to obtain X_{t+1-h}^k. Finally, the desired expectation is computed as

$$f(X_{t+1} \mid X_t) \simeq \frac{1}{\mathcal{T}} \sum_{k=1}^{\mathcal{T}} \tilde{f}(X_{t+1} \mid X_{t+1-h}^k), \qquad \text{(B.16)}$$

where $\mathcal{T}$ is the number of random draws.

While the distribution of the state process X under actual probabilities is used in estimation, as we have stressed throughout, risk-neutral expectations are used in pricing. Estimation of a dynamic term-structure model using historical data therefore requires that one specify explicitly the *market prices of risk* that link the actual and risk-neutral measures. For the case of affine models, Duffee (2002) proposed a flexible specification of the market price of risk that preserves the requisite affine structure under the risk-neutral measure. Specifically, for the case of two-factor affine diffusions of our hybrid type (C) of Section 7.2.1, the market-price-of-risk process Λ is assumed to be of the form

$$\Lambda(t) = \sqrt{S_t}\lambda^0 + \sqrt{S_t^-}\lambda^X X_t, \qquad \text{(B.17)}$$

where λ^0 and λ^X are constant 2×2 matrices and S_t^- is a diagonal matrix with ith diagonal element defined as

$$S_{ii,t}^- = \frac{1}{\alpha_i + \beta_i \cdot X_t}, \qquad \text{if } \inf_{x \in D} (\alpha_i + \beta_i \cdot x) > 0, \qquad \text{(B.18)}$$
$$= 0, \qquad\qquad \text{otherwise,}$$

where the coefficients α_i and β_i determine the instantaneous variance $S_{ii,t} = \alpha_i + \beta_i \cdot X_t$ of X_{it}, as in (B.18). The infimum taken in (B.18), over points in the state space D of the affine state process X, rules out arbitrage opportunities that might otherwise arise as the risk (volatility) in the economy approaches zero (see Cox et al., 1985). The state space of an affine process D is normally defined, as in the examples of Section 7.2.1, by nonnegativity restrictions on some coordinates of the state vector X_t, and no restrictions on other coordinates. (That is, D is typically of the form $\mathbb{R}_+^n \times \mathbb{R}^{k-n}$ for nonnegative integers k and $n \leq k$.) So, for example, if the ith risk factor X_{it} is a CIR process, then $\alpha_i = 0$ and β_i is the vector whose ith element is 1 and whose other elements are zero, so, from (B.18), we would have $S_{ii,t}^- = 0$.

In order to interpret this specification of the market prices of risk, it is instructive to use the various special cases of two-factor affine reference models introduced in Section 7.2.1. In case (A), X is Gaussian and the matrices λ^0 and λ^X are unconstrained. Excess returns are time varying in this model, because of time variation of the risk premia, even though the instantaneous variances of the risk factors ($S(t)$) are constant. With the common practice of assuming that $\Lambda(t)$ is proportional to the factor volatilities $\sqrt{S(t)}$, we would have $\lambda^X = 0$ in (B.17). This common formulation forces constant mean excess bond returns, which is clearly counterfactual.

At the other end of the *volatility spectrum* is case (B), for which the two factors are independent CIR processes with time-varying volatilities. In this case, obtaining well-defined bond prices *requires* that $\lambda^X = 0$. With λ^0 free, this means that the market prices of risk are proportional to the factor volatilities or, equivalently, excess returns are proportional to the factor variances [see (7.7)]. Thus, the variation in the factors affects expected excess returns only through the factor variances.

In the hybrid case (C), assuming that $\inf_x (\alpha_2 + \beta_2 \cdot x) > 0$, λ^0 is again free, but λ^X has the structure

$$\lambda^X = \begin{pmatrix} 0 & 0 \\ \lambda_{21}^X & \lambda_{22}^X \end{pmatrix}. \tag{B.19}$$

It follows that both risk factors affect the market price of risk of X_2 (even though the conditional variance of X_2 is constant), while the market price of risk of X_1 is proportional to the volatility of X_1.

Recently Dai and Singleton (2002) and Duffee (2002) found that, within the affine family of models, having nonzero elements of λ^X is critical for getting a model to match the historical variation in expected excess returns on bonds. Their findings point toward the use of cases (A) or (C) over (B) in actual empirical applications. Accordingly, we focus on a hybrid model [a three-factor extension of case (C)] in Chapter 13 for our analysis of future exposures on credit-sensitive positions.

C

HJM Spread Curve Models

AN ALTERNATIVE APPROACH to the pricing of defaultable bonds focuses on the term-structure forward spread rates, as in models of the style of Heath-Jarrow-Morton (HJM).[1] We suppose that a defaultable zero-coupon bond maturing at s has a price at time t (assuming default has yet to occur) of the form

$$d(t, s) = \exp\left(-\int_t^s [F(t, u) + S(t, u)]\, du\right), \qquad (\text{C}.1)$$

where, for each fixed T, $F(t, T)$ is the default-free forward rate, in the sense of HJM, and therefore $S(t, T)$ is the spread forward rate. (The model does not actually say anything about the pricing of forward contracts on defaultable debt, at least not without some convention for how a forward contract on a bond would settle in the event of default of the underlying bond before delivery.)

Fixing the date s of maturity, we suppose that the process $\{F(t, s) : 0 \leq t \leq s\}$ satisfies the usual[2] HJM dynamics given by

$$dF(t, s) = \mu_F(t, s)\, ds + \sigma_F(t, s)\, dB_t^*, \qquad (\text{C}.2)$$

where B^* is a risk-neutral standard Brownian motion in $\mathbb{R}^m$, for some number m of risk factors. Here, μ_F and σ_F satisfy the usual HJM technical conditions. (The volatility process σ_F need not be deterministic.) We have the standard HJM risk-neutral default-free forward-rate drift restriction

---

[1] As noted earlier in the text the HJM model is due to (Heath et al., 1992). This defaultable version is based on results in Duffie (1998b) and Duffie and Singleton (1999). For more, see Bielecki and Rutkowski (2000a,b, 2002).

[2] One can add jumps to the model and extend the calculations easily.

$$\mu_F(t, s) = \sigma_F(t, s) \cdot \int_t^s \sigma_F(t, u) \, du. \tag{C.3}$$

We suppose that the spread forward rates satisfy the same sort of model, with

$$dS(t, s) = \mu_S(t, s) \, dt + \sigma_S(t, s) \, dB_t^*,$$

for a given $\mathbb{R}^m$-valued *spread volatility process* $\{\sigma_S(t, s) : 0 \le t \le s\}$. By using Itô calculus, it can then be shown, under technical conditions, that the model-implied risk-neutral default intensity is $\lambda_t^* = S(t, t)/\ell_t^*$, where ℓ_t^* is the risk-neutral expected fraction of market value lost at default. The risk-neutral drift restriction for forward spread rates is

$$\mu_S(t, s) = \sigma_S(t, s) \cdot \int_t^s \sigma_F(t, u) \, du + \sigma_F(t, s) \cdot \int_t^s \sigma_S(t, u) \, du. \tag{C.4}$$

A related drift restriction arises in the case of a model based on a specified rate of default recovery of face value, or of a default free bond, as in Duffie and Singleton (1999).

With a model for the default-free forward rates and forward spread rates in place, one can define a stopping time τ such that (S, F, τ) has the "correct" joint distribution and, in particular, such that τ has the implied risk-neutral intensity process λ^*. One method for constructing τ in terms of (F, S) is as follows. First, one can let Z be exponentially distributed with parameter 1 and independent of F and S. Given Z and S, one can then let $\lambda_t^* = S(t, t)/\ell_t^*$ and finally define τ by

$$\tau = \inf \left\{ t : \int_0^t \lambda^*(s) \, ds = Z \right\}, \tag{C.5}$$

that is, the first time that the compensator $\int_0^t \lambda^*(s) \, ds$ reaches Z. The risk-neutral intensity of τ is, with this construction of τ, indeed given by λ^*.

In principle, this algorithm allows for joint simulation of defaultable forward rates and default times, which may be important for the valuation of certain credit derivatives, such as spread options. It is not necessary to simulate τ in order to price defaultable bonds, of course, because the bond prices themselves can be computed directly from the forward rate and spread curves.

The *instantaneous correlation* process ρ_{SF} between spreads and default-free forward rates is defined, for each s and $t \le s$, by

$$\rho_{SF}(t, s) = \frac{\sigma_S(t, s) \cdot \sigma_F(t, s)}{\|\sigma_S(t, s)\| \, \|\sigma_F(t, s)\|},$$

assuming nonzero volatilities. Alternatively, one could take the total spread volatility process v_S, defined by $v_S(t, s) = \|\sigma_S(t, s)\|$, and the correlation process ρ_{SF} as inputs, satisfying technical conditions, and from these determine a consistent process for σ_S. That is, provided the Brownian motion B^* is of dimension $m > 1$, one can always construct an $\mathbb{R}^m$-valued process σ_S with $\|\sigma_S(t, s)\| = v_S(t, s)$ and

$$\sigma_S(s, t) \cdot \sigma_F(s, t) = \rho_{SF}(t, s)v_S(t, s)\|\sigma_F(t, s)\|.$$

Given the default-free forward-rate process F, the spread volatility process σ_S, and the initial spread curve $\{S(0, t) : t \geq 0\}$, the model for any forward spread $S(t, u)$ is determined. Of course, one wants restrictions under which $S(t, s)$ is nonnegative for any nonnegative initial spread curve. Roughly speaking, it is enough that $\sigma_S(t, u) = 0$, for any u, whenever $S(t, s)$ is zero. Then, from the risk-neutral drift restriction given above for $\mu_S(t, s)$, for each fixed s, we have $\mu_S(t, s) \geq 0$ whenever $S(t, s) = 0$, so 0 is a natural boundary for $S(\cdot, s)$, giving the desired nonnegativity.[3]

---

[3] See Miltersen (1994) for technical conditions for the analogous nonnegativity of default-free forward rates.

References

Abken, P. (1993). Valuation of Default Risky Interest Rate Swaps. *Advances in Futures and Options* **6**, 93–116.

Ahn, D.-H., R. F. Dittmar, and A. R. Gallant (2002). Quadratic Gaussian Models: Theory and Evidence. *Review of Financial Studies* **15**, 243–288.

Akerlof, G. (1970). The Market for 'Lemons:' Qualitative Uncertainty and the Market Mechanism. *Quarterly Journal of Economics* **89**, 488–500.

Altman, E. (1968). Financial Ratios, Discriminant Analysis and the Prediction of Corporate Bankruptcy. *Journal of Finance* **23**, 589–609.

———. (1989). Measuring Corporate Bond Mortality and Performance. *The Journal of Finance* **44**, 909–922.

———. (1991). Defaults and Returns on High-Yield Bonds Through the First Half of 1991. *Financial Analysts Journal*, November–December, 67–77.

Altman, E., and V. Kishore (1995). Defaults and Returns on High Yield Bonds: Analysis Through 1994. Working Paper, New York University Salomon Center.

Amemiya, T. (2001). Endogenous Sampling in Duration Models. Working Paper, Department of Economics, Stanford University.

Amemiya, T., and J. Powell (1983). A Comparison of the Logit Model and Normal Discriminant Analysis When the Independent Variables Are Binary. In S. Karlin, T. Amemiya, and L. Goodman (Eds.), *Studies in Econometrics, Time Series, and Multivariate Statistics*. New York: Academic Press.

Amihud, Y., and H. Mendelson (1991). Liquidity, Maturity and the Yields on U.S. Government Securities. *Journal of Finance* **46**, 1411–1426.

Andersen, P., Ø. Borgan, R. Gill, and N. Keiding (1993). *Statistical Models of Counting Processes*. New York: Springer.

Andersen, T., L. Benzoni, and J. Lund (2002). An Empirical Investigation of Continuous-Time Equity Return Models. *Journal of Finance* **57**, 1239–1284.

Anderson, R., and S. Sundaresan (1996). Design and Valuation of Debt Contracts. *Review of Financial Studies* **9**, 37–68.

Artzner, P., and F. Delbaen (1995). Default Risk Insurance and Incomplete Markets. *Mathematical Finance* **5**, 187–195.

Artzner, P., F. Delbaen, J. Eber, and D. Heath (1999). Coherent Measures of Risk. *Mathematical Finance* **9**, 203–228.

Arvanitis, A., J. Gregory, and J. Laurent (1999). Building Models for Credit Spreads. *The Journal of Derivatives* **6**, Spring, 27–43.

Asquith, P. (1995). Convertible Bonds Are Not Called Late. *Journal of Finance* **50**, 1275–1290.

Bakshi, G., and D. Madan (2000). Spanning and Derivative-Security Valuation. *Journal of Financial Economics* **55**, 205–238.

Bakshi, G., C. Cao, and Z. Chen (1997). Empirical Performance of Alternative Option Pricing Models. *Journal of Finance* **52**, 2003–2049.

Bakshi, G., D. Madan, and F. Zhang (2001). Investigating the Sources of Default Risk: Lessons from Empirically Evaluating Credit Risk Models. Working Paper, University of Maryland.

Barlow, R., and F. Proschan (1981). *Statistical Theory of Reliability and Life Testing.* Silver Spring, Md: Holt, Rinehart and Winston.

Basle Committee on Banking Supervision and IOSCO (1995). Treatment of Potential Exposure for Off-Balance Sheet Items.

———. (1996). Amendment to the Capital Accord to Incorporate Market Risks.

———. (1997). Survey of Disclosures about Trading and Derivatives Activities of Banks and Securities Firms.

Bates, D. (1996). Jumps and Stochastic Volatility: Exchange Rate Processes Implicit in PHLX Deutschemark Options. *Review of Financial Studies* **9**, 69–107.

———. (1997). Post-'87 Crash Fears in S&P 500 Futures Options. *Journal of Econometrics* **94**, 181–238.

Beaglehole, D. R., and M. S. Tenney (1991). General Solutions to Some Interest Rate Contingent Claim Pricing Equations. *Journal of Fixed Income* **1**, 69–83.

Behar, R., and K. Nagpal (1999). Dynamics of Rating Transition. Working Paper, Standard & Poor's.

Bernanke, B. (1990). On the Predictive Power of Interest Rates and Interest Rate Spreads. *New England Economic Review*, 51–68.

Bielecki, T., and M. Rutkowski (2000a). Modeling of the Defaultable Term Structure: Conditionally Markov Approach. Working Paper, Department of Mathematics, Northeastern University.

———. (2000b). Multiple Ratings of Defaultable Term Structure. *Mathematical Finance* **10**, 125–139.

———. (2002). *Credit Risk: Modeling, Valuation, and Hedging.* New York: Springer.

Black, F., and J. Cox (1976). Valuing Corporate Securities: Liabilities: Some Effects of Bond Indenture Provisions. *Journal of Finance* **31**, 351–367.

Black, F., and M. Scholes (1973). The Pricing of Options and Corporate Liabilities. *Journal of Political Economy* **81**, 637–654.

Blume, M., and D. Keim (1991). Realized Returns and Defaults on Low-Grade Bonds: The Cohort of 1977 and 1978. *Financial Analysts Journal*, March–April, 63–72.

Blume, M., D. Keim, and S. Patel (1991). Returns and Volatility of Low-Grade Bonds: 1977–1989. *Journal of Finance* **46**, 49–74.

Blume, M., F. Lim, and C. MacKinlay (1998). The Declining Credit Quality of US Corporate Debt: Myth or Reality. *Journal of Finance* **53**, 1389–1413.

Bohn, J. (1999). Empirical Assessment of a Simple Contingent-Claims Model for the Valuation of Risky Debt. Working Paper, University of California, Berkeley.

Bollerslev, T. (1986). Generalized Autoregressive Conditional Heteroskedasticity. *Journal of Econometrics* **31**, 307–327.

Bollerslev, T., R. Chou, and K. Kroner (1992). ARCH Modeling in Finance: A Review of Theory and Empirical Evidence. *Journal of Econometrics* **52**, 5–59.

Boyarchenko, S. (2000). Endogeneous Default under Lévy Processes. Working Paper, Department of Economics, University of Pennsylvania.

Brandt, M., and P. Santa-Clara (2001). Simulated Likelihood Estimation of Diffusions with an Application to Exchange Rate Dynamics in Incomplete Markets. Working Paper, Wharton School, University of Pennsylvania.

Brennan, M., and E. Schwartz (1977). Convertible Bonds: Valuation and Optimal Strategies for Call and Conversion. *Journal of Finance* **32**, 1699–1715.

———. (1980). Analyzing Convertible Bonds. *Journal of Financial and Quantitative Analysis* **15**, 907–929.

Briys, E., and F. de Varenne (1997). Valuing Risky Fixed Rate Debt: An Extension. *Journal of Financial and Quantitative Analysis* **32**, 239–248.

Bulow, J., and K. Rogoff (1989a). A Constant Recontracting Model of Sovereign Debt. *Journal of Political Economy* **97**, 155–178.

———. (1989b). Sovereign Debt: Is to Forgive to Forget? *American Economic Review* **79**, 43–50.

Cantor, R., and F. Packer (1996). Determinants and Impact of Sovereign Credit Ratings. *FRBNY Economic Policy Review*, October, 37–53.

Carey, M. (1998). Credit Risk in Private Debt Portfolios. *Journal of Finance* **53**, 1363–1388.

Carty, L., and J. Fons (1994). Measuring Changes in Corporate Credit Quality. *The Journal of Fixed Income* **4**, June, 27–41.

Cathcart, L., and L. El-Jahel (1998). Valuation of Defaultable Bonds. *The Journal of Fixed Income*, June, 66–78.

Chava, S., and R. Jarrow (2001). Bankruptcy Prediction with Industry Effects, Market Versus Accounting Variables, and Reduced Form Credit Risk Models. Working Paper, Cornell University.

Chen, R.-R., and L. Scott (1993). Maximum Likelihood Estimation for a Multifactor Equilibrium Model of the Term Structure of Interest Rates. *Journal of Fixed Income* **3**, December, 14–31.

———. (1995). Interest Rate Options in Multifactor Cox-Ingersoll-Ross Models of the Term Structure. *Journal of Derivatives* **3**, Winter, 53–72.

Chernov, M., and E. Ghysels (1998). What Data Should Be Used to Price Options? Working Paper, Department of Finance, Pennsylvania State University.

Cheung, S. (1996). Provincial Credit Ratings in Canada: An Ordered Probit Analysis. Working Paper, Bank of Canada Working Paper 96-6.

Collin-Dufresne, P., and R. Goldstein (2001). Do Credit Spreads Reflect Stationary Leverage Ratios? Reconciling Structural and Reduced Form Frameworks. *Journal of Finance* **56**, 1929–1958.

Collin-Dufresne, P., and B. Solnik (2001). On the Term Structure of Default Premia in the Swap and LIBOR Markets. *Journal of Finance* **56**, 1095–1116.

Collin-Dufresne, P., R. Goldstein, and J. Martin (2001). The Determinants of Credit Spread Changes. *Journal of Finance* **56**, 2177–2208.

Constantinides, G. (1992). A Theory of the Nominal Term Structure of Interest Rates. *Review of Financial Studies* **5**, 531–552.

Cooper, I., and A. Mello (1991). The Default Risk of Swaps. *Journal of Finance* **46**, 597–620.

Cossin, D., and H. Pirotte (1996). Swap Credit Risk: An Empirical Investigation on Transaction Data. Working Paper, HEC, University of Lausanne.

Counterparty Risk Management Policy Group (1999). Improving Counterparty Risk Management Practices. Working Paper, Counterparty Risk Management Policy Group.

Cox, J., and M. Rubinstein (1985). *Options Markets*. Englewood Cliffs, N.J.: Prentice-Hall.

Cox, J. C., J. Ingersoll, and S. Ross (1981). The Relation between Forward Prices and Futures Prices. *Journal of Financial Economics* **9**, 321–346.

———. (1985). A Theory of the Term Structure of Interest Rates. *Econometrica* **53**, 385–407.

Crouhy, M., S. Turnbull, and L. Wakeman (1998). Measuring Risk Adjusted Performance. Working Paper, Global Analytics, CIBC.

Crouhy, M., D. Galai, and R. Mark (2000). A Comparative Analysis of Current Credit Risk Models. *Journal of Banking and Finance* **24**, 57–117.

———. (2001). *Risk Management*. New York: McGraw-Hill.

Dai, Q., and K. Singleton (2000). Specification Analysis of Affine Term Structure Models. *Journal of Finance* **55**, 1943–1978.

————. (2002). Expectations Puzzles, Time-Varying Risk Premia, and Affine Models of the Term Structure. *Journal of Financial Economics* **63**, 415–441.

Das, S., and G. Geng (2002). Modeling the Processes of Correlated Default. Working Paper, Santa Clara University.

Das, S., and R. Sundaram (1999). Of Smiles and Smirks: A Term Structure Perspective. *Journal of Financial and Quantitative Analysis* **34**, 211–239.

Das, S., and P. Tufano (1996). Pricing Credit-Sensitive Debt When Interest Rates Credit Ratings and Credit Spreads Are Stochastic. *The Journal of Financial Engineering* **5**, No. 2, 161–198.

Das, S., L. Freed, G. Geng, and N. Kapadia (2002). Correlated Default Risk. Working Paper, Santa Clara University.

Davis, M., and V. Lo (1999). Infectious Default. Working Paper, Research and Product Development, Tokyo-Mitsubishi International Plc, London.

————. (2000). Modeling Default Correlation in Bond Portfolios. Working Paper, Imperial Collge, London.

Delbaen, F., and W. Schachermayer (1999). A General Version of the Fundamental Theorem of Asset Pricing. *Mathematische Annalen* **300**, 463–520.

Delianedis, G., and R. Geske (1998). Credit Risk and Risk Neutral Default Probabilities: Information about Rating Migrations and Defaults. Working Paper, Working Paper 19-98, Anderson Graduate School of Business, University of California, Los Angeles.

DeMarzo, P. (1998). Pooling and Tranching of Securities. Working Paper, Haas School of Business, University of California, Berkeley.

DeMarzo, P., and D. Duffie (1991). Corporate Financial Hedging with Proprietary Information. *Journal of Economic Theory* **53**, 261–286.

————. (1999). A Liquidity-Based Model of Security Design. *Econometrica* **67**, 65–99.

Demchak, B. (2000). Modelling Credit Migration. *RISK*, February, 99–103.

Derivatives Policy Group (1995). A Framework for Voluntary Oversight of the OTC Derivatives Activities of Securities Firm Affiliates to Promote Confidence and Stability in Financial Markets. New York.

Deutsche Bank Research (1999). Global Emerging Markets-Debt Strategy. Working Paper, Deutsche Bank.

Dewatripont, M., and J. Tirole (1993). *The Prudential Regulation of Banks*. Cambridge: MIT Press.

Duffee, G. (1998). The Relation between Treasury Yields and Corporate Bond Yield Spreads. *Journal of Finance* **53**, 2225–2242.

————. (1999). Estimating the Price of Default Risk. *The Review of Financial Studies* **12**, 197–226.

————. (2002). Term Premia and Interest Rate Forecasts in Affine Models. *Journal of Finance* **57**, 405–443.

Duffie, D. (1996). Special Repo Rates. *Journal of Finance* **51**, 493–526.

————. (1998a). Defaultable Term Structure Models with Fractional Recovery of Par. Working Paper, Graduate School of Business, Stanford University.

————. (1998b). First-to-Default Valuation. Working Paper, Graduate School of Business, Stanford University.

Duffie, D., and N. Gârleanu (2001). Risk and Valuation of Collateralized Debt Obligations. *Financial Analysts Journal* **57**, 41–62.

Duffie, D., and M. Huang (1996). Swap Rates and Credit Quality. *Journal of Finance* **51**, 921–950.

Duffie, D., and R. Kan (1996). A Yield Factor Model of Interest Rates. *Mathematical Finance* **6**, 379–406.

Duffie, D., and D. Lando (2001). Term Structures of Credit Spreads with Incomplete Accounting Information. *Econometrica* **69**, 633–664.

Duffie, D., and J. Liu (2001). Floating-Fixed Credit Spreads. *Financial Analysts Journal*, May–June, 76–88.

Duffie, D., and J. Pan (2001). Analytical Value-at-Risk with Jumps and Credit Risk. *Finance and Stochastics* **5**, 155–180.

Duffie, D., and K. Singleton (1997). An Econometric Model of the Term Structure of Interest Rate Swap Yields. *Journal of Finance* **52**, 1287–1321.

————. (1998). Simulating Correlated Defaults. Working Paper, Graduate School of Business, Stanford University.

————. (1999). Modeling Term Structures of Defaultable Bonds. *Review of Financial Studies* **12**, 687–720.

Duffie, D., M. Schroder, and C. Skiadas (1996). Recursive Valuation of Defaultable Securities and the Timing of Resolution of Uncertainty. *Annals of Applied Probability* **6**, 1075–1090.

Duffie, D., J. Pan, and K. Singleton (2000). Transform Analysis and Asset Pricing for Affine Jump Diffusions. *Econometrica* **68**, 1343–1376.

Duffie, D., D. Filipović, and W. Schachermayer (2003a). Affine Processes and Applications in Finance. Working Paper, Stanford University, forthcoming, *Annals of Applied Probability*.

Duffie, D., L. Pedersen, and K. Singleton (2003b). Modeling Sovereign Yield Spreads: A Case Study of Russian Debt. *Journal of Finance* **58**.

Dybvig, P., J. Ingersoll, and S. Ross (1996). Long Forward and Zero-Coupon Rates Can Never Fall. *Journal of Business* **69**, 1–25.

Eaton, J., and M. Gersovitz (1981). Debt with Potential Repudiation: Theoretical and Empirical Analysis. *Review of Economic Studies* **48**, 289–309.

Ederington, L., and J. Goh (2000). Is a Convertible Bond Call Really Bad News? Working Paper, University of Oklahoma.

Ederington, L., and J. Yawitz (1987). The Bond Rating Process. In E. I. Altman (Ed.), *Handbook of Financial Markets and Institutions*, Chapter 23, pp. 3–57. New York: Wiley.

Ederington, L., G. Caton, and C. Campbell (1997). To Call or Not to Call Convertible Debt. *Financial Management* **26**, Spring, 22–31.

Eichengreen, B., and A. Mody (2000). Would Collective Action Clauses Raise Borrowing Costs? NBER Working Paper No. 7458.

Eisenberg, L. (1995). Connectivity and Financial Network Shutdown. Working Paper, The Santa Fe Institute.

Eisenberg, L., and T. Noe (1999). Clearing Systems and the Transmission of Systemic Risk. Working Paper, The Risk Engineering Company, and the School of Business, Tulane University.

Elton, E., M. Gruber, D. Agrawal, and C. Mann (2001). Explaining the Rate Spread on Corporate Bonds. *The Journal of Finance* **56**, 247–277.

Eom, Y., J. Helwege, and J.-Z. Huang (2002). Structural Models of Corporate Bond Pricing: An Empirical Analysis. Working Paper, College of Business and Economics, Yonsei University, Seoul, Korea.

Estrella, A. (1994). Taylor, Black, and Scholes: Series Approximations and Risk Management Pitfalls. Working Paper, Federal Reserve Bank of New York.

Estrella, A., D. Hendricks, J. Kambhu, S. Shin, and S. Walter (1994). The Price Risk of Options Positions: Measurement and Capital Requirements. *Federal Reserve Bank of New York Quarterly Review*, Summer–Fall, 27–43.

Ethier, S., and T. Kurtz (1986). *Markov Processes: Characterization and Convergence*. New York: Wiley.

Feller, W. (1951). Two Singular Diffusion Problems. *Annals of Mathematics* **54**, 173–182.

Finger, C. (2000). A Comparison of Stochastic Default Rate Models. Working Paper, Working Paper 00-02, Riskmetrics Group.

Fischer, E., R. Heinkel, and J. Zechner (1989). Dynamic Capital Structure Choice: Theory and Tests. *Journal of Finance* **44**, 19–40.

Fisher, M., D. Nychka, and D. Zervos (1994). Fitting the Term Structure of Interest Rates with Smoothing Splines. Working Paper, Board of Governors of the Federal Reserve Board, Washington, D.C.

Fons, J. (1991). An Approach to Forecasting Default Rates. Working Paper, Moody's Investors Services.

———. (1994). Using Default Rates to Model the Term Structure of Credit Risk. *Financial Analysts Journal* **3**, September–October, 25–32.

Friedman, B., and K. Kuttner (1993). *Business Cycles, Indicators, and Forecasting—Does the Paper-Bill Spread Predict Real Economic Activity?* Chicago: University of Chicago Press.

Froot, K., D. Scharfstein, and J. Stein (1993). Risk Management: Coordinating Corporate Investment and Financing Policies. *The Journal of Finance* **48**, 1629–1658.

Galai, D., and M. Schneller (1978). Pricing of Warrants and the Value of the Firm. *Journal of Finance* **33**, 1333–1342.

Gârleanu, N., and L. Pedersen (2001). Adverse Selection and Re-Trade. Working Paper, Graduate School of Business, Stanford University.

Garman, M. (1996). Improving on VaR. *RISK* **9**, May, 61–63.

Geske, R. (1977). The Valuation of Corporate Liabilities as Compound Options. *Journal of Financial and Quantitative Analysis* **12**, 541–552.

Gibson, R., and S. M. Sundaresan (1999). A Model of Sovereign Borrowing and Sovereign Yield Spreads. Working Paper, Graduate School of Business, Columbia University.

Global Credit Research (1998). Historical Default Rates of Corporate Bond Issuers, 1920–1997. Working Paper, Moody's Investor Services.

Gluck, J., and H. Remeza (2000). Moody's Approach to Rating Multisector CDO's. Working Paper, Moody's Investor Services.

Goldman Sachs (1994). Valuing Convertible Bonds as Derivatives. Working Paper, Quantitative Strategies Notes, Goldman Sachs.

Gordy, M. (2000). A Comparative Anatomy of Credit Risk Models. *Journal of Banking and Finance* **24**, 119–149.

———. (2001). A Risk-Factor Model Foundation for Ratings-Based Bank Capital Rules. Working Paper, Board of Governors of the Federal Reserve System, Washington, D.C.

Grinblatt, M., and N. Jegadeesh (1996). The Relative Pricing of Eurodollar Futures and Forward Contracts. *Journal of Finance* **51**, 1499–1522.

Gupton, G., and R. Stein (2002). LossCalc: Moody's Model for Predicting Loss Given Default (LGD). Working Paper, Moody's Investors Services, Global Credit Research, New York.

Harrison, M., and D. Kreps (1979). Martingales and Arbitrage in Multiperiod Securities Markets. *Journal of Economic Theory* **20**, 381–408.

Haugen, D., and L. Senbet (1978). The Insignificance of Bankruptcy Costs to the Theory of Capital Structure. *Journal of Finance* **33**, 383–393.

He, J., W. Hu, and L. Lang (2000). Credit Spread Curves and Credit Ratings. Working Paper, Chinese University of Hong Kong.

Heath, D., R. Jarrow, and A. Morton (1992). Bond Pricing and the Term Structure of Interest Rates: A New Methodology for Contingent Claims Valuation. *Econometrica* **60**, 77–106.

Heldring, O. (1997). Safe Settlement. *RISK*, February, 22–27.

Helwege, J., and C. Turner (1999). The Slope of the Credit Yield Curve for Speculative-Grade Issuers. *Journal of Finance* **54**, 1869–1884.

Heston, S. (1993). A Closed-Form Solution for Options with Stochastic Volatility, with Applications to Bond and Currency Options. *Review of Financial Studies* **6**, 327–344.

Hilberink, B., and C. Rogers (2001). Optimal Capital Structure and Endogenous Default. Working Paper, University of Bath.

Huang, J., and M. Huang (2000). How Much of the Corporate-Treasury Yield Spread Is Due to Credit Risk?: Results from a New Calibration Approach. Working Paper, Graduate School of Business, Stanford University.

Huge, B., and D. Lando (1999). Swap Pricing with Two-Sided Default Risk in a Rating-Based Model. *European Finance Review* **3**, 239–268.

Hull, J., and A. White (1995). The Impact of Default Risk on the Prices of Options and Other Derivative Securities. *Journal of Banking and Finance* **19**, 299–322.

Hurt, L., and A. Felsovalyi (1998). Measuring Loss on Latin American Defaulted Bank Loans. Working Paper, Citibank Global Strategies.

Ingersoll, J. (1977). An Examination of Corporate Call Policies on Convertible Securities. *The Journal of Financial Economics* **5**, 289–322.

Innes, R. (1990). Limited Liability and Incentive Contracting with Ex-Ante Choices. *The Journal of Economic Theory* **52**, 45–67.

International Monetary Fund (2001). Involving the Private Sector in the Resolution of Financial Crises. International Monetary Fund.

Israel, R., J. Rosenthal, and J. Wei (2001). Finding Generators for Markov Chains via Empirical Transition Matrices. *Mathematical Finance* **11**, 245–265.

Jackson, P., and A. Emblow (2001). The New Basel Accord. *Derivatives Use, Trading, and Regulation* **7**, 118–126.

Jarrow, R., and S. Turnbull (1995). Pricing Options on Financial Securities Subject to Default Risk. *Journal of Finance* **50**, 53–86.

———. (1997). When Swaps Are Dropped. *RISK* **10**, May, 70–75.

Jarrow, R., D. Lando, and S. Turnbull (1997). A Markov Model for the Term Structure of Credit Risk Spreads. *Review of Financial Studies* **10**, 481–523.

Jarrow, R. A., D. Lando, and F. Yu (2000). Default Risk and Diversification: Theory and Applications. Working Paper, Cornell University.

Johnson, R. (1967). Term Structures of Corporate Bond Yields as a Function of Risk of Default. *The Journal of Finance* **22**, 313–345.

Jones, E., S. Mason, and E. Rosenfeld (1984). Contingent Claims Analysis of Corporate Capital Structures: An Empirical Investigation. *The Journal of Finance* **39**, 611–625.

Jonsson, J., and M. Fridson (1996). Forecasting Default Rates on High-Yield Bonds. *The Journal of Fixed Income*, June, 69–77.

J. P. Morgan (1997). CreditMetrics Technical Document, New York.

Kalbfleisch, J., and R. Prentice (1980). *The Statistical Analysis of Failure Time Data*. New York: Wiley.

Kaplan, R., and G. Urwitz (1979). Statistical Models of Bond Ratings: A Methodological Inquiry. *Journal of Business* **52**, 231–261.

Kavvathas, D. (2001). Estimating Credit Rating Transition Probabilities for Corporate Bonds. Working Paper, University of Chicago.

Kealhofer, S. (1995). Managing Default Risk in Portfolios of Derivatives. In *Derivative Credit Risk, Advances in Measurement and Management*, pp. 49–66. London: Risk Publications.

Keswani, A. (2002). Estimating a Risky Term Structure of Brady Bonds. Working Paper, Lancaster University.

Kiesel, R., W. Perraudin, and A. Taylor (2000). The Structure of Credit Risk: Spread Volatility and Rating Transitions. Working Paper, London School of Economics.

Kim, J., K. Ramaswamy, and S. Sundaresan (1993). Does Default Risk in Coupons Affect the Valuation of Corporate Bonds? A Contingent Claims Model. *Financial Management* **22**, 117–131.

Kliger, D., and O. Sarig (1997). The Information Value of Bond Ratings. Working Paper, Wharton School, University of Pennsylvania.

Kusuoka, S. (1999). A Remark on Default Risk Models. *Advances in Mathematical Economics* **1**, 69–82.

Lando, D. (1998). Cox Processes and Credit-Risky Securities. *Review of Derivatives Research* **2**, 99–120.

Lando, D., and T. Skødeberg (2000). Analyzing Rating Transitions and Rating Drift with Continuous Observations. Working Paper, Department of Statistics, University of Copenhagen.

Langetieg, T. (1980). A Multivariate Model of the Term Structure. *Journal of Finance* **35**, 71–97.

Leippold, M., and L. Wu (2001). Design and Estimation of Quadratic Term Structure Models. Working Paper, Fordham University, New York.

Leland, H. (1994). Corporate Debt Value, Bond Covenants, and Optimal Capital Structure. *Journal of Finance* **49**, 1213–1252.

Leland, H., and D. Pyle (1977). Information Asymmetries, Financial Structure, and Financial Intermediaries. *Journal of Finance* **32**, 371–387.

Leland, H., and K. Toft (1996). Optimal Capital Structure, Endogenous Bankruptcy, and the Term Structure of Credit Spreads. *Journal of Finance* **51**, 987–1019.

Lennox, C. (1999). Identifying Failing Companies: A Re-Evaluation of the Logit, Probit and DA Approaches. *Journal of Economics and Business* **51**, 347–364.

Li, H. (1995). Pricing of Swaps with Default Risk. Working Paper, Yale University.

———. (2000). A Model of Pricing Defaultable Bonds and Credit Ratings. Working Paper, John M. Olin School of Business, Washington University, St. Louis, Mo.

Litterman, R., and T. Iben (1991). Corporate Bond Valuation and the Term Structure of Credit Spreads. *Journal of Portfolio Management*, Spring, 52–64.

Litterman, R., and K. Winkelmann (1998). Estimating Covariance Matrices. Working Paper, Goldman Sachs, Risk Management Series.

Litzenberger, R. (1992). Swaps: Plain and Fanciful. *The Journal of Finance* **47**, 831–850.

Lo, A. (1986). Logit versus Discriminant Analysis: A Specification Test and Application to Corporate Bankruptcies. *Journal of Econometrics* **31**, 151–178.

Longstaff, F., and E. Schwartz (1995). Valuing Risky Debt: A New Approach. *The Journal of Finance* **50**, 789–821.

Lopez, J., and M. Saidenberg (1999). Evaluating Credit Risk Models. Working Paper, Economic Research Department, Federal Reserve Bank of San Francisco.

Lowenstein, R. (2000). *When Genius Failed.* New York: Fourth Estate.

Lucas, D., and J. Lonski (1992). Changes in Corporate Credit Quality 1970–1990. *Journal of Fixed Income* **1**, Issue 2, 7–14.

Lyden, S., and D. Sariniti (2000). An Empirical Examination of the Classical Theory of Corporate Security Valuation. Working Paper, Advanced Strategies & Research Group, Barclays Global Investors.

Madan, D., and H. Unal (1998). Pricing the Risks of Default. *Review of Derivatives Research* **2**, 121–160.

Marshall, J. (1993). *The Swaps Market*—2nd edition. Miami: Kolb Publishing Co.

McBrady, M., and M. Seasholes (2000). Bailing-In. Working Paper, University of California, Berkeley.

McDonald, C., and L. Van de Gucht (1996). The Default Risk of High-Yield Bonds. Working Paper, Louisiana State University.

Mella-Barral, P. (1999). Dynamics of Default and Debt Reorganization. *Review of Financial Studies* **12**, 535–578.

Merrick, J. J. (1999). Crisis Dynamics of Implied Default Recovery Ratios: Evidence from Russia and Argentina. Working Paper, Stern School of Business, New York University.

Merton, R. (1974). On the Pricing of Corporate Debt: The Risk Structure of Interest Rates. *The Journal of Finance* **29**, 449–470.

Merton, R., and A. Perold (1993). Theory of Risk Capital in Financial Firms. *Journal of Applied Corporate Finance* **5**, 16–32.

Miltersen, K. (1994). An Arbitrage Theory of the Term Structure of Interest Rates. *Annals of Applied Probability* **4**, 953–967.

Miltersen, K., K. Sandmann, and D. Sondermann (1997). Closed Form Solutions for Term Structure Derivatives with Log-Normal Interest Rates. *Journal of Finance* **52**, 409–430.

Modigliani, F., and M. Miller (1958). The Cost of Capital, Corporation Finance, and the Theory of Investment. *American Economic Review* **48**, 261–297.

Moody's Investors Service (1993). Structured Finance Research and Commentary—Special Comment: A Framework for the Analysis of the Default Risk of Securitized Assets. Working Paper, Moody's Investors Service.

————. (1994). The Status of Swap Agreements under the U.S. Bankruptcy Code. Working Paper, Moody's Investors Service.

Myers, S., and N. Majluf (1984). Corporate Financing and Investment When Firms Have Information Shareholders Do Not Have. *Journal of Financial Economics* **13**, 187–221.

Nakazato, D. (1997). Gaussian Term Structure Model with Credit Rating Classes. Working Paper. Industrial Bank of Japan.

Neal, R., D. Rolph, and C. Morris (2000). Interest Rates and Credit Spreads. Working Paper, Kelley School of Business, Indiana University.

Nickell, P., W. Perraudin, and S. Varotto (2000). Stability of Ratings Transitions. *Journal of Banking and Finance* **24**, 203–228.

Nielsen, L. T., J. SaaRequejo, and P. Santa-Clara (1993). Default Risk and Interest Rate Risk: The Term Structure of Default Spreads. Working Paper, INSEAD, Fontainebleau, France.

Norros, I. (1986). A Compensator Representation of Multivariate Life Length Distributions, with Applications. *Scandinavian Journal of Statistics* **13**, 99–112.

Nyborg, K. (1996). The Use and Pricing of Convertible Bonds. *Applied Mathematical Finance* **3**, 167–190.

Ogden, J. (1987). Determinants of the Relative Interest Rate Sensitivities of Corporate Bonds. *Financial Management* **16**, Spring, 22–30.

Page, M., and D. Costas (1996). The Value-at-Risk of a Portfolio of Currency Derivatives under Worst-Case Distributional Assumptions. Working Paper, Susquehanna Investment Group, Philadelphia, and Department of Mathematics, University of Virginia.

Pagès, H. (2001). Can Liquidity Risk Be Subsumed in Credit Risk? A Case Study from Brady Bond Prices. Working Paper, Bank for International Settlements.

Pan, J. (2002). The Jump-Risk Premia Implicit in Options: Evidence from an Integrated Time-Series Study. *Journal of Financial Economics* **63**, 3–50.

Paul, A., D. Mullins, and E. Wolff (1989). Original Issue High Yield Bonds: Aging Analysis of Defaults, Exchanges, and Calls. *Journal of Finance* **44**, 923–952.

Pearson, N., and T.-S. Sun (1994). An Empirical Examination of the Cox, Ingersoll, and Ross Model of the Term Structure of Interest Rates Using the Method of Maximum Likelihood. *Journal of Finance* **49**, 929–959.

Pedersen, A. (1995). A New Approach to Maximum Likelihood Estimation for Stochastic Differential Equations Based on Discrete Observations. *Scandinavian Journal of Statistics* **22**, 55–71.

Phelan, M. J. (1995). Probability and Statistics Applied to the Practice of Financial Risk Management: The Case of J. P. Morgan's RiskMetrics. Working Paper, The Wharton Financial Institution Center, University of Pennsylvania.

Pitts, C., and M. Selby (1983). The Pricing of Corporate Debt: A Further Note. *The Journal of Finance* **38**, 1311–1313.

Protter, P. (1990). *Stochastic Integration and Differential Equations.* New York: Springer-Verlag.

Punjabi, S., and J. Tierney (1999). Synthetic CLOs and Their Role in Bank Balance Sheet Management. Working Paper, Deutsche Bank, Fixed Income Research.

Pye, G. (1974). Gauging the Default Premium. *Financial Analyst's Journal* **30**, 49–50.

Reisen, H., and J. Maltzan (1999). Boom and Bust and Sovereign Ratings. Working Paper, Technical Paper No. 148, OECD Development Centre.

Rendleman, R. (1992). How Risks Are Shared in Interest Rate Swaps. *Journal of Financial Services Research* **5**, 5–34.

Rochet, J.-C., and J. Tirole (1996). Interbank Lending and Systemic Risk. *Journal of Money, Credit, and Banking* **28**, 733–762.

Roubini, N. (2000). Bail-In, Burden-Sharing, Private Sector Involvement in Crisis Resolution and Constructive Engagement of the Private Sector. Working Paper, New York University.

Ruml, E. (1992). Derivatives 101. Working Paper, Bankers Trust New York Corporation.

Sarig, O., and A. Warga (1989). Some Empirical Estimates of the Risk Structure of Interest Rates. *The Journal of Finance* **44**, 1351–1360.

Schönbucher, P. (1998). Term Structure Modelling of Defaultable Bonds. *Review of Derivatives Research* **2**, 161–192.

Schönbucher, P., and D. Schubert (2001). Copula-Dependent Default Risk in Intensity Models. Working Paper, Department of Statistics, Bonn University.

Schorin, C., and S. Weinreich (1998). Collateralized Debt Obligation Handbook. Working Paper, Morgan Stanley Dean Witter, Fixed Income Research.

Scott, L. (1996). The Valuation of Interest Rate Derivatives in a Multi-Factor Cox-Ingersoll-Ross Model that Matches the Initial Term Structure. Working Paper, University of Georgia.

———. (1997). Pricing Stock Options in a Jump-Diffusion Model with Stochastic Volatility and Interest Rates: Application of Fourier Inversion Methods. *Mathematical Finance* **7**, 345–358.

Shaked, M., and J. Shanthikumar (1987). The Multivariate Hazard Construction. *Stochastic Processes and Their Applications* **24**, 241–258.

———. (1993). Multivariate Conditional Hazard Rate and Mean Residual Life Functions and Their Applications. In R. Barlow, C. Clarotti, and F. Spizzichtho (Eds.), *Reliability and Decision Making* , Chapter 7. London: Chapman and Hall.

Shane, H. (1994). Comovements of Low-Grade Debt and Equity Returns of Highly Leveraged Firms. *Journal of Fixed Income* **3**, 79–89.

Sharpe, W. (1964). Capital Asset Prices: A Theory of Market Equilibrium under Conditions of Risk. *Journal of Finance* **19**, 425–442.

Shimko, D., N. Tejima, and D. Van Deventer (1993). The Pricing of Risky Debt When Interest Rates Are Stochastic. *Journal of Fixed Income* **3**, 58–65.

Shumway, T. (2001). Forecasting Bankruptcy More Accurately: A Simple Hazard Model. *Journal of Business* **74**, 101–124.

Singleton, K. (2001). Estimation of Affine Asset Pricing Models Using the Empirical Characteristic Function. *Journal of Econometrics* **102**, 111–141.

Singleton, K., and L. Umantsev (2002). Pricing Coupon-Bond Options and Swaptions in Affine Term Structure Models. *Mathematical Finance* **12**, 427–446.

Smith, C., C. Smithson, and L. Wakeman (1988). The Market for Interest Rate Swaps. *Financial Management* **17**, Winter, 34–44.

Solnik, B. (1990). Swap Pricing and Default Risk: A Note. *Journal of International Financial Management and Accounting* **2**, 79–91.

Sorensen, E., and T. Bollier (1994). Pricing Swap Default Risk. *Journal of Derivatives*, May–June, 23–33.

Stiglitz, J., and L. Weiss (1981). Credit Rationing with Imperfect Information. *American Economic Review* **71**, 393–410.

Stock, J., and M. Watson (1989). New Indexes of Coincident and Leading Economic Indicators. *NBER Macro Annual*, 351–395.

Sundaresan, S. (1991). Valuation of Swaps. In S. Khoury (Ed.), *Recent Developments in International Banking*. Amsterdam: North-Holland.

Tolk, J. (2001). Understanding the Risks in Credit Default Swaps. Special Report, Moody's Investors Services, March 16, 2001, New York.

Tsiveriotas, K., and C. Fernandes (1998). Valuing Convertible Bonds with Credit Risk. *Journal of Fixed Income* **8**, September, 95–102.

Vasicek, O. (1977). An Equilibrium Characterization of the Term Structure. *Journal of Financial Economics* **5**, 177–188.

Wilson, T. (1997a). Portfolio Credit Risk, I. *RISK* **10**, September, 111–117.

———. (1997b). Portfolio Credit Risk, II. *RISK* **10**, October, 56–61.

Zhou, C. (2001). The Term Structure of Credit Spreads with Jump Risk. *Journal of Banking and Finance* **25**, 2015–2040.

Index

Page numbers followed by *n* indicate notes; those followed by *f* indicate figures; those followed by *t* indicate tables.